Releasing the
PROPHETIC DESTINY *of a* NATION

– SECOND EDITION –

DESTINY IMAGE BOOKS BY TIM & DUTCH SHEETS and CHUCK D. PIERCE

TIM SHEETS

Prayers & Decrees That Activate Angel Armies: Releasing God's Angels into Action

Angel Armies: Releasing the Warriors of Heaven

Angel Armies on Assignment: The Divisions and Assignments of Angels and How to Partner with Them in Your Prayers

Planting the Heavens: Releasing the Authority of the Kingdom Through Your Words, Prayers, and Declarations

Heaven Made Real: A Biblical Guide to the Afterlife and Eternity

The New Era of Glory: Stepping into God's Accelerated Season of Outpouring and Breakthrough

Come Home (Coauthor Rachel Shafer)

God's Got This: Power Decrees to Overcome Problems, Step Into Purpose, and Receive Promises (Coauthor Rachel Shafer)

TIM & DUTCH SHEETS and CHUCK D. PIERCE

Releasing the Prophetic Destiny of a Nation: An Intercessor's Handbook to Pray for All 50 States in America

Dutch Sheets & Chuck D. Pierce
with Tim Sheets

Releasing the
PROPHETIC DESTINY *of a* NATION

— SECOND EDITION —

An Intercessor's Handbook
to Pray for
All 50 States in America

© Copyright 2024 – Tim Sheets, Dutch Sheets, Chuck D. Pierce

All rights reserved. This book is protected by the copyright laws of the United States of America. This book may not be copied or reprinted for commercial gain or profit. The use of short quotations or occasional page copying for personal or group study is permitted and encouraged. Permission will be granted upon request. Scripture quotations marked NKJV are taken from the New King James Version®. Copyright © 1982 by Thomas Nelson. Used by permission. All rights reserved. Scripture quotations marked KJV are taken from the King James Version. Scripture quotations marked MSG are taken from *The Message,* copyright © 1993, 2002, 2018 by Eugene H. Peterson. Used by permission of NavPress. All rights reserved. Represented by Tyndale House Publishers, Inc. Scripture quotations marked NLT are taken from Holy Bible, New Living Translation, copyright © 1996, 2004, 2015 by Tyndale House Foundation. Used by permission of Tyndale House Publishers, Inc., Carol Stream, Illinois 60188. All rights reserved. Scripture quotations marked NASB1995 are taken from the New American Standard Bible®, Copyright © 1960, 1971, 1977, 1995 by The Lockman Foundation. All rights reserved. Scripture quotations marked NASB are taken from the New American Standard Bible®, Copyright © 1960, 1971, 1977, 1995, 2020 by The Lockman Foundation. All rights reserved. Scripture quotations marked AMPC are taken from Amplified Bible, Classic Edition; Copyright © 1954, 1958, 1962, 1964, 1965, 1987 by The Lockman Foundation. Scripture quotations marked AMP are taken from the Amplified Bible; Copyright © 2015 by The Lockman Foundation, La Habra, CA 90631. All rights reserved.

DESTINY IMAGE® PUBLISHERS, INC.
PO Box 310, Shippensburg, PA 17257-0310

"Publishing cutting-edge prophetic resources to supernaturally empower the body of Christ"

This book and all other Destiny Image and Destiny Image Fiction books are available at Christian bookstores and distributors worldwide.

For more information on foreign distributors, call 717-532-3040.

Or reach us on the Internet: www.destinyimage.com

ISBN 13 TP: 978-0-7684-7743-6
ISBN 13 EBook: 978-0-7684-7744-3

For Worldwide Distribution, Printed in the USA

1 2 3 4 5 6 / 27 26 25 24

DEDICATION

This book is dedicated to the apostles, prophets, and intercessors who are willing to stand and cry "Restore!" in our nation.

ACKNOWLEDGMENTS

WE EXTEND A GREAT THANKS TO:

Our families who released us and sacrificed during our time of going.

Our staff who made the administration of this task possible.

All those in each state who facilitated our visits.

CONTENTS

Preface. 11

Part I Divine Encounters 13

1 The Ride *(Dutch Sheets)*. 14
2 The Call *(Chuck D. Pierce)* 29
3 Planting the Heavens *(Tim Sheets)* 49
4 Can a Nation Be Restored? *(Chuck D. Pierce)*. 65
5 The Adjustment *(Dutch Sheets)* 95
6 Connecting with Heaven and Earth *(Dutch Sheets)*. 105
7 Receiving the Anointing to Stand Strong *(Chuck D. Pierce)* . 115
8 Time Catches Up with the Decree *(Dutch Sheets)*. 141
9 The Reigning Church *(Tim Sheets)*. 151

Part II Intercessor's Handbook. 173

10 State by State—History and Future Destiny 174
11 Declarations and Decrees for the Nation 522
   Endnotes 529
   About the Authors 553

PREFACE

by

Larry Sparks

Why a new edition of a book containing "old" prophetic words? Simple. God has not changed His mind about what He said concerning the United States of America. How long do we pray into a specific prophetic word? *Until* the moment that the word comes to fruition. We cannot grow weary in praying God's word back to Him. Study the history of revival and awakening; it is highlighted by bold, audacious voices who took God at His word and would not relent bombarding Heaven with targeted, specific, bold intercession **until** they *saw* what they were crying out for. Let it be said of you, in this hour, that you would truly *see* what you have been crying out for in prayer.

When Dutch Sheets and Chuck Pierce embarked on their historic 50-state tour prior to the original publication of this book, they compiled both prophetic words and relevant data for each of the 50 states in the United States for the purpose of providing you with a blueprint on how to pray effective, targeted, and strategic prayers for America.

We changed the book's subtitle, and with good reason. This is truly an intercessor's guide to praying for the nation—and whether you know it or not, *you* are an intercessor. It is not like the "fivefold ministry," where some are prophets, apostles, teachers, pastors/shepherds and teachers; every believer is called to pray and intercede.

The original manuscript remains completely intact, except we added some very helpful teaching from Dr. Tim Sheets about how your prayers plant the heavens, and furthermore, provide you with some powerful decrees that you can make over America.

It's an urgent hour. It's time for the voice of Jesus' Ekklesia to arise and decree what *He has said* concerning the destiny of the nation!

Larry Sparks, MDiv
Publisher, Destiny Image

PART I

DIVINE ENCOUNTERS

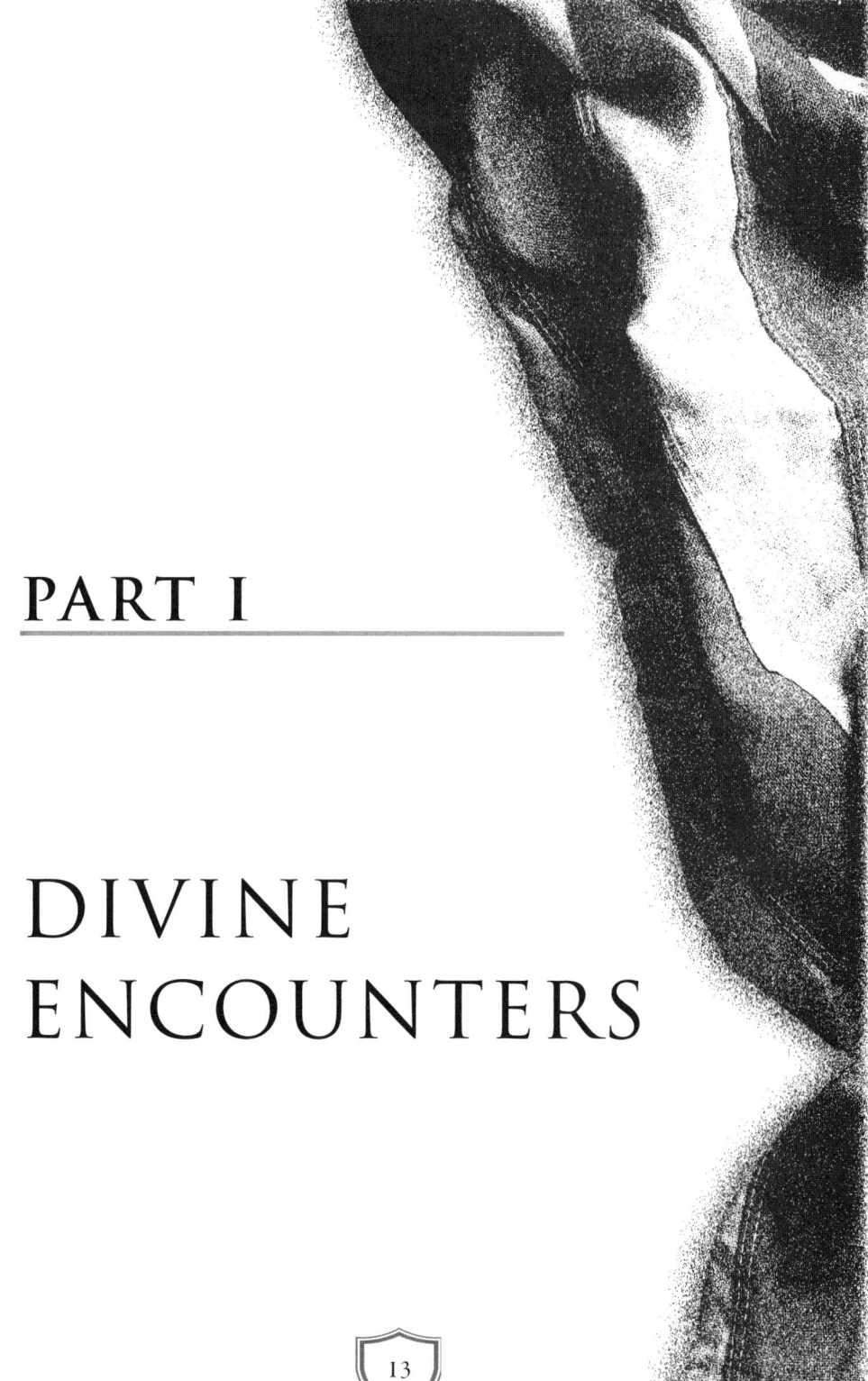

– 1 –

THE RIDE

(Dutch Sheets)

I knew I was in for a wild ride when the Lord showed me a mental picture[1] of myself riding with Christ on His white horse—I just didn't know how wild! But when the Holy Spirit spoke to both Chuck Pierce and me in October 2002 to go to all 50 states in order to network intercessors and leaders, pray for breakthrough, and further shift the nation toward revival, I began to realize just how wild—and long—the ride would be.

My part of this adventure actually began in September 1998 when I was speaking for Peter Wagner at a conference in Rochester, New York. Suddenly, during the worship, I was given a vision of America. It was as though I was looking down from Heaven onto the United States. I then saw the Lord in the middle of the nation, dressed for war and riding His white warhorse.

Both Christ and the horse wore very intense expressions, much like Christ is described as wearing in Revelation 19:11-16. He was fearsome and majestic beyond words. So was His horse, which was shifting, prancing, and obviously wanting to run. It was evident that Christ was either waiting for some signal or was in the process of deciding for Himself where to go first.

Suddenly, He looked toward the East, prodded the horse, and they dashed to Washington, DC, where He struck the earth with a staff, causing flames to spring up from the earth. I knew the flames represented both cleansing and revival. He then paused while deciding where to go next, then charged to another part of the nation where He struck the ground again, with the same results. This was repeated, with no visible pattern, until He had crisscrossed the nation many times, and the flames had sprung up all across the nation.

RIDING WITH CHRIST

A short time later I received the same picture or vision of the Lord on His horse ready to begin this ride. This time, however, I was in the vision standing next to Him and His horse, when He looked at me and said, "Get onto My horse with Me."

With absolute incredibility I responded, "Lord, I can't ride Your horse with You!" Hanging around with prophets—all of whom, like Chuck Pierce, seem to be on the weird side!—has helped me grow somewhat accustomed to cerebral-stretching events such as this. But not even their strangeness prepared me for this one!

"Sure you can," He replied, and immediately reached down, put His arm around me, and pulled me up onto the horse. I was surprised that He did not put me behind Him, but rather in front where He could hold me securely between His arms as we rode. Then off we went, making the same ride across the nation that I had previously seen.

Through this vision it was obvious the Lord was telling me I was going to make this ride with Him across America. I am not implying, by the way, that this is the fulfillment of Revelation 19:11-16, which

speaks of Christ riding a white horse; that obviously comes later in history. Nor did I assume that I would be the only believer—or even the primary one—making this ride with Christ. Though I realized I was a leader in the modern-day prayer movement and knew I might play a leadership role in this effort, I also realized that I represented the entirety of the prayer movement—that we would ride with Him in this endeavor. In other words, Christ was going to release the fire of cleansing and revival, but as is always the case, He would be doing so *through His people*, partnering with them on this amazing ride.

A DIVINE ENCOUNTER

Another key event along my journey occurred in January 1999. While ministering at another conference convened by Peter Wagner, this one in Colorado Springs, I had an encounter with the Lord that forever changed me. At the conclusion of the meeting, I sat on the edge of the platform to rest for a few minutes while other leaders began to pray for the attendees. As I sat there, I began to feel a heavy weight on my chest. I didn't know if it was physical or spiritual in origin, but I laid back on the platform to see if I could ascertain what was happening. It wasn't long before I knew the weight was spiritual.

As I laid there, God began a very powerful impartation to me that lasted for an hour and a half. As strange as it sounds, it was so strong at times that I was fearful of dying. Just as the prophet Isaiah feared for his life in the Lord's presence (see Isaiah 6:1-7), and John "fell at His feet as dead" when encountered by the Lord (Revelation 1:17), I, too, was overcome by His presence and feared for my life. I wept for much of the time, on occasion shook and trembled, and felt throughout the experience that everything inside me was being removed and replaced by a new substance, which I now believe was a new measure of the life of God.

At one point I saw a cross suspended over me, which was then shoved into my spirit—not as if stabbed, but the entire cross was placed into me. This was the point at which I was afraid I might die, and indeed, I believe something of me did, for at the end of the experience the Lord spoke to me and said, "Now you belong to Me. You will go where I tell you to go, do what I tell you to do, say what I tell you to say, and you will fear no man." He informed me that He had placed a mantle upon me for this nation and that He would begin to send me on specific missions.

RECEIVING GOD'S HEART

I had one more significant encounter with the Lord that prepared me for this "ride." It occurred in October 2000, just before the national presidential elections. During a Wednesday night service, I walked to the podium to begin a message when a strange feeling began to overtake me. I paused, trying to discern what was happening, and within seconds was weeping uncontrollably as God began to impart to me His heart for America. I did not feel anger, though I'm sure we as a nation have angered Him, but instead I felt His great love—the kind of love a father might feel for a prodigal child.

I began to weep so hard that I could not regain my composure. Someone else closed the service, everyone went home, and I was left alone. For three and a half hours I wept over America—so hard at times that I was afraid I was injuring myself. I felt as though my heart was literally breaking. I did not know one could cry from so deep a place inside.

Author and lecturer Leo Buscaglia once talked about a contest he was asked to judge. The purpose of the contest was to find the most caring child. The winner was a four-year-old child whose next-door neighbor was an elderly gentleman who had recently lost his wife. Upon seeing the man cry, the little boy went into the old gentleman's yard, climbed onto his lap, and just sat there. When his mother asked him what he had said to the neighbor, the little boy said, "Nothing, I just helped him cry."[2]

For three and a half hours I helped God cry.

During this incredible experience, the Lord revealed several things to me concerning the upcoming presidential elections. I knew:

1. These elections were not going the way He wanted.

2. If the elections did not go His way, His purposes for America, and other parts of the world also, would be frustrated. I felt that if the right person wasn't elected, America would begin another spiritual spiral downward, similar to what began in the 1960s. And I knew that this one would also last for decades.

3. The warfare existing over this election was very great, similar to what was described in Daniel 10, and was truly a battle for the soul of a nation.

4. The present level of prayer wasn't enough to turn the tide, and an urgent prayer alert had to be issued to believers around the nation.

I issued this prayer alert,[3] and millions of people around the world responded. Our prayers were effective, God was merciful, and I believe we were given His choice as president.[4]

RECEIVING THE KEY

During this four-week period of prayer, God began to speak to me very clearly about our spiritual authority as believers. He gave me a series of confirmations, so many in fact, that they made this one of the most amazing seasons of my life. The following is the account of these confirmations, which is included in a chapter I wrote in *Destiny of a Nation*, a book compiled by Peter Wagner, chronicling the amazing events orchestrated by the Holy Spirit leading up to this election:

* On a cross-country flight, I happened to notice that my departure time was 2:22. I then was seated in row number 22 and the total travel time was 2 hours and 22 minutes. My first thought was, *What a strange coincidence!* Then the Lord reminded me that He had been speaking to me about the election from Isaiah 22:22, *"Then I will set the key of the house of David on his shoulder, when he opens no one will shut, when he shuts no one will open"* (NASB 1995). *Would God do something like this to bring me confirmation?* I wondered.

* A couple of days later I received a phone call from Sam Brassfield, a spiritual father in my life. While in prayer, Sam had felt the Lord prompt him to call and give me Isaiah 22:22, emphasizing the phrase, *the key of David*. He said, "Dutch, God is giving you a key of authority in this nation."

* Soon afterward, I went to Washington, DC, on a ministry trip, and there a trusted intercessor friend of mine gave me a gift at the meeting. She said the Lord had impressed her months earlier to buy it for me, with the instruction

that He would let her know when to give it to me. It was a beautiful silver key, and her words to me were, "This is the key of the city!" I knew it represented the key spoken of in Isaiah 22:22.

* Another man, knowing nothing about this, came to me after that meeting with three keys and said, "This morning I felt impressed to bring you these three keys." He, too, realized they symbolized spiritual authority. Again, I knew they pictured Isaiah 22:22. Matthew 16:19 is another pertinent Scripture about keys which came to mind, *"I will give you the keys of the kingdom of heaven; and whatever you bind on earth shall have been bound in heaven, and whatever you loose on earth shall have been loosed in heaven"* (NASB).

* A week later I was in San Diego with Chuck Pierce. Chuck told me that God had led him to give me a key. He had been given this key in New York by people who said it represented a revival anointing for America. Chuck said, "The Lord impressed me to give it to you."

* After that service, another man gave me three more keys, saying he had been impressed by the Lord to do so. Incredibly, the number "222," and no other numbers, was on each of these keys!

* A couple of weeks later I was in California again to meet and pray with my friend, Lou Engle. Lou said to me, "God has been speaking to me about Isaiah 22:22. I've even had dreams about the number 22 and this verse. And at a meeting I did recently, the number of my hotel room was 222."

* I came home from that meeting, shared this with our church and a young man in our congregation said to me,

"Just today God directed me to Isaiah 22:22. I felt it was a verse for our church."

- ★ Another lady in the service had been awakened from a dream at 2:22 a.m., and shared her experience with me.

- ★ Still another lady in the service, a visiting pastor's wife from New England, had also had a dream the previous night. In her dream there was a man with an old set of keys. She asked him, "What are you doing with those?" He replied that he was going to throw them away because they were just old keys. In the dream she said to the man, "Please don't throw them away. They are precious. May I have them?" He then gave her the keys.

Over the course of a few weeks, I had no less than 25 remarkable confirmations that God was speaking to me about keys of authority and relating this to Isaiah 22:22. He was clearly saying, "I am giving you authority—keys—to impact the nation."

Though the occurrences were happening to me, I realized the message was not just for me, but for the entire Body of Christ. We truly have been given keys of authority from God to legislate from the heavenlies (in the realm of the spirit), opening doors that can't be closed by satan or any person, and closing doors through which evil and destruction might otherwise enter.

TO THE WHITE HOUSE

As I stated earlier, our prayers were effective, and I believe God gave us His choice as president. Then came the hanging chads and the amazing

battle for the state of Florida, which would of course determine the final outcome. On December 2, 2000, after so much confirmation and prayer, I became convinced that it was time for an extremely bold act of prayer and prophetic declaration. I, along with two other people, went to the White House grounds late that Saturday night and, standing at one of the gates, began to pray Isaiah 22:22 along with Psalm 34.

We first prayed for then Vice President Al Gore and his family. We blessed him in numerous ways and asked God to fulfill the destiny He had purposed for him. We then, however, spoke out, took the authority of the keys, and spiritually closed the door of the White House to him, decreeing that he would not enter there to lead this nation.

We then proceeded to decree that the door to the White House was open to George W. Bush, and that he would enter it as president of the United States. This intense prayer time lasted about 30 minutes.

Presumptuous? Arrogant? Some would no doubt feel that it was. However, by that time, I was thoroughly convinced God had confirmed again and again that we had this authority in the spirit and that we were to exercise it. I was willing to obey God even if it might look foolish to others. Agreeing with the prayers of millions of people that presumably by then had been stored in the heavenly prayer bowls mentioned in Revelation 5, we simply made the declarations that turned out to be the final release. A few days later, the Supreme Court made its decisive ruling and Vice President Gore conceded.[5]

What a ride!

GO TO ALL 50 STATES

Now, getting back to the events of October 2002, the Lord led both Chuck and me to go to all 50 states. We were together in Washington, DC, talking about what the Lord was speaking to us about the nation. Incredibly, both of us declared—almost in fear and dread—that God had spoken to us to go to every state. We realized we were to take the spiritual keys we had been given and "ride" across this nation with the Lord, striking the ground and trumpeting the message of revival. The consensus we had, which we were confident was from the Lord, was to:

- ✯ Gather and network intercessors and leaders in each state.
- ✯ Seek specific insight and messages for every state. Indeed, we spoke three times in each state, and though some points and truths were repeated a few times, no two messages were ever fully repeated; most were completely different.
- ✯ Receive and deliver prophetic discernment relating to prayer, events, actions, and strategies for breakthrough in each state.

A FINAL CONFIRMATION

Knowing that we had received a mandate from the Lord, we began making plans for the Tour. Interestingly, a few months later in January 2003, another confirmation was given to me about Isaiah 22:22 and keys of authority. I was in Washington, DC, for a prayer gathering. One particular morning, we were scheduled to tour the State Department. Actually, the real purpose of the tour was to pray for the Department as we walked through the building. When I awoke that morning, however, I had the clear impression, *Don't go to the State Department; go to the White House to pray.*

I prayed about this for a few minutes and also called my wife, Ceci, looking for confirmation. She felt this was from the Lord, as did I, so I decided to obey the prompting. Upon asking the Lord the reasons for going, I felt He was leading me, based upon Isaiah 22:22, to close the door to unwise counsel flowing to the president and open the door to God's will and counsel.

The rest of the group headed for the State Department while I hailed a taxi and left for the White House. It was a very cold and windy day, and I would be praying outside. It wasn't a good day to forget my overcoat! The more I prayed, the colder I got, which was affecting my attitude. In addition, there were lots of people milling around taking pictures, and a group of protestors was shouting one-liners and singing songs.

On top of that, security was strong—I felt that every move I made as I paced in front of the fence was being scrutinized. As I prayed quietly, I was almost sure the entire Secret Service was watching this strange man—me—pacing in the cold, obviously alone but speaking to someone. I could only imagine that they pictured a microphone or walkie-talkie on my body somewhere, enabling me to communicate with someone else, who was waiting to detonate a bomb or commit some other act of terrorism.

Suffice it to say that after about 30 minutes of this, I had had enough. I felt nothing but cold and frustration—no anointing, feeling of peace, or any other confirmation in my heart that I was accomplishing anything. My conversation with myself went something like this: *Sheets, who do you think you are? You're not accomplishing a thing. God gives you a verse a couple of years ago, uses it in your life, and you then think you can do anything you want with it. You're moving in presumption, not obedience. You should be over at the State Department with the rest of the team. You might as well go back to your room and get out of this bitter cold.*

As I turned to go, tail tucked between my legs, a young woman, her baby stroller next to her, approached me from behind. When I turned around, she was so close I almost ran into her.

"Excuse me, sir," she said. My first thought was that she was going to ask me for money. Was I ever wrong!

"I hope you don't think I'm weird," she said, "but is your name something like, Dutch Pierce?"

After getting over my initial shock, I then had to deal with the incredible offense of being confused with Chuck Pierce! Actually, the fact that this lady wasn't really even sure of who I was made what was about to happen much more believable and impactful!

"My name is Dutch Sheets," I said, "and I minister some with a guy named Chuck Pierce. Do I know you?"

"Oh, yeah, that's right—Dutch Sheets. No, you don't know me. I hope you don't think I'm weird," she repeated, "but I heard you speak a couple of years ago, and you talked about a verse in Isaiah—2:22 or 22:2—something like that."

She was getting my attention! "It was 22:22," I said.

"Yeah, that's right—22:22, the verse about keys to open and close doors. Well, this morning the Lord awakened me early, reminded me of that verse and your message, told me to go to the White House, and said, 'I'll show you what to do when you get there.'

"I've never done anything like this," she said, "and I don't come here regularly to pray. But the impression was so strong that I bundled up

my baby and came to see what would happen. I have really struggled with what I'm doing," she continued.

"It's cold, my baby is probably cold, and I've been questioning if I really heard the Lord. Then I saw you and thought, *Is that the man who preached about this verse in Isaiah?* I've been watching you for the last 30 minutes, asking God if I'm supposed to approach you, and if so, wondering what to say. I even called my husband, asking him if I should speak to you. He told me that I must! So here I am.

"I know you already know this, and I feel really strange telling you, but the only thing coming to me is that the Lord wants to remind you of that verse and tell you, you really do have the keys to open and close doors in the spirit."

I was blown away! And deeply embarrassed.

"Ma'am," I said, "I've been praying that verse for the last 30 minutes—in complete unbelief. You have fulfilled your assignment. Now get your baby home where it is warm. I'm going to go back and complete my assignment, this time in faith."

I did so. Later, I signaled a taxi and headed toward my hotel. On the way back, I received one of the hardest spankings from the Lord I've ever received. It went something like this: "Don't you ever make Me get mama and her baby out of bed again, and send them into the cold to teach you 'Faith and Obedience 101,' especially after I've already given you two or three dozen confirmations relating to the situation."

Ouch!

Suffice it to say, this was an important reminder to me, and a tremendous encouragement before beginning the Tour. I knew Chuck and I had authority from the Lord to take His key of authority around this nation, doing whatever He instructed us to do. "Dutch Pierce" took the ride!

The results were profound and truly life-changing. The Lord faithfully led and met with us in every state, releasing revelation, and orchestrating the meetings in ways neither of us had ever seen before.

This book is the account of that amazing assignment. Chapters in Part I contain some of the most significant revelations and messages the Lord gave us, including insights from Tim Sheets, my brother, who is also on assignment for God. Part II includes specific words and insights we received for each state.

Our desire is that you will use the insights and revelations, working them into your prayers for your state and the nation, and turn the key of authority. Much has been accomplished in the past four years to turn America back to God, but there remains much to do. It will be the prayers of the saints that turn the tide! The words of Abraham Lincoln, spoken during the difficult days of the Civil War, are appropriate for today:

> I do not doubt that our country will finally come through safe and undivided. But do not misunderstand me...I do not rely on the patriotism of our people...the bravery and devotion of the boys in blue...[or] the loyalty and skill of our generals...But the God of our fathers, Who raised up this country to be the refuge and asylum of the oppressed and downtrodden of all nations, will not let it perish now. I may not live to see it...I do not expect to see it, but God will bring us through safe.[6]

Like Lincoln of old, my faith is in God—not in America's great military, our incredible wealth and abundant resources, our amazing innovation and perseverance, or any other natural asset. My faith, like his, is in the God of our fathers, who is riding across this nation once again, lighting fires of cleansing and revival. And just as He did way back then, He will bring us through once again.

Why don't you ride with Him?

– 2 –

THE CALL

Riding with the Lord across the Nation

(Chuck D. Pierce)

What an interesting chapter you have just read! You can see the sovereign call of God on Dutch Sheets's life to pray for our nation. Dutch's call has a governmental intercessory mandate that God has released for a particular nation. In this case, the call is extended from Heaven to earth to this individual to stand in the gap for a nation. Notice that Dutch left an open-ended question at the end of the last chapter: *Why don't you ride with Him?* Hopefully in this chapter, I will help you understand God's call to find your place in the gap, on the wall, and in our nation.

Intercession is defined as "mediating, going between, pleading for another, representing one party to another for, but not limited to, legal situations."[7] Intercession means to interpose and reconcile. "Meditation defines intercession and intercession defines mediation."[8] In his book, *Intercessory Prayer*, Dutch shares:

> The Hebrew word for intercession, *paga*, means "to meet." As we have already seen by studying the English word, intercession is not primarily a prayer a person prays, but something a person does that can be done through prayer.

This is also true in the Hebrew [obscured]. Although the word intercession has come to [obscured] in our minds, its Hebrew word does not nece[obscured] prayer at all. It has many shades of meaning, [obscured] can be done through prayer…Intercession c[obscured]g. Intercessors *meet* with God; they also me[obscured]s of darkness. "Prayer meetings" are aptly named![9]

This is one of the reasons we felt we needed to have "meetings." We knew if we could gather God's people in a state to meet with God, His glory would be released in that state in a new way and His voice could be heard. The Lord has an eye to find someone on earth who will stand on His behalf. Isaiah 59:14-16 (NKJV) says:

> *Justice is turned back, and righteousness stands afar off; for truth is fallen in the street, and equity cannot enter. So truth fails, and he who departs from evil makes himself a prey. Then the Lord saw it, and it displeased Him that there was no justice. He saw that there was no man, and wondered that there was no intercessor; therefore His own arm brought salvation for Him; and His own righteousness, it sustained Him.*

When the Lord sees a nation submerged in injustice, oppressions, or lies, His first choice is to find a person to take a stand in the place that has been broken. This is called a breach or gap. He will always have a plan to bring redemption, even if He has to take the stand Himself. However, His will is that we stand and co-labor with Him until situations of injustice become just in His eyes.

Ezekiel 22:23-30 is a good example of this. Israel's leadership had become wicked in their operation of administration and stewardship

– 2 –

THE CALL

Riding with the Lord across the Nation

(Chuck D. Pierce)

What an interesting chapter you have just read! You can see the sovereign call of God on Dutch Sheets's life to pray for our nation. Dutch's call has a governmental intercessory mandate that God has released for a particular nation. In this case, the call is extended from Heaven to earth to this individual to stand in the gap for a nation. Notice that Dutch left an open-ended question at the end of the last chapter: *Why don't you ride with Him?* Hopefully in this chapter, I will help you understand God's call to find your place in the gap, on the wall, and in our nation.

Intercession is defined as "mediating, going between, pleading for another, representing one party to another for, but not limited to, legal situations."[7] Intercession means to interpose and reconcile. "Meditation defines intercession and intercession defines mediation."[8] In his book, *Intercessory Prayer*, Dutch shares:

> The Hebrew word for intercession, *paga*, means "to meet." As we have already seen by studying the English word, intercession is not primarily a prayer a person prays, but something a person does that can be done through prayer.

This is also true in the Hebrew language. Although the word intercession has come to mean prayer in our minds, its Hebrew word does not necessarily mean prayer at all. It has many shades of meaning, all of which can be done through prayer...Intercession creates a *meeting*. Intercessors *meet* with God; they also *meet* the powers of darkness. "Prayer meetings" are aptly named!⁹

This is one of the reasons we felt we needed to have "meetings." We knew if we could gather God's people in a state to meet with God, His glory would be released in that state in a new way and His voice could be heard. The Lord has an eye to find someone on earth who will stand on His behalf. Isaiah 59:14-16 (NKJV) says:

> *Justice is turned back, and righteousness stands afar off; for truth is fallen in the street, and equity cannot enter. So truth fails, and he who departs from evil makes himself a prey. Then the Lord saw it, and it displeased Him that there was no justice. He saw that there was no man, and wondered that there was no intercessor; therefore His own arm brought salvation for Him; and His own righteousness, it sustained Him.*

When the Lord sees a nation submerged in injustice, oppressions, or lies, His first choice is to find a person to take a stand in the place that has been broken. This is called a breach or gap. He will always have a plan to bring redemption, even if He has to take the stand Himself. However, His will is that we stand and co-labor with Him until situations of injustice become just in His eyes.

Ezekiel 22:23-30 is a good example of this. Israel's leadership had become wicked in their operation of administration and stewardship of the nation. Her priests had violated the holiness in the sanctuary. Holiness and vileness could not be distinguished in the worship form of that day. Her prophets were whitewashing everything linked with the moral future of the nation. They were operating in divination and lies. The people of the land were committing adultery and mistreating the poor. Ezekiel 22:30 (NKJV) says, *"So I sought for a man among them who would make a wall, and stand in the gap before Me on behalf of the land, that I should not destroy it...."* In other words, if the Lord could find just one person who would take a stand in this gap, He would begin a reversal of fortune for the nation. I will explain this later; as you read through this book and pray for our nation, we are decreeing that a reversal of fortune becomes a way of life for you.

A gap or *perets* is a break or breach. A gap forms when the enemy breaks through God's protective shield or hedge. Gaps form when communications break down and confusion enters into situations. Gaps form when legal structures develop contrary to God's absolute law and authority. Gaps form when domination and abuse occur between races. Gaps form when individuals gain revelation illegally or use occult means to determine their path. Gaps form when fatherlessness overtakes a society and we see our inner cities falling into greater decay. Gaps form when corruption or lack of integrity invades the structures of society. Gaps form when spiritual leaders do not harness their desire and fall into immoral situations. Gaps form when covenant-breaking spirits produce division in God's Kingdom plan. You get the point. To rectify these situations, God begins His process by searching for people who will receive His same heart, and stand until the situation on earth is changed and reflects Heaven's perfect plan.

Unless someone is willing to allow the Lord to get their feet planted in a situation that is opposite of His plan in the earth realm, darkness multiplies and evil forces build a throne opposite to the ruling Throne of the Holy God. Instead of us worshiping our Creator, satan develops a strategy of worship to divert God's covenant plan from coming into fullness. The enemy uses this throne to connect and rally his allies on earth—the enemies of God's plan. But God! If we respond to His call, satan's plan is foiled, and we see the hedge that has been broken rebuilt. This call involves time, money, a strain on our nerves, a determination, and sometimes a depletion of strength. However, the benefits of the call are worth anything that we could ever give or sacrifice.

Dutch also says in *Intercessory Prayer* when discussing Ezekiel 22:

> God's holiness, integrity, and uncompromising truth prevent Him from simply excusing sin. It must be judged. On the other hand, not only is He holy, but He is also love and His love desires to redeem, to restore, and to show mercy.... The passage is clearly saying, "While My justice demanded judgment, My love wants forgiveness. Had I been able to find a human to ask Me to spare his people, I could have. It would have allowed Me to show mercy."[10]

In other words, if we do not take our stand, then He has to release destruction to bring restoration of His purpose on earth.

AN INTERCESSORY CALL

I am an intercessor. Even though I'm known by many around the world as an apostolic prophetic leader in the Body of Christ, I would have to determine my ultimate call is intercessor. The Lord spoke to me from Ezekiel 13:5 (NKJV): *"You have not gone up into the gaps to build a wall for the house of Israel to stand in battle on the day of the Lord."* This happened when I was in my late 20s. Of course, I did not understand the fullness of what this verse meant, but I did embrace the call.

While I was in a denominational church, God began to bring people into my life to develop this call. Actually, God's initiation of my call occurred during my second year of college. I was at a Baptist Student Union State Convention in 1972. When the speaker gave the invitation, I heard these words form in my spirit, "I have called you for the healing of the nations."

Although I had not fully determined the course I felt I should pursue in college, I was already studying courses related to Pre-Med. I went forward and surrendered to the words I heard, by signing a missions card. However, I had no understanding of the call. My mind definitely resisted the thought of studying for eight years and then ending up in a foreign nation as a medical missionary. I could not get away from this experience though, and even when I switched to the field of Business the next year, my change in direction did not change God's plan.

The call of God is progressive. This actually means that you have a starting place, but God matures you into the fullness of His plan. God has a plan over each one of our lives. He also has a plan for people groups and a plan for nations. When He is knitting us together in our mother's womb, that plan is being initiated. The call of God is the highest part of God's plan for us individually. God then matures our individual call as we align corporately in the Body of Christ.

We were never made to be independent. God made us so that our gifts and destinies would align with others. The hand needs the arm; the eyes need the mind; and so on. Once we find our place in the Body of Christ and we see that "room has been made for our gift," our call is extended to the city and territory that we are part of. As we become stewards and faithful to demonstrate God's covenant plan in every aspect of our life, He can extend our call even to a nation.

Therefore, the functionality of our gift can increase and be used in a greater scope, function, or sphere of authority.

Over the past 30 or so years, I have watched the Lord develop His call in my life for the "healing of the nations." He first assigned me to pray for my extended family who had been scattered. The Lord showed me that if I would take my stand, He would restore my family. I will explain this further. He then had me take a stand on behalf of a friend who was going in a wrong direction. God had me stand and intercede for this friend until he surrendered to the call of God to minister the Word of God. He then had me take a stand on behalf of the church that my wife and I were attending. This church then experienced growth, entered into a major building program, and the Lord began to visit and pour out His Spirit in a new way in the midst of the Body.

The Lord then asked me to stand and pray for the Church and nations of the former Soviet Bloc countries. At this point, I stepped over into a dynamic of understanding the healing of the nations. I rallied prayer and worked along with other organizations to see oppressed Christians in those areas released from prison. After the 1989-1991 changes that occurred in these nations, the Lord arranged circumstances so that I would meet a lady named Cindy Jacobs, who introduced me to Peter Wagner and Bobbye Byerly. They then opened the door for me to become a prayer leader for the 10/40 window, the most unevangelized area in the world. Since that time, God has assigned many nations for me to pray for. My faith has increased as I have progressed in His calling to believe for the healing of the nations and the release of captives from satan's dominion.

GO TO ALL THE STATES

At the end of 2002, when I was flying into Washington, DC, to attend a few meetings, the Lord impressed me with these words, "For this nation to change, I need you to visit every state and rally My army." This was a very stretching moment in my life. I have many commitments. I speak and travel worldwide. I have a large family, a vibrant church, and serve on many ministry boards. Therefore, I knew the Lord would have to fully confirm His word to me.

He began to do some very peculiar things to let me know He was working to assign me my next "gap" to stand in. Dutch Sheets met me in DC where we were having leadership gatherings and ministering. He asked me this question: "What do you hear the Lord saying?" I could only respond that He was asking me to go to every state of our nation. With a very peculiar look on his face, he said, "The Lord has spoken the same thing to me!" Thus, our lives would change the next two years with the promise that if we would go, the nation that we loved would also change.

THE CALL OF GOD

As you can see, the call of God is extremely personal but has great corporate and national ramifications. I have found that God can do more by my going than my staying. If He asks me to go, He prospers my family. They seem to thrive because of my obedience to the Lord. In *The Best Is Yet Ahead: Pressing Toward Prophetic Fulfillment*, you can read about my wife's journey and my journey out of barrenness and into conception and multiplication, which happened after I obeyed the Lord's call to, "Follow Me."[11]

With each call of God, we receive grace and power to accomplish His purpose. Here are examples of four different calls that we find extended in the Word of God. The characteristics of these calls reflect the very heart and character of God being displayed on earth.

Abraham—A Call to Covenant

In Genesis chapters 11 and 12, we find one of the most incredible sections of the entire Word of God. Decadence, false worship, and people building a prototype that did not reflect Heaven necessitated a call from Heaven into the earth realm. God found a man in Ur of Chaldees and said to him, "Get out!" "Come out of everything around you and follow Me" seemed to be the words echoing from Heaven. The Lord said that if Abraham would follow Him, he would not only be a blessing on earth but he would be a blessing to all the families on earth.

Abraham's obedience affected each of us. This gave us a door and connection to receive the same blessings God was speaking to Abraham. In Galatians 3:13-14 (NKJV) we find, *"Christ has redeemed us from the curse of the law, having become a curse for us (for it is written, 'Cursed is everyone who hangs on a tree'), that the blessing of Abraham might come upon the Gentiles in Christ Jesus, that we might receive the promise of the Spirit through faith."*

Abraham's obedience created an alignment of the Throne of Heaven with man on earth. Abraham's obedience to the call created a covenant agreement that would extend from generation to generation. When we obey the call of God, His covenant blessings manifest on earth.

Nehemiah—A Call to Restoration

When we disobey or violate God's covenant agreement with us and deviate from His path of life, we find His blessings stop and decay begins. Nehemiah is a wonderful character who was displaced along with God's covenant people, Israel, after they continually went against God's plan on earth. Nehemiah, whose name means "Yahweh comforts," received God's call when he was in Shushan, the winter capital of Persia. A friend, Hanani, came and told him of the great distress, reproach, and brokenness that had occurred in Jerusalem. This news produced such a burden in Nehemiah that all he could do was pray and weep.

Many times the call of God comes from a distressing situation around us. We feel compelled to be part of the "fixing" of the situation. When Nehemiah went in to do his job before the king, the king noticed Nehemiah's distress and favored him by allowing him to go and help his people rebuild what had been torn down. When we heed the call of God, we can bring back to life what has been destroyed and restore His purposes on earth.

Isaiah—A Call to Holiness

Isaiah was called to be a prophet to Israel. One of the prophet's roles on earth is to prevent the people of God from veering off God's perfect path. Isaiah had prophesied many times the will of God to the people. Then God did something new in Isaiah's life to create a different paradigm. Isaiah saw the Lord judging King Uzziah for attempting to fulfill a role that was not his call. When Isaiah realized God's power and order, He "saw the Lord" in a whole new way. You can find this story in Isaiah chapter 6. Verse 3 (NKJV) summarizes Isaiah's vision by stating the cry of the angels, *"Holy, holy, holy is the Lord of hosts; the whole earth is full of His glory!"* This affected Isaiah both spiritually as well as physically. His voice was changed. His unclean lips were sanctified. The prophet then submitted himself to say, *"Here am I! Send me"* (Isaiah 6:8). The call of God is a holy call that purifies our expression of God's character, purpose, and will on earth.

Peter—A Call to Harvest

Then there is Peter. So many of us identify with Peter—his struggles and emotional roller-coaster ride. However, even Peter, with all of his issues, was called. In John chapter 1, we find that when Jesus first met Peter, He spoke to the very depths of Peter's purpose and called him to follow Him into that purpose. Peter became a disciple. A disciple learns how to walk on his or her path so they can be sent into the fullness of God's plan. Of course, you know the history of Peter. Jesus met him in his business. Jesus met him in his fear. And in Matthew chapter 16, Jesus acknowledged his revelatory gift and connection with the Father. The Lord promised him that He would build the Church upon his revelation. Of course, Peter fell twice and denied the Lord three times after this. However, this did not stop the Lord's call. In John chapter 21, we find the Lord speaking to Peter three times, asking him a simple question, "Do you love Me?" Through their conversation, the Lord showed Peter His purpose. He said, "Feed My sheep." And then He said to Peter, "Follow Me." The call of God leads us into harvest.

THE REDEMPTIVE CALL

I call the Lord's relationship with Peter an expression of developing our redemptive call. When the Lord first met Peter as recorded in John chapter 1, through an introduction by Peter's brother, Andrew, the Lord looked at Peter and said to him, *"'You are Simon, the son of Jonah. You shall be called Cephas' (which is translated, A Stone)"* (John 1:42 NKJV). Jesus spoke into Peter's full redemptive plan.

Redemption is buying back something that has been lost. *Padah* is a Hebrew word that expresses the legal and commercial use of the redemptive concept in relation to the redemption of persons or other living beings. For example, if a person owned an ox, which was known to be dangerous, yet he did not keep the ox secured, and the ox gored the son or daughter of a neighbor, both the ox and the owner would be stoned to death. If, however, the father of the slain person agreed to accept an amount of money, the owner of the ox could pay the redemption price and live (see Exodus 21:29-30,32).

Ga'al is another Hebrew word that indicates a redemption price involving family members and the responsibility of next-of-kin. A kinsman was responsible to redeem the estate that his nearest relative might have sold because of poverty (see Leviticus 25:25; Ruth 4:4). It was the kinsman's responsibility also to ransom a kinsman who may have sold himself (see Leviticus 25:47-48).

The Old Testament book of Ruth is the most striking example of a kinsman who used his power and Jewish law to redeem. Boaz demonstrated one of the duties of the kinsman—that of marrying the widow of a deceased kinsman. A correlation is sometimes made between the redemption of Ruth by Boaz and the redemption of sinners by Christ.

God called Jeremiah to demonstrate his confidence in God's promise by going out from Jerusalem to his ancestral village, Anathoth, and acting as next-of-kin to redeem or ransom the family land by paying the redemption price for it (see Jeremiah 32:6-15). Such commercial practices easily passed over into religious concepts. God would redeem Israel from her iniquities.

Kipper (or "cover") is another word that is used strictly in religious concepts and practices. It is the word from which *Kippur* is derived in *Yom Kippur*, Day of Atonement, or Day of Covering, perhaps the most sacred of the holy days in Judaism. (The verb form in the Old Testament is always used in a religious sense, such as the covering of sin or the making of atonement for sin.) The Lord has *bought back* or *paid in full* the price for your life. He has done the same thing for this nation.

The New Testament centers redemption in Jesus Christ. He purchased the Church with His own blood (see Acts 20:28), gave His flesh for the life of the world (see John 6:51), as the Good Shepherd laid down His life for His sheep (see John 10:11), and demonstrated the greatest love by laying down His life for His friends (see John 15:13).

The purpose of Jesus in the world was to make a deliberate sacrifice of Himself for human sin. He did something that sinful people could not do for themselves. He brought hope to sinners, providing redemption from sin and fellowship with the eternal Father. As the suffering Servant, His was a costly sacrifice, the shameful and agonizing death of a Roman cross. New Testament redemption thus speaks of substitutionary sacrifice demonstrating divine love and righteousness. It points to a new relationship with God, the dynamic of a new life, God's leniency in the past, and the call for humility for the future.[12]

GOD HAS A PROPHETIC ARMY

Another reason that I believe going from state to state materialized is because of a word that God gave me in October 2000, before the presidential election. I had been meeting in states with apostles, prophets, and intercessors for many years; and in Oklahoma, we began to intensify meetings after the bombing of the Murrah Building—which was the worst terrorist attack ever recorded in our land up until that point. During the meeting, the Spirit of God fell on me, and I began to prophesy. God began to speak about setting a new course in our nation.

He began to share that He would review our nation state by state. He added the following, "Judgment will come based on the complacency of the Church from state to state. I am setting a new course of righteousness." He said that He would look at each state based upon how they gathered and worshiped, as well as how they dealt with the issue of robbing His covenant plan from the next generation (the issue of abortion and illegal bloodshed).

This word was also given in the context of an impending war that would break out in our nation. After giving a time frame of the next 18 months, He said, "This will be a war of great spiritual magnitude. The war will be over the boundaries of the future, for the enemy has shifted boundaries. There is a war over the justice of this land. I will establish justice in the midst of My people. Therefore there will be war over laws that have been established wrongly. Know you are warring with an antichrist system. Therefore, do not fear this supernatural war that I am calling My people to be engaged in."[13]

After I gave this prophecy, God got more specific with me, and I prophesied that the Lord would break out in our land by September 18, 2001. Therefore, like Nehemiah and Isaiah, I received such a burden to pray for our nation and our children.

HOW GOD IS MOVING THE CHURCH FROM FELLOWSHIP TO ARMY

To be victorious in war we need to know our God, ourselves, and our enemy. So, who are we? What is "the Church"? In Matthew 16:13-20, Peter tapped into who the Lord really is. The Lord responded by saying, *"Blessed are you, Simon Bar-Jonah, for flesh and blood has not revealed this to you, but My Father who is in heaven. And I also say to you that you* are Peter, and on this rock I will build My church, and the gates of Hades shall not prevail against it. And I will give you the keys of the kingdom of heaven, and whatever you bind on earth will be bound in heaven, and whatever you loose on earth will be loosed in heaven"* (Matthew 16:17-19 NKJV).

Therefore, the Lord is saying that through this confession of revelation He will call out and gather a group who will express His purposes to the gates of hell. He will give these called-out ones keys of authority to bind and loose on earth. This will allow them to forbid and permit. They will forbid the purposes of satan to continue, and they will permit God's full diverse expression of Himself to be seen on earth.

Many people often confuse the Church with the Kingdom of God. They are not the same. The Kingdom is the overall structure that the Church is attempting to express on earth. The Church exists to see the Kingdom established and operating on earth. The Church facilitates the Kingdom. There is conflict in the earth realm between kingdoms. The Kingdom of God and the kingdom of satan are at war! The Church operates as the armed forces of God in that war. The Church is the governing, legislating, mediating force that God has ordained and aligned to accomplish His purposes on earth.

In *The Worship Warrior*, John Dickson and I write, "Worship and war go together. But for war we must have an army. An army is a nation's personnel organized for battle."[14] You can see the concept of the Church is one of power, legislation, and corporateness. We are a decreeing, demonstrating power on earth.

In *The Future War of the Church*, Rebecca Wagner Sytsema and I write:

> The Greek word *ekklesia* ("Church") means those gathered to accomplish something or a group of people who

THE CALL

are called out for a purpose. The first time this notion of a people called out appears in the Bible is when the children of Israel come out of Egypt. They were called out in order to move into God's inheritance that He had promised their forefather Abraham. This promise had been passed down to Isaac and then to Jacob. The promise then moved with the sons of Jacob/Israel from the place of fulfillment into a foreign land, the land of Egypt, as had been prophesied in Genesis 15. ...So even though the people of promise had remained in Egypt for 400 years, they had to be called out in God's perfect time, so that they could journey to the place of the promise's fulfillment.

What did God do to call out His promise from one place and send to its place of fulfillment?

First of all, we see that He changed governments over the people:

Now it happened in the process of time that the king of Egypt died. Then the children of Israel groaned because of the bondage, and they cried out; and their cry came up to God because of the bondage. So God heard their groaning, and God remembered His covenant with Abraham, with Isaac, and with Jacob. And God looked upon the children of Israel, and God acknowledged them (Exodus 2:23-25 NKJV).

...This calling-out place is also the first time we see God's heart to order His people for war. He chose Moses and Aaron to be their leaders, *"the same Aaron and Moses to whom the Lord said, 'Bring out the children of Israel from the land of Egypt according to their armies'"* (Exodus 6:26 NKJV). In other words, the order of the family clans was

important for the future of their victories according to the promises He had ordained for them.

God called the children of Israel out of Egypt because He had planned to govern them Himself. He had ways to govern them and He raised up the order and method of government for His people so they could accomplish His purposes.[15]

We find this government being extended into the earth with gifts of grace by the Lord Jesus Christ when He was ascending after His death and resurrection. This ascension has brought Him to the right hand of the Father, making Him available to us to legislate God's Kingdom today.

Ephesians 4:11-16 (NKJV) says:

> *And He Himself gave some to be apostles, some prophets, some evangelists, and some pastors and teachers, for the equipping of the saints for the work of ministry, for the edifying of the body of Christ, till we all come to the unity of the faith and of the knowledge of the Son of God, to a perfect man, to the measure of the stature of the fullness of Christ; that we should no longer be children, tossed to and fro and carried about with every wind of doctrine, by the trickery of men, in the cunning craftiness of deceitful plotting, but, speaking the truth in love, may grow up in all things into Him who is the head—Christ—from whom the whole body, joined and knit together by what every joint supplies, according to the effective working by which every part does its share, causes growth of the body for the edifying of itself in love.*

Armies have always been organized in different ways at different times. When we talk about a changing paradigm or wineskin in the

Church, we are talking about God's army being organized in a way to express themselves to the dark forces of the age they represent. John Dickson and I go on to say in *The Worship Warrior:*

> The writer of the book of Hebrews, in the New Testament, looked back on the heroes of faith and proclaimed that through faith they "turned to flight the armies of the aliens" (Heb. 11:34). John's vision of the end times included the armies of heaven following the King of kings to victory over the beast and the false prophet (see Rev. 19:11-21). In Revelation we also find that the six angels sounded a trumpet and released the four angels who had been prepared to go forth and bring a level of destruction to Earth. Universal spiritual warfare resulted from this trumpet blast. The army was always comprised of the people of God, prophets, soldiers, heavenly hosts and other leaders.
>
> In the Greek, the word for army is *strateuma*, which means an armament, a body of troops organized in a systematic way. When we study this word we see that it is also linked with strategy. So an army gains strategy and then moves in order to accomplish victory.
>
> Today God is raising up an army of worshiping warriors. No force on Earth will be able to withstand this army. In the New Testament we find this principle: God had His Church, or *ekklesia* group, called out and assembled together as one man. This army was called out to complete the purpose of God in the earthly realm (see Heb. 8:1-13).
>
> This group was called to worship Him. They also are called to enlist others. They are established under His authority (see Matt. 16:13-21). They have a sure foundation (see Eph.

2:20). They demonstrate His redeeming death by exercising the power of His resurrection. They know that He is the head. They are members. They fellowship together to gain strength and access the mind of their leader. They are fighting against an enemy and his hierarchy. They are bold witnesses, and they have a hope of their leader's return to fill and restore all things in the earthly realm.

They worship unrestrained, so they can obey and further their master's Kingdom plan. They are a Bride ready for war at all times to avenge the enemy and defeat his plan of darkness. Arise, worshiping warriors! Let the Church arise!¹⁶

GATHERING A SYNERGISTIC PRAYER ARMY

Because God is concerned about our worship from state to state, you can see why He would raise up a couple of people who could help us gather together. I have been involved over the last several years in assisting and developing an intercessory prayer army around the world. My involvement intensified in 1992 when I began to work with Peter Wagner and Cindy Jacobs in what was known as the Spiritual Warfare Network. In 1995, this involvement increased again as we began to shift the prayer movement into a new dimension by finding leaders in every state who could help us pray very specifically for key issues. This developed into the United States Strategic Prayer Network (USSPN), which is one of the larger prayer networks in our nation. The communication system for this network began to develop as I was working with Peter Wagner and Ted Haggard in what is known as the World Prayer Center.

In 1996, when Cindy Jacobs was appointed as the U.S. Coordinator of the USSPN, we had two goals: to mobilize a leader and network of pray-ers in every state, and to have a solemn assembly in every state by the year 2000. Since then, we have continued to establish and accelerate the process of connecting strategic prayer leadership throughout every state and region of the United States. This has enhanced our ability to communicate about major issues. We have established State Coordinators (and a Coordinator for the District of Columbia), along with teams of strategic-level intercessors.

Because America is a federation of states, we believe each state must be dealt with individually for the healing of the nation. These prayer groups open up paths of reconciliation and bridge any gaps created by iniquitous sins and patterns that would defile the land and allow the enemy legal right to develop and maintain strongholds in our midst. These iniquitous patterns cause gender, racial, and spiritual division. We have accomplished much reconciliation, and we are now coming together corporately to enter into breakthrough praying throughout the states of this nation. The wars are intensifying, but the army is growing.

As National Apostle of the USSPN, I am excited about how we have moved forward to network our nation for spiritual breakthrough and transformation. And when Pastor Dutch and I began to travel to every state, we saw the army develop in a new way.

TODAY, IF YOU WILL HEAR MY VOICE!

Just as the Church transitions from one wineskin to another so that they can receive the revelation that is pertinent in their age, I believe the prayer force must also transition. God's intercessors usually hear first because they have heeded the call to stand in the gap.

As we began to ride across the land, Dutch and I covenanted with each other and the Lord that we would listen carefully to His current word for each state. In Second Peter 1:12 (NKJV) we find, *"For this reason I will not be negligent to remind you always of these things, though you know and are established in the **present** truth."* "Present" means the now word of the hour, to express the manifold wisdom of God for this age. Therefore, we knew we were supposed to seek God's current word for each state, address the army in each state, and then connect each state to the overall whole of our nation.

Proverbs 29:18 (AMPC) says, *"Where there is no vision [no redemptive revelation of God], the people perish; but he who keeps the law [of God, which includes that of man]—blessed (happy, fortunate, and enviable) is he."* God is expressing to our nation that He would not have one perish. He also wants us to return to His covenant plan. Another purpose of this journey was to review the prophetic history of our nation and link that history into today's current word. We will discuss this more in a following chapter.

Once you receive the word of God, you decree the word of God. The power of that decree sets in motion God's plan on earth for today. We looked at the resources that we had—a well-developed internet communications structure and apostolic and prophetic leaders whom we knew in every state. We knew that intercessors, using the internet communications system, would begin to talk among themselves and rally for their states. We also knew that if we could find the key apostolic and prophetic leaders in each state, we could gather God's army. God was faithful to back what He had called us to do.

You will read several examples in the following chapters of what God has done. Then in Part II of this book you will find a state-by-state history and prophetic destiny for each hour. Use this book to pray through our nation and see its covenant destiny released in a new way.

– 3 –

PLANTING *the* HEAVENS
(Tim Sheets)

And I have put My words in your mouth; I have covered you with the shadow of My hand, that I may plant the heavens, lay the foundations of the earth, and say to Zion, "You are My people"
(Isaiah 51:16 NKJV).

Isaiah 51:16 speaks revelation to us right now, in this day and time. However, the fullness of what God was saying to the prophet Isaiah is not going to be manifested until He comes back in His millennial reign. Notice He says, *"I have put My words in your mouth."* The word for *mouth* is the Hebrew word *peh*, and it means "the taste center of the body" (Strong's H6310). You eat food by putting it in your mouth, chewing it up, and swallowing it. Where words are concerned, the mouth is literally the speech center of the body.

Peh also has a figurative meaning—the opening of the body to sound forth a command, an instruction, a prophetic word or insight, or some other communication. The mouth does this by forming and amplifying words to a person, organization, congregation, nation, government, or other similar entity. God distinguishes two different realms where the words take effect, realms not talked about very much in our times but clearly emphasized by God right from the beginning—the heavens or the earth.

PRAYERS ARE WORD SEEDS

In this verse in Isaiah, God talks about words sounding forth from the mouths of His sons and daughters, His heirs, into the realm of the heavens or the earth. This again emphasizes that words are seeds—word seed decrees. This also includes prayer because prayers are words of communication seeded into the heavens and into the earth. Prayer is speech to God making a request, but it is also, at times, a decree of God's promises. Prayers express confidence in God's answering abilities, or they may ask for divine intervention into a situation.

The mouth (*peh*) is the opening of the body to sound forth God's Word as seeds that grow to fullness until they are manifested in the heavens or on earth. The mouth is, therefore, the opening through which we sow the seed of God's Word into a region. Lucifer and his kingdom seek to silence Christ's Body (the Church). They want our mouths closed. They don't want us to speak. Part of a demon's assignment is to shut the mouth of Christ's Body. Too many in the Body of Christ have fallen into that error and actually embraced it.

From the very beginning, God's original intent was for His sons and daughters, His heirs, to open their mouths and declare His words onto the earth. He has put His Word in your mouth so that He may plant it in the heavens and on the earth. The word for *plant* is the Hebrew word *nata*, and it means "to plant, to fix, or to set in place" (Strong's H5193). God Himself was the original Gardener, and we have inherited that job from Him as His heirs.

GRANDPA'S GARDEN

Whenever I think about planting, I think of my grandfather Henkel. He worked at a hardware store in Waverly, Ohio, and he needed to make extra income. For probably 25 years or so, he would sell plants in the spring. He always began the process in the winter time. I can remember, as a little kid, my grandpa sitting in the living room flipping through books of seeds and wondering aloud, "Do I want this kind of tomato plant?" "Is this the kind of seed I'm going to buy?" He would decide what kinds of seeds he was going to order.

Then, as soon as the weather broke, he would go out into what he called "hot beds," which were four or five feet wide and ten feet long, and that's where he planted everything. He would dig up all the dirt and he would burn it and mix in fertilizer and then he would go out and plant those seeds. He would cover the seeds up with plastic, and he was careful to water them and take care of them. When those plants got to maybe six to eight inches tall, he would put up his sign on the front porch: "Plants for Sale."

People came from all around Waverly, Ohio, to buy my grandpa's plants. My grandfather's seeds planted a lot of gardens in Waverly. Hundreds of people ate from them. People would come and get the little plants that he would wrap in newspaper, and they would take them home to their gardens and set them out. Of course, he saved some of the plants to set out in his own garden. He always had one of the best gardens anywhere around, and he fed his family out of that garden year-round. Whatever they didn't eat they would can and save for later.

GOD'S SPOKEN WORDS

In the beginning, God planted the stars. His Word said "be" and it was. He set the stars, sun, and planets into place. He planted galaxies and moons with His Word. He planted the heavens and He planted the earth with His word seed decrees. He told the prophet Isaiah in Isaiah 51:16, *"I have put My words in your mouth...that I might plant the heavens,* [and] *lay the foundations of the earth."* Foundations on the earth were established according to God's decreed word. The condition of the heavens and the earth were dependent upon the Word of God, His spoken word, and it still is today.

The entire universe is made to hearken to the voice of God's Word. Heaven and earth are made to respond to the voice of God's Word. Angel armies are made to respond to the voice of God's Word. Amazingly, human beings, made in God's image and likeness, are also carriers of God's voice when they are activated at the new birth.

As His seed on the earth, we are to open our mouths and plant the heavens and the earth with God's Word. We are to declare the words of God into the heavens and the earth, mankind, nations, government, congregations, and people everywhere to set in place foundations for stable government and society. We are to be stewards of what God said was to be. If the foundations are not set according to God's Word, then at some point that society is going to crumble under the weight of iniquitous roots. Jesus said that such a house will not be built upon rock; it will be built upon sand, and when the storm comes it is going to fall (see Matthew 7:26).

The Body of Christ is to open their mouths and plant God's Word into the earth. Like my grandfather planted produce (good seeds) into all of Waverly, we, too, are to plant God's good word seeds into our cities and regions. *"I have put My words in your mouth that I might plant the heavens and the earth."* Words are the seeds we plant with.

PLANTING WORDS IN A REGION

Years ago, before I ever understood that words are seeds, I remember I was asked to go to a very small church in southern Ohio. I knew the pastor, and they had a special event going on and wanted me to come share. I don't remember what the event was, but I remember praying, "Okay, Lord. What should I share with these people?" As I prayed about, it I received revelation concerning the church ruling and reigning with Christ Jesus in this life (see Romans 5:17). I got a download of understanding and it just kept coming.

Afterward I began to think, *I need to help the Lord out here.* It's something I don't attempt to do much anymore, but I said, "Lord, that's not what these people need to hear. They won't understand this. This is not even on their radar screen. This is not where they are."

He said something to me all those years ago that I have never forgotten, and it has been instruction for me concerning my apostolic calling and assignment ever since. He said, "They will understand what I help them to understand and what I reveal to their hearts." In other words, don't you worry about them getting fed—I will take care of that.

I have seen that over the years. I don't know how many times I have preached a sermon and somebody has come up and said, "That is exactly what I needed to hear," and proceeded to tell me what they got from the message. In the meantime, I'm thinking, *That is not even what I said! It's not even my point!* But it was God's point to them. However many people are there, that's how many sermons you're preaching because they're thinking concerning their own life situations, their own experiences, and what God is saying to them.

God said, "They'll understand what I help them understand and what I reveal to their hearts." But then He said, "I need you to plant this word into the region."

Now that gave me pause. I began to think, *Can I do that? Lord, can I plant a message in the heavens and the earth realm of a region? Do You really want me to plant a message, to plant doctrine from Your Word into the atmosphere of a region?*

Very clearly He said to me, "Yes. I want to grow it there. It has been requested by My people, and I need you to sow it into the region. I need you to set the foundations. I need you to lay the biblical foundation for it. It's what apostles and prophets do." I remember thinking at the time, *They do? I didn't know that.* Then the Scripture came to mind that the church is built upon the foundation of the apostles and the prophets (see Ephesians 2:20). He clearly said, "I need you to sow this into the region."

SEEDING THE ATMOSPHERE

I had never thought about it. It had never crossed my mind. I had never heard anybody else talk about this. But I knew a new level of understanding was being given to me, one that years later would help me with my apostolic calling. Sometimes when I am preaching, I will have the awareness that while I am talking God is going to help people understand or get something out of it, but I am also seeding the atmosphere of a region. I'm preaching a message, but I am really planting revival seeds everywhere. I'm planting God's will into the region. I am setting the foundations in the spirit realm. Sometimes I feel like I am laying a foundation in the spirit realm or into the atmosphere so that there can be productivity. I am preaching and planting the heavens.

I'm preaching and planting the earth, in and around this country, for reformation and awakening.

So many times I have the awareness that God is saying, "Plant this into the region. Don't worry about it. Just plant it into the spirit realm. I want to grow it there. It's been requested by My people." Some Sunday mornings, on my way to speak, I experience understanding and begin to think, *I'm preaching this one to seed the region. I am preaching this to seed into the state. I am preaching this to seed it into the atmosphere of the United States of America.* It's not always that way, but sometimes it is. I had to learn that. It is something apostles and prophets do, but it is also something all sons and daughters are supposed to do—apostles and prophets just model it.

BUILDING A FIREWALL

This has helped me with the AwakeningNow Prayer Network, which we began in Ohio in 2008 and is spreading into the surrounding states. This network now has hundreds of churches in the region. The word from Prophet Chuck Pierce was, "Build a firewall around the entire state."

I didn't know how to build a firewall around the whole state, but in prayer the Holy Spirit said, "Go to all 88 counties and hold prayer assemblies." We are currently doing that—we take apostolic teams and worship teams to the prayer assemblies and we make 50 or 60 decrees into that county.

We are there to plant God's Word in the heavens and the earth of that region, and we do that with bold, faith-filled decrees of what God says. We plant prophetic words into that region. We plant that region with the will of God. We, along with the remnant believers who gather, are there to sow the atmosphere of that region with God's word seed decrees so that the rains of Heaven can come and activate them and grow them to fullness. In a sense, we are planting gardens everywhere—gardens that will be beautiful and feed and bless the people of God. Without this understanding of words as seeds or praying into the atmosphere, there is little doubt that I would be doing what I am now doing.

JESUS' PLANTING METHOD

This method of planting the heavens was also taught by Jesus. Remember that He first planted the heavens and the earth in Genesis 1. He is the Word. He planted the entire universe with word seed decrees, saying "be" and it was. In Matthew 6:10 (NKJV), He taught us to pray this way, *"Your kingdom come. Your will be done on earth as it is in heaven."* That's a different kind of prayer because it's not really a petition—it's a declaration. It's not a foretelling of the future—it's a commanding decree. It's calling something to be, calling something to exist. In other words, He said to declare, "Will of God, be done. Will of God, come."

When Jesus walked the earth, we see that His words caused things to happen. Wherever He went, He opened His mouth and He sounded forth decrees that brought miraculous results. In John 6:63 (NKJV) He tells us, saying this, *"The words that I speak to you are spirit, and they are life."* Understand the magnitude of that statement. When Christ spoke, when He opened His mouth and decreed, Holy Spirit moved into the atmosphere. His mouth opened the atmosphere for Holy Spirit to begin to move.

Remember, Holy Spirit hovers until He hears the Word of God. When He hears the Word of God declared, He moves, just like He did upon the chaos and darkness in the beginning. Christ's mouth opened ways for the Kingdom to come. His mouth proclaimed an invitation, "Holy Spirit come. Move here."

What Jesus said produced after its kind. The superior reality of the Kingdom of God, a spiritual Kingdom that visibly affects the entire earth, began to move and transform the earth realm. The Word became a reality and produced what He decreed. The seed in the words produced it. Jesus was modeling ministry for you and me, His joint heirs.

JOINT HEIRS

> *For you did not receive the spirit of bondage again to fear, but you received the Spirit of adoption by whom we cry out, "Abba, Father." The Spirit Himself bears witness with our spirit that we are children of God, and if children, then heirs—heirs of God and joint heirs with Christ, if indeed we suffer with Him, that we may also be glorified together* (Romans 8:15-17 NKJV).

"Joint heirs" is the Greek word *sygkleronomos*, and it simply means a coheir (Strong's G4789). It is also the Greek word for "identical." We are *identical heirs* with Christ. Because of God's grace and the free gift of righteousness through the cross, believers (born-again ones) have now been made to be identical heirs with Christ Jesus. Christ mentors those heirs (us) through the example of His earthly life, showing us how to open our mouths and sound forth Spirit-alive words. Yes, we as coheirs can speak with the presence of the power of the Holy Spirit and can plant the heavens and the earth realms. That's staggering. That's hard to get your mind around.

When the sons and daughters of God open their mouths and decree God's Word, it can change the atmosphere of a region. Our decrees act as a catalyst that sets in motion a chain of events to bring God's Word to pass. They open the heavens so blessings can rain down, miracles can be produced, and we can receive revelation and enlightenment. Our decrees attract angel armies to ascend and descend and assist the heirs of salvation in that region (see Hebrews 1:14).

As God's heirs, as His children on the earth, we are commissioned to plant the heavens with His words, to seed them with declarations of truth. We must declare, on the basis of God's Word, the rightful rule of King Jesus over the earth, the region, and over the kingdom of darkness. We are commissioned to do it. It is well past time, but the sons and daughters of God are just waiting for Christ's return, just waiting for Him to come back. We are commanded to occupy until He comes (see Luke 19:13). We are commanded to rule and reign with Him in this life (see Romans 5:17).

We are to rule over principalities and powers, mights and dominions of darkness, binding them with superior authority just like Jesus bound them when He opened His mouth and declared that they must go. Sitting silent with closed mouths has never been an option for real heirs.

CREATE WITH WORDS

In Isaiah 55, God tells us that His declared word becomes creative. This now starts to get very interesting. Just as God created with His words, saying *"be"* and it was, so you and I, His legitimate seeds on the earth, are restored in purpose and identity to create with our words. Our words, in alignment with God's Word when declared in faith, become creative seeds that grow and produce after their kind. Our words become creative when they are in agreement with God's Word and in alignment with Holy Spirit and His revelation to us. They open creative spheres in a region. Think about it—how could God's creative seed literally be placed in you and you not be creative in nature? The Creator seed is in us; it is our nature to be creative with our words.

> *For as the heavens are higher than the earth, so are My ways higher than your ways, and My thoughts than your thoughts. For as the rain comes down, and the snow from heaven, and do not return there, but water the earth, and make it bring forth and bud, that it may give seed to the sower and bread to the eater, so shall My word be that goes forth from My mouth; it shall not return to Me void, but it shall accomplish what I please, and it shall prosper in the thing for which I sent it* (Isaiah 55:9-11 NKJV).

> *It is the same with my word. I send it out, and it always produces fruit. It will accomplish all I want it to, and it will prosper everywhere I send it* (Isaiah 55:11 NLT).

> *So will My word be which goes out of My mouth; it will not return to Me void (useless, without result), without accomplishing what I desire, and without succeeding in the matter for which I sent it* (Isaiah 55:11 AMP).

So will the words that come out of my mouth not come back empty-handed. They'll do the work I sent them to do, they'll complete the assignment I gave them (Isaiah 55:11 MSG).

GOD'S PROMISE TO US

Words are given assignments! What a promise! "My words shall not return void." *Return* is the Hebrew word *shuv,* and it means "turn around" (Strong's H7725). The promise to you and me—the born-again ones, His sons and daughters—is that the word you decree will not turn around. It cannot be reversed. It's not going to boomerang. The word for *not* is the Hebrew word *lo,* and it simply means to negate something (Strong's H3808). It's a particle of negation in the Hebrew language. It makes a positive statement negative. For example, *"I am absolutely going to do this, maybe."* That's *lo.*

Hear this: God says, "There are not going to be any maybes or I won'ts. If I said it, that's what's going to happen. If it's My word decreed, it's not going to be turned around on you. It shall not be negated. Hell will not negate it. Lucifer will not negate it. Government won't negate it. Demons won't negate it. Humanism cannot negate it. Nothing can negate it."

The word for *void* is the Hebrew word *raykawm,* and it means "empty, ineffectual, and to leak out" (Strong's H7387). God says, "My word that My sons and daughters decree in My name does not return empty." In other words, He is saying, "I don't give empty promises. No, they're all full. They're all effective, and they do not leak. They don't leak out." He tells Isaiah and He tells us today, *"My promises don't leak. They never return empty."*

"It shall accomplish" is one word in the Hebrew text and it's the word *asah,* meaning to yield out of oneself (Strong's H6213). That's what God does—He brings out of Himself. He creates from within Himself with His words. That's what Hebrews 11:3 (NKJV) is talking about. *"By faith we understand that the worlds were framed by the word of God, so that things which are seen were not made of things which are visible."*

The entire universe came out of God. All of creation came out of God. His words framed it. His words decreed it and described it and it produced its kind. All visible, material things were decreed by God to be. They all came out of Him as He decreed His words as seeds. Of course, if the whole universe came out of God then most certainly He can create whatever we need. How hard can that be? Our God can create any word that He speaks. No word of His is empty. When we decree God's Word, creative forces begin to flow. Even if what is needed doesn't exist, God's Word can create it.

The word *asah* also means "to become, to come to pass, to yield, or to bear" (Strong's H6213). *Asah* draws a picture of a fruit tree—it will yield whatever kind it is. The seed contains the tree that will grow from it. The fruit is also in the seed and it becomes what it is. *Asah* is also the word for "execute" or "furnish." God's Word is furnished with power to execute and to bring that word to pass. God's Word, when decreed by His seed in alignment with His will, becomes what it is.

God says it will prosper in the thing for which He sent it. *Prosper* is the Hebrew word *tsaleach,* and it means "to push forward, to break out, to be good, to be successful, or to be profitable" (Strong's H6743). God's Word decreed becomes profitable. It breaks out of confinement. That's the way soil is pictured in the Scriptures. Soil is a confinement for the seed, but the seed breaks out of confinement to produce what it is. Word seeds break through blockages in the heavens and the earth and they are made good. They are successful. They yield and release creative abilities.

THE POWER OF OUR DECREES

We have to understand the power in our decrees of God's Word. We almost haven't even dared to go there. Perhaps it seems too good to be true because we are accustomed to living with a negative theology that we are just downtrodden Christians waiting for Jesus to come. If that's how we think, we have not understood who we really are and who God made us to be. We have not realized that His DNA is literally transmitted into us. Our decrees, just like Jesus Christ's decrees (our identical heir), can become creative forces that break openings in the heavens or the earth for God's purpose and His plan to produce.

We have this promise: when we stand in faith and decree what God says, when we refuse to back off, when we refuse to abandon that word seed, when we water the seed with our faith, our prayers, our praise, our confession, and our steadfast trust, the seed will produce after its kind. It becomes what it is or what it describes. Never give up on a seed you plant. Never give up on God's Word. Never. Don't negate it. We are supposed to make decrees that break loose hell's grip. We can bring forth God's promises in fullness upon the earth.

As God's sons and daughters, we ought to walk this planet expecting to reap God's abundant life that His Word describes to us. We should expect:

- ★ God's word seeds that we decree to produce after their kind
- ★ The word of promise to come to pass, no matter what it is

- ★ The word seeds we sow to become fruitful and multiply
- ★ God's Word on healing to produce the fruit of healing
- ★ His Word that we decree on good success to bear the fruit of success

We should walk this planet declaring the promise and purpose of God and what His Word says. This is true in all aspects of our lives—for example, parenting. My wife, Carol, shared the following story with me that she found on Joanna Gaines's Facebook page. Joanna and Chip Gaines are the popular hosts of HGTV's *Fixer Upper* (a show I have never seen). Joanna writes:

> There's an Adonis Blue butterfly bush I planted by the girls' window almost five years ago when we were renovating the farmhouse. I wanted butterflies by the girls' windows that they could see and enjoy. I never told them about the bush and, honestly, I forgot about it over the years.
>
> This morning, I found my little Emmie sitting by her window, looking excitedly at the bush and saying, "Here she is! My little hummingbird comes every morning, Mom!" First, I didn't know she looked out for her bird every morning. Second, I forgot all about the bush and never told her if she looked out the window she would see the prettiest butterflies and hummingbirds gathered around it.
>
> It's hard not to think, this is a lot like parenting. You sow seeds early on and work hard to be intentional and then, over time, you move on to new lessons and challenges. Then one day you look up and the seeds you planted in your little children's hearts are now in full bloom. Be

encouraged today to keep pressing in and tending to their hearts. It will be worth it. —Joanna Gaines[17]

Parenting seeds planted are still growing years later; even as an adult they are still there.

We should expect deliverance, freedom, prosperity, harvest, miracles, healings, signs, wonders, favor, strength, restoration, satisfaction, fullness, preservation, ways provided for us, help provided for us, abundance to come our way, rest for our souls, and wisdom for answers. Why? It is the seed that is in you. It's the nature of God. Remember, God's *spora* is in you. Expect the parenting seed of your Father to produce His nature. Expect His Word to produce His life everywhere. Expect bountiful gardens to come up all around you to feed and prosper your life. Words are seeds. They grow and they become after their kind.

Prophet Chuck Pierce recently released this prophetic word, which illustrates the importance of your words as seeds:

> Many seeds have been planted, and many seeds are now waiting for a chance in the atmosphere so they can sprout. These seeds are not lying desolate but are waiting for an atmosphere of refreshing and rejoicing that will cause them to break forth. This is a time I'm sending out those who will go to those places where seeds are sown, and from the seeds being sown they will open a portal so the rain of My Spirit can come. Then they will harvest and bring back to the storehouse what needs to be brought back. Seeds are waiting. Your portal will carry the water to bring forth the harvest of grain that has fallen into the earth for a season of death. From the death of past fields a great harvest will come! Amen!

– 4 –

CAN a NATION BE RESTORED?

(Chuck D. Pierce)

For you to come into God's full plan that He has for your life, I believe Acts chapter 17 is very important to understand. Verses 24-28 say:

> *God, who made the world and everything in it, since He is Lord of heaven and earth, does not dwell in temples made with hands. Nor is He worshiped with men's hands, as though He needed anything, since He gives to all life, breath, and all things. And He has made from one blood every nation of men to dwell on all the face of the earth, and has determined their preappointed times and the boundaries of their dwellings, so that they should seek the Lord, in the hope that they might **grope** for Him and find Him, though He is not far from each one of us; for in Him we live and move and have our being, as also some of your own poets have said, "For we are also His offspring"* (Acts 17:24-28 NKJV).

He has a perfect time and place that He has determined for you. When you are at the right place at the right time, you can "grope for

Him and find Him." When you grab hold of God, you can bring His blessings down into the earth realm. Old cycles can break. Restoration begins and starts a process to bring you full circle into God's perfect plan. God does not look at how long sin or iniquity has been in place; He looks for someone who will grab hold of Him and start His process working on earth. To "grope" means to touch God. When we touch God and He touches us, Heaven and earth come into agreement. *Grope* is a covenant word also. Not only do Heaven and earth agree, but covenant blessings are released as well.

CAN A NATION REALLY BE RESTORED?

This is a good question and we believe the Bible answers this question. God says in Isaiah 66:7-9 (NKJV):

> *"Before she was in labor, she gave birth; before her pain came, she delivered a male child. Who has heard such a thing? Who has seen such things? Shall the earth be made to give birth in one day? Or shall a nation be born at once? For as soon as Zion was in labor, she gave birth to her children. Shall I bring to the time of birth, and not cause delivery?" says the Lord. "Shall I who cause delivery shut up the womb?" says your God.*

If God can birth a nation in a day, He can change a nation when it strays. Of course, this is linked with our covenant relation to Him. Isaiah also says that the nations are as a drop in the bucket to the Lord. Nations are no more difficult to deal with than individuals.

However, restoration is a different process than conception and birth. Since the Garden of Eden, mankind has been in need of restoration from the time we are born. God knits us together in our mother's womb, and I believe He knits our purpose within us. I also believe He knits His ability to press past every plan of the enemy that would stop us from coming into that purpose. When we rely on His ability, we overcome the enemy's plan.

God's ultimate intent was for the Garden to be filled with His glory. His glory would then work its way out and cover the entire earth. This is still His purpose today, but we are working from a standpoint of restoration. Land needs glory to represent the fullness of God. So when a people develop a nation and align that nation with God's covenant plan, they start the restoration process of bringing God's glory into the earth realm. However, when they divert from God's covenant plan, the glory lifts and decay begins. Therefore, we have other elements we have to process before we see restoration occurring. We must deal with illegal bloodshed, idolatry, immorality, and covenant breaking.

Any time these issues enter into God's covenant relationship and plan for a nation, they have to be addressed and reconciliation has to occur.

Acts 3:19-21 (NKJV) says,

> *Repent therefore and be converted, that your sins may be blotted out, so that times of refreshing may come from the presence of the Lord, and that He may send Jesus Christ, who was preached to you before, whom heaven must receive until the times of **restoration** of all things, which God has spoken by the mouth of all His holy prophets since the world began.*

After the resurrection, when Jesus ascended to the right hand of the Father, He left the Holy Spirit to be His agent of reconciliation. The Holy Spirit shakes us and convicts us of communion blocks—those things that prevent us from touching and talking with God. He first restores our ability to contact God. Then He begins to restore every thing and place that we are a part of. Rebecca Wagner Sytsema and I write several chapters about the power of loss and God's process of restoration in *Possessing Your Inheritance*. We talk about moving from grief to glory. This comes when God begins to visit us in the place that He has determined for us.

When the true manifest presence of God visits us as humans, His glory radiates from that presence. At times God does visibly reveal His glory. Such a display of His presence is often seen as fire or dazzling light, perhaps as a cloud or mist, or sometimes as an act of His mighty power. But even when we do not visibly see manifestations of God's glory, the visitation leaves us with an impression of His glory burned into our hearts. It is the inward hidden work in our heart that produces the Christlike attributes that move us from glory to glory.[18]

The dictionary definition of *restoration* is "to revive and return to life" or "to bring back to a former or original condition." This definition falls short of all that restoration in God means. God intends to do more than bring us back to a former or original condition. Restoration begins multiplication! When you study the process of restoration, you discover that once the process begins, you have the right to double, quadruple, and even enter into a sevenfold completion of all of God's purposes. In my own life, I became even more committed to the 50-State Tour because the Lord said to me, "I am opening a door to this nation's future. My desire is for its latter to be greater than its former."

RESTORING, RECONCILING, AND ALIGNING A NATION STATE BY STATE

There is usually a process in everything. Process is the course of something developing and eventually coming into its full operation. Process includes preparation, discipline, order, change, development, and operational steps that bring you to a destination. Therefore, we go through a process to reach our destiny. That process usually includes restoration, reconciliation, and some sort of release.

States have destinies. Our nation was created sovereignly.

The United States Constitution says:

> We the People of the United States, in Order to form a more perfect Union, establish Justice, insure domestic Tranquility, provide for the common defence, promote the general Welfare, and secure the Blessings of Liberty to ourselves and our Posterity, do ordain and establish this Constitution for the United States of America.

In the Declaration of Independence we find,

> We, therefore, the Representatives of the United States of America, in General Congress, Assembled, appealing to the Supreme Judge of the world for the rectitude of our intentions, do, in the Name, and by Authority of the good People of these Colonies, solemnly publish and declare, That these United Colonies are, and of Right ought to be Free and Independent States; that they are Absolved from all Allegiance to the British Crown, and that all political connection between them and the State of Great Britain,

is and ought to be totally dissolved; and that as Free and Independent States, they have full Power to levy War, conclude Peace, contract Alliances, establish Commerce, and to do all other Acts and Things which Independent States may of right do. And for the support of this Declaration, with a firm reliance on the protection of divine Providence, we mutually pledge to each other our Lives, our Fortunes and our sacred Honor.

Therefore, we should view the destiny of our state as part of the whole of what God has planned for our nation. This is the same concept as members of a body. Also, we should look at the Body of Christ in each state. When we align the Body of Christ in our nation, we find a peculiar people ready to do God's will from Heaven, in the land that we occupy here on earth. We represent God in this nation. We, the Body of Christ, should be the driving force to even maintain our Constitution and the Declaration of Independence. Any time a state deviates from God's plan first and then His sovereign order in this nation, the Body of Christ should rise up in that state and say, "Let us return and be restored to the Lord."

In this book, you will read several examples of how the Lord has released the destiny of states. (See Chapter 10, "State by State: History and Future Destiny.") We knew that the 50-State Tour gatherings would be a key to our nation's restoring its breastplate of righteousness. The major goal of the state meetings would be to align the Body properly and to decree the Lord's redemptive plan for each state. This would stir up the faith in the Body of Christ in each state and cause them to take their stand on behalf of their land.

So that our nation might be transformed, God's order must first be established in each state. When strategic intercessors are aligned with apostolic leaders, breakthrough begins. Intercessors carry the burden of God, prophetic people make key declarations, and apostles set the decrees in motion. In other words, intercessors keep the heavens open; prophets begin to express God's heart, making key declarations into the atmosphere; and apostolic leaders pull upon that revelation or blueprint of Heaven and bring it into an established form in the earth realm.

The following section describes how a typical meeting went in each state. After we connected with apostolic leadership in a territory, many times we would begin addressing an issue that had stopped God's redemptive covenant plan. We would declare restoration! Usually reconciliation would follow. Then God would release His purpose. We also would obey the word of God and pray for the authorities in our nation. In the example below, you will find how we began with state purposes and actually moved from there into God's plan for our nation. Then the meeting in a supernatural way would touch the whole world.

TEXAS STATE MEETING—A GREAT MODEL

At the Texas 50-State Tour gathering, these elements clicked. Alice Patterson, our USSPN Apostolic Coordinator for the state of Texas, sponsored the state meeting in San Antonio on December 8-9, 2003. The meeting was held at New Life Christian Center, headed by Apostles LaSalle and Portia Vaughn. These were key apostolic leaders with an incredible church. We began our restoration process by reconciling issues concerning the Host People of the land. Jay Swallow, a Native apostolic leader, led this. We then moved from the Host People of the land to reconciliation between Hispanics and Anglos. Being in San

Antonio where cultures clash and many breaches have occurred gave us a need to identify with past sins and problems. Much reconciliation occurred concerning the Hispanic issue of our nation and the leaders of that ethnic group taking their prophetic apostolic place in our nation.

Cindy Jacobs, a well-known apostolic prophetic intercessor, was there on the night of December 8 and began to prophesy and unlock a new anointing for the state of Texas. Dutch began to teach and preach on the night of December 9. When he did, a prophetic anointing began to fill the room. It was as if *I knew* God's heart and mind and why we were there. I actually felt I was being lifted into the heavenlies and standing before the Lord. I grabbed hold of Alice and said, "I am going up before God." In this spiritual place I heard Him say, *"I am going to tell you why you are here. Do not think; just go and decree what I tell you."*

Declaring the Mantle of a State

Dutch Sheets began by declaring the redemptive gift of the state of Texas:

> Jesus, we want more of Your Christ anointing of the prophetic. Jesus, the Prophet, come to Texas. Come with Your holy zeal, come with Your fire, come with Your revelation—Jesus, the Prophet, the Prophet of God. The very testimony of You is the Spirit of prophecy. Jesus, come and mantle Texas tonight with another level, another degree of the prophetic anointing to be forerunners for America. Impregnate this state with a transformation anointing. Impregnate this state with the ability to prophesy and decree change to the rest of the nation. Impregnate this state with revelation so that their words don't fall to the ground. Impregnate them with a power that no matter what the hordes of hell say,

that something changes in the Spirit. The decrees of man, the unrighteous spirit, the decrees of ungodly judges begin to pale and fall before You. Let the idols of man fall and be broken next to the Ark of Your Presence. Lord, I just say according to Your word, a nation could be born from this state. I say there is a governmental anointing on the state of Texas—on the Church of Texas—to rise up in her position in heavenly places and begin to legislate and begin to affect, to begin to release the government of God (that) changes the government of man.

Connecting the State into the Whole Purposes of Our Nation

Pastor Dutch began to pray for President Bush:

> I say there is an anointing, whether he knows it or not, on our president to do it—that comes from the state of Texas. And he is mantled with a prophetic anointing to hear from Heaven. And where he is—I break off of him and shield him even now from any ability of the enemy to deceive him or lead him down wrong paths. And I decree that if he has gone down a wrong path, You're just going to correct it because You put him there and You love him and You've called him and he loves You. And I say that the prophetic anointing of God rests upon the man. I say, Lord, would You speak to this nation and the nations of the earth through that man. Lord, we just say now, Your word is in us as a seed and we are now pregnant with life. A nation is in our womb. We are a prophetic people, and we're going to build bridges into the

> new. We are ready. We receive a new mantle of Your Spirit to mantle the state of Texas once again with a new level of the prophetic anointing. We say the old is broken and the new has come, and the reproach is broken and the breaches are dealt with, and the new mantle is coming to the state of Texas in Jesus' name.

The Stirring of the Prophetic Anointing and the Release of a "Now" Word

I then began to prophesy:

> Watch the bridges that begin to fall. For even now there are some that are sitting on pillars that will not stand in days ahead. These will become signs to you. For bridges will be coming down so that I can reroute what I need to do at this time. There is strength in this state to turn the battle at the gate. Allow your strength to rise up…the heavens are opening tonight and the revelation is beginning to pour out.

Declaration of the Lord's Purpose for Bringing Us Together

I next shared the Lord's reasons for bringing us together:

> Now, when Pastor Dutch was sharing with us about Detroit and how we were at a certain place at a certain time [April 3-5, 2003], and God gave us revelation about how the key had been turned over and even caused the voice of that region to be lost, we were there [in Detroit] right when it was time, and they [the coalition troops] were stalled going through

the gate into Babylon. And I felt like we made a break, and as we broke through and as we repented, as the key people came forward, it allowed us to enter in and bring confusion and to declare a dropping of a stronghold.

However, since that time we have seemed to lose ground in that nation of Babylon, in that nation of Iraq...there was a quickening when he said that.

And He said, "Just as you were there then, I have you here now. And what has fallen into confusion where ambushes have come, I have said to you tonight and I say to you tonight I am raising up a people here tonight that can put a stop to the ambushes from this place in San Antonio. In this place tonight you have been given the power to stop what has been scattered, and call things back into place. Start with yourself and declare scattering will flee. Decree that scattering, that is a part of the vision that you're a part of, will now have to go. And now where the enemy has tried to bring scattering even into the leadership of this state—decree it stopped tonight. And now declare over this nation that the power of scattering that would even create plans to go this way and that way and another way, decree that the ambushes are now being stopped in Jesus' name. And declare, instead of ambush, that President Bush will have a clear mind tonight."

Speaking from the Seer Anointing

And then the Lord showed me a nest, and it was a nest of snake eggs. And the Lord said,

> There are four snake eggs that are lying wait, and that from this state I am giving you the power tonight to crush those snake eggs. I would even say to you in this state tonight you will be able to decree to Babylon, and that strongman that has not been found will now be found in the next seven days.

Warring with the Prophetic Word

Pastor Dutch continued,

> Expose him. We declare exposure. We declare the eggs are being crushed under our feet in Jesus' name. Under our feet, under our feet, under our feet....Break it. We say witchcraft is broken that hides him in Jesus' name.

Local Leadership Begins to Agree with the Decree

Pastor Darrell Feemster then stated,

> Fort Hood, Texas, the 4th I.D. [Infantry Division], is in Iraq. And this next month the 1st Cavalry, as he [Chuck] spoke about a nation in our loins—I wonder if God could birth a Christian nation in Iraq with the 1st Cavalry from Texas, the 4th I.D. from Texas, that God would birth a Christian nation in Iraq. Father, we pray. We speak blessing over our soldiers. Lord, they are soldiers of our nation, but they're soldiers of Texas. They are the forerunners around Baghdad and Tikrit. They're watching for Saddam Hussein. Father, their materials, their weapons are already over there. They're going to pick up their weapons. And Lord, they're going to take the

> victory. They're going to raise up a nation, and that nation is going to be named after Your name in the name of Jesus. We bring down that spirit of Babylon in the name of Jesus.

National Military Authority Comes Into Agreement with Prophetic Revelation

Greg Jackson, who was dressed in military uniform, declared,

> As a witness to the prophetic word in this house, as a representative of the Armed Forces in the state of Texas, I declare in the name of the Lord, it shall be!

Whole Corporate Body Expresses Themselves in Worship

A *roar* went up from the crowd. That *roar* entered the atmosphere and, I believe, was traveled by the Spirit of God all the way to Iraq. Worship was then released in an incredible way. The roar of God is a prophetic release that creates a covering of God's authority in the earth realm. Amos 3:7-8 (NKJV) says, *"Surely the Lord God does nothing, unless He reveals His secret to His servants the prophets. A lion has roared! Who will not fear? The Lord God has spoken! Who can but prophesy?"*

Results Were Heard Worldwide

Troops from the 4th Infantry went in and found Saddam Hussein three days later! Even though many were praying around the world, I believe it takes corporate gatherings at times to express God's purpose on earth.

WORSHIP AND INTERCESSION CAUSES LAND TO SHIFT INTO GOD'S PURPOSE

In *The Worship Warrior* John Dickson and I write:

> When we worship and intercede, we tear down the snares that have been erected on earth by our enemy. God has a process of manifesting His will on Earth. Worship invades each one of the steps of that process. The process is as follows:
>
> 1. **Intercessory Burden**. God releases His burden from heaven. One of the words related to intercession is "burden bearing." This means to sustain, bear or hold up against a thing. Dutch Sheets writes that "this is likened to when a person will tie a stake to a tomato plant to sustain it from the weight it carries. The strength of the stake is transferred to the plant, and thus, 'bears' it up." Sheets goes on to write that another [meaning] for burden is "to bear, lift or carry" something with the idea being to carry it *away* or *remove* it....The intercessory work of Christ reached its fullest and most profound expression when our sins were "laid on" Him and He bore "them away." Therefore, the Lord will lay His burden on us for something in the earthly realm, and we are to stand and pray until we get rid of it. I do not believe we can withstand this burden without intimate worship.
>
> 2. **Revelation Released**. When we are bearing the burden of the Lord, we are *lifting* that burden up to Him for change. He begins to release revelation to us that will give us strategy to see the individual or the city or the nation or

the situation change. The Holy Spirit begins to help us. He is our advocate. He is our comforter. He is our helper. He is our counselor. He is our intercessor. He helps us in our weakness, so we can withstand the weight of this burden. When we don't know how to pray, He reveals the will of the Father to us. This is another way of saying what we find in Romans 8:26-28: Revelation can come to us naturally or supernaturally. But it only comes when we touch God in some way or form of intimate worship—whether it be reading the Bible, walking and praying, singing or whatever.

3. **Prophetic Declaration**. Once we have revelation, we can make declaration. We can call things as they should be. The Lord formed the world by faith. As we ascend in worship, faith abounds. We can then speak what is not into the form that it should be. This is the creative power of the Word when filled with Christ's life. As we worship we hear, and the life of God abounds on earth.

4. **Apostolic Execution**. Once the Word and will of God is being released in Heaven, our burden begins to lift. The gift of apostles is key in days ahead. Apostolic authority is key to establishing God's will on earth. Apostles have territorial authority. They also execute the prophetic will of the Lord in the earthly realm. Apostles are called to worship and war.

5. **Divine Fulfillment**. One of the gifts of the apostle is the gift of building. Once God has released His will from heaven, we have interceded and stood in the gap to see that will established, we've made prophetic declarations, and apostolic leadership has gone forth into new vision, then

we begin to see the divine will of God fulfilled on earth. We then drop on our knees and worship and thank God.[19]

Dickson and I go on to say in *The Worship Warrior*:

> God's sound permeates from heaven and orders much of what goes on in the earthly realm.
>
> When He is ready to bring restoration to Earth, He releases His sound. Physical sound is created when something vibrates.
>
> Sometimes we can see the vibration, and sometimes we cannot. When we clap our hands or stomp our feet, vibration occurs. This causes air to move. The source of the sound vibrates and pushes the molecules through the air and into our ears, and our brains then interpret it as sound. Sound, when unorganized, produces noise. Sound, when organized, produces music....
>
> There were songs of triumph after victory in battle (see Exod. 15:1; Judg. 5:1). Miriam and the women celebrated the downfall of Pharaoh and his horsemen "with timbrels and with dances" (Exod. 15:20), and Jehoshaphat returned victorious to Jerusalem "with stringed instruments and harps and trumpets" (2 Chron. 20:28). Music, singing and dancing were common at feasts (see Isa. 5:12; Amos 6:5). In particular, they were features of the vintage festivals (see Isa. 16:10) and of marriage celebrations. Kings had singers and instrumentalists (see 2 Sam. 19:35; Eccles. 2:8). The shepherd boy had his lyre (see 1 Sam. 16:18). The young men at the gates enjoyed their music (see Lam. 5:14).[20]

I want to add two other points that occur in addition to the five previous:

> 6. **Gates Open for the King of Glory.** I call this heavenly portals opening for the Lord to visit. *"Lift up your heads, O you gates! And be lifted up, you everlasting doors! And the King of glory shall come in. Who is this King of glory? The Lord strong and mighty, the Lord mighty in battle. Lift up your heads, O you gates! Lift up, you everlasting doors! And the King of glory shall come in. Who is this King of glory? The Lord of hosts, He is the King of glory"* (Psalm 24:7-10 NKJV).
>
> 7. **The Lord of Hosts, Yahweh Sabaoth, the Captain of all the angelic armies, the armies of Israel, the hosts of nations, ruler of everything in Heaven and on earth, sends help on our behalf.** The King then accesses our life, city, corporate worship, or nation.
>
> When we worship, He begins to order and align His armies for victory. "Hosts" signifies an organized group under authority. God has a multitude of ready and able servants. This suggests that the Lord is the Commander-in-Chief of the armies in Heaven.

THE CALL TO FULFILLMENT

In the second chapter we talked about the call of God. The purpose of the call of God is to fulfill His will on earth. Restorative prophecy releases redemption. When a prophetic word is released from Heaven into the earth realm, we find that God is:

1. Working to restore our lives *personally*,
2. Working *corporately* to mature us,
3. Working *territorially* to release His glory and break hindering spirits, and
4. Working *generationally* to connect us.

This pattern is found in Joel chapters 2–3. Once that prayer army is raised up and we begin to prophesy, spirits of desolation begin to flee. A great example of this is in Ezekiel chapter 37. Most states had areas that could be related to the "dry bone" scenario. Notice how Ezekiel dealt with processing the situation that he saw.

In *The Best Is Yet Ahead*, Becky and I explain about the four levels of prophecy that we can see working in the life of Ezekiel in his vision of the Valley of Dry Bones.

> If Ezekiel had stopped at any point before God's full purpose had been accomplished, he would have failed. Ezekiel went through a four-step process at each new level of prophecy. These four steps are the same ones we need to follow if we are going to stay on track with prophetic fulfillment in our own lives:
>
> **1. He received prophetic revelation.** Ezekiel sought God and was open to receiving prophetic instruction. In fact, he *expected* God to speak to him. How often in our daily lives do we *expect* to hear God? God is speaking to us today! We need to learn how to listen for God's voice and direction in our lives in order to receive the instructions that will move us forward.
>
> **2. He obeyed the voice of the Lord.** God told Ezekiel what to say and do in order for the next step to be accomplished.

This seems so basic, and yet it is a critical step that we must understand. Ezekiel could not have moved to the fourth level of prophecy without first obeying God at the first, second, and third levels. If you are having difficulty gaining new revelation and hearing the voice of the Lord, go back and be sure you have done all that the Lord has required of you thus far. For example, if we have fallen out of relationship with someone, and the Lord reveals to us that we have to go get right with that person, we should not go back to the Lord looking for new revelation until we have obeyed Him in the last revelation. If we want to continue to move forward toward prophetic fulfillment, we'd better go get right with that person.

3. He watched God's purpose being accomplished and assessed the situation. At each level of obedience, Ezekiel saw miracles happen as God's will was accomplished. Even so, he knew that all of God's purposes had not yet been fulfilled. He saw the bones come together. This in itself must have been a great and miraculous sight. But when he looked closer, he saw that even with this great miracle, there was no breath. Then he saw breath come into them. A great army of living, breathing beings replaced a dead pile of dry, useless bones. And yet there was hopelessness and infirmity. It was not until Ezekiel saw the Lord break infirmity and death off of the great army and bring them into the land He had promised them that the process of prophetic fulfillment was complete. Even though we may see great miracles along the way, we need to be sensitive to the Holy Spirit's leading as to whether or not His will has been fully accomplished.

4. He listened for his next instruction. Miracle after miracle did not stop Ezekiel from seeking God for the next step. He did not bask in the awesome works of God in a way that stopped him from looking forward. Of course we need to stop and thank God for His great power and allow ourselves to be drawn into worship. But, we can't let the glory of something that has already occurred keep us from moving toward a greater level of glory.[21]

I believe the 50-State Tour and the state gatherings were just the beginning of realigning the mind of the Body of Christ with God's redemptive plan for the states. Faith overcomes and shifts us into a whole new dimension of God's reality.

God is realigning or shifting our nation. A shift is a change of place, position, or direction. A shift also includes an exchange, or replacement, of one thing for another. A shift is a change of gear so that we can accelerate. A shift can also be an underhanded or deceitful scheme. Therefore, in our shift, we must recognize that the enemy is plotting to stop it. God is ready for us to shift through our choice to enter into a new dimension of faith. Let us not lean on our understanding but shift into this new dimension of faith!

REPENT AND ALLOW THE LORD TO SHIFT YOUR THOUGHTS!

During our 50-State Tour meeting in Providence, Rhode Island, the Spirit of the Lord began to align us with the redemptive history of that state. (The history of Rhode Island is incredible!) In the process of the message, the Lord began to speak that this would be one of the first states where there would be a sweeping move of repentance.

The *simple* meaning of repentance is to *change your mind*. So many times we develop a belief system that is not aligned with the absolute Word of the Lord; or we start off believing right but then add other worldly knowledge to our knowledge of who God is and develop other thought patterns. This is how strongholds and iniquitous patterns develop. Second Corinthians 10:3-6 (NKJV) says:

> *For though we walk in the flesh, we do not war according to the flesh. For the weapons of our warfare are not carnal but mighty in God for pulling down strongholds, casting down arguments and every high thing that exalts itself against the knowledge of God, bringing every thought into captivity to the obedience of Christ, and being ready to punish all disobedience when your obedience is fulfilled.*

These thought processes have to be dismantled if we are ever going to express the mind and heart of God.

Repentance has three phases: intellectual, emotional, and volitional. First, there is an *intellectual* aspect of repentance. When we gain knowledge that something in our own life or thoughts is not right, we have to change the way we think to incorporate that knowledge.

Next, there is an *emotional* aspect to repentance. Our emotions actually store many of our memories. When we are wounded, we remember. When we experience trauma, we remember.

When we violate a principle of God and suffer the consequences, our emotions are affected. In other words, we can know we need to forgive, but our emotions never give up the wound.

The third aspect of repentance is *volitional*. Our will must change. There has to be an action based upon your new thought processes. This is why so many prophets demonstrate through prophetic actions the required change of mind that God is requesting His people to make. This also means that you cannot voice a change of mind and then continue to practice the same old sin pattern.

When we repent, we change our mind and take a turn onto our new path of victory. The Lord accomplished this in many ways throughout the Word of God. He would bless His people abundantly, as He did with Peter in Luke chapter 5. He would bring judgment. He would dry up heavens or change atmospheres. And at all times, the Lord is longsuffering, in order to provoke us to think the way He thinks.

In *Restoring Your Shield of Faith*, Robert Heidler and I share that to enter into a new dimension of faith we must:

> *Develop His mind-set.* We can't lean on our own understanding because we will never make the right choice with our limited knowledge. Philippians 2:5-8 makes it clear: *"Let this mind be in you which was also in Christ Jesus, who...made Himself of no reputation, taking the form of a bondservant....He humbled Himself and became obedient."* Romans 12:2 declares, *"Do not be conformed to this world, but be transformed by the renewing of your mind, that you may prove what is that good and acceptable and perfect will of God."* This simply means we cannot let Satan's scheme shape our thinking to be that of the world. Also, we cannot allow outward appearances to deceive us, causing us to miss what God is doing. We must prove the voice of God and practice in everyday life what God's will from heaven is declaring to us. Romans 8:7 explains: *"The carnal mind is*

enmity against God." We declare that the Lord will put His finger on every area of carnality in our thinking.

We must also learn to *express His heart*. I love to prophesy. We war with our prophecies. Many of us never enter into a new place because we don't know how to war with the word God has given us. However, we forget that prophecy is not just speaking truth. Prophecy is expressing the mind and heart of God. We need to let the Lord deal with our emotions so that they do not interfere with His communicating His heartbeat. We declare that all self-pity and hope deferred are being removed from us. Bitterness and unforgiveness are leaving so that we can express what God is thinking. We will not let inordinate affection cause us to misalign. The heart can have weights or attachments that create shifts. These shifts can prevent us from entering into a new dimension of faith. I declare a free heart over all of us.[22]

This causes us to *develop a Kingdom mentality*. The Kingdom of God is within us. We build the Church, but we receive keys to the Kingdom. We need to study the Kingdom. Matthew 11:12 (NKJV) declares, *"...now the kingdom of heaven suffers violence, and the violent take it by force."* The Kingdom advances in victory. This occurs through violent spiritual conflict and warfare. When the Church acts as God's warring agent, the Kingdom increases. Let us lift up our shield and sharpen our sword because they are both important in God's Kingdom conflicts ahead.

RECONCILIATION FOLLOWS REPENTANCE

Once we know that God wants changes on earth and we agree with Him, we must move forward with Him to reconcile or realign His purposes. *Reconcile* means to "restore friendship and fellowship." I think this should begin first with the Lord instead of each other. Reconciliation brings the change of mind into a thorough visible manifestation. When we reconcile, we open the door for a full release. The Lord reconciled the world and changed its relationship to God by going to the cross. We have been reconciled to God. This is how loss becomes salvageable.

The person in the Bible who has most affected my prayer life, other than Jesus, is Daniel. I just love how he operated in victory in Babylon. He was truly "in the world, but not of it." He was disciplined, sensitive, consistent, uncompromising, bold, supernatural, attentive to the past, but always pressing toward God's expected end for the people of Israel. We find a great pattern when we look at how he repented and reconciled the situation of God's covenant people while he lived in Babylon. This was also a good pattern of what happened during the 50-State Tour. In Chapter Five, Dutch will explain in detail how this Daniel type of praying works. Again, reconciliation realigns the door of Heaven with earth.

The Lord is *forming* new doors or portals in the heavenlies as we pray, war, decree, and advance in His order. To *form* means to "develop or mold the shape or outline of something," or to "give meaning, character, or nature to something." Another way of thinking about a season of formation is to see something (including the conditioning of our mind and body) as it will be in days ahead. A *forming* season includes conceiving, training, and disciplining.

This was what the Lord showed me when He visited me in December 2003. Many enemies are behind this door that is forming, but the Lord says: *"Do not focus on your enemies during this season, but watch the door form and **be ready to enter into this new opportunity. I will give you grace over your enemies.**"* This is the time for a major conversion of souls. Ephesians 6:12 (NKJV) reminds us, *"For we do not wrestle against flesh and blood, but against principalities, against powers, against the rulers of the darkness of this age, against spiritual hosts of wickedness in the heavenly places."*

He understood how prophecy was important in our prayer lives. He knew we had to use the prophecies spoken to war for our future! Take, for example, the situation when Jeremiah prophesied that the people of Israel would go into captivity, but would be released in 70 years. Daniel uncovered the prophetic writings of Jeremiah while Israel was still held captive in Babylon. He learned that Jerusalem was to lie desolate for 70 years, and that the 70-year period had now come to an end. Because of Jeremiah's prophetic declaration, Daniel knew that now was the time to act. Jeremiah's understanding of the future had turned into a "now" word for Daniel.

Daniel did four specific things to bring an end to Israel's captivity:

1. *He prayed and fasted.* Jeremiah was specific in saying that the Lord would turn a deaf ear to His people for 70 years. Now, however, Daniel knew that the *kairos* time had come to beseech the Lord for an end to captivity.

2. *He repented for himself and his people.* Once he knew the mind of God, Daniel confessed and repented not only for his own sin, but for the sins, iniquities, and failures of the Israelites that resulted in their captivity in the first place.

3. *He received an angelic visitation.* God honored Daniel's efforts and sent His archangel, Michael. After three weeks of prayer, fasting, and repentance, an angel appeared to Daniel to tell him what was written in the "Book of the Future." In other words, he told Daniel what would happen to his people.

4. *He received revelation of the future.* Because of Jeremiah's prophecy, Daniel understood the times in which he was living. Because he understood the times, he saw his window of opportunity and began to seek the Lord with great fervency. When he did, he gained an understanding of the future God had for his people, and through obedience to God's commands, he could move them forward, out of their captivity.

When the word of God is released through prophecy, it is never forgotten. It is stored in Heaven until God is ready to release it back into the earth. In the Body of Christ, we have received many prophetic words, both through Scripture and through modern-day prophets, that are about to come to pass on earth. We need to understand the times, seize our *kairos* opportunities, and move into the future with victory! Even though times ahead will change rapidly and may be difficult, we have great confidence that God will give us the revelation we need to move forward. When we are overwhelmed by our present circumstances and apparent defeats, we must hear the Lord speak to us, just as He did to Jeremiah, "Is there anything too hard for Me?"

In Daniel chapter 7, we also find revelation of the Ancient of Days. I believe this is very important and needed revelation for us to be victorious in prayer in days ahead. In Daniel 7:9-14 (NKJV), we find that Daniel had a revelation of God's everlasting reigning power. He states:

> *I watched till thrones were put [set] in place, and the **Ancient of Days** was seated....One like the Son of Man...came to the **Ancient of Days**....Then to Him was given dominion and glory and a kingdom, that all peoples, nations, and languages should serve Him. His dominion is an everlasting dominion, which shall not pass away, and His kingdom...which shall not be destroyed.*

This name of God, "Ancient of Days," is a phrase that describes the Everlasting God, One advanced in days or knowledge, the Father of Years, and One who forwards time or rules over it.

The name implies dignity, endurance, judgment, and wisdom. *"Behold, God is great, and we do not know Him; nor can the number of His years be discovered"* (Job 36:26 NKJV).

The Ancient of Days has a covenant with the earth. In this covenant, the earth will be full of His purposes, and He will be longsuffering until all have heard. The heart of God is to form covenant with all peoples on the face of earth and establish a house of prayer for each one (see Isa. 56:5-8), including those in your city. That is why we must learn how to prophesy to that which has been scattered through these thrones of iniquity. Just as Ezekiel did in Ezekiel chapter 37, we must speak to the dry bones and command them to be brought back to life. This kind of prophetic declaration not only reestablishes God's covenant purpose for a territory, but also brings those within the territory out of their hope deferred, causing them to rebuild that which the enemy has destroyed.

The Ancient of Days releases ancient wisdom for present-day victory. A Scripture that has revolutionized my prayer life is First Corinthians 2:6-10 (NKJV):

We speak wisdom among those who are mature, yet not the wisdom of the age, nor the rulers of this age, who are coming to nothing. But we speak the wisdom of God in a mystery, the hidden wisdom which God ordained before the ages for our glory, which none of the rulers of this age knew; for had they known, they would not have crucified the Lord of glory. But as it is written: "Eye has not seen, nor ear heard...the things which God has prepared for those who love Him." But God has revealed them to us through His Spirit....

God gives us several keys as we pray:

- God has wisdom greater than any worldly wisdom we encounter.
- Powers and principalities do not have access to this wisdom.
- The authority of demonic forces is limited.
- There is wisdom that has been hidden since the beginning of time, for His glory.
- Through the redemptive cross of Jesus Christ, we have access to this wisdom.
- God is prepared to release this wisdom to us as we get to know Him intimately, through prayer.
- This wisdom will overthrow high places and release captives.
- Wisdom dismantles demonic structures and overthrows thrones of iniquity.

When the Lord showed this to me, I knew that any demonic force holding a territory captive could not withstand the wisdom that God would release to His people. I knew that if the Spirit of the Lord burdened me to pray for a city or a state or a nation, I had authority to gain the keys for the release of its inhabitants. This is a day when the Lord is extending a fresh call of prayer to His people.

God is revealing the true condition of our states and saying: *"Overcome every obstacle that is keeping these people from coming to know Me. Open the door for My house to be built within them so they may experience My love throughout eternity. Through prayer, gain wisdom that will overthrow the thrones of iniquity wherever they have been established. Then establish My throne that many may worship Me and gain life everlasting!"* This is how entire cities will experience conversion. This is how we will overthrow thrones of iniquity and see God's covenant plan for whole territories flourish in days ahead.

In Daniel chapter 10, we find Daniel seeking God with intensity for 21 days. It was then that the Ancient of Days sent the aid of Michael, the archangel. Revelation was then released into the earth realm—revelation that we are walking in today.

CAN WE AS A NATION CONTINUE TO SHIFT AND REALIGN TO GOD'S PERFECT PLAN?

The answer is YES—*if we are willing to war to receive God's covenant blessing*. Abraham is a great example (see Genesis 14–15).

The answer is YES—*if we find our place in the gap*. Nehemiah is a great example (see Nehemiah 1–2). He received God's burden and found favor from the king to accomplish the task.

The answer is YES—*if the Church is willing to shift from its discipling-teaching mentality to an apostolic-sending mentality* (see John 20–21). Jesus discipled the Twelve until it was time to send them. Then He released them and sent them.

The answer is YES—*if we allow the Spirit of God to align us in God's order*. We find an order of God in First Corinthians 12: first apostles, second prophets. Any time God says "first," He means that's the key to the prototype of the future. We must see apostles and prophets align in our region. Then teachers and pastors will rise up with new anointing, and we will see miracles and healings that unlock evangelism.

The answer is YES—*if we will allow the Lord to shake disinterest, confusion, legalism, condemnation, discouragement, and disillusionment.* Once God began to shake the people in the days of Haggai, He assured them that their latter would be greater than their former. He shook them into a desire to complete His purposes (see Haggai 1–3).

The answer is YES—*if we are willing to be like the woman at the well and drop our pot and run quickly* (see John 4). This woman tore down her prejudices, overcame her past, experienced a new reality of the Lord, left her mundane daily exercise of getting water, and ran and evangelized her whole city.

The answer is YES—*if we are willing to bind the strongman who has robbed us of our spoils*. In Matthew 12:25-29, we find that we should *first, bind the strongman...then go in and take his spoils*. We are entering into a season of plundering the enemy's camp.

The promises of God are "yes" and "amen." Shout "yes" and see our nation realign and shift into God's purposes!

– 5 –

THE ADJUSTMENT

(Dutch Sheets)

I think I'm finally adjusted. For many years people have adjusted me. In fact, I've been adjusted so many times—I've had adjustments to my adjustments—that I think I may finally be fully adjusted.

My dad adjusted my attitude when I was growing up. He used a belt, menacing looks, strong words, the loss of privileges, and monetary deprivation. In recent years, my wife has adjusted my thinking more than once. She uses looks and words, also. Because of her I have adjusted my thinking toward the art of communication, the importance of remembering certain dates, the use of remote controls, the number of shoes a woman needs in order to function, and the broad-ranging effects of hormones.

My dentist has adjusted my bite so my teeth will last longer and my jaws will feel better. He also took a bite out of my wallet.

My chiropractor has adjusted my back and neck so I will feel better. One time he said I had a subluxation. "Is that good or bad?" I asked.

"Bad."

"Can you take it out?" I said, trying not to show my alarm. "No. You don't extract subluxations—where have you been, the dentist? But

if you'll come in 50 times I can adjust it," he assured me. I don't know if I still have the subluxation, but I'm adjusted. So is my bank balance.

My insurance adjuster did his thing the other day. I always wondered why they called them adjusters; but when the pipes froze and burst in my garage, he adjusted my thinking, explaining to me what the insurance company was and wasn't going to give me to fix my pipes, the sheetrock, and my car, which was scratched from falling debris. By explaining to me what all the clauses, exceptions, and deductions meant, it seems that most of what I had been paying for was the peace of mind that comes from knowing he would be there to personally explain to me what he couldn't do. I certainly felt adjusted.

The policeman adjusted my thinking toward speed (thank God for civil servants!), my jeweler toward the value of rocks, and Starbucks toward the price of a cup of coffee...as you can see, I'm pretty well-adjusted.

THE HEAVENLY CHIROPRACTOR

God adjusts us also. He has adjusted me many times—my heart, my thinking, my direction, even my hopes and dreams. He also adjusts nations. Chuck spoke in the last chapter about repentance, restoration, and reconciliation, all of which involve adjustments that lead to life, and he did so in the context of a nation's being healed or restored. That was the purpose of the 50-State Tour—healing adjustments and holy realignments.

There is a fascinating word in the New Testament, *katartizo*, that relates to this. It means "to adjust; to put a thing in its appropriate position."[23] The word is used in context with mending nets (see Matthew

4:21), repairing schisms or relational breaks (see 1 Corinthians 1:10), and even restoring broken lives (see Galatians 6:1). The word has also been used to describe the restoration of a dislocated joint or a broken bone. So, as you can see, the concept of this word involves proper alignment, including realignment, resulting in healing or restoration.

It should come, then, as no surprise that God uses that word to describe the proper alignment of the seasons of time. In other words, He declares in advance His plans for the future of nations and peoples of the earth. Hebrews 11:3 says, in its more literal and accurate rendering, that the "ages" (Greek—*aiones*) were "properly aligned or connected" (Greek—*katartizo*) by the word or decree of the Lord. In other words, God decreed the flow of history.

HISTORY MUST BE HEALED

At times, however, breaches occur that cause the need for corrections in this flow of history. Simply stated, history needs to be healed. Whether it be on a corporate level, such as the Fall of humanity, wars, racial division, etc., or on a more individual level in the sense of broken relationships, loss, etc., the fact is that history often needs healing. This corporate level of healing is what is referred to in verses like Isaiah 58:12 (NASB): *"Those from among you will rebuild the ancient ruins; you will raise up the age-old foundations; and you will be called the repairer of the breach, the restorer of the streets in which to dwell."* (See also Isaiah 61:4.) This would also be the concept spoken of in Second Chronicles 7:14 (NASB): "[If] *My people who are called by My name humble themselves and pray and seek My face and turn from their wicked ways, then I will hear from heaven, will forgive their sin and will heal their land."*

God, the holy Chiropractor of history, heals our dislocations—our subluxations. He *katartisis*-es the *aiones*. This occurs through repentance, reconciliation, forgiveness, prayer, fasting, prophetic decrees, and other biblical actions, all of which are effective because of the blood of His Son, Jesus Christ.

So it came as no surprise to Chuck and me when the Lord spoke to us often on the Tour to *katartizo*—shift or adjust—a state back into its God-appointed purpose and destiny. Due to the positive effects of much prayer, fasting, repentance, etc., on the part of many, it was now time for the fruit of these actions to occur: realignment...repairing...rebuilding...restoring...the healing. The fact is, we and many other intercessors around the nation found ourselves in a glorious time of history where we could stand in the gap for a land so that it could be healed, rather than destroyed (see Ezekiel 22:30-31), and broken places could be *katartisis*-ed—realigned spiritually—with the plan and purposes of God.

As you will see when you read in the last chapter of this book the summaries of what the Lord spoke to each state, He would often speak prophetically of His purpose for them, how that plan had been altered or aborted, and what to do now in order to restore it. Prayers were then offered, decrees were issued (see Job 22:28), and oftentimes specific strategies for recovery were released.

TENNESSEE RECEIVES AN ALIGNMENT

Though it isn't practical to highlight each state, a good example of this occurred in Tennessee. On the way to the meeting, I asked the Lord what He wanted to say to Tennessee. I clearly heard Him instruct me to tell the people that He had broken a curse off the state that week, and that blessing would now be released to it.

I questioned the Lord, asking Him to give me something more: What kind of curse? What caused it? Why was it broken that week? I certainly didn't want to imply that a curse was broken just because we had arrived! Nor did I want to tell a group of people that they had been under a curse without some sort of explanation as to "what" and "how."

Again the Lord spoke to me clearly. "Tell them they have been under a curse that resulted from breaking covenants with the Native American people." (A biblical example of this can be found in Second Samuel 21:1 where David was told that he and his generation were under a curse because his predecessor Saul broke a covenant with the Gibeonites. The result was a severe famine in the land.)

The Lord then continued by telling me, "Because, however, the state of Tennessee has stood with and blessed Israel, I have been able to break this curse and release blessing." And He was very clear about the timing—that very week. He then reminded me of Genesis 12:3 where He stated that anyone blessing Abraham's seed would enable Him to bless that person or people who blessed them.

I stated all this in the meeting that Thursday evening, doing so in faith and obedience, with no natural knowledge of anything that would confirm it. After I spoke this portion of the message, one of the local leaders and spiritual fathers in the Church of Nashville, Don Finto, came hurriedly to the platform. He didn't even wait for the message to conclude! "This past Monday," he said, "I was in a meeting where our Lieutenant Governor signed a formal declaration saying the state of Tennessee would stand with Israel."

All of us were amazed. Most of the people gathered were like me—they had no prior knowledge of this. You can imagine the faith and excitement that were released; if this portion of the word about Tennessee blessing Israel, and the fact that it occurred that week, were accurate, then the portion about breaking a curse and releasing a blessing probably were as well. Chuck ran to the platform and began to prophesy. Jim Goll, another trusted prophet, did as well. The Holy Spirit began to speak of ways in which the curse had manifested, then how the blessing would replace it. We prayed, decreed, worshiped—it was incredible!

Katartizo was taking place. History was being healed; destiny was being reconnected with. And though the work had begun earlier in the week with Tennessee's declaration, there was still the need for prophetic words, prayers, and decrees to be offered in order to bring understanding about the curse, as well as launch the state into the new blessing.

MICHIGAN RECOVERS ITS VOICE

Another example of history being dealt with, and realignment occurring, took place in Michigan. The Lord had spoken to me, while en route to the meeting, that Michigan had lost its voice. This seemed strange, so again I questioned the Lord. All He would say was that Michigan had lost its voice, which I assumed meant either its prophetic anointing or its influence.

"Tell them they gave it away," He said, "and speak tonight on 'How to Reclaim Your Voice.'"

I had no idea what any of this was about, and had never spoken on the subject before, but I hurriedly put together a message. (As you can imagine, these meetings were very challenging. Everywhere we went,

Chuck and I had to construct messages in very short amounts of time, sometimes in just a few minutes as God would sometimes wait until the worship began to speak His word to that state.)

After this message, Chuck came forward and said that he knew when Michigan lost its voice. "Twenty years ago," he said (which was an approximation), "the mayor of Detroit gave Saddam Hussein the key to the city!" Not only had this occurred, but prior to this tragic act in the region's history, there had been a strong root of anti-Semitism established through others.

Though I'm sure this former mayor did not intend to—at the time it was not yet known just how evil Saddam Hussein was—through this event, authority and influence over this region was given to the spirit behind Islam. It should come as no surprise that the greatest concentration of Muslims in America is located there. A dislocation had occurred in history, opening the way for the voice of the Lord to be lost and the voice of Islam to prevail.[24]

It was also amazing to us that the very night God gave me this word and we began the process of dismantling this stronghold and reestablishing the government of God, our troops surrounded Baghdad and went in the next morning to take the city. While we were dealing with this stronghold spiritually, our troops were doing so naturally!

At this point, the entire meeting for the state of Michigan took on the direction of breaking this wrong alliance and reestablishing covenant with the Lord. Michigan was being realigned, adjusted, and healed.

Since that time the fruit of this meeting has been increasing. Races are coming together in unprecedented ways, including Jews and those of Muslim descent. Chuck and I were recently in a powerful series of meetings with Barbara Yoder in the Detroit area where Native

Americans, Jews, African-Americans, Caucasians, and former Muslims all came together in order to bring further healing to the region.

Katartizo!

AMERICA MUST CROSS OVER

There is an Old Testament word and concept that captures the essence of what happens when we align or realign with God and His purposes. The word is *abar*, and it means "to cross over; penetrate."²⁵ It is the root word for Abraham's descriptive term "the Hebrew" in Genesis 14:13. He was called "the Hebrew" because he had crossed *out of* his homeland and *into* a new region when instructed to do so by the Lord.

Although this word is often used in a generic sense of transitioning from one place to another, it has also been used sometimes to denote very significant "crossings" that became landmark events in people's lives, as was referenced in Abraham. Some examples are:

- ✯ The Lord "passed between" (*abar*) the pieces of the covenantal sacrifice Abram offered to God (see Genesis 15:17). It is as though God was saying, "You have, in obedience, crossed over to Me, Abram; now I'm crossing over to you in covenantal alignment." Crossing over can be a covenantal act.

- ✯ God "passed by" (*abar*) Moses in Exodus 33:19-22, showing him His goodness and glory. When God crosses over to us, facets of His nature and character are revealed.

- ✯ A new generation "crossed" (*abar*) into their inheritance in Joshua chapters 1–4. In Joshua 3:4, the Lord instructed

Israel to watch or follow the ark of the covenant "for you have not passed [*abar*] this way before." Each generation must have its own crossing over. They were not true Hebrews just because their forefathers were—and neither are we.

* The air passing through the jubilee trumpet was described as *abar*. Crossing over can be the release of the breath of God to us, bringing freedom and new beginnings.

These and other usages of *abar* have significance for America. God needs for us as a nation to "cross" back into a meaningful and covenantal relationship with Him. When we do, we receive the benefit of His covenantal crossing to us. We cannot rely on what our forefathers and foremothers have done to dedicate this nation to God; we must have our own crossing over in our day. As we do, Christ our Jubilee will breathe on us again, bringing true freedom and restoration.

TO RECEIVE THE RIVER WE MUST ACCEPT GOD'S RULE

Finally, there is one other usage of *abar* that is significant and needs highlighting. Ezekiel chapter 47 is the great passage that describes the increasing levels of the river of God flowing out of the temple. The verses are filled with symbolism—the river flows into desert regions and brings life; everything it touches is healed; there will be many fish (souls)—of what occurs when this river flows.

But another of the interesting points of the passage is that the prophet had to pass through (*abar*) each new level of the river. Many have speculated as to why this was required. One of the interesting explanations has to do with the fact that between each level there was a thousand cubits, which led to the next level and another crossing. One thousand, being a multiple of ten, is the number of divine order and government in biblical numerology. This would suggest that for every new level of God's river—life, healing, and restoration—to be released, there must be an acceptance of God's order and government. In other words, His plan and rule must be followed.

In the United States of America, we have not yet been able to experience spiritual recovery and restoration back into the fullness of God's blessing, though many have asked Him for it. This is because we must do more than ask; there is an order and pattern that must be followed. As that pattern occurs, however—humbling ourselves, praying, seeking His face, and repenting (see 2 Chronicles 7:14), just to name some of the things required—we are then positioned (*katartizo*) for more of God's healing to occur.

It is clear to us that God is realigning and positioning America so we can cross over into a new era of revival and blessing. He is adjusting us, bringing healing to our broken places and dislocations. America is about to see another great awakening, which will result in many salvations and the turning of a nation back to its God and its destiny. Curses are being broken, blessings are being released, and our God-given voice is being restored.

What a privilege to partner with Him!

– 6 –

CONNECTING *with* HEAVEN *and* EARTH

(Dutch Sheets)

*while we look not at the things which are seen, but at the things which are **not seen**; for the things which are seen are temporal, but the things which are not seen are eternal*
(2 Corinthians 4:18 NASB).

*for we walk by faith, **not by sight***
(2 Corinthians 5:7 NASB).

*Now faith is the assurance of things hoped for, the conviction of things **not seen***
(Hebrews 11:1 NASB 1995).

There is a relatively unknown dimension that must be understood in order to fully partner with God and experience the fullness of His blessing. It is the unseen realm of the spirit—invisible yet real, hidden yet very active. Much of what happens on earth is influenced by it; certainly anything of eternal significance or which controls the destinies of people and nations is controlled within this realm.

Most people, including Christians, give little thought to this unseen world that governs the one we see. Many individuals, especially in cultures such as ours which emphasize higher levels of education and intellectualism, are actually cynical of this arena of invisible activity. But the Bible is filled with descriptions and accounts of this dimension—in fact, it is the story of the Bible. Indeed, apart from it, there is no God, satan, angels, demons, fall of humankind, birth of Christ, redemption through the cross, miracles, or the resurrection of the dead. Yet again, surprisingly, most Christians in America live their lives without giving much thought to how much this realm affects us, let alone how we can influence it.

Yet here is an important truth: *The more we learn to function in the invisible realm of the spirit, recognizing and applying the principles that govern it, the more we can partner with God, positively impact our world, avoid the snares and influence of the evil one, and enjoy the blessings of our salvation.* Doing business for the Lord in this arena was the primary purpose of our 50-State Tour. A few examples from Scripture that reveal just how much this dimension impacts our natural world will help us understand why it was such an emphasis.

AMALEKITES DEFEATED BEFORE AN INVISIBLE FORCE

In Exodus 17:8-16, we find the account of Israel warring against the Amalekites. The strategy for the battle was that Moses, Aaron, and Hur would go up on a hill above the battlefield, taking with them "the staff of God," while Joshua and the army would go below to fight. When Moses held aloft the staff, Israel prevailed; when he grew tired and lowered it, Amalek began to dominate the battle. So Aaron and Hur positioned themselves on each side of Moses in order to help him keep the staff of God raised, thereby ensuring Israel's victory.

What are we to deduct from this? The staff used by Moses represented the power and authority of Jehovah, the great I Am, in much the same way a king's scepter represents the same. It was this very rod that was used to deliver Israel, judge the gods of Egypt, part the Red Sea, and strike the rock bringing forth water. By raising this staff of God, Moses was exalting the Lord and His strength and power. He was declaring that, in spite of the very literal battle below, there was an unseen realm from which they could draw on another power source for victory. In contrast, the lowering of the rod symbolized the army of Israel fighting in their own strength and authority.

The picture is clear: While there were *visible*, flesh-and-blood people fighting with tangible, physical weapons, and on a very real battlefield, the action of Moses on the mountain was releasing an *invisible* force that was determining the outcome of the battle. Notice that actually both realms were influencing the other: Actions occurring in the *visible* realm (Moses lifting the staff) activated God's *invisible* authority and power, which in turn, determined the outcome in the *visible* realm (the battle). Both arenas—the natural and the spiritual, the seen and the unseen—were affecting the other. And they still do today. Millions of good and bad events occur on Planet Earth every day due to this two-way cause and effect.

UNSEEN ALLIES

Another clear example of this is found in Second Kings 6:8-23. The king of Aram sent an army to kill Elisha; and when Elisha and his servant woke up in the morning, a great army had surrounded them. "Alas, my master!" cried the servant. "What shall we do?"

Elisha, enabled by the Holy Spirit to see in the spirit realm, responded that there were many more on his side than the number of his enemies. He then prayed that the eyes of his servant would be opened to see this spiritual dimension, and God answered his prayer. The servant saw a mighty host of angelic forces, which at the request of Elisha, proceeded to strike the enemies with temporary blindness. Again, an *invisible* realm was actually controlling what occurred in the *visible*, and vice versa.

HEAVENLY COMBAT

Still another striking account of spiritual activity controlling what happened in the natural realm, and vice versa, is found in Daniel 10:10-21. Daniel had been seeking insight from God for 21 days concerning visions he had received. When an angel finally came to Daniel with the answer, the following amazing explanation was given to him by the angel:

> *He said to me, "O Daniel, man of high esteem, understand the words that I am about to tell you and stand upright, for I have now been sent to you." And when he had spoken this word to me, I stood up trembling. Then he said to me, "Do not be afraid, Daniel, for from the first day that you set your heart on understanding this and on humbling yourself before your God, your words were heard, and I have come in response to your words. But the prince of the kingdom of Persia was withstanding me for twenty-one days; then behold, Michael, one of the chief princes, came to help me, for I had been left there with the kings of Persia. Now I have come to give you an*

understanding of what will happen to your people in the latter days, for the vision pertains to the days yet future" (Daniel 10:11-14 NASB1995).

Incredible! For three weeks a war had gone on in the unseen realm of the spirit, keeping the angel from breaking through to Daniel with the answer to his prayers. In his commentary on these verses, Zodhiates says, "These princes or angels engaged in heavenly combat, and the implication is that what was happening to these nations on the earth was affected by this heavenly struggle."[26]

WE MUST LEARN TO PARTNER WITH HEAVEN

Indeed, there is great activity, including warfare, going on around us in the invisible realm of the spirit *all the time*. And the key to an overcoming life, to partnering with God, and certainly to receiving spiritual breakthrough, is learning to operate in this arena. We often do so without realizing it—through worship, the quoting of Scripture, preaching the gospel, prayer and fasting, acts of kindness, and many other spiritual activities—but what we haven't learned to do as effectively is intentionally operate in this realm by obeying biblical principles, and by asking God what is needed in a given situation and then obeying His instruction.

Just before the Tour began, God had been trying to give me a higher level of understanding concerning this dimension of spiritual life. On one occasion, while studying the subject, I felt impressed to read the five references to "heavenly places" in Ephesians, without reading the in-between text. What I found was an amazing sequence of verses that sounded like one unbroken passage. Here are the five verses together:

Blessed be the God and Father of our Lord Jesus Christ, who has blessed us with every spiritual blessing in the heavenly places in Christ....which He brought about in Christ, when He raised Him from the dead and seated Him at His right hand in the heavenly places....and raised us up with Him, and seated us with Him in the heavenly places in Christ Jesus....so that the manifold wisdom of God might now be made known through the church to the rulers and the authorities in the heavenly places.... For our struggle is not against flesh and blood, but against the rulers, against the powers, against the world forces of this darkness, against the spiritual forces of wickedness in the heavenly places (Ephesians 1:3,20; 2:6; 3:10; 6:12 NASB 1995).

Taken together, these power-packed verses reveal several important things about operating in this invisible realm of the spirit. First of all, the Lord informs us that we have been given everything we need to operate in this arena. He then states that Christ has been positioned there with all authority, and we who have been seated there with Him, share in this authority. This is followed by a declaration that we, the Church, will manifest God's great wisdom to the opposing forces that operate there. And finally, in the last reference, the Holy Spirit identifies these invisible enemies that we will overcome by using God's wisdom, power, and authority.

Amazing!

The Lord began emphasizing to me the necessity of operating more effectively in this spiritual dimension. He also led me to Matthew 16:18-19 (NASB), which states:

> *I also say to you that you are Peter, and upon this rock I will build My church; and the gates of Hades will not overpower it. I will give you the keys of the kingdom of heaven; and whatever you bind on earth shall have been bound in heaven, and whatever you loose on earth shall have been loosed in heaven.*

Having studied these verses for years, I was somewhat surprised to find that the most literal rendering of verse 19 is, "And I will give thee the keys of the Kingdom of heavens [plural]. And whatever thou shalt bind on the earth shall be as having been bound in the heavens [plural]; and whatever thou shalt loose on the earth shall be as having been loosed in the heavens [plural]."[27]

Notice that Jesus was not referring to Heaven where God's throne is, but to the spiritual realm around us, and He spoke of our involvement there. The two verses describe the Church as having authority (keys) to govern for Christ in the heavens—the invisible realm of the spirit—though doing so from earth. And He promised us that when doing so, the powers of hell would not overpower us.

Then the Holy Spirit led me to yet another passage, Micah 2:13 (NASB1995): *"The breaker goes up before them; they break out, pass through the gate and go out by it. So their king goes on before them, and the Lord at their head."* While studying the subject of spiritual breakthrough, I had examined this verse in detail but had failed to notice one thing. It refers to the Lord as our "head," also calling Him "the breaker." The Amplified Classic translation actually says, *"the Breaker [The Messiah],"* confirming that this verse is referring to Christ. But what the Holy Spirit finally zeroed me in on was the little word *up* (Hebrew—*alah*), which means to ascend or rise up.

I finally realized what the Holy Spirit was endeavoring to say to me: We must follow Christ, the Breaker, up into the heavenly places, so we can partner with Him and experience breakthrough there. *Breaking through in the invisible realm of the spirit always creates breakthrough in the visible, natural realm.*

"THE DOOR IS UP HERE!"

After speaking to me from these verses, the Holy Spirit gave me one more lesson concerning this truth shortly after the Tour began. We were at our second stop, the state of Oklahoma. Chuck was at the podium prophesying, and in the prophecy he said something about God opening a door. I immediately pictured something occurring in the natural realm that would create an open door or opportunity. I actually envisioned a door opening in front of me.

Instantly I heard the Holy Spirit say, "There you go again." Being the intelligent person I am, I immediately discerned that I had messed up! "The door opening is not a physical occurrence," He said. "It is a spiritual occurrence in the heavens. You must learn to go through it *up there* before you'll be able to go through it *down here.*"

Just as the Holy Spirit was speaking this to me, Chuck said, "Let's bring Dutch up to speak now." Then he hesitated. "No," he said, "before he comes up, I need to share one more verse, Revelation 4:1 (NKJV). It reads, *'After these things I looked, and behold, a door standing open* **in heaven***. And the first voice which I heard was like a trumpet speaking with me, saying, "Come* **up here***, and I will show you things which must take place after this."'* Now, Dutch, come on up and share."

I was blown away. The Holy Spirit then spoke to me one more time, "See, the door I'm trying to show you is not *down there*—visible, natural, earthly. It is *up here*—invisible, spiritual, heavenly. I'm trying to teach you to go up into that realm in your thinking, listening, praying, and decreeing, and to partner with Me there, just as I showed you in Ephesians, Matthew, and Micah. If you will learn and do this, you will properly connect Heaven and earth."

That had my attention! What an interesting phrase—*connecting Heaven and earth.*

"This will give you the results you're seeking: realignment, restoration, the healing of a nation, and the release of My glory," He continued.

CONNECTING HEAVEN AND EARTH RELEASES GOD'S GLORY

The release of God's glory is no small thing! Moses cried out for it in Exodus 33:18, *"Show me Your glory"* (NASB). Though in Moses' mind it no doubt referred to God's splendor and majesty, the glory of God encompasses so much more. The word in Hebrew is *kabowd,* and it means "weighty or heavy." It carries the meaning of authority, as is implied when we say someone with great authority "carries a lot of weight." The word can even mean to be wealthy or prosperous, from the sense of being heavy with goods. When Heaven and earth connect, causing a release of God's glory, His weighty presence is felt and great authority is released.

The New Testament word for glory, *doxa,* is just as significant. It has in its root meaning the recognition of something or someone for what they really are. When the glory of the Lord is released, He is recognized! The Church will recognize Him, sinners will recognize Him, and His weighty presence will change things.

THE CAPTURE OF SADDAM HUSSEIN

This is what occurred in Texas on the Tour. I was delivering my message when Chuck received a word from the Lord. "The heavens opened," he said, "and the Lord picked me up into the spirit realm."

"Go up, prophesy what I give you, and don't think about it," the Lord said to him. (Chuck knew later that this was because he probably wouldn't have been bold enough to say what he ended up saying had he thought about it first.) He then proceeded to the platform and prophesied the capture of Saddam Hussein within seven days!

Chuck then turned around and looked at me with a shocked expression that I interpreted as, *I don't believe I just said that.* Then he handed the microphone back to me, expecting me to do something! I didn't know what to do—except pray. And pray we did! We bound the demonic powers that were keeping him hidden, and decreed his capture.

Three days later Saddam was pulled from his hole in the ground!

Authority—the weighty glory of God released on earth. Breakthrough—Heaven and earth connecting to bring God's heavenly will into earthly situations.

Prayer and declaration in San Antonio, Texas, led soldiers on the other side of the world to a man hiding in a hole. The armies of Heaven, the armies of earth, and a group of intercessors all joined together to defeat the forces of evil.

We must learn to partner with the invisible forces of God. There are more *for* us than *against* us, and we must learn the ways of the spirit in order to draw from this invisible world. If we do, this nation will continue to turn back to God, awesome breakthroughs will occur, and another great awakening will unfold.

Join us in this worthy and eternal cause!

– 7 –

RECEIVING *the* ANOINTING *to* STAND STRONG

Understanding the Issachar Anointing

(Chuck D. Pierce)

Understanding the times and seasons is key for victory in our personal lives and territories! However, most of us do not understand the biblical timetables. I will try to explain them as we move through this chapter.

When God spoke to Dutch and I to go to all 50 states, I knew there was an urgency in accomplishing the will of God in the earth realm. On the other hand, why would we need to go and why would we need to gather God's people? Couldn't God do everything Himself if we did not go?

God is sovereign! Of course He could do everything if He chose to. He is quite capable of shaking and rearranging the earth. He said: "Let there be *light!*" And there was *light!* But there was a condition in the Word of God—*us!* He created us and placed us in the earth realm to watch after and cultivate "His garden," the earth. To continue to do that successfully, we must follow Him. *Place* seems to be important with God. Our function or sphere of authority also seems very key to receiving all the Lord has for us. Abraham had to follow God's command and leave Ur of the Chaldees before God released the promise and came into covenant agreement with him. He told Abraham that He wanted him to get to a *place* called Canaan.

Following the will of God, Jesus came to earth to redeem us from the power of sin and death. Can you imagine leaving Glory to reveal glory in the midst of chaos? In turn, Jesus said, "Follow Me." And then He commissioned us to *go!* There seems to be a destination or *place* for each of us to serve and reflect our faith on earth. Jesus said, "I will make you fishers of men." In other words, "Follow Me and I will cause you to catch mankind."

> *The God Who produced and formed the world and all things in it, being Lord of heaven and earth, does not dwell in handmade shrines. Neither is He served by human hands, as though He lacked anything, for it is He Himself Who gives life and breath and all things to all [people]. And He made from one [common origin, one source, one blood] all nations of men to settle on the face of the earth, having definitely determined [their] allotted periods of time and the fixed boundaries of their habitation (their settlements, lands, and abodes), so that they should seek God, in the hope that they might feel after Him and find Him, although He is not far from each one of us. For in Him we live and move and have our being...* (Acts 17:24-28 AMPC).

Not only does *place* seem to be very important to the Lord as we see in the Acts 17 Scripture, but *time* is also very important. The Lord is not "in time" as we are in time. *He is time.* He knows the end from the beginning. However, He has made us to be set into a timed sequence in His plan on earth. He expects us to seek Him during the time frame that He has determined for our lives. Dutch will explain this in the next chapter. He uses a wonderful example from our state gathering in Alaska.

GOD DETERMINES TIMES AND SEASONS

In *God's Timing for Your Life*, Dutch shares:

> The word *chronos* refers to the general process of time or chronological time. The word *kairos* refers to the right time, the opportune or strategic time, the now time. As I was doing this [studying these two words for time], God began to reveal a very important truth to me. I have always completely separated these two concepts—chronological time and the right time—but God has been showing me that this is not accurate. Often, they are simply different phases of the same process. *Kairos*, in many ways, is an extension or continuation of *chronos*. As the processes of God's plans unfold, *chronos* becomes *kairos*.
>
> The new is connected to the old and, in fact, is often the result of what happened in the old. *Kairos*, the opportune time, is literally born of *chronos*, the general time. When we're in a nonstrategic general season of life's daily routine, plodding along in the *chronos* time, God doesn't totally start over with a *kairos* season. His overall agenda does not change. He simply takes us through one phase of a process in which our perseverance and faithfulness have allowed Him to shift us into the next phase—a strategic season. He changes the time and season, transforming *chronos* into *kairos*.[28]

Do you really believe that your life can make a difference if you are at the right place at the right time? *Relentless Generational Blessings* by Arthur Burk is a very interesting book that reveals how God intends each of us to have a generational impact in this world. This very positive book encourages us to see generational blessings in our families as opposed to the negative traits and failures that seem to derail success. This book discusses how we not only inherit a toxic waste dump we do not deserve (our generational curses) but we also inherit a gold mine that we have not earned (our generational blessings).[29]

You should recognize your life this way. You should also recognize that each state that makes up this nation has incredible blessings in the midst of strife and defilement, and each generation has a responsibility to bring forth those blessings. That is why we are on earth. I always define success as being at the right place, at the right time, doing the right thing. That is what we actually tried to do on the 50-State Tour. We tried to be in each state at the right time and decree what God was saying so that the people could move forward in God's perfect will.

THE ISSACHAR ANOINTING

First Chronicles 12:32-33 (NKJV) refers to *"the sons of Issachar who had understanding of the times, to know what Israel ought to do, their chiefs were two hundred; and all their brethren were at their command."*

One of the first prophecies I received over my life was from a well-known individual who was being used in the Charismatic movement in the 1970s. He prophesied that I would understand *time* and have an *anointing for timing*. On the Israelites' march in the desert, Issachar was on the east with Judah and Zebulun, his brothers. They led the march toward the Promised Land (see Numbers 2:5; 10:14-15). This Issachar anointing is very important if we are going to advance in victory. I am probably known for this *anointing for time* in the Body of Christ and have attempted to study to show myself approved. Actually, one of the most important issues of my life is that I seem to recognize when *I am not* in God's timing.

Issachar means "he will bring reward." Men of Issachar, approximately 200, knew how to ascertain the periods of the sun and moon, the intercalation of months, the dates of solemn feasts, and could interpret the signs of the times. In addition, Jacob prophesied, *"Issachar is a strong donkey, lying down between the sheepfolds. When he saw that a resting place was good...he bowed his shoulder to bear burdens, and became a slave at forced labor"* (Genesis 49:14-15 NASB 1995). This anointing is very important if we are going to carry God's burdens in the earth realm, and bring them to birth at the appropriate time.

Dutch goes on to say in *God's Timing for Your Life*:

> The Bible speaks not only of *chronos* and *kairos*, but also of a *pleroo*, or fullness of time. Galatians 4:4 reads, "But when the fullness of the time came, God sent forth his Son, born of woman, born under the law." This word "fullness" indicates fully completing or finishing something. Whereas *kairos* indicates opportunity to perform a task or produce fruit, *pleroo* means it has been accomplished. This could be linked to the process of bringing forth children.
>
> After conception, a woman goes through all three states of timing: *chronos*, *kairos* and *pleroma*. For nine months, she faithfully endures the challenging but important developmental stage of *chronos*. Much is happening in the hidden place of the womb, but she cannot yet hold and fully enjoy the fruit she knows is coming. She then moves into

the *kairos* stage of labor and delivery. She hasn't yet come to fullness, but it is near. This *kairos* time is very difficult and dangerous, however. Opportunity doesn't guarantee success. There will be much work, pain and pushing if the fullness stage of birth is to be reached.... Finally a woman goes from the *kairos* season into the *pleroma* stage of fullness, and the baby is born. It is always worth the pain of the process when this occurs.[30]

Issachar was positioned on Shechem at Mount Gerizim *"to bless the people"* (Deuteronomy 27:12). To summarize, the Issachar anointing understands the timing of God and the government of God, carries the burden of the Lord, and releases the blessings of God into the earth realm at the intersection or crossroads of every season.

In the Word of God, the timing element is built around the Feasts. The Old Testament contains two calendars—a civil and a religious one—and this can complicate our understanding of the origins of the New Year. Rosh Hashanah begins what is known as the Head of the Year and culminates with the Feast of Tabernacles. This is different from the first month of the year, which actually begins at Passover. When we read the Bible while understanding this concept of time, we seem to better recognize God's purposes on earth. Hebraic numbers have word and pictorial meanings. This helps us understand time and stay focused prophetically. We should begin the Head of the Year with God's revelation for that year. We should pass over or cross over into the fullness of the year with this revelation guiding our path.

In September 2001, we entered the Hebrew Year 5762. Of course, most of us remember the beginning of this year by the World Trade Center event in New York City. However, what this year actually meant was that we were entering into a *seven-year war season*. I attempted to have the book, *The Future War of the Church*, ready to help the Body shift into a mindset for war. This book is still very helpful today. Much of what was written to prepare us is now an actuality in our daily operation.

In October 2000, I was attending a state meeting in Oklahoma when I heard the Lord speak the following: *"I have keys in My hand. I'm reviewing authority from city to city, state to state, and region to region...War will now break out in these next 18 months. This will be a war of great spiritual magnitude. The war will be over the boundaries of the future—for the enemy has shifted boundaries."*

In January 2001, I continued to hear the Lord say, *"There will be a* **restoration** *of the* **war mantle** *of the Body of Christ...."*

In Oklahoma the Lord also said:

> *"I AM setting My course for judgment upon the states of this land. I will be judging the states of this land and judgment will be evident by February 2002. Judgment will come based upon the complacency of the Church from state to state. For you have thought judgment would come based upon the civil government that is in place, but I would say to you that judgment will come because of the complacency of My people*...It is important now how you motivate those around you to respond to Me," saith the Lord.
>
> "For that is how I will determine those that go into drought and who go into natural disaster—based upon the response of My people now. ***I say to you also I will release judgment from state to state based upon the response that I see concerning My Spirit dwelling on this earth****...For I say it is My Spirit that is the restraining force in this land, and based upon

> how My Spirit is welcomed in a territory is how I will begin to allow demonic forces to rise up and how I will begin to dethrone demonic forces…So I say to you, do not be a people who operate in false judgment, for My judgment will come only based upon complacency and My judgment will only come upon the welcoming of My Spirit into your territories.
>
> "…This will be a time of determining the authority at the gates of your cities and states. The rulership of the gates is being determined ***now***. …There is a war over the justice of this land. I will establish justice in the midst of My people; therefore, there will be war over laws that have been established wrongly. …Know that you are warring with an antichrist system; therefore, do not fear this supernatural war that I am calling My people to be engaged in. Align yourself properly for war."

Therefore, I knew we had entered a key *kairos* time that we could not afford to miss. I think this was the propelling word that entered deep into my spirit that would not let go of me. This generated in me a burden for our nation for this particular season. (You can read about a portion of that burden in *Destiny of a Nation*.)

In *God's Timing for Your Life*, Dutch says:

> At the Pool of Bethesda, Jesus came to the man who had been in his paralyzed condition for 36 years and asked him what seemed to be a strange question: *"Do you want to get well?"* (John 5:6 NIV). The man's answer revealed that although he was waiting at the pool, he really had no hope of being healed. He was in a *kairos* moment, close to fullness, but hopelessness had set in. Jesus asked him this question to make him realize that, although he was

waiting for the miraculous stirring in the pool, he had lost all hope of actually being healed. Only seconds away from experiencing the new, just a handclasp away from total restoration, the man was too disillusioned to recognize it. Somewhere along the way, as he went through the process of time, he lost his expectation. There wasn't anything within him that could respond in hope to Jesus' question. When God brings a shift, we must be ready to shift with Him. If we're not careful, we won't believe that He can bring us from the *chronos* stages through the *kairos* seasons and into fullness.[31]

A NEW SEASON OR DAWN IS BREAKING

We have now entered into the second phase of this seven-year war season. I believe we need a new anointing to break open God's full purposes in this time. At each breaking day of a new season, we need to have a renewed commitment to the One who made us and gives us life. Psalm 37:5-6 (Living Bible) says: *"Commit everything you do to the Lord. Trust him to help you do it, and he will. Your innocence will be clear to everyone. He will vindicate you with the blazing light of justice shining down as from the noonday sun."* The word *new* is defined as "different from one of the same which existed before; or made fresh." The following are eight new issues to look for in your life at this time:

1. *New relationships.* May your relationship with the Lord be new and fresh, and may He supernaturally connect you horizontally with others who will cause you to come into a greater level of success.

2. *New acts.* May the Lord divinely intervene in your life with signs, wonders, and miracles.
3. *New identity.* May His fullness flow through your personality. May your soul be restored.
4. *New weapons for the war ahead.* The trumpet is sounding a new sound. Listen carefully. May you receive everything you need to defeat your enemies.
5. *A new garment of favor to go with your new identity.* May you radiate with favor and have entryway into new opportunities.
6. *A new sound.* May you hear the sound of victory and shout this sound from the rooftops.
7. *A new anointing.* May you be anointed in a way that every yoke is broken.
8. *A new level of authority.* May you receive the ability to stand in dominion in the sphere of authority that you have been granted by God.

These are things that we all should be looking for the Lord to reveal to us in a *kairos* time on earth.

DECREEING, DECLARING, AND PROCLAIMING

God has chosen us as the necessary link to bring His will from Heaven to earth. He wants us to commune with Him, listen carefully to His voice, gain prophetic revelation, and decree that revelation into the earth. This will unlock miracles and release His blessings. Once we hear

God, we can intercede, but we can also prophesy. Prophesying is declaring His mind and His heart. As we speak, He forms His will on earth. We should always be willing to say, "Yes and amen" to His promises. When we receive prophetic revelation, we need to decree the prophetic revelation. This was the pattern that we operated in, once we gathered together in our meetings from state to state.

> *I will declare the decree: the Lord has said to Me...* (Psalm 2:7 NKJV).

> *You will make your prayer to Him, and He will hear you, and you will pay your vows. You shall also decide and decree a thing, and it shall be established for you; and the light [of God's favor] shall shine upon your ways. When they make [you] low, you will say, [There is] a lifting up; and the humble person He lifts up and saves. He will even deliver the one [for whom you intercede] who is not innocent; yes, he will be delivered through the cleanness of your hands* (Job 22:27-30 AMPC).

> *Then He saw wisdom and declared it; He prepared it, indeed, He searched it out* (Job 28:27 NKJV).

A *decree* is an official order, edict, or decision. A decree is something that seems to be foreordained. This is what makes decrees prophetic. *Decree* can also mean to order, decide, or officially appoint a group or person to accomplish something. A decree is linked with setting apart or ordaining something or someone. A *declaration* is an announcement, a formal statement, or a proclamation. This statement sometimes is what a plaintiff releases in his complaint, which results in a court action. A *proclamation* actually brings something into a more official realm. A proclamation can ban, outlaw, or restrict. This is linked with the process of binding and loosing.

Once we hear the word of the Lord decreed, declared, or proclaimed, God begins to establish this word in the earth realm. This causes God's people to press in for a full manifestation of what He is longing to accomplish in our midst. All through the Word of God you find decrees, declarations, and proclamations. Cyrus sent out a decree that caused God's people to return from captivity and rebuild the city of Jerusalem and the temple of God. Caesar sent out a decree that positioned Mary and Joseph in the place where prophecy could be fulfilled through the birth of Jesus. Elijah declared that the heavens would be shut up. The priests proclaimed what God was ordaining.

As Dutch and I traveled to each state, we knew that this was our mandate. We were assured by the Spirit that God had a unique "word" for each state.

We are in a time of prophetic declaration and apostolic proclamation. God's people are becoming bold to say what He is saying. This creates an open Heaven and brings Heaven and earth into agreement. I call this an open portal or door in Heaven. In *Restoring Your Shield of Faith*, Robert Heidler and I write:

> Revelation is a book that provides deep insight into the nature and tactics of the enemy. In the book of Revelation the apostle John had a supernatural visitation during an extreme time of persecution. In the midst of this persecution, he began to see that the Lord God omnipotent reigns! He seemed to agree with Paul that those who would follow the Lord in their daily life would enter into and be involved

in continuing spiritual conflict. As the Lord visited John, He gave him a message concerning the seven key churches of that region. This message also reveals to us God's heart concerning the Church today.

We then find John sharing with us in Revelation 4:1 the following: *"After these things I looked, and behold, a door standing open in heaven. And the first voice which I heard was like a trumpet speaking with me, saying, 'Come up here, and I will show you things which must take place after this.'"* This open heaven causes our faith to soar.

Faith overcomes! The shield of faith is closely related to the concept of a door—the Greek name being *thureos*, from *thura*, a square shield that can also be seen as a door. A door is an opening for entering or leaving a house, tent or room. The door is used symbolically in the Bible in many ways. We find the Valley of Achor, a place of trouble (see Josh. 7:26), is later promised as "a door of hope" (Hos. 2:15). It will become a reason for God's people to trust Him again. Our trouble can be turned into an entry point into a new place of victory.

Jesus called Himself "the Door" (John 10:7,9). Faith in Him is the only way to enter the kingdom of God. God gave to the Gentiles "the door of faith" (Acts 14:27), or an opportunity to know Him as Lord. Jesus stands at the door and knocks (see Rev. 3:20). He calls all people to Himself, but He will not enter without permission. We need to give the Lord permission to take us through new, opportune doors and allow Him to come in and give us the power to go through these doors. Let us open the door of our heart so that we can go through our new door of opportunity.

Paul constantly sought new doors of service! These were open doors for him to go through so that he could minister in the name of Jesus Christ. First Corinthians 16:9 reads, *"For a great and effective door has opened to me, and there are many adversaries."* There are many doors of opportunity ahead for each one of us. However, the adversaries behind those doors will overtake us unless our door of faith is in place.

Let us lift up our shield, or door, of faith. We do not need to be afraid to go through the opening and into the new places to which the Lord would lead us. Even though many adversaries will be on our path in days ahead, our shield of faith will quench all of their fiery darts. Jeremiah 46:3 (NIV) is encouraging: *"Prepare your shields, both large and small, and march out for battle!"* Let us go forth with confidence, with our shield lifted high, and our victory will be assured.[32]

The following are a few declarations that we made during the 50-State Tour. It will benefit you to make these declarations in your life, over the Church of your city, your state, your region, and this nation.

1. *The river is changing courses!* Ready yourself for the next war ahead! Don't remain in your last war cycle. Make sure you are allowing or causing or choosing for the old to end! Deal with all of your dangerous emotions so they will not present great challenges to you in the future. Let's move into our next phase of victory!

2. *Receive a new anointing...* for victory over death cycles and the fear of death...for victory over demonic forces that

would try to stop you in the future…for increase and harvest so you begin to fill His storehouse…and for an Issachar anointing to interpret the times so you know what decisions to make.

3. When the enemy encircles you, declare you will find security in the Lord. The enemy will attempt to surround you, so *be sure to develop your shields of protection*. Musk Oxen form a circle around a cow that is giving birth. This provides protection so the next generation can come forth. To intercessors and prayer groups, you must be like the Musk Ox in your region.

4. *Be surrounded and sealed by the Holy Spirit.* Develop a new level of discernment through worship. Reality is produced when we worship in Word (Truth) and Spirit. End old cycles. Do not cycle through your wilderness again. Break the cycle of Mount Sinai. (Don't go around that mountain again!) Head toward and up Mount Zion. In the face of your enemy, violently praise! Let praise bind the strongman and then plunder, take, and repossess your spoils.

5. Let the Lord take His *compass* and drop His plumbline in your midst. Allow Him to set a new direction and *chart your course for the future* (see 1 Corinthians 16:5-18).

6. Do not fear; go up against what has *seemed* to be invincible in your past (see Joshua 5–7).

7. Let His supernatural **love** overwhelm and encompass you. This will release a dimension of *compassion* that the Church has lost. This will cause the healing mantle to be restored back to the Church. This will open the door for prodigals to return (see Matthew 9; Luke 15).

8. Review your boundaries. This is a season of *divine commandments*. The Lord will be restructuring our boundaries so the law can be fulfilled in our hearts. This will allow us to take back ground from the enemy who has shifted laws and time (see Daniel 7).

9. Come *full circle*. The Lord will give you a second chance to confront and deal with that thing that defeated you in the last season!...or you will go around that same mountain again.

10. This is a season of the Spirit supernaturally rekindling the *power gifts*. The war will take a supernatural turn. Example: There is a fine line between word of knowledge and ESP (see 1 Corinthians 12,14). On the Tour, we asked the Lord to release His gifts in the Body of Christ in our nation.

11. Ask the Lord to bring forth new revelation from the pulpit of your region. Supernatural *teaching will defy religion*. The Lord will reveal a different dimension of the Word to expound upon (see Mark 2).

12. Ask the Lord to bring forth a *new expression of worship*. Be expressive in *praise* and rejoice in the midst of your battles. Do not hide your emotions (see 2 Chronicles 20). The roar of the Lion of Judah will win your battles!

13. Declare the generations will connect and war together (see Isaiah 59:15-21). The word *generation* is linked with *circle* (see Esther 9).

14. This is a time to *plunder*. Read Exodus 3–12. (*The Future War of the Church* explains dethroning the gods of Egypt.) First Samuel 30 shows how David gained control of his emotions and recovered his loss.

15. *Gain new prayer strategies, prepare the way, and expect victory* (see 2 Kings 3)! Do not let the enemy's retaliation cause you to back up.

Worship and sound are important. Throw open the window and receive the sound of the Lord! Let the Wind bring the sound that you need through your window. Your conscience is like a window between soul and spirit. Make sure nothing is clouding your conscience. Open your mouth and release the shout of victory! This is the season of confession and decree. What we say now determines our future. If we will cleanse our conscience, then the revelation that has not been able to influence our minds will find entrance. Though the enemy is roaming like a mighty lion seeking whom he may destroy, there is a *roar* in you to be released at this time. This *roar* will defy the enemy. Go past that which seems invincible in your life. Get in the river of change that is flowing by your door and let it take you to your next place. Get a shield of protection around you and birth the new that the Lord has for you. Your latter end (future) will be greater than your beginning.

One of the things that the Lord keeps speaking to me is that blessings are surrounding us, but we must learn how to open the door so they can manifest in our sphere of influence and the territory of which we are a part. I pray that the blessings of God manifest in each one of you (see 3 John 2).

> *To you I will cry, O Lord my Rock.... Hear the voice of my supplications, when I cry to You, when I lift up my hands toward Your Holy sanctuary. ...The Lord is my strength and my shield...with my song I will praise Him. The Lord is their strength, and He is the saving refuge* [or defense] *of His anointed* (Psalm 28:1-2,7-8 NKJV).

May you have confidence in prayer. May you find your place in His sanctuary and boldly enter the throne room of grace. May you be filled with renewed joy. May all the trials and discouragement of this past season and any hope deferred be gone from you. May your soul rejoice and prosper. May the work of your hands prosper. May He work in you mightily to do His will. May the gifts of God within you be released and activated. May a new anointing arise within you and favor be seen upon you. May He defend His anointed. May your shield of faith be polished and renewed.

> *Fear not, for I am with you; be not dismayed, for I am your God. I will strengthen you, yes, I will help you, I will uphold you with My righteous right hand. ...Those who war against you shall be as nothing.... Fear not, I will help you* (Isaiah 41:10,12-13 NKJV).

The following are decrees to accomplish our future or expected end.

1. We must understand the power of violence and become violent in the Spirit by *praising God* in new ways. This will be a season of violence. This will be a season of intense learning. This will be a season of falling and getting back up. This will be a season to overcome fear. This will be a season to learn a different way of prospering financially.

2. We must allow the Lord to discipline and make us *watchmen*. You must know who you are watching after and are connected with, and you must know who is watching after you. Get your assignment quickly.

3. This is a season in which we must understand *signs*. Signs are pointers that identify and uncover godliness and the

redemptive plan of God that is in the world. We must not miss our signs at this time! We must not be afraid of the supernatural, but rather begin to enter into that dimension that will get us to our new "there." This will begin individually and work into a corporate demonstration.

4. This is a season where we will begin to *interpret supernatural revelation*. We must ask God for the gift of interpretation. The Lord will be releasing a new revelation in the earth realm so we understand times and seasons. Dreams will become very significant. There will be a revival of words of knowledge. Words of wisdom will begin to give us clear directive strategy for the words of knowledge being received. These two gifts will balance each other this season. For understanding, read Daniel chapters 6–11.

5. There will be *much shifting* in the *Church* and in the lands of the earth at this time. Many will become dissatisfied with traditionalism and will seek God's supernatural power. Therefore, God will shift many into new places. On the other hand, there are many in the Body of Christ who are critical, judgmental, negative, and condemning. Unless they are delivered, they will wander in this next season and not be able to find their place. If we will pray Isaiah 58 and let God lead each one of us into the type of fast that He has for each of us, we will be delivered and positioned properly for the future. *Realign yourself!* God is changing territorial boundaries.

6. This is a season when God shows us how to *end curses*. There are certain curses that the Lord is ready to bring to an end in the land. Joel chapter 2 is very important. This is a year to transfer evil into blessing. Do not be afraid to face the curse

that has hindered your progress. Decode the occult structure linked with the curse. Evaluate its destruction, and begin the rebuilding cycle for your future.

7. This is a season of *treading*. There are new paths to be made at this time. As we walk and advance, that which does not seem to be in place will begin to become a path of light. We will also go to places we have not been before. The Lord will begin to penetrate ungodly nations and bring His glory to places that have never experienced Him. This will be a season of pioneering into new places after judgment and wrath have occurred. This is the time when we begin to face the antichrist system that will be a hindrance to God's Kingdom advancing in the earth realm. Fear not, and tread forth!

8. This will be season of *threshing*. "To thresh" is used figuratively in the Bible to relate to providential chastisement, crushing oppression, judicial visitation, and the labors of ministers. Grain, wine, and oil were all related to threshing, and were products of the soil. Key threshing floors in our areas must be uncovered at this time. There is a new sound that is coming to the earth linked with threshing.

9. This is a season of a *different* type of *worship* than we've ever known. The Tabernacle of David is being established. Individual worship will turn into corporate worship. Corporate worship is a key to the transformation of our regions.

10. This is a season where the *roar* of the *Lion* becomes very distinguishable. The enemy will roar loudly, but the Lion of Judah will roar louder. We must learn the Lion of Judah's sound. It is in us, and it must be drawn out of us. *Ferret*

out criminals. Psalm 101 is a key chapter. Pray this for your region, and that every evil thing will be exposed.

STAND AND WITHSTAND

We must learn to stand and withstand. Ephesians 6:10-18 (NKJV) says:

> *Finally, my brethren, be strong in the Lord and in the power of His might. Put on the whole armor of God, that you may be able to **stand** against the wiles of the devil. For we do not wrestle against flesh and blood, but against principalities, against powers, against the rulers of the darkness of this age, against spiritual hosts of wickedness in the heavenly places. Therefore take up the whole armor of God, that you may be able to **withstand** in the evil day, and having done all, to **stand**.*
>
> ***Stand** therefore, having girded your waist with truth, having put on the breastplate of righteousness, and having shod your feet with the preparation of the gospel of peace; above all, taking the shield of faith with which you will be able to quench all the fiery darts of the wicked one. And take the helmet of salvation, and the sword of the Spirit, which is the word of God; praying always with all prayer and supplication in the Spirit, being watchful to this end with all perseverance and supplication for all the saints.*

As said at the beginning of this chapter, there is usually a condition in the Word of God—*us!* James 4:7-8 (NKJV) admonishes us to,

*"**Submit** to God. Resist the devil and he will flee from you. Draw near to God and He will draw near to you. Cleanse your hands, you sinners; and purify your hearts, you double-minded."* So for us to stand, we must submit. The word *submit* means to stand under. The word *stand* means to go against. The word *withstand* is the same word used for *antihistamine*. The Lord is saying, "Stand under My rule and authority. Be in authority and under authority. Stand against the governments of hell that would resist My purposes on earth. Let Me build your resistance to satan's schemes on earth. Overthrow his purposes. Let Me draw near to you and let My presence overtake you."

BE ANOINTED

To stand and withstand, we must be anointed. Isaiah 10:27 proclaims that the anointing breaks the yoke! The Hebrew word *mashiach* refers to one who is anointed with oil, symbolizing the reception of the Holy Spirit, enabling him to do an assigned task. Kings (see 1 Samuel 24:6), high priests, and some prophets (see 1 Kings 19:16) were anointed. In the case of Cyrus, he was anointed with God's Spirit and commissioned an "anointed deliverer" of Israel (see Isaiah 45:1).

The patriarchs were called "anointed ones." As I said earlier, we need to *receive a new anointing*. This anointing will give you victory over death cycles and the fear of death. May you be anointed to have victory over demonic forces that would try to stop you in the future. May you be anointed for increase and harvest so you begin to fill His storehouse. May you have an Issachar anointing to interpret the times so you know what decisions to make. The Hebrew word *mashach* means "to smear with oil or paint." May the hand of the Lord paint you with His anointing, and may your enemies know you have been set apart.

The following are several other uses of the term *anoint* that will broaden your understanding for receiving a new anointing:

1. The anointing represents physical refreshment after washing. In Ruth chapter 3, Ruth made her shift. Naomi told her to take off her widow's garment, wash, and anoint herself. Ruth then went to the threshing floor and found her redeemer. You have toiled too long. I decree that all weariness breaks from you. May His redemptive plan and key connections come clear in your life.

2. *Chrio*, or anoint, is used metaphorically in connection with "the oil of gladness," similar to "a lotion for a sick horse." May the anointing restore your joy. May you be delivered from any form of weakness that could hinder you.

3. The anointing is used to cause eyes that have lost vision to be open again. The church in Laodicea had its eyes anointed with eye salve. May your vision be renewed. May all dead works from the past year be broken. May you receive revelation of new methods that will make you more productive and effective. May a new passion be rekindled.

4. "To rub on" is used for the blind man whose eyes Christ "anointed." May you be healed from any loss of vision or past failures and anointed for your future.

5. *Murizo* is used for "anointing" the body for burial in Mark 14:8. May you receive an anointing, allow a natural death of certain issues that the Lord would like to fall into the ground, and then spring forth in new ways.

6. *Chrisma* means "an anointing from the Holy One" and indicates that this anointing renders them holy, separating

them to God. May the Holy Spirit be very efficient in enabling you to possess knowledge of the truth. May this truth unlock the doors that have remained shut to you. May you be separated and favored above the world around you.

7. The anointing means to "grow fat." May every yoke binding you, break from around you, and you go free like a calf let out of a stall.

I can honestly say, I sensed the anointing rise in God's people in every state of this great nation. We have received so many responses since the 50-State Tour. This book could not capture all the things that have come forth. Dutch and I both have acknowledged all over the nation our thanks to each person who stood and co-labored with us to see our nation shift. We have many examples of states making incredible shifts. One example of a generation shifting was provided by Bill Yount:

> A vote for righteousness on November 2nd seemed to shake down an avalanche of angels over Washington, DC, as the White House began to be decorated with yellow-gold ribbons. I heard the Father proclaiming, "Salvation is coming to My House...The White House will become a Light House with a burning fire, branding nations for eternity during the next four years!" I believe we will see a whole nation born again in one day in the next four years somewhere on earth!

Bill goes on to say:

> I sensed the Father decreeing, "I will restore the years that the cankerworm and palmerworm have eaten from this nation, and I will redeem time and will cause these four years to stand still on My spiritual timetable to accomplish what no other four years could ever do. These next four years will be known as the longest four years in America's history because of what I will accomplish! I will cause one day to seem like a month in government time. Remember one day with Me is as a thousand years and a thousand years as one day (2 Peter 3:8)! Because My people have begun to awaken and turn to Me in prayer and have begun to turn from their wicked ways (complacency being the most wicked way in her), I will begin to heal the land with signs and wonders and miracles. Healings in My Body will begin to be contagious, spreading throughout the land with medical breakthroughs with whole cities coming under the power of My influence! If My people keep humbling themselves and keep praying and keep turning from their wicked ways and keep pressing their foot on the neck of the enemy, My Kingdom will come to earth as it is in heaven! I promise you, you will see heaven on earth! Keep turning to Me...We are on a holy roll."[33]

WE MUST KEEP GOING!

This is a time when *we must* continue to advance. *We must* identify the apostolic leaders who are developing prototypes or models for this generation. The four walls of the Church *must* expand to encompass all societal structures. *We must* identify apostolic kingdom prototypes where Church leaders and economic leaders are working together to bring transformation to their community. *We must* identify the apostolic leaders who are willing to shift their minds from maintenance/pasturing to dominion. *We must carefully watch signs on earth* and identify new fields and people groups where the time is ripe for Kingdom invasion. (*Can the Lord birth a nation in a day?*) *We must* identify the nations where the Spirit of God is raising up leadership to ready our nation and other nations to be discipled.

Just as we are seeing certain natural elements influence our times and seasons on earth, we must also advance spiritually. Spiritually, we must go beyond our current levels of celebration and religious ritual (see John 2). We must go beyond our poverty way of thinking and enter into a harvest multiplication thoughtmode (see 1 Kings 17). We must also go beyond our debt mentality and know that the Lord can free us to accomplish His purposes (see 2 Kings 4). We must come to the end of ourselves and know that God has a better plan (see Luke 5). We must be willing to push past any halfway point in our lives and have a desire to complete the task at hand. We must go beyond our past failures and structures of unbelief that would hold us captive and prevent us from accomplishing our future (see Acts 12). We must be aware of every opportunity that the Lord has set before us and not miss the open windows and doors of Heaven that come into our spheres of influence (see 2 Kings 13).

The Lord knows the beginning from the end. He is Alpha and Omega. Let's cooperate with Him and experience the best in our generation.

– 8 –

TIME CATCHES UP *with* *the* DECREE

(Dutch Sheets)

As was usually the case, Chuck and I didn't know what word or message we would release when we arrived in Alaska. And, as was also typical, he made me go first. His usual cop-out to me when I tried to reverse the order was, "No, you go first. I'll get mine while you're up there."

Though I teased Chuck often about this order, it really was right that I go first. The normal pattern was that when I began to preach and decree under a prophetic anointing, his incredibly strong and accurate prophetic gift would engage, enabling him to discern much about the state.

He would often begin to prophesy, even during my message. At times, he would see or discern strongholds over a region, including how they were established and could be broken; he also frequently tapped into the future plans and purposes of God for a city or state, along with how to move into them. Chuck and I have a great rapport with each other, and these "interruptions" didn't bother me at all. To the contrary, it was wonderful, and would often lead us into times of powerful intercession.

So, as usual, Chuck insisted that I go first in Alaska. He had arrived before me on the day the meetings were to begin and attended a prayer

meeting that afternoon. When I met with him shortly before the evening meeting, as was my habit, I asked if he was seeing or hearing anything in the spirit about the state.

"Yes," he said, "God spoke to me in the prayer meeting today and said, 'Alaska is My alpha and omega state.'"

"What does that mean?" I responded. "What is an alpha and omega state?"

"I don't know, but you need to speak on it tonight."

"How am I supposed to do that when I don't even know what it means!" I complained.

Chuck gave me his usual, unsympathetic response to my insecurity about not knowing what to share or what some statement from the Holy Spirit meant: "God will show you."

"Yeah, easy for you to say," I murmured while walking away, "and I suppose you'll get your part while I'm up there."

He was right, however. As stretching as it was, God did show me, and Chuck did get his part while I was speaking.

ALASKA IS AN INITIATING STATE

"The Alpha and the Omega" is a phrase from Revelation 22:13 (NASB) and is a title of Christ. The entire verse reads, *"I am the Alpha and the Omega, the first and the last, the beginning and the end."* Alpha and omega are the first and last letters of the Greek alphabet, thus the meaning of this title is explained in the latter portion of the verse as *"the first and the last, the beginning and the end."*

During those two days, several things were revealed to us about the ways in which God intended Alaska to represent Him as the alpha and omega. One of the more significant revelations was that it was to be a state of *beginnings—an initiating, forerunning* place for the purposes of God. In other words, God's desire was that Alaska, with a mantle and calling to initiate, was to be a birthing center for His eternal purposes. This means, in essence, that the Body of Christ there has a calling to launch the Church into the new purposes and moves of the Spirit.

One example of this is the modern-day, worldwide prayer movement. Not many people are aware that Alaska, largely under the leadership of Mary Glazier and her organization, Intercessors for Alaska, was in many ways a forerunner of this movement for America and other parts of the world. Before the Strategic Prayer Network and other prayer networks had the momentum they enjoy today, Mary and her group had already blanketed Alaska with prayer and were seeing great fruit.

A LESSON IN GEOGRAPHY

The Lord began to reveal, however, that this ability to represent Christ as the Alpha—the first, the beginning—had been hindered. One of the interesting ways He began to speak to me about this was through the geography of the state. West of the mainland is an island that is part of Alaska but is on the other side of the International Date Line. When you cross this line traveling to the island, you move into *tomorrow*, even though you're still in Alaska. If you're on the island, west of the date line, and go eastward to the mainland you move into *yesterday*. Amazingly, Alaska has in it both the beginning and the end of a day—simultaneously. The very geography of the state pictures Christ, the Alpha and the Omega!

In fact, Alaska has yesterday, today, and tomorrow in it all at the same time: If you're west of the line, it is *yesterday* on the mainland; if you're east of the line on the mainland, it is *tomorrow* on the island; and wherever you are it is *today!* How's that for confusing!? Again, the very geography of the state pictures the nature of the eternal God—the Ancient of Days, the great I Am, He who is the same yesterday, today, and forever.

I share all of this, not to bore you with "Biblical Geography 101," but to give you the framework with which to understand what the Holy Spirit spoke to me for Alaska. He focused my attention on this interesting picture and said to me, "Tell Alaska to move forward into *tomorrow*, not into *yesterday*."

The Lord then began revealing to me the existence of an iniquitous cycle that often caused the Body of Christ in Alaska to get stuck in what He had done yesterday. This meant that whenever God tried to move them into new truth (tomorrow), they would many times abort it by moving right back into the old (yesterday). This was hindering their ability to see, birth, and be a gateway for the "beginning" nature of God's character to the nation.

The Body of Christ in Alaska is certainly not unique in this, and Jesus warned us of the propensity for our wineskin to become old (see Matthew 9:17). But it was very urgent that they break out of this pattern, for they are called to play a role in pioneering the new for all of us.

WE CAN ALWAYS MOVE FORWARD

After revealing this portion of Alaska's destiny and the stronghold that was opposing it, the Lord used this prophetic insight, as He often did on the Tour, to launch us into messages, prayers, and decrees—all for the purpose of breaking this cycle and releasing them into His current plans and purposes.

This pattern and redemptive process is very relevant to all of us. God wants to reveal His purposes, expose the tactics of the enemy to abort them, and give us His strategy for recovery and fulfillment. And He wants to do so, not only for states, but for individuals as well. His desire is that our "latter" always be greater than our "former" (see Haggai 2:9); and when we listen to and obey Him, it can be, even if there has been loss or setback.

Haggai 2:9 was given during a season when God's purposes were not being fulfilled in Israel. The nation had just come through a period of judgment known as the Babylonian captivity and was moving into restoration. The Medo-Persian king, Cyrus, had issued a decree allowing the Jews to return to Jerusalem and rebuild the Temple. This account can be found in Ezra chapters 1–3.

Because of opposition from neighboring peoples, however, work on the Temple stopped for 16 years (see Ezra 4:4-5). God then raised up the prophets Haggai and Zechariah to bring a word of rebuke, correction, and challenge to restart the project. The Israelites were told that the reason for their lack of blessing and provision was because they had abandoned God's project for their own (see Haggai 1:1-11). They responded by repenting and renewing their efforts, thereby ending this 16-year delay.

Based upon their response, the prophet Haggai then gave a wonderful prophecy about how God was going to bless them and the project, ending the word with this great verse in Haggai 2:9 (NASB1995): *"'The latter glory of this house will be greater than the former,' says the Lord of hosts, 'and in this place I will give peace,' declares the Lord of hosts."*

This is a promise not just for those Israelites, however, but is a timeless principle in God. His plan and desire are always that we go from glory to glory (see 2 Corinthians 3:18), faith to faith (see Romans 1:17), and that the latter is always greater than the former. Our redemptive and restorative God never loses! The only question is always: Will we cooperate with Him?

ROWING INTO THE FUTURE

As part of this unfolding revelation in Alaska, the Holy Spirit emphasized two verses, Isaiah 46:10 and Jeremiah 29:11, which became very helpful in understanding what He was saying:

> *Declaring the end from the beginning and from ancient times things which have not been done, saying, "My purpose will be established, and I will accomplish all My good pleasure"* (Isaiah 46:10 NASB).

> *"For I know the plans that I have for you," declares the Lord, "plans for prosperity and not for disaster, to give you a future and a hope"* (Jeremiah 29:11 NASB).

The words translated "end" and "future" are the same Hebrew word, *achariyth*, and when fully understood bring powerful insight. The New King James Version translates this word as "destiny." Zodhiates says the following about it: "the general meaning is 'after,' 'later,' 'behind,' 'following.' The Hebrew way of thinking was like a man rowing a boat; he backs into the future. Therefore, what is 'behind' and what is 'future' come from the same root *achar*."[34]

Fascinating—what is behind and what is future comes from the same word. Actually, within its meaning is captured the concept of eternity—in both directions, past and future—depicting the eternal nature of God and the spirit realm.

It is very encouraging that our destiny and future are in the hands of an eternal God who declares "the end from the beginning!" And while it does seem that we row backward into our future—by faith, without fully seeing in advance what is coming—we nevertheless know that our destiny is secure in God, and that our end can always be greater than our beginning.

TIME CATCHES UP WITH THE DECREE

As I meditated on this verse, Isaiah 46:10, especially the part about God decreeing the end (*achariyth*) from the beginning, the Holy Spirit impressed upon me an interesting phrase: *Eventually time catches up with My decree*. In other words, the eternal, timeless God declares the end from the beginning; and as I continue to row into my future, I will eventually row into that which He has destined and decreed for me.

All believers have experienced this. God often reveals to us His intentions for our lives, whether personally or prophetically through someone else, far in advance of when He intends for them to occur. When they don't immediately come to pass, many of us become confused. Abraham, who was promised Isaac 25 years in advance, certainly did. So did David, who was anointed to be king over Israel 20 years before it transpired. The frustration and confusion sets in because this timeless God doesn't always bother to tell us that what He is promising may be years ahead, just as He didn't with these two men.

A BAD TRIP

I recall an experience I had with the Lord in September 1973 that pictures this truth. Having recently recommitted my life to Christ, I was sitting in a parked car informing a friend of my rededication. This person had done a lot of hallucinogenic drugs and began experiencing a horrible flashback while I was speaking. He began writhing, thrashing, and screaming in the backseat of the car. Looking back on it now, it was probably demonic.

An amazing calm came over me—I now believe it was the gift of faith—and I knew with certainty that I had authority over this "bad trip." I spoke to my friend, not knowing whether he could hear me or not, telling him I was going to pray and rebuke the effects of the drugs. I did just that, commanding the flashback to end. It stopped immediately, and my surprised friend sat staring at me with a calm but puzzled expression. "What happened?" he murmured.

In the context of this event, the Holy Spirit began speaking to me about my future (*achariyth*). He spoke to me of things I would experience, and of the different facets of the calling and anointing He had planned for me. Then the long wait began! Some of the things He spoke to me are just now beginning to occur.

We must always remember that God often speaks far in advance of time's fulfillment. In the meantime, we must keep rowing—by faith—into our future. And just as a rower stays on course by using a reference point behind him, we do also. For us, that reference point is often the promise or word of the Lord from our past. But if we keep rowing, time will catch up with the decree of the Lord, and we will row into our destiny. Alaska did, so can you.

DECREE THE DECREE

Chuck wrote about decrees in the last chapter. Adding to what he has said, there is one more verse I want to share with you, Job 22:28 (NASB 1995) that states, *"You will also decree a thing, and it will be established for you; and light will shine on your ways."* The word *thing* in this verse is *omer*, and means a word, promise or decree.[35] This portion of the verse could be translated, "You will decree a decree." When time catches up to the decree of the Lord for our lives—when the opportune time for fulfillment has come—we must decree the decree, agreeing with and declaring what God has said about us. As we come into agreement with His plans by declaring our faith in them, we are releasing the creative power of His word, which as the verse goes on to say, will cause them to be established.

This is what Chuck, I, and others did time after time on the Tour: We heard His plans, discerned His timing, and decreed the decree. The number one question we asked of the Lord was: "What are You saying to [this state] right now?" Once this was discerned, decrees could be made in agreement with His plans and purposes—which He declared from the beginning—releasing the creative power of His word.

RECEIVE THE HOLY SPIRIT'S HELP

This, by the way, makes clear why the prophetic anointing is so important if we are to see God's purposes established. The sons of Issachar are wonderful biblical examples of this. They were able to discern the times, which then enabled them to also know what to do (see 1 Chronicles 12:32). We, too, must walk in this ability to discern the timings of the Spirit, which is such an important prerequisite to knowing what to do. Make this a goal for your life, and the Holy Spirit will faithfully reveal to you the times and seasons. As He does, like Israel in Haggai's day, your latter can be greater than your former.

Keep rowing—time will catch up with His decree for you!

– 9 –

THE REIGNING CHURCH

Christ's Ekklesia

(Tim Sheets)

When Jesus came into the coasts of Caesarea Philippi, he asked his disciples, saying, Whom do men say that I the Son of man am? And they said, Some say that thou art John the Baptist: some, Elias; and others, Jeremias, or one of the prophets. He saith unto them, But whom say ye that I am? And Simon Peter answered and said, Thou art the Christ, the Son of the living God.

And Jesus answered and said unto him, Blessed art thou, Simon Barjona: for flesh and blood hath not revealed it unto thee, but my Father which is in heaven. And I say also unto thee, That thou art Peter, and upon this rock I will build my church; and the gates of hell shall not prevail against it. And I will give unto thee the keys of the kingdom of heaven: and whatsoever thou shalt bind on earth shall be bound in heaven: and whatsoever thou shalt loose on earth shall be loosed in heaven (Matthew 16:13-19 KJV).

As sons and daughters of God, we are commanded to forbid or to permit things on earth. God's original intent for His people is to reign with Him and exercise dominion, declaring God's

Word into the nations. God's purpose for the Church is for it to be involved in government. It is vitally important to see the Church in context with Jesus Himself. That context is a King and His Kingdom.

Understand, please, that Jesus does not talk about His Church first. He establishes His Kingdom first. He does that for nearly three years, and then at the very end of His ministry He mentions the Church. You would think He would start off talking about His Church, but He doesn't. John the Baptist and the disciples all preached the Gospel of the Kingdom. They preached, saying, "Repent, for the Kingdom of Heaven is at hand." It is near you. It is here right now.

UNDERSTANDING KINGDOM

Jesus came to start a Kingdom that Isaiah said would have no end. A quick review of the Book of Matthew highlights the overwhelming importance the Godhead placed upon this. It's why Jesus didn't start explaining His Church first. You cannot understand what real Church is until you understand Kingdom. The Church is a part of His Kingdom. The world right now is in an absolute mess because we have not understood that the Church is to be a ruling and reigning branch of His Kingdom upon the earth. In fact, Kingdom has been minimized by the nominal (in name only) Church in our times. Christ's intent that His Church should rule and reign has been completely distorted. Most believers have been taught the exact opposite. I was raised in church and I was taught the exact opposite. Hell has worked for centuries to suppress this truth, and yes, satan has even used the Church to suppress this truth.

The message of the Kingdom today and the ruling and reigning mandate upon the Church has been put off into the future. We need to see what Jesus says. I am more interested in what Jesus says than what man, the devil, or our government says. It seems to me to be common sense that Jesus would define what He means by the Church that He is building. He did say, *"I will build my church; and the gates of hell shall not prevail against it."* Why would we allow anyone else but Jesus Himself to define what He means? That makes no sense to me. What He meant is a bit complicated, but it's not hard to understand if we have the right definitions. It's been clouded up because of man's ideas that have gotten in the way of the truth.

The answer to all the chaos and confusion in our world today is the Church rising up to be what Christ says the Church is to be. It is abundantly clear to anyone who will take an honest look at Scripture that Jesus came to start a Kingdom. He came to build a spiritual Kingdom that would represent Him on the earth, a spiritual Kingdom that would visibly affect the earth.

When you think about a spiritual Kingdom, do not think *unreal*—think *real but unseen*. For example, while you can't see Heaven right now, decisions made in Heaven can and do affect things on the earth. Christ's Kingdom is a spiritual Kingdom that does visibly affect the world, even though it's invisible to the natural eye. It is a real Kingdom. It is not a phantom Kingdom, nor is it one that is off in the future somewhere as most today describe it.

A KINGDOM WORLDVIEW

Jesus Christ came teaching the reality of the Kingdom because He wanted this truth to be the worldview of His sons and daughters. If we don't understand this, Christianity does not work as originally intended, at least not to its fullest extent. The dominion mandate and the great commission to go into all the world and disciple nations will not happen without a Kingdom worldview. That's why lucifer and his powers fight the message of the Kingdom so hard. He doesn't want us reigning with Christ in this life. He doesn't want us exercising dominion. He doesn't want us to understand what Jesus originally meant. He wants us to be ignorant and passive.

Jesus did not come to start a Kingdom that would be dormant for 2,000 years. That would make no sense. He expects His Kingdom to rule and reign with Him on this earth right now. Through prayer decrees and planting God's word seeds, He expects His joint heirs to keep good foundations maintained upon the earth so that government can be built on a solid social structure. He expects them to, in His name, forbid some things and permit some things. He expects His influence to enter into a culture and change that culture through His born-again ones teaching exactly what He says. He expects His Church to act like it's supposed to act and to work for what His Word says must be accomplished.

KINGDOM

The word for *kingdom* is the Greek word *basileia* meaning royal dominion, to rule, the realm of a king, and a kingdom's reign (Strong's G932). The English word is composed of two other words—*king* and *-dom*, a suffix meaning "domain." A *king's domain* is his kingdom. A kingdom is a government that rules a territory, an area, or a nation. The Scriptures teach emphatically that Jesus is a King, He has a Kingdom, and He rules a territory. Naturally, His rule is boundless. His domain is everywhere—in Heaven and upon the earth. He even rules hell itself because He has the keys, which represent authority.

Jesus being King of Heaven is not argued very much among Christians. But that He is King over the earth is often dispensationalized. It's put off into the future as though the earth is not yet a part of His domain or jurisdiction, which is exactly wrong. To say that would limit His authority, and you can't do that because Jesus Himself said, *"All authority has been given to Me in heaven and on earth"* (Matthew 28:18 NKJV). He spoke that word in the present tense, so that must mean that He is King of Heaven and He is King of earth right now. He is sovereign over it all right now.

How does that work? It's supposed to work through His Kingdom's Church, which is His body (see Ephesians 1:23). The Church is to be Christ's ruling body on the earth. Remember from Romans 8:17, we are *"heirs of God, and joint-heirs with Christ."* We are identical heirs with Christ right now, and in His name we are to rule on the earth. Yes, we are going to rule with Him through eternity, but we need to reign with Him now as well. We should not dispensationalize it away into the future.

JESUS PREACHED KINGDOM

Christ declared the Kingdom before He ever introduced His Church. I think most would agree that His very first sermon was a sermon that He thought through very carefully. Jesus is brilliant. He is a genius. No one can communicate like Him. No one ever spoke like He spoke. No doubt His first sermon was designed with a very clear purpose. It's found in Matthew 4:23-24 (NLT):

> *Jesus traveled throughout the region of Galilee, teaching in the synagogues and announcing the Good News about the*

Kingdom. And he healed every kind of disease and illness. News about him spread as far as Syria, and people soon began bringing to him all who were sick. And whatever their sickness or disease, or if they were demon possessed or epileptic or paralyzed—he healed them all.

Notice He preached the Gospel of the Kingdom and He never stopped preaching the Kingdom. Moffatt's translation reads, *"He made a tour through the whole of Galilee...preaching the gospel of the Reign."* The Church has preached many things—it preaches most of the things found in the Bible—but it has not preached the Gospel of the reign, the rule, or the governing. Jesus preached the Sermon on the Mount, beginning with Matthew 5:3 (NLT), saying, *"God blesses those who are poor and realize their need for him, for the Kingdom of Heaven is theirs,"* and ending that with verse 10, saying, *"God blesses those who are persecuted for doing right, for the Kingdom of Heaven is theirs."* He begins and He ends with the good news of the Kingdom.

In chapter 6 of Matthew, He preaches on prayer, saying, *"In this manner, therefore, pray: Our Father in heaven, hallowed be Your name. Your kingdom come. Your will be done on earth as it is in heaven"* (Matthew 6:9-10 NKJV). The Greek speaks that in a declarative way. In other words, He said, "Kingdom, come." That's what we are to declare. "Kingdom, come to our region. Kingdom of God, come and reign over this territory."

Then Christ preaches in Matthew 7:12 what we simply call the Golden Rule, *Do unto others as you would have others do unto you.* He also says in Matthew 7, *"You can enter God's Kingdom only through the narrow gate. The highway to hell is broad, and its gate is wide for the many who choose that way. But the gateway to life is very narrow and the road is difficult, and only a few ever find it"* (Matthew 7:13-14 NLT).

The Kingdom way is a narrow way. He is not talking about something off in the future. He is talking about the Kingdom way right now:

> *Not everyone who calls out to me, "Lord! Lord!" will enter the Kingdom of Heaven. Only those who actually do the will of my Father in heaven will enter. On judgment day many will say to me, "Lord! Lord! We prophesied in your name and cast out demons in your name and performed many miracles in your name." But I will reply, "I never knew you. Get away from me, you who break God's laws"* (Matthew 7:21-23 NLT).

If you do things that are not authorized, you are apostate and you're sent away from Him. In others words, you are a phony. You can't be a part of His Kingdom and do unauthorized things. You can't ordain homosexuals; it's unauthorized. You can't preach Chrislam; it's unauthorized. You can't say everybody is going to Heaven, no matter what; it's unauthorized. If you can't enter into Heaven and you are sent away, then there is only one other choice—hell. No, not everyone is going to Heaven; our King says so. It's unauthorized to say it, and if you do then the King says, "I will say get away from me. You're not entering the Kingdom of Heaven." You must preach what is authorized and plant the uncompromised Word of the Living God. You can't suppress what it's saying. If you do, He could send you away.

Jesus began His Galilean ministry by preaching in Matthew 9:35 (NKJV), *"Then Jesus went about all the cities and villages, teaching in their synagogues, and preaching the gospel of the kingdom, and healing every sickness and every disease among the people."* Why would He be preaching the Gospel of the Kingdom if it was for the future? Especially when He demonstrated that the Kingdom of Heaven was among them by healing the sick and diseased.

Later, Jesus sent His twelve disciples out to preach. He empowered them when they went to cast out devils and to heal the sick. And what were they to preach? In Matthew 10:7 (KJV) Jesus said, *"And as ye go, preach, saying, The kingdom of heaven is at hand."* It is near you—right at your fingertips. You can touch it. Demonstrate that by casting out demons and healing the sick. The Message Bible reads, *"Tell them that the kingdom is here."* The J.B. Phillips translation says, *"Proclaim that the kingdom of Heaven has arrived."* That doesn't sound like it's off in the future to me.

Christ made these statements 2,000 years ago, so He can't be talking about the future. He said to them, "Declare the Kingdom of God is here now," and then the book of Matthew continues with one parable after another concerning the Kingdom of God and what the Kingdom of God is like.

The point is, Jesus did His very best to get His disciples to understand the Gospel of the Kingdom. He wanted them to think Kingdom. He insisted that they renew their minds to that worldview. Over and over He said that He came to plant a Kingdom on the earth—a Kingdom that cannot be shaken. A Kingdom that He said will never come to an end. So when He begins to speak of the Church, without question the context is the Kingdom of God. The Church is part of His Kingdom upon the earth.

CHRIST'S CHURCH

The picture of a kingdom that grows and prospers on earth is strengthened by the word Jesus chose to refer to His Church. After three years of teaching the Kingdom, He used a political, judicial, and governmental word to introduce His Church into the earth. That astonishes a lot of people. But remember, God wants His sons and His daughters reigning with Him. We are made in His image and He is the Ruler, Governor, and the King, so the nature to govern is planted into our being the day we are born again. It's part of our spiritual DNA.

The word Jesus uses for "church" emphatically reflects that. That word is *ekklesia,* and it is translated "church" 113 times in the New Testament (Strong's G1577). Jesus, the disciples, and the apostles used *ekklesia* to describe the Church. It is not a religious word. It is not even a sacred word, and in the Bible it never denotes a building or a specific place of worship. Of course, it has come to mean that today. We say, "I am going to church today," or someone may ask, "Where do you attend church?"

Technically, that is not possible because *you are the Church.* The word *church* originally meant an assembly of those called out for a purpose. Yes, a part of that purpose is worship, a part of it is teaching, and a part of it is discipline, but those are not the whole purpose, and place is never a factor. You can worship any place. If Christ meant to speak of a place, He would have used the word *synagogue* or *temple.*

The English word *church* does not appear in New Testament translations until 1557 in the Geneva New Testament. That is the first time the word *church* is ever used—1,500 years after Christ. Until then, *ekklesia* was translated as assembly, congregation, an assembly of called out ones, or specially assembled ones.

The Geneva New Testament was translated in Geneva, Switzerland. The translators were greatly influenced by Theodore Beza and John Calvin, the protestant leaders in Geneva. Beza essentially invented the word *church*, specifically to refer to certain religious orders governed by a hierarchy (such as the Catholic Church or the Puritans). These orders had individual churches all around the world, but one central government that controlled them all through many levels of religious authority. To describe this, Beza used the Greek word *kyridakon* to come up with the English word *church*, but it is never found in the New Testament.

The king of England at the time was King James, a very religious man. He liked the word *church* and was fond of hierarchies (not surprising, as he was a king himself), and in 1611 he ordered that the King James Authorized Version be written with fifteen rules the translators were bound to. One of those rules was that the New Testament Greek word *ekklesia* always be translated with the English word *church*, and that rule stuck in other translations from then on.

Once the word *church* was in place in the English Bible, anyone who read it would read "church" every time the original authors used *"ekklesia."* Over time, the word *church* gained a broader meaning, evolving to mean a location, a hierarchal religious order, a place of worship, a holy place, or a building. None of these ideas are even close to anything Jesus meant when He spoke of *ekklesia.*

Notice the distinction between *ekklesia*, an assembly or group of people, and *church*—a location with a building (and probably some people in it). This is subtle, but it is a dangerous confusion that has caused most people today to hear *church* and think place, not Kingdom. Hell's definition confines the most powerful governing body on the earth, the *ekklesia,* to within the walls of a building on Sunday morning.

Christ never said, "I will build My synagogue or temple, and the gates of hell will not prevail against its walls." He said, *"I will build My ekklesia, and the gates of hell will not prevail against it"* (Matthew 16:18 KJV). Knowing who Jesus is and His brilliance, we have to conclude that He did not use this word accidentally to describe His Church. It was stated on purpose, it was Godhead planned, and no other word is ever used. It's *ekklesia* in all four Gospels, in Acts, in Romans, in the Epistles, in Timothy, Titus, Hebrews, and Revelation. It is never another word. We must understand the meaning of *ekklesia* if we are going to understand what Jesus intended His Church to be.

By the way, just so you know, I do love the word *church*. I can't think of another word, and I'm not on a campaign to change it. We need a good English word and church fits, but we have to understand what it originally meant when Jesus used it. What we call church today He called *ekklesia*. Make no mistake about it—He knew exactly what He was saying and what He meant. The true meaning of *ekklesia* is so radical that many people are scared to even go there.

EKKLESIA

What does *ekklesia* mean? It is from two Greek words: *ek* and *kaleo*. *Ek* means out and *kaleo* means to call out (Strong's G1537, G2564). It means to be called out and assembled for a purpose. The word *ekklesia* first occurs in the 5th century (500 years) before Christ. Again, it was a political term, not a religious term. It is a word describing those with the final say in Greek government. The definition of *ekklesia* in classical Greek is, "An assembly of citizens summoned by the town crier to legislative assembly at the gate." The gate, of course, is where people of authority sat. It would be like where our city building is, where the mayor and the city council do business. The capital of Ohio would be the gate of Ohio. It is from where our governor, Senate, and House govern. Washington, DC, would be called the gate of the United States in Bible days. Citizens 18 years of age and up could answer a call to gather or assemble to pass legislation, always by upraised hand.

Colin Brown states in the *New International Dictionary of New Testament Theology* volume 3, "The ekklesia denotes in the usage of antiquity the popular assembly of the competent full citizens of a city. It met at regular intervals but could also be called quickly in cases of emergency." The ekklesia's sphere of competence included:

A. Decisions on suggested law and final decisions on new law.

The final decision of all law was left to the ekklesia. Don't think Jesus didn't know what He was talking about. "My Church is to have the final decision on laws in the nation or region." He said it, not me!

B. Appointments to official positions.

Voting was for magistrates or for those who held an office. It was the ekklesia's responsibility to vote for those who held office.

C. Both internal and external policies in the region including contracts, treaties, war and peace, and financial matters for the region.

They were all decided by the ekklesia. It is not conceivable that Jesus didn't know what the word *ekklesia* meant when He used it. He understood it very well.

D. The ekklesia would rule on cases of treason.

If someone was involved in treason, they would be brought before the ekklesia, and they would vote and decide their guilt or innocence.

E. It could summon for its army to assemble for war.

The ekklesia had command of the military, which is certainly a lot of authority.

F. The ekklesia ruled on societal and cultural matters for its geographical location or territory.

Jesus said, "My ekklesia is to set the cultural standards for a region." He understood what it meant.

G. The ekklesia chose by upraised hands who would sit at the Areopagus (the high court of Athens).[36]

The capital of Greece was Athens, the gate of Greece. The high court there was similar to our Supreme Court today. It was the Supreme Court of Athens, Greece.

The *Areopagus* literally means "the Rock of Ares." Athens was a city where the temples of many gods were, and it had cultural facilities that defined the culture of the nation—including the high court. The Areopagus was where the high court of Greece sat to deliberate.

Notice, the ekklesia was not the high court—it was the assembly of the people—but it decided who would be on the high court. Those in the Areopagus were selected by the ekklesia. Both groups had their legal roles, with a nuanced interplay, but from what we can discover, the ekklesia remained the final authority. For example, the high court (Areopagus) could investigate corruption or treason, but then the evidence was taken to the ekklesia for sentencing.[37]

Some citizens were required to attend the ekklesia, but many more were not—their presence was voluntary. The decisions of government were up to those who answered the call to assemble and rule. That's why

I have taught for years in favor of voting in elections. It is our responsibility, commanded by our King, to be responsible for who sits on the court. Biblically, voting is a responsibility. If you are a Christian, raise your hand and make a decision. Nothing secret. Raise your hand and be seen. Publicly decide.

Also, the Areopagus in Athens was the gateway of Greece where philosophies were debated. Pope John Paul II said that today's media is our modern-day Areopagus. This is very insightful because the people in the media are now the ones who are spinning the new philosophies. The media is now trying to decide who holds official positions and who sits on the United States Supreme Court. The media promotes godless ways, and it's telling the Church to be quiet. They have stolen the authority of the Areopagus, and we can't stand for it.

The apostle Paul was so concerned about the cultural conditions and the idol worship in Athens that he went and preached a sermon at the Areopagus, saying:

> *...When I arrived here the other day, I was fascinated with all the shrines I came across. And then I found one inscribed, to the god nobody knows. I'm here to introduce you to this God so you can worship intelligently, know who you're dealing with* (Acts 17:23 MSG).

In ancient Greek terms, Paul preached a sermon about Jesus Christ at the Supreme Court. The apostle Paul did not stay out of the judicial system. He exercised his God-given authority to speak into it. He raised his hand. In essence he said, "Let me tell you about this unknown God. Let me tell you that the philosophies that you are spinning are godless. Let me encourage you to change your ways." He preached a message at the high court calling them out for their godless laws. It's probably why he got beat up, but he did it.

A GOVERING BODY

We need to understand the kind of authority an ekklesia held in order to fully grasp what Jesus meant when He used the word. "When the Greek city-states found their governments had become too corrupt and oppressive, they would call for an ekklesia, an assembly outside the civil authority of the city. If enough people came out and refused to accept the existing centralized civil authority, that government would collapse."[38] Due to the ekklesia's authority, civil leaders could be replaced to ensure the ekklesia's rule was enforced. Wow. That's pretty strong authority. Remember, Jesus said His *ekklesia* would forbid some things and permit some things.

There are some people we should forbid from holding office. There are others we should permit.

Thayer's Greek Lexicon defines *ekklesia* as "an assembly of people convened at the public place of council for the purpose of deliberating." *Deliberating* means thinking through things very carefully. The *ekklesia* is to think through cultural standards and then raise their voice by voting on those standards. It is not biblical to not vote. Godless politicians have been placed into office because believers sit at home and don't vote.

The Romans, who were the governing power when Christ made the statement in Matthew 16:18, also had ekklesias. Don't think Jesus didn't know it. He knew it very well. When Rome would conquer a territory, they would send in a group of administrators, legislators, or regulators of culture. How did they regulate?

- ★ They regulated by shaping the culture. "Here is what the culture is going to be allowed to do."
- ★ They shaped the education system of the region. "Here is what you will teach."
- ★ They administered laws, societal standards, and taxes.

The idea was to make that province look like Rome, reform it to be a little Rome, and make it compatible with Roman rule. They called that governing council the ekklesia. The Jewish people were under a Roman ekklesia too. Don't think Jesus didn't realize that.

Now we have a more complete context for what Jesus is saying. We see what *ekklesia* meant at the time, and we see that the first mention of church is within the context of the Kingdom of God. So the contextual definition is this: "The Kingdom of God's governing, ruling body is the *ekklesia,* established by King Jesus to look after His Kingdom on earth." We have to get that. The ruling Kingdom is not for a future time in Heaven because it won't be necessary there.

Every kingdom has six distinct areas that bring identity to it:

1. A king—our King is Jesus and we have no other king but Jesus.
2. Geographical boundaries—our Kingdom does also; it's everywhere.
3. Laws and commands—our Constitution is the Word of Almighty God—the Bible.
4. A society or culture that shapes it—ours is in our hearts, transmitted there by Holy Spirit who governs our conscience.

5. A political government—it legislates and has standards it maintains. If you are part of any Christian effort that has no standards, it is not part of His Kingdom

6. An economy—ours is called tithes and offerings. Ten percent.

Jesus said, "The body who stewards this for Me is My Church, My *ekklesia,* My called-out ones.

The born-again citizens of My Kingdom will worship Me as their King, represent Me as their King, and in My name they will steward their territorial or geographical boundaries. They will steward the laws and commands to ensure they are biblically based. They will steward societal and cultural values to conform to and be shaped by My ways and Word. They will call to account political governments. They will decide official positions and remove some from official positions by voting. Some have got to go. It's the Church's responsibility. They will, in My name, steward economies, insisting on ethical financial behavior by voting over what is acceptable."

Apostle Joseph Mattera writes that by using the word *ekklesia*, "Jesus called His followers the new congress of His kingdom."[39] That's the best definition I've seen yet. Jesus says believers are to come together and they are to rule with Him in His name on the earth. Where in the world can you possibly find separation of church and state in any of that? We have fallen so far short of what Jesus meant by "church" that it is embarrassing. We have wrongly bought the idea that we are to stay out of politics, legislation, and cultural decisions when, in fact, the very word for *church* in Scripture is a political word—a ruling body, a governing body, a legislative body. It is a congress, and make no mistake—Jesus knew exactly what that was.

Read this testimony from a personal friend of ours.

CANDICE'S STORY

As CEO of a pro-life agency, I often dream that I am rescuing babies. From accidents, from animals, from predators. It's a residual effect of the work we do. The cause permeates your very being and you struggle with how to accomplish more.

In 2015, as I watched the Heartbeat Bill lay dead in the Ohio Senate for the fifth straight year, I wondered who would ever rise up to speak for the innocent unborn. We had a conservative majority, and yet supposed pro-life members were not bold enough to protect an unborn child whose heart could be heard beating?

One night, I had a dream of a different kind. It was only a voice saying, "Whom shall I send, and who will go for us? Then said I, Here am I; send me" (Isaiah 6:8 KJV). The word *us* ripped at my heart. Sixty million babies have died and their voices have never been heard.

In my own life, God has always made me do the thing of which I am most afraid. Looking back, I see how God was with me, preparing me all my life. He equipped me, even when I did not realize it.

A vacant seat was upcoming in our local House race and my husband and I decided that I should try to win the seat. I had never run for public office and it was a long shot. I knew I would be defined as a "one-issue candidate." When we filed to run, we were immediately attacked from all sides but we kept our eyes on the finish line.

Much to our shock, the Church began to mobilize on my behalf. Both evangelicals and Catholics took my pro-life stance to heart and they formed a formidable volunteer base of over 1,000 workers. I ran against a person with strong name recognition and good financial backing. In fact, I was outspent nearly two to one.

On primary day, we went home exhausted after weeks of nonstop campaigning and watched the returns roll across the bottom of our television screen. I won with nearly 60 percent of the vote and I will leave for the Ohio Statehouse in just a few days.

"God is preparing His heroes and when the opportunity comes, He can fit them into their places in a moment. And the world will wonder where they came from" (A.B. Simpson).

I am only one person but I have an army behind me. We must be willing to risk it all. If we lose, we lose. But we must fight. There is no other way. This is the thing the enemy fears the most.

—Candice Keller,
State Representative, Ohio's 53rd House District

By using the word *ekklesia* Jesus was clearly saying, "Church, get involved and shape your culture. If it is wrong, don't hide. Raise your hand. Be vocal. Be public and forbid it. Rebuke things in My name. Forbid some things in My name and permit what is biblical. Affect public policy. Make sure you have the final say. Make the final choice. Get involved in the laws of your land. Get involved in matters of war and treaties. Speak up against corruption. Don't be passive and say nothing. If it's corrupt, say so. Vote it gone. Rule against it in My name. Only back those in any kind of official capacity who will obey My Word.

"Ekklesia, church, speak up against adultery in your capital, your gates. Rule against ridiculous philosophies that are coming out of your capitals and ideas or philosophies that justify sin and pollute the culture. Speak up and raise your hand. Vote and rule against it. You're My legislative body on the planet. You're My congress. Regulate the laws of your land. Regulate the culture you are going to live in. Say no to social corruption. Transform your territories. Shape them to look like a little bit of Heaven on earth. Shape the culture you are living in. Decide societal issues. Decide the economy. Decide tax issues, and only back those who honor the Word of God."

Remember, the prophet Samuel told King Saul, "Do not take any of the spoils of war. You kill every animal, all the goats; you don't take any of it" (see 1 Samuel 15). But King Saul did. He kept the animals for himself, and what did Samuel do? He stepped up and said, "The Lord now rejects you from being king." He ruled against him. He said that he was no longer permitted to be the king of Israel and he began to work to overthrow him and he did. Saul's government did not prevail. The Kingdom of God did prevail and David took his place. There are times when we have to say, "That is it. You are rejected from being a leader over us."

Christ says to believers, "You may not be the judge who sits on the bench, but you make sure you decide who it is." Make sure you decide who it is by publicly voting on it. Be vocal. You're God's ruling body, so act on it. The world has said repeatedly, "Church, you stay out of politics." They are going to say it more and more through today's media. But Jesus says, "Church, get involved in politics. You're an ekklesia. You're on earth to be My congress."

In our times, the Church has misplaced this teaching. We have missed the cultural mandate of our King. We've allowed hell to steal it from us, and we've allowed humanism and the secular church to redefine us. It is time to stop the heresy. It is time for some of us to raise our hands and declare the truth no matter who likes it or who doesn't like it.

The cultural mandate of the Scriptures is that the Church is called to be the moral center of the culture and the backbone of its laws by influencing every discipline and jurisdiction with a biblical worldview. It's time we were about the business of doing it and quit apologizing for it.

It's time to be what Christ Jesus says we are—an ekklesia raising our hands to affect public policy, judge corruption, pass and enforce legislation that lines up with God's Word, shape the culture, speak against idolatry and vain philosophies, and speak against judges who legislate unrighteousness. We have been authorized in Jesus' name. We have been called to that purpose.

I know that we will never have a utopia upon this planet until Jesus comes back. But we can affect the world and its governments, and we are expected to.

PART II

INTERCESSOR'S HANDBOOK

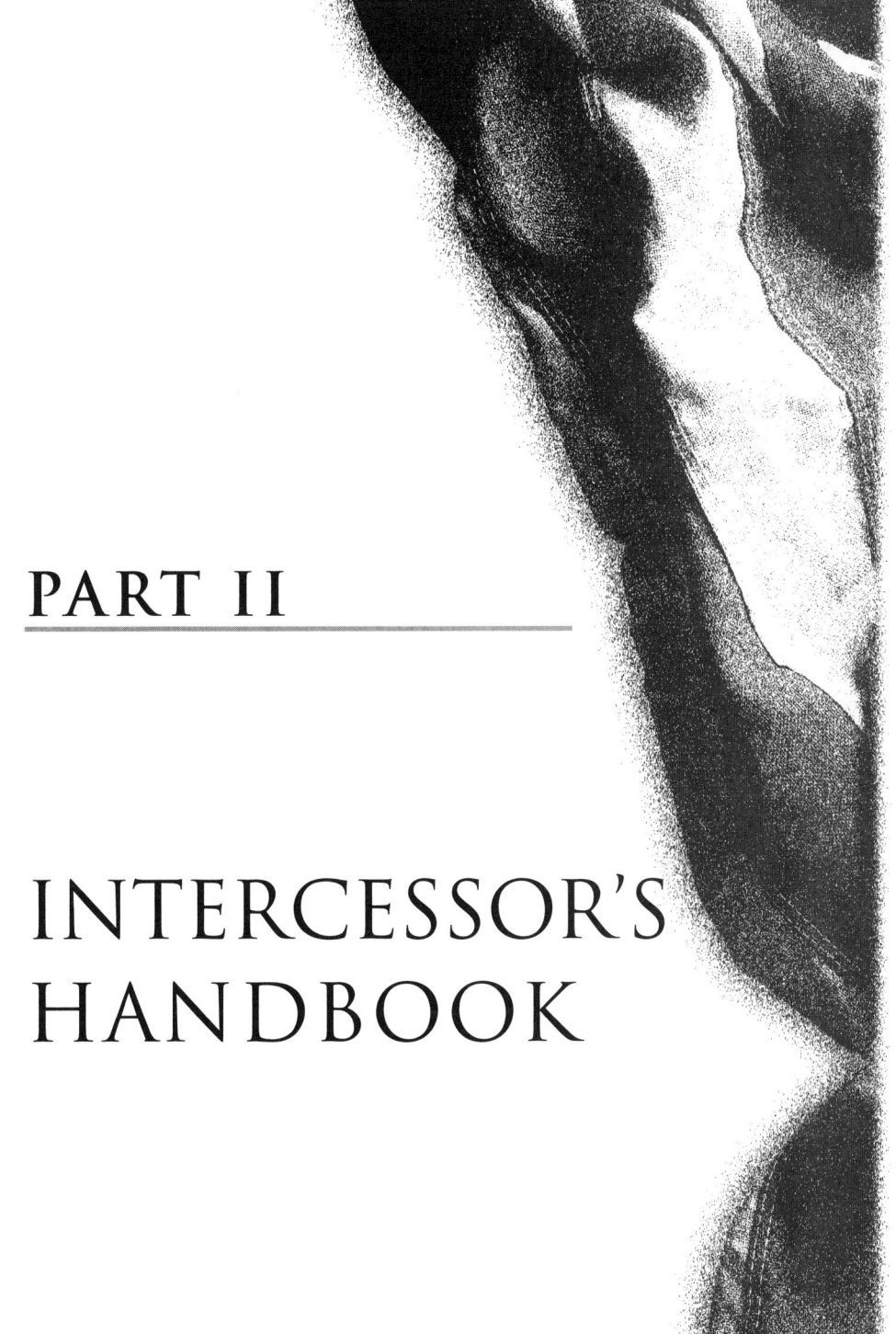

– 10 –

STATE *by* STATE

History and Future Destiny

In this second part of the book, Chuck and I share some of what the Holy Spirit spoke prophetically to each state, as well as other insights relating to its history and calling. Use this information to pray and decree, agreeing with what He has said. As we all do our part, we can see each state and this entire nation turn back to God.

You can help turn the tide and be a history maker!

We are grateful for each of our United States Strategic Prayer Network (USSPN) Coordinators and for their help in hosting and/or promoting the 50-State Tour gatherings. These men and women also helped in submitting or contributing to the following state-by-state reports and histories.

ALABAMA

Alabama: Name of Indian tribe
Statehood: December 14, 1819 (22nd state)
Motto: *Audemus Jura Nostra Defendre* (We Dare Defend Our Rights)
Familiar Name: The Heart of Dixie
50-State Tour: The Reformer and Justice State, July 22-23, 2003

> *Thou shalt no more be termed Forsaken; neither shall thy land any more be termed Desolate: but thou shalt be called Hephzibah, and thy land Beulah: for the Lord delighteth in thee, and thy land shall be married* (Isaiah 62:4 KJV).

The Lord is well able to redeem the reproach of the past.

Few, it seems, share such a legacy of shame as the state of *Alabama*, but she has not been forsaken; her God has heard the groaning and is come down to deliver. There is a growing witness that His hand is very much at work in this state. Even through *Levi*, who with Simeon shared in the shame of cruelty and shedding of innocent blood, redemption would be known and a true priesthood would be revealed. It is true; healing and restoration are coming; purpose and destiny are at hand.

The following are some key concepts the Spirit of the Lord released for Alabama:

Beauty — "The spirit of infirmity that is dwelling on this state will break," saith the Lord. "The birthing that needs to come forth for this nation will come forth...you will become the Gate Beautiful and Alabama will be known as one that rose from the ashes and became a beautiful gate to this land." (Prophesied by Chuck Pierce.)

Bridges — "And I am going to change your barriers into bridges—the dividing walls and barriers shall be changed into bridges." (Prophesied by James Goll.)

- ✶ Please agree with us in prayer for the fulfillment of God's heart in the state of Alabama concerning "Beauty and Bridges" or "Beauty and Bands." In Scripture, the Lord wrote these words upon staves—by writing "Beauty/Favor," He referred to *covenant*, and by writing "Bands/Union," He referred to *brotherhood* (see Zechariah 11:7-14).

- ✶ Please agree in prayer that Alabama will move from the ashes of injustice and shame of reproach to a sunrise of justice and the beauty of holiness, covenant, and union—both with God and with one another. It is time!

Gates of Justice — "In these gates where there is so much injustice locked up, I am opening these gates to usher in Justice to the South... Justice is coming through the Southern Gates." (Prophesied by Negiel Bigpond, Yuchi Peace Chief.)

- ✶ Please agree in prayer that Alabama and the South will be found faithful in opening the gate for *justice* to be ushered into the nation. It has pleased the Lord to bring redemption from where such injustice and atrocity first found entrance.

Reformer — "I keep hearing the word 'reform, reformer, reforming, reform'—the ability to reform. There is a reforming anointing on Alabama, a true Hezekiah reformer anointing, the ability to tear down the old and establish the new. That's what reformers do—they deal with the old and bring in the new." (Prophesied by Dutch Sheets.)

Voice — "Ask the Lord for a full voice in Alabama—to become a complete, forerunning, reforming people with a full voice to deal with the old and bring in the new." (Prophesied by Dutch Sheets.)

Bones — "While digging in the earth for something precious (re-digging wells for breakthrough and national revival), I struck something that hindered all progress. As I continued, I discovered what blocked further digging were bones—bones of injustice. Then I noticed something written on the first bone...upon it was inscribed, ALABAMA." (Prophesied by Lou Engle.)

- ★ Please agree in prayer for breakthrough regarding "justice" in Alabama, for it is a key to breakthrough for the nation in regard to these things.

Justice and the Judicial Crisis

To judge, within the Scripture, means more than to condemn the guilty; it is also to defend the rights or cause of the innocent. There is a fierce passion in Alabama to judge or defend the rights or cause of self or another. The state motto, "We Dare Defend Our Rights," certainly reflects this as does history. (The flash points in Alabama in relation to the Civil War, then later, civil rights, and more recently, with Judge Moore, were all issues related to real or perceived "rights.") This zeal to judge or defend one's rights or cause is rooted in her redemptive gift, but may be (and has been) perverted. Understanding this and what God had intended for good, gives great insight into both the purpose and the perversion.

- ★ Please agree in prayer that Alabama will judge righteously and not according to appearance and that she will execute justice toward the stranger, widow, and orphan in pleading their cause. Also, may she take up the right and cause of the Native American, the African-American, the wavering courts of our nation, and the unborn, who cannot speak for themselves. Please agree that we will also take responsibility for the places where we have erred, that we may see healing, and even restitution, come.

Judge Roy Moore provided the flash point that finally brought national awareness to the judicial crisis and our nation's courts. This case was not about the Ten Commandments, but whether *the state has the right to acknowledge God publicly.* (Note: All 50 of our State Constitutions acknowledge God.) After the Supreme Court did not accept his case, thus allowing the inconsistency to continue, he announced legislation that would be introduced nationally to address it.

- ★ Please agree in prayer that this legislation will successfully bring this issue before Congress, and that where the Judicial Branch has cowered rather than addressing the issue, the Legislature would finally confront it. This is not about legislating righteousness, but defining the rights and jurisdiction the Constitution already details that are currently being ignored by many federal courts.

Even without Judge Roy Moore running for election, Alabama elections are stirring up the same issues. With Moore's witness of moral courage and willingness to stand on principle in public office, the issues are escalating in the state (and even nation).

★ Please agree in prayer for godly governmental and political leaders to be raised up in this year's elections, especially in this time of critical decision. Pray also that Alabama would respond to the recent events with Moore in a way that honors God, and doesn't stop short of the promise and true testimony of Jesus Christ.

Redemptive Gift and Call

Alabama comes from the Native Choctaw tongue meaning "thicket clearer"—one who clears a path, prepares a way, or clears a field. The redemptive gift of prophet, as detailed in Romans, seems to fit repeatedly with Alabama's role through history, whether for good or evil. Whether the birthing of a number of movements with national consequence, or first to stand with Israel multiple times, the perceived rights and moral issues that fuel this call bring tremendous possibility when in right relation to God.

★ Please agree in prayer that Alabama would see and perceive truly, as the Lord sees, for her greatest stumbling blocks have appeared when she has been blinded by her own strength or is *standing* rightly but *perceiving* wrongly (as in zeal for state's rights but blind to the injustice of slave's rights). Also please agree for the full maturing of this call.

The Heart (Not Just Dixie)

In seeking the Lord regarding how to pray for the state of Alabama in relation to the nation, strong direction has come to pray for Alabama as you would pray for the "heart" as a member of the Body. This gives

further understanding of part of her intended role, but also insight into why Alabama has struggled, especially with "matters of the heart" (i.e., especially issues of relationship, covenant, and justice/prejudice that pertain to the heart).

> ✯ Please agree in prayer that Alabama's heart would "beat" again—that she would not be a divided heart, but a heart *united* to fear Him, and that we would guard her with all diligence. Pray and agree that from her might flow a wellspring of Life, that the *law* would be written upon her, that the priestly breastplate of *justice* would truly cover her (as it did the heart of Aaron the high priest), that the word and commandments of the Lord would be hidden within her (including the State Judicial Building in Montgomery), and for the wisdom to understand the times, knowing when things birthed must transition to those who are a "head" with the grace to govern or rule.

Brief Alabama History[40]

The earliest inhabitants of Alabama were Native Americans. The first journey inland by Europeans was made by Spanish explorers in the 16th century under Hernando De Soto. By the 18th century, few of the peoples De Soto had met were still organized under the same names, with most Native peoples now members of four major Native American Nations: the Cherokee, the Chickasaw, the Choctaw, and the Creek Confederacy. The French colonized Alabama in 1682 as part of Louisiana, but the French Indian War in 1763 gave the British ownership; and all of Alabama north of Florida became Reservation Lands for the Indians. White settlement in this reservation without permission of the Native Americans was forbidden by king's order. After the Revolutionary War in 1783, Alabama was given to the United States, who formed the Mississippi Territory, which included present-day Alabama and Mississippi.

In the early 1800s, the Louisiana Purchase, War of 1812, and Creek War all had a profound impact on Alabama, which became a separate Territory. On December 14, 1819, Alabama became the 22nd state of the Union. The state capital moved from Huntsville, to Cahaba, to Tuscaloosa, and finally to Montgomery. With an influx of settlers, the population more than doubled, and pressure intensified with Native Americans. Under President Andrew Jackson (1829-1837), these Indian nations were forced to give up their lands and move west of the Mississippi. Cotton became the cash crop of Alabama and the plantation system, which was organized around slave labor and adopted from Virginia. Southern states were convinced that slavery was essential for agriculture and the North was just trying to dominate the economy, so the platform of Southern Rights led Alabama to finally secede from the Union following Lincoln's election in 1860.

Alabama called the other states to Montgomery in 1861 to form a Southern nation, the Confederate States of America, with Montgomery as the first capital of the Confederacy. In the reconstruction following the Civil War, Alabama refused to ratify the 14th Amendment extending rights to blacks, and was put under military rule until finally readmitted to the Union in 1868. Railroads were built and industry began to emerge afterward, though a system of sharecropping continued and segregation of public facilities was the standard at the end of the century.

Industrial and economic growth in the early 1900s was halted by the Depression, and Alabama's delegation in Congress provided leadership in the recovery with the New Deal and TVA. In the 1950s, Civil Rights efforts began to focus on integration and with the flash point of Rosa Parks and the Montgomery Bus Boycott, Dr. Martin Luther King Jr. led both the state and nation toward radical reform. Resistance to the Supreme

Court ruling on segregation required President Kennedy to enforce it with the National Guard, but it still wasn't until 1970 that most blacks attended integrated schools. Aggressive pursuit of industry continued in the late 20th century with the manufacturing and service industries providing the greatest contribution to the economy.

May the Gates of Justice open wide! *"Let justice run down as waters, and righteousness as a mighty stream."*

ALASKA

Alaska: Aleut meaning "greatland"
Statehood: January 3, 1959 (49th state)
Motto: North to the Future
Familiar Name: The Land of the Midnight Sun
50-State Tour: The Alpha and Omega State, August 13-16, 2003

"Alaska is My 'Alpha and Omega' state." (Submitted by Chuck D. Pierce.)

Alaska is a place where things begin and where things end. This state actually has an island on the other side of the International Dateline. Consequently, it literally has the beginning and ending of each day; Alaska has yesterday, today, and tomorrow within it. God says, *"Tell My people to move **forward** and not **back** into yesterday!* Something aborts you from moving into the new, and you slip back into the old pattern. *Break the cycle* and move into the *new!*" The Lord says, **"Alaska is the Gateway of the Nation to the Ancient of Days!"**

God has given Alaska an assignment as a sentinel and a vanguard for North America. Alaska will open doors for the glory of the Lord to sweep through North America. From Alaska, the Spirit of God will fall, and your people will be sent to train prophets and intercessors. New cycles will begin in Alaska.

Brief Alaska History[41]

The largest, coldest, and most northerly state, Alaska is the only U.S. territory that once belonged to Russia, and it is by far the closest to Russia. (Only 55 miles separate the U.S. and the territory that was once the USSR, at the Bering Strait.)

The early inhabitants of Alaska were the Inuits, the Aleuts, the Tlingit, and Haida. The Inuits lived on the land from Alaska across North America to Greenland. They were hunters. The Aleutian Islands were populated by the Aleuts who lived by hunting sea creatures. The Tlingit and Haida lived in coastal regions and sustained life by fishing and hunting game.

Alaska was discovered by Vitus Bering in 1741. He had not seen the coast covered in fog in 1728 as he sailed near it looking for a northeast passage. It was hidden from his ship, *Gabriel*. Since he had not seen the coast, due to the fog, Bering set out again in 1741. Bering had two vessels specially built for this expedition—*St. Peter* (captained by Bering) and *St. Paul* (captained by Alexei Chirikof). These two ships became separated by violent storms and they never saw each other again. However, the ships' logs show that they arrived in Alaska within a day of each other in July 1741.

Russians began coming to Alaska to hunt for furs. The Aleuts were enslaved by some of these Russian fur traders, and some of the animal populations were nearly destroyed.

The first Russian colony was on Kodiak Island. In later years, Russian Orthodox priests came to the area to convert Alaskan natives to Christ.

Alaska was formally ceded to the United States on Friday, October 5, 1867—according to the Julian calendar, which was in effect in Russia. However, the date became October 18, 1867 by the new Gregorian calendar, which Alaska adopted when it became part of the United States in 1867. A new date and time was put into effect by decreeing that Friday, October 6, 1867 would be followed by Friday, October 18 of the same year. This was a shift of 12 days in the calendar year. An adjustment was also made to the International Dateline at this time. It was relocated from one side of Alaska and moved to the waters of the Bering Strait, so that the entirety of Alaska could be on the same day as the United States. Alaska was sold to the U.S. for $7,200,000, or two cents an acre.

Juneau was founded after gold was discovered in the area. Sixteen years later gold was found in the Klondike area of Canada, near Alaska. Miners found gold in Nome and Fairbanks as well, which created the gold rush. Many people moved to the area in search of wealth. Once people began to move to Alaska, Congress took more interest in the territory.

In 1912, the U.S. Congress passed the Second Organic Act. This Act allowed Alaska to have a territorial legislature. In this act, "the federal government retained the power to regulate the territory's fish, game, and fur resources, a function no organized territory had been thus far denied" according to Eric Gislason in his writing on the history of Alaskan statehood.

Alaska was thrust into World War II when Japanese forces bombed Dutch Harbor and Unalaska on the Aleutian Chain on June 3-4, 1942. It was considered harmful for the American public to be aware that Japan actually occupied American soil. The American people were not told, during the war, of the occupation of the Aleutian Islands of Alaska. The 42 people living on Attu were taken prisoner when the Japanese invaded.

On June 7, 1942 as people departed from church, they were taken captive. They were taken to Japan and forced to work digging clay. After a year, people began to find out what had happened to the Attu people on the island. In July 1942, the remainder of the Aleut people were taken to internment camps in Southeast Alaska. Of the 42 people taken from Attu, only 25 survived. On August 10, 1988, the U.S. Congress passed an act for "Restitution for World War II internment of Japanese-Americans and Aleuts." This document recognized that there was no remedy for the injustices suffered by the Aleuts during World War II.

The following is a copy of the Alaska Native Claims Settlement passed in 1971. It delineates what the federal government and the Native tribes agreed to. It states:

> **Alaska Native Claims Settlement Act (ANCSA):** The Native Claims Settlement Act of 1971
>
> was a full and final settlement of all claims to any rights, title, interest or privilege by people of Native origin in the state of Alaska, and extinguished any claims of Alaska Natives to special hunting or fishing rights. This Act is a legal settlement in the nature of a treaty; it therefore takes precedence over any previous or subsequent laws of Congress.

    A. Declaration of Congressional Policy in § 1 states that "the settlement should be accomplished...*without establishing any permanent racially defined institutions, rights, [or] privileges....*"

    B. The settlement provided for payment by the federal government to Alaska Natives of four hundred sixty-two million, five hundred thousand dollars ($462,500,000) in cash payments, and another five hundred million dollars ($500,000,000) in assignments of mineral royalties and lease payments received by the State of Alaska. It also granted title to millions of acres of land to regional and village Native corporations established under the Act.

    C. In exchange, the Native peoples of the state specifically waived forever any and all aboriginal claims based on previous use or occupancy (in other words, traditional use), or based on any previous statute or treaty. These forfeited claims include claims to any right, title, use or occupancy in or to land and water areas of the State of Alaska.

A recent vision was given about painted warhorses that were released from Heaven for all those in attendance. Many people had visions of their horses and great excitement filled the auditorium as each realized that they were called to ministry and equipped by the Lord Himself.

★ Please pray that they will step out of their comfort zone and begin to function as warriors in the Kingdom with wisdom, being led by the Spirit and not by their imaginations.

ARIZONA[42]

Arizona: Papago meaning "little spring"
Statehood: February 14, 1912 (48th state)
Motto: *Ditat Deus* (God Enriches)
Familiar Name: The Grand Canyon State
50-State Tour: The Greenhouse State, January 24-25, 2003

Our time in Arizona was coordinated by BridgeBuilders, headed by Hal and Cheryl Sacks. Cheryl also serves as the USSPN State Coordinator for Arizona and the USSPN Coordinator for the Southwest Region. The meeting was held at Word of Grace Church. There was great attendance from all across the state.

The Lord began to encourage the people by saying: "This is a prophetic city [Phoenix] and state!" However, the people of Arizona are not fully perceiving what the Holy Spirit is saying at this time, and they will not reap the harvest in certain areas as a result of this lack of perception. Since the flow of revelation is not steady, a shift is needed. This region is very connected laterally, but not vertically. Arizona must learn to hear prophetically and then do battle in the heavenlies.

We entered into a time of cleansing the state of the quenching of the Holy Spirit.

Competition has led to accusation: "This state is more important than you know. You control the flow of the river. I long for the River to rise within you. You regulate and cause it to flow out to other places. But accusation has dammed the river. Declare that this death over the Church from accusation will lift. The mantle and shroud of death is lifting this hour. The spirit of barrenness is being broken."

Isaiah 35 has often been prophesied over the state:

> *The desert and the parched land will be glad; the wilderness will rejoice and blossom.... Then the eyes of the blind be opened and the ears of the deaf unstopped. Then will the lame leap like a deer, and the mute tongue shout for joy. Water will gush forth in the wilderness and streams in the desert* (Isaiah 35:1,5-6 NIV).

Dutch Sheets decreed a marriage of prophetic intercession with the administrative/pastoral. The apostolic gifting that had been locked up in the pastors of the region was prophetically opened. We declared the gate of revelation was opening!

Cheryl Sacks then declared that Arizona needed to shift from a Church that *survives* to a Church that *overcomes*; it is a well-watered garden and takes authority. The Lord encouraged them to expand their hearing, for if they do not, they will not expand their faith (since faith comes by hearing). They need to learn to hear God's prophetic voice in multiple ways.

I (Chuck D. Pierce) then taught on the issue of there coming a time when the old ends (just as when John the Baptist was beheaded) and the new begins.

I then prophesied to Cheryl Sacks for the state: "You are about to build a greenhouse over this state, a covering of deliverance over Arizona. Find 14 key anchor points around the borders and throughout the state that will erect the tent. You will lead a group and troop in these points, and then they will go out from these points. I am removing the old covering. I am beginning to erect a new covering. You will mobilize and I will anoint you with favor to go. There is a troop arising! What has been a desert will become a fruitful planting. Deliverance is forming. By next April, deliverance will be flowing in this state and many will recognize who I AM."

Brief Arizona History[43]

The motto of Arizona is *Ditat Deus,* which means "God enriches," and our Creator has certainly endowed this state with a history of creative entrepreneurs, a heritage of sacrificial Christian leadership, sources of wealth in mineral deposits, and breathtaking displays of beauty found in natural wonders such as the Grand Canyon.

The first known inhabitants of the land were the Sinagua (which means "without water" in Spanish) in the north and the Hohokam ("the people who have gone away" in Hopi) in the central part of the state. The Hohokam were ingenious people who discovered how to harness the water of the Gila and Salt Rivers and use it to irrigate their fields and grow a variety of crops. They were knowledgeable astronomers, skilled jewelry makers, and the first entrepreneurs, traveling even as far as the Pacific Ocean to trade their handicrafts with other tribes.

There is even some evidence that the Hohokam trained the Sinagua in farming techniques. Their belief system was filled with mythological stories about receiving power from various animals and birds through dreams, and they also worshiped three main gods through magical songs and ritual dances. One god was Siuuhu, who was believed to have created mankind a second time after the original people were destroyed by a great flood that covered the earth. Both the Hohokam and the Sinagua mysteriously disappeared around the year AD 1400.

In the 1500s, Spanish explorers arrived, many of whom had been lured by legends about seven cities of gold and the expectation of sudden wealth. Probably the most famous of these was Francisco Vásquez de Coronado. Though Coronado was seen by his peers as a failure for not discovering the fabled riches, his reports gave the Spanish a vivid description of the area's geography and the Indians of the region.

Not all of the explorers were opportunists though; some were Christians who had miraculous healing gifts. One was Alonzo del Castillo Maldonado. One evening he declared a blessing on the sick, Christians prayed, and by morning all were well.

The next to arrive in the 1600s were the Franciscans, Dominicans, and Jesuits, who were motivated by missionary zeal. The first three Franciscans came to the resistant and suspicious Hopi Indians in northeastern Arizona. When Friar Francisco de Porras healed a blind boy, hundreds of Hopis were converted to Christianity in a short time. Porras became the first martyr in Arizona after eating food poisoned by angry Hopi shamans.

Probably the most famous Jesuit was Father Eusebio Francisco Kino. Known as the Great Apostle to the Pima Indians, Father Kino made his first trip to Arizona in 1691. He established missions in the Tucson area, but also made itinerant trips to preach. In his 24 years of labor, it is estimated that he rode or walked 75,000 miles to reach the Indians.

The Spanish soldiers and other settlers in the area lacked the kindness of the friars, mocked the natives, crowded them out of the missions, and confiscated the best farm lands. One Spanish lieutenant infuriated the Indians with his use of the whipping post and stocks. To make matters worse, Captain Javier Fernando de Rivera, who had no respect for the padres or Indian ownership of the land, arrived with his 1,000 horses and mules that trampled Indian crops. On July 17, 1781, angry Indians retaliated against the Spaniards. They killed most of the inhabitants of the two missions as well as Rivera and his soldiers. After the massacre, travelers avoided the Yuma Crossing for the next 40 years.

It should be remembered that during this time Arizona was still part of Mexico under the control of the Spanish Empire. When Mexico won its independence from Spain, the Mexican Congress decreed on

December 20, 1827, that all foreign missionaries be expelled. So, this ended the missionary endeavors of the various Catholic orders from Spain. The United States acquired a portion of what is now Arizona under the terms of the Treaty of Guadalupe Hidalgo and the remainder of the land through the Gadsden Purchase in 1853.

Not many are aware that the Civil War actually had a part to play in the formation of Arizona. One battle of the war was fought at Picacho Peak, a site located between Phoenix and Tucson, on April 15, 1862. The Tucson area was largely made up of settlers from the South, who were naturally sympathetic to the Confederate cause, while the areas farther north consisted of pro-Union settlers from the East Coast. The Tucson settlers tried to persuade Congress to create a Confederate Territory of Arizona with Tucson as the capital. But in the 1860s, large quantities of gold were discovered in the north near the present city of Prescott.

In Washington, DC, it was decided that the Union should secure its claims to Arizona and its mineral wealth. Congress quickly passed a bill, called the Organic Act, which divided New Mexico in half and created a Territory of Arizona from its western half. One prominent lobbyist for this bill was Charles D. Poston who became known as the "Father of Arizona" for his work in making Arizona a separate territory.

Fascination with the Aztec culture became part of Prescott's first Masonic lodge, which named itself the Atzlan Lodge. Aztlan was a mythical site where the devil appeared to the Aztecs in the representation of an idol. Masonry and other secret societies were very popular in the western towns of Arizona and much of the settlers' social life revolved around lodge activities.

In 1889, the territorial capital was moved permanently to Phoenix, a place named for the mythological bird that rose up out of the ashes.

In a similar way, Phoenix arose from the ruins of the Hohokam. While on an excursion in 1867, Jack Swilling, a prospector and former Confederate army officer who fought in the Picacho Peak battle, saw before him the expansive Salt River Valley and discovered the ruins of prehistoric Indians canals. Swilling, a resourceful man with the innovative spirit of an entrepreneur, suddenly had the idea to re-dig the ancient canals and divert water from the Salt River to irrigate land for farming. He soon organized the Swilling Irrigation Canal Company and moved into the valley.

With this new access to water, many settlers moved into the area. Swilling felt the new town site for Phoenix should be located around his home because of the many Hohokam ruins in the area. But two other factions had their own opinions about the best location for the new town, and some heated discussions ensued. Finally, a location, which is still the current downtown area of Phoenix, was selected. By 1875, Phoenix was a thriving community of 16 saloons, four dance halls, a brewery, a jail, a lithograph, two banks, a bakery, a butcher shop, and a general store.

Precious little happened in Arizona without a struggle, and the territory's admission to statehood was no exception. Many petitions for admission were largely ignored for about 20 years. Then in January 1910, Congress authorized the Arizona territory to hold a constitutional convention for the purpose of drafting a state constitution. This new constitution passed the Congress, but President Taft vetoed it because it contained a provision allowing the recall of judges. The majority of Arizonans favored this provision. But in a general election, Arizonans voted to amend the constitution in accordance with the president's wishes. Finally, on February 14, 1912, Arizona was admitted as the 48th state of the Union. In a humorous turn of events, voters reinserted the recall of judges back into their constitution on November 5, 1912.

After World War II there was a significant increase in population as many veterans who had been stationed in Arizona returned after the war. This tremendous population growth has continued to this day with Phoenix being the sixth largest city in the nation. Every day, the population of Arizona grows by 425 people. Many of the new residents are from other nations. According to the 2000 Census, the Asian/Pacific Islander population is Arizona's fastest growing racial group, but there has also been an 88 percent rate of growth in the Hispanic population over the past decade.

ARKANSAS[44]

Arkansas: Sioux meaning "south-wind people"
Statehood: June 15, 1836 (25th state)
Motto: *Regnat Populus* (Let the People Rule)
Familiar Name: The Land of Opportunity
50-State Tour: The State of Exposing and Dislodging the Serpent, February 24-25, 2004

> "Arkansas, you've been in captivity long enough. Today is a new day, even though the past has contained many mistakes. A new mantle is going on this state and is raising up a leadership for the future that thinks the way I [the Lord God] think." (Prophesied by Chuck Pierce.)

During the 50-State Tour in February 2004, the Lord gave Dutch Sheets four promises for Arkansas. Declare them with us:

1. "I am going to restore the foundations."

    — God is returning Arkansas to once again be the "Land of Opportunity."

2. "I am going to realign and restore Arkansas with its God-ordained purpose."

    — Arkansas is a state of refuge where God will re-infuse hope.

    — Prayer teams will go from Arkansas to leading cities all over the nation to "break in."

    — Arkansas has a deliverance anointing upon it.

3. "I am going to expose and dislodge the serpent."

    — Leviathan, the strongman over Arkansas whose "cunning aspect" is to distort communication, will be cast down.

    — "Dislodge" speaks of the strong Masonic structure in this state, yet to be undone.

    — God will deal with witchcraft.

    — Light, revelation, and the gift of discerning of spirits will be released.

    — The Lodge will be dislodged.

4. "It's time for Arkansas to blossom."

    — Declare Isaiah 35 over this state; it is Arkansas redemptive Scripture.

    — The river will come to Arkansas and flood the desert with life; no more mirages!

    — The rivers that flow from this state will heal the land.

God has emphasized three realms in which He desires to be moving apostolically within this state—the *church*, the *marketplace*, and the *political arena*.

Brief Arkansas History[45]

From evidence left in mounds and bluffs, including pottery and stone implements, we know that people have been living in the region that is now Arkansas for thousands of years. The ancestors of the Indians were first to inhabit the region. The abundant wildlife and fertile soil made the area a wonderful home for these people, who gradually developed from primitive hunter-gatherers living in caves to much more sophisticated farmers living in large, permanent villages. As the eastern lands became settled, more Indians moved to sparsely inhabited Arkansas. The Indians who lived here included the Folsom people, Bluff Dwellers, Mound Builders, Caddos, Quapaws, Osage, Choctaw, and Cherokee.

In 1541, the Spanish explorer Hernando De Soto was the first European to set foot in Arkansas. He led an unsuccessful, yearlong expedition for gold. One hundred thirty-one years later, two Frenchmen named Marquette and Joliet visited Arkansas briefly. In 1682, at the mouth of the Mississippi, LaSalle claimed the Mississippi Valley for France, but was later assassinated by two of his companions. In 1686, Henri De Tonti set out from Fort Saint Louis on the Illinois River to meet LaSalle at the mouth of the Mississippi. After he failed to locate LaSalle, De Tonti, the "Father of Arkansas," established the first European settlement in Arkansas—Arkansas Post, which was comprised of six residents.

Over the next hundred years, development of the region was sluggish as the number of settlers slowly increased. In 1762, the entire Louisiana Territory was ceded to Spain, and Spanish governors offered free land and no taxes to encourage settlers to inhabit the area. In 1799, there were approximately 386 white people living in Arkansas. In 1803, the Louisiana Purchase brought a large amount of land to the United States, and, in 1819, Arkansas was organized as a territory. Its northern, eastern, and southern borders were the same as they are now; but to the west, some of what is now Oklahoma was included. In that same year, the *Arkansas Gazette*, once considered the oldest newspaper west of the Mississippi, was founded by William E. Woodruff. Two years later, in 1821, the territorial capital was moved from Arkansas Post to Little Rock.

By 1836, the Arkansas Territory had the required 60,000 residents necessary to become a state, and after writing an acceptable constitution, was declared the 25th state in the United States. The new state enjoyed a 30-year period of prosperity, and by 1860 had a population of 435,000 (25 percent of whom were slaves). The majority of the residents were planters who lived in the rich bottomlands of the east and southeastern portion of the state and farmers who lived in the central and northern hills. A much smaller number of residents were lawyers, doctors, merchants, missionaries, and teachers.

Arkansas was drawn into the Civil War in May 1861 by its decision to secede from the Union. Troops were mustered and civilians devoted their energy and resources to providing food, clothing, weapons, and horses for the soldiers. Two major battles, Pea Ridge and Prairie Grove, were fought in Arkansas. In 1863, the Confederate government of Arkansas moved to Washington (a city in the southwestern corner of Arkansas); and, in 1864, the Union government was established in Little Rock. After the Civil War ended in 1865, the era called Reconstruction began and dramatic changes were made in the South. The Democrats returned to power in 1874, the same year the present constitution was adopted. Even as early as 1875, Arkansas was billed as the

"Land of Opportunity" when an active campaign was launched outside the state to attract new residents to Arkansas.

In 500 years, Arkansas has grown from a vast wilderness to a thriving state with a population in the millions. It is home to the Wal-Mart Corporation, the world's largest retailer, as well as multimillion/billion dollar companies such as Tyson, Beverly Enterprises, and Arkansas Best. Advancements in farming, lumbering, manufacturing, tourism, and government have gained Arkansas a viable place in the international market.

CALIFORNIA[46]

California: Name of an island paradise in *Las Ser gas de Esplandian,* a 16th century novel
Statehood: September 9, 1850 (31st state)
Motto: *Eureka* (I have found it)
Familiar Name: The Golden State
50-State Tour: The Crossing Over State, February 1-2, 2004

> "Tell California: it's time to **cross over**! I've brought this state to a place; I've accomplished some things by My Spirit; the potential is there for them, and tell them: ***It's time to cross over***." (Prophesied by Dutch Sheets.)

Genesis 14:13 is the first time Abraham was called a *Hebrew*. The root word is *abar*, and means "to cross over, into, pass over, through Egypt, over Israel, moving from one place to another"; also Hebrew word for "penetrate." It's the Old Testament word for "impregnating." Abraham was called a Hebrew because he was *willing* to move out of a place of comfort and cross over to something new! One definition is: "one from the other side." Hebrews *cross over* into the new—"pioneer spirit"— ready to go when God says, "Go." In Joshua 3:5, *abar* means "You haven't been this way before."

Every generation must have its "crossing over." You must choose! Are we going to cross over? We must get this Hebrew anointing on us in California.

To Joshua: *"It's your turn to take them over."*

To California: *"It's your turn now to take this state across!"* (Prophesied by Dutch Sheets.)

> "This is My hour to fix a fracture in San Diego; the fracture **must be addressed now** or else the enemy will come in through this crack! **San Diego** must cross over! I'm going to move with an unprecedented move of healing in **San Francisco**. This move of healing in San Francisco will defy the religious spirits and focus in this land! The Body is cursing the people of this city and keeping them from coming into freedom! Therefore, this is My hour to cross San Francisco over!" (Prophesied by Chuck D. Pierce.) **Shout**: "San Francisco will cross over!"
>
> "Cross into miraculous, deliverance, miracles, salvation; you need to cross out of the religious spirit. You're going to break into *freedom*!" (Prophesied by Dutch Sheets.)
>
> "I would say to you there's an anointing for **Northern California** moving toward **Sacramento**. Sacramento, I am ready to roll into your city! You will be known as a city of worship. Cross over Sacramento!" (Prophesied by Chuck D. Pierce.)

"I'm going to bring a reformation into the **Catholic people of California.** The Catholic people will fall under My power. And the spell that has been on the Catholics of California will begin to break. A reformation of **government change** will invade the Catholic Church of California and shake this nation and even affect the world. I say to the Catholics of California: Cross over! And I would say to **San Jose**: You will be a city like a magnet. I will even treat you like a magnet school, for many will be streamlining their ideas together, and think tanks will begin to come into this city. Many will lay down their agendas and innovations—new and fresh—that will change the course of travel, change the course of history—will arise from San Jose. I say to you: **Become a refuge** for the thinkers of this land, and allow Me to invade their minds. I say to San Jose: Cross over! And I would say: I'm ready to cross over the **youth in California.** And I say: I will target the **Black community in L.A.** I say: Cross over into the Black community, and call forth and unlock the captives there so the youth in the Black community of California can affect the way that the police departments of this land are being operated. I say: Cross over Black community of L.A. I say: Youth—move across! And I would say to you: I am dropping an evangelistic mantle on the **Hispanic community** of this state. I say: The Hispanic community will rise up with great boldness and strength, and that passion will be liberated, and they will unlock many captives and draw them into My Kingdom. I say to the Hispanic community: Cross over!

"I say to the 'groin' [and I don't know where this is—you'll have to look at this on the map]; I say to the 'groin' of California: There will be a fracture, and it will create a shaking, and it will seem like the state is weakened; but from the very 'groin' of California a net will be placed in, and that net will produce a new strength, and I say, from that area I will cause this state to rise up and stand with Me in the day of adversity. I say to the 'groin' of California: Though you tear this year, you will rise up with new strength in the future. California: Cross over! And I would say to California: *War is in your midst—it will be known that war is in California. But, I say to you: Though this state has been passive toward My purposes in the past, it will be known that God's warriors have arisen in California! CROSS OVER!*" (Prophesied by Chuck D. Pierce.)

Crossing Over

When we *"cross over to the Lord and He crosses to us"*—the same word is used there that was used of Moses when the Lord came to him or "passed to him" or "crossed over" to him and began to speak.

> If you'll cross over, California, He's going to cross over to you, and He's going to begin to put a seed in you that will *impregnate* you with life! He's going to give you everything you've been crying out for—for the next generation! He's going to awaken something. There's a generation there that's so ready, ripe for the *seed of life*—they are just waiting for something to come and ignite the flame! And it is going to be the word of the Lord that is released; and all of a sudden, we are going to see a *double portion mantle of God come to another generation.* We are "pregnant" with it now! Maybe that's why this word is here in California; maybe it has something to do with

"The Call"; maybe it has something to do with what God has been doing among others in this state; maybe we are close, maybe we are "***pregnant***" with an anointing to do something with the next generation that is going to totally dethrone and throw her off the wall—the spirits and principalities, the spirit of death, the spirit of Molech, the love of Mammon, and worship of idols. Maybe we're about to see a generation empowered with the double portion anointing of Elisha with a Jehu mantle that will say, "Come ride with me in my chariot, and I will show you the zeal of the Lord!" He's coming to us with His seed. (We're going to decree and prophesy to this next generation.) (Prophesied by Dutch Sheets.)

The first time the word *reproach* is used in the Bible, it's directed toward a *barren womb*; the opposite of a barren womb is one that has been "impregnated." God is saying,

"I am ready to cause My seed to come in, and what has been barren I am ready to break open. I am ready for the hostility of the womb of California to change today. Signs and wonders will come over barren wombs in California, and it will be a sign that the womb of California is no longer hostile to My conception." One other thing the Lord would say, "The womb of California has been defiled, and I would say I am ready to cleanse the defilement out of the womb, and I would say some have made decisions to hold this defilement in place in government, and I'm ready to shift the powers of defilement in this state! I would say train yourself to 'box' this year, for I am ready to remove the current 'Boxer' that's in the ring of this state. However, you must be willing to get into the ring; you must be willing to stand and box and then watch; watch things begin to change. I say, cross over into the ring and box this year. I would say, what has been fine in this state is no longer fine with Me. Take your stand and trade 'fine' for the 'best' I have. I say, the womb of the state has been defiled. I say, I am ready to cleanse the womb, break the defilement, cause the hostility of the womb to change. I am ready to birth My purpose in this state.

"I call California, Naboth's vineyard, this year [see 1 Kings 19–21]. *There will be great contending of evil forces to gain legal control over California this year."* The tax structure becomes very important. The legality of government becomes very important this year because the enemy wants Naboth's vineyard. It was right next to Ahab's kingdom and Ahab tried everything he could to get it. Jezebel (manifestation of Minerva on the state shield) finds a way to take it through religious accusation. *"There will be a rising up of religious structures in California this year that will try to move into a government office/arena so that California is being controlled in a way that is not lawful from Heaven."*

"The last three years, California has been hanging in the balance. Tell them, this year, I am giving them a reprieve—a window to pour out super-abundant grace on them. This is a year of fertilizing and plowing up every hard piece of land. After this year, I will review the state of California, but not until February 2005."

We must raise up that intercessory strength in every county in California this year. God has people who will mobilize and get people in place.

> "There will come a layer of darkness across the state if you do not contend for it. I am giving My people time to get in order. Plow up, dig up, and fertilize this year. I am calling My people to leap forward."
>
> "In October [2004] there will come such conflict in this state that it will cause this nation to take a shift and cause this nation to awaken in a new way. I say, get ready. I am contending with this vineyard and I do not want Ahab to have it!" (Prophesied by Chuck D. Pierce.)

BRIEF CALIFORNIA HISTORY

The first Europeans to explore parts of the coast were Juan Rodriguez Cabrillo in 1542. The first to explore the entire coast and claim possession of it was Francis Drake in 1579. Beginning in the late 1700s, Spanish missionaries set up tiny settlements on enormous grants of land in the vast territory north of Spanish (Baja) California proper. Upon Mexican independence from Spain, the chain of missions became the property of the Mexican government, and they were quickly dissolved and abandoned.

California was the name given to the northwestern part of the Spanish Empire in North America. Following the Mexican-American War of 1847, the region was divided between Mexico and the United States. The Mexican portion, Baja (lower) California was later divided into the states of Baja California and Baja California Sur. The western part of the American portion, Alta (upper) California, became the U.S. state of California in 1850.

In 1848, the Spanish-speaking population of distant upper California numbered around 4,000. But after gold was discovered, the population burgeoned with Americans and a few Europeans in the great California gold rush. A California Republic was founded and the Bear Flag was flown that featured a golden bear and a star. The Republic came to a sudden end when Commodore John D. Sloat of the United States Navy sailed into San Francisco Bay and claimed California for the United States. In 1850, the state was admitted to the Union.

During the War Between the States, popular support was divided 70 percent for the South and 30 percent for the North, and although California officially entered on the side of the North, many troops went east to fight with the Confederacy. Lincoln sent troops from Massachusetts to California which he called his "California Column."

The connection of the far Pacific West to the eastern population centers came in 1869 with the completion of the first transcontinental railroad. Out West, residents were discovering that California was extremely well suited to fruit cultivation and agriculture in general. Citrus, oranges in particular, were widely grown, and the foundation was laid for the state's prodigious agricultural production of today.

In the period from 1900 to 1965 the population grew from fewer than one million to become the most populous state in the Union, sending the most electors to the Electoral College to elect the President. From 1965 to the present, this population completely changed and became one of the most diverse in the world. The state is liberal-leaning, technologically and culturally savvy, and a world center of engineering businesses, the film and television industry and, as mentioned, American agricultural production.

COLORADO

Colorado: Spanish meaning "red"
Statehood: August 1, 1876 (38th state)
Motto: *Nil sine Numine* (Nothing without Providence)
Familiar Name: The Centennial State
50-State Tour: The State of Breaking the Drought, October 9-10, 2003

"I would say to Colorado that this is a year that I am going to address bitter roots in this state. I am going to go back to deep-rooted bitterness, and I say to you, you can repent of it. It can be removed. If you do not remove bitterness—every dry place of this state—you can put your finger on it—it will be linked with a bitter root that has not been dealt with. If drought comes, I say to you, look for the bitterness, and I will send water in the place of drought. I would say to you, this is your season for bitterness to be removed and for sweetness to flow. This is a season for My word to go out from here and flood the nations in a new way. I would say, this is a season of revelation. Enter in and receive, and I will surprise your enemy that has held you captive in the past....

"Watch, Colorado, this year, because it could go either way. Don't rationalize the drought that dwells above you and manifests in the earth realm because it has not been decided yet how the overall state is going to embrace the covenant of God. You will be able to discern that better this year by the atmospheric change and how the rain that is in Heaven above you touches the earth. It will be a sign to you this year. Cry out for the rain that is in the atmosphere to come down

> on the earth of Colorado as a sign because that says you are entering into a new dimension of tabernacle as a state." (Prophesied by Chuck D. Pierce.)

BITTER ROOTS AND DROUGHT [47]

This word prophesied by Chuck D. Pierce was given at Colorado's 50-State Tour meeting on October 9, 2003. The state of Colorado had a time frame through April 2004 to uproot strongholds of bitterness. When bitterness was removed, it would break both the physical and spiritual drought in the state. In January 2004, the forecast that the serious five-year drought in Colorado would end in 2004 seemed unlikely, but we had the prophetic word of God and His promise. A subsequent gathering by Apostles Dutch Sheets, Jay Swallow, and Jean Steffenson led an intercessory remnant in dealing with these bitter roots, by closing doors and renouncing bitterness. There was sincere reconciliation between the peoples of Colorado—the Asian, Spanish, Jew, Native, and African American. The leaders in Colorado continued to deal with the bitter roots in their communities and the rain of God's blessing started in May 2004. The rains have continued through the summer overturning the drought in Colorado. On January 13, 2005, the newspaper headlines of the *Colorado Springs Gazette* even read "Snowpack 'Fabulous' So Far," and the accompanying article discussed how officials are optimistic that the state may have turned the corner on drought.

A Treasure in This Nation[48]

Another word released was that *"Colorado is a treasure in this nation."* Chuck declared, *"Let the treasure of this state be mined properly and brought forth this season. Pray for what has been blocking the mining of the treasure in this state—both old and new to come forth—and the treasure of this state will be seen throughout this land."* Dutch had a dream that President Clinton (the current president in the dream) asked him, "What do you bring me from Colorado?" Dutch said, "Something old and something new." One of God's redemptive purposes for Colorado concerns the many old treasures buried underground. In 1540, the explorer Coronado led an expedition north from Mexico into Colorado in search of the Seven Cities of Cibola where the streets were allegedly paved with gold. But this treasure remained hidden until the Colorado Gold Rush of 1859. In the brief years that followed, billions of dollars from the gold and silver mines of the Colorado Rockies made its way to many nations. The dazzling white marble of Colorado was the source for the Lincoln Memorial and Tomb of the Unknown Soldier. The metal alloy, molybdenum, was used extensively to strengthen metal manufactured for wartime use during the World War era. Again the land yielded its treasure in the oil boom of the 1970s and '80s.

> "I am focused to bring forth My harvest in this state. And that which would prevent it, the old methods and the old weapons that would prevent this harvest, I would say to you, let go. I am going to send a wind that will blow the spirit of Nazareth off of this state. This state has accepted and become familiar with what I am doing in its midst. The wind that comes is a sign that the familiarity of unbelief that is linked into this state is being blown away. I am changing the mantle. I say, let go and enter into the new mantle." (Prophesied by Chuck D. Pierce.)

We prayed, "Father, we say this revelation is important and we now declare that the new dragnet that you have for

> Colorado Springs will come into place, and Lord, we decree Colorado Springs a treasure in this United States. We say, let the treasure of this state be mined properly and brought forth this season. What has blocked the mining of the treasure that is in this state, we command you to be gone in Jesus' name; and we say, Colorado, you are a treasure. Both old and new will now come forth, and the treasure of this state will be seen throughout this land in Jesus' name" (Chuck D. Pierce).

Brief Colorado History[49]

Early Inhabitants, European Exploration, and U.S. Conquest

Colorado's earliest inhabitants were the Basket Makers, Native Americans who settled in the mesa country before the beginning of the Christian era. Later people known as cliff dwellers inhabited the area, building their pueblos in canyon walls.

The first European to enter the region was probably the Spanish conquistador Francisco Vásquez de Coronado in the 16th [century]. Spain subsequently claimed (1706) the territory, although no Spanish settlements were established there. Part of the area was also claimed for France as part of the Louisiana Territory. At the end of the French and Indian Wars (1763), France secretly ceded the Louisiana Territory, including much of Colorado, to Spain. The French regained the whole area in 1800 by the secret Treaty of San Ildefonso concluded with Spain.

The United States bought the area [north] of the Arkansas River and [east] of the Rocky [Mountains] in the Louisiana Purchase of 1803. The federal government sent expeditions to Colorado which generated some public interest in the new territory, and they explored routes opened earlier by the famous mountain men, trappers, and fur traders who included William H. Ashley, James Bridger, Jedediah S. Smith, Kit Carson, and the Bent brothers. Bent's Fort, in Colorado, was one of the best-known Western trading posts. Settlement in the area did not begin, however, until the United States acquired the remainder of present-day Colorado from Mexico by the Treaty of Guadalupe Hidalgo in 1848.

Gold, Settlement, and Statehood

In the early 1800s a small farming settlement had been established in the San Luis valley, but most settlers pushing westward across the Great Plains continued on to the more fertile lands of Oregon, Washington, and California. It was the discovery of gold that first brought large numbers of settlers to Colorado. Prospectors led by Green Russell discovered gold in 1858 at Cherry Creek, where part of the city of Denver now stands, and after another strike the following year, the mining boom began.

At the time of the gold rush the area in which the gold fields were located was part of the U.S. Kansas Territory. A group of miners organized the gold fields as Arapahoe co. of Kansas Territory. The region was divided into districts, and miners' and people's courts were set up to provide quick justice. The miners sought separate territorial status in 1859 and formed the illegal Territory of Jefferson, which operated until the bill for territorial status was passed by Congress in 1861. William Gilpin, the first territorial governor, chose the name Colorado [Spanish for "red" or "colored"]. Measures proposing statehood for Colorado were introduced in the U.S. Congress in 1864, and again in 1866 and 1867 when they were vetoed by Andrew Johnson. A bill granting Colorado's statehood was finally passed by Congress in 1876.

When the first settlers came to Colorado, the Ute lived in the mountain areas, while the Comanche, Cheyenne, Arapaho, and Kiowa inhabited the Great Plains. Warfare between plains and mountain ethnic groups was continuous. The tribes of the plains combined their forces in 1840 to halt the invasion of their homelands and hunting grounds by settlers, and violence ensued. The warfare finally culminated in the Native Americans' defeat after the Indian Wars (1861-1869) and the Buffalo War (1873-1874). Colorado's Native Americans now live mainly on the Southern Ute reservation and in the Denver area.

Decline and Diversification

While Colorado was seeking to establish a government and engaged in conflict with Native Americans, the state's mining boom was in sharp decline. The surface gold had been extracted in the middle 1860s, and mining areas became, and in many cases remain, studded with ghost towns—machinery abandoned and shacks deserted. Other towns, such as Central City with its famous opera house dating from the city's days of opulence, managed to stay alive.

The completion (1870) of a railroad link from Denver to the Union Pacific in Cheyenne [Wyoming], and later railroad construction helped to stimulate the extension of farming and the growth of huge cattle ranches as well as to encourage an influx of settlers. Between 1870 and 1880 population increased almost fivefold. Denver briefly became the largest receiving market for sheep, and a smelting industry was established.

In the 1870s the discovery of silver-bearing lead carbonite ore at Leadville started a new mining boom. Prosperity was short-lived, however, for in the 1890s, despite a rich silver strike at Creede and the discovery of the state's richest gold field at Cripple Creek, Colorado suffered a depression. In 1893 the U.S. government stopped buying silver in order to restore confidence in the nation's currency, which had been placed on the gold standard in 1873. The silver market subsequently collapsed, dealing a severe blow to Colorado's economy.

Labor conflicts, disputes over railway franchises, and warfare between sheep and cattle interests also plagued the state at the turn of the century. Many of labor's battles in this period were fought in the mines of Colorado, and the lawlessness and ruthlessness that prevailed among both employers and miners were reminiscent of the early days of the mining camps. When the silver market broke, Colorado turned politically to fusion Populist-Democratic leaders advocating a return to bimetallism. The free-silver movement, however, was unsuccessful, and by 1910, with the improvement of national economic conditions, Colorado settled down to a predominantly agricultural economy.

The Twentieth Century

Large national parks, established in the early 1900s, have provided a continuing source of revenue; tourism has grown steadily. During World War I the price of silver soared again and the economy prospered. The stock-market crash of 1929 and the droughts of 1935 and 1937 brought hardships, but the economy recovered again during World War II, when the state's foods, minerals, and metal products were important to the war effort.

In the mid-1960s Colorado experienced a large influx of new residents and rapid urban growth and development, especially along a strip (c.150 mi/240 km long) centered on Denver and stretching from Fort Collins and Greeley in the north to Pueblo in the south. This growth, combined with the area's high altitude, caused pollution problems, most notably smog. The discovery and exploitation of oil created a boom in the 1970s, which collapsed in the early 1980s. Diversifying industry, swelling in-migration and accompanying construction, and tourism and recreation have since enabled Colorado to rebound, and between 1990 and 2000 it had the third largest percentage of growth of any state in the union.

CONNECTICUT[50]

> **Connecticut:** Mohican meaning "long river place" or "beside the long tidal river"
> **Statehood:** January 9, 1788 (5th state)
> **Motto:** *Qui transtulit sustinet* (He who transplanted still sustains)
> **Familiar Name:** The Constitution State
> **50-State Tour:** The State of Favor, April 4-5, 2004

This state carries a greater mantle of revival than any other state in New England.

God is going to cause something in Connecticut that will cause this nation to take notice of this state.

Right now God is ready to do something sovereignly in Connecticut that will cause the very root of His nation to rise up in a new way.

This state is getting ready to make a shift. We're getting ready to walk in favor. We're getting ready to have the favor of God wrapped around our feet instead of the snares of the past.

There will be a gathering in Yale that will ripple throughout the earth. Connecticut is getting ready to pass over. Get ready! God says this is a state that He is ready to give favor, connect and penetrate, and pull together. "*I have been pulling together a plan and am now ready to drop the plan on the state."* (Prophesied by Chuck D. Pierce.) Our being brought into national attention is a sign. This state has favor like a film above it. It is hovering over the ground. The Lord will put the favor that is hovering over the state onto the ground. *"My people walking in favor—they will walk city to city and it will be like a net over the state; and hundreds will be drawn into My Kingdom because of it."* (Prophesied by Chuck D. Pierce.) The Lord is about to open a door to new authority. Get ready! It will be known that the glory of the Lord will be poured out over Connecticut.

As a sign of favor resting on the state, both the men's and women's basketball teams at the University of Connecticut went on to win the NCAA Division 1 Championships.

The Lord is about to open a door to new authority. *"I am going to open a door over this state, for everyone who asks receives, Connecticut is ready."* (Prophesied by Chuck D. Pierce.) Matthew 7:7-8 says, *"Ask, and it will be given to you; seek, and you will find; knock, and it will be opened to you. For everyone who asks receives, and he who seeks finds, and to him who knocks it will be opened."*

> Lord, we ask You for favor on this land. We are ready to find You in the midst of this state. We are knocking, and looking for You to open the door!

Brief Connecticut History[51]

The gateway to New England, this state has a place in history all out of proportion to its small size. European settlement began when the Dutch built a fort near today's capital, Hartford, in the early 1630s. Soon after, in 1639, English settlers, recognizing their need for some form of government, wrote the world's first modern constitution, the *Fundamental Orders*. This was the first written document in history to create a government of limited powers, but its primary goal was the preservation of "the liberty and purity of the Gospel of our Lord Jesus...." Thus Connecticut became known as the Constitution State.

Our early history is full of overt Christian references. Our state motto, *Qui transtulit sustinet*, means "He who transplanted still sustains," and likely refers to Psalm 80, in which God took a vine out of Egypt and planted it in the Promised Land. Connecticut men flew a flag with this motto at the siege of Boston in 1775, cheering it for they knew it said God was on their side.

As Connecticut grew and changed from an agricultural and seafaring state to an industrial powerhouse, its people created a legacy that provides the images of so many aspects of our American national character: the serious Puritan, the sturdy Yankee farmer, the ingenious inventor. Nor is this mere mythology—Connecticut's innovators gave us gadgets like the cotton gin and the submarine. In more modern times our Puritan flavor has been greatly enriched by European immigration and African American and Hispanic migration. But while Connecticut Yankees may now be rare, their spirit lives on in our prized values of thrift and hard work.

A major part of our prophetic character is revealed in one of our older nicknames, the Provision State—a name we received by, among other things, being a main supplier for the Continental Army, supposedly saving the troops at Valley Forge. Connecticut has always been a major supplier of U.S. armed forces and continues to receive large military contracts today, manufacturing helicopters and submarines. Our historic role as a supplier and storehouse is also seen in the development of the insurance industry, which made Hartford the "Insurance Capital of the World." Major insurance companies such as Aetna still make their headquarters here.

Connecticut's economy has created some of America's wealthiest towns, and it is often considered to be the richest state in the United States. But this wealth is not without its problems, as patterns of inequality have placed poor cities next to unbelievably wealthy suburbs. Our calling to be providers is always challenged by the temptation to be the polar opposite—Yankee traders driven by greed. We have recently been shamed by corruption scandals, which resulted in the resignation of our governor and the jailing of several mayors. And greed is always a temptation in a state with two enormous casinos—one of which is the largest resort casino in the world.[52]

However, many hopeful signs have appeared in the last several years, as believers from all denominations and cultures have been meeting together to pray, organize, and encourage each other in new ways. God has favored us with victories in the public arena as we have sought to maintain biblical morality in the face of aggressive opposition. Christians here have a new faith!

DELAWARE[53]

Delaware: Named after Lord De la Warr
Statehood: December 7, 1787 (1st state)
Motto: Liberty and Independence
Familiar Name: The First State
50-State Tour: Releasing the Firstfruit of a Nation, June 2-3, 2003

Delaware was the first state to ratify the United States Constitution. Because of this action, Delaware became the first state in the Union, and is, therefore, accorded the first position in such national events as presidential inaugurations.

Chuck Pierce prophesied that Delaware would ascend in worship as he walked up the church steps on an afghan blanket depicting the state of Delaware during the 50-State Tour Delaware Gathering.

Dutch Sheets declared, *"The word for Delaware is this: You're going to reconnect to your roots and you are a firstfruits state. I have recently been in London at Christ Church in Oxford University. As I was walking through it, I saw a stone that said, 'Here John and Charles Wesley were ordained.' I hit my knees immediately. [They are the fathers of the Methodist church.] I felt the anointing of the Lord. My daughter said, 'You're re-digging a well, aren't you, Dad?' You better believe I was. I was laying hold of everything that's ever been here."*

Delaware is known as the "Cradle of Methodism." In 1805, the revival fire of the Methodists was burning so hot that 10,000 to 15,000 would gather for a week of meetings. It is recorded that the shouts of the saints and the cries of repentant sinners could be heard three miles away.

At the Delaware gathering, Dutch Sheets was asked to stand at the top of the steps. Pastors, leaders, and intercessors grabbed hold of his ankles to tap into the anointing that he had received in London while kneeling. It was a moment beyond time.

Chuck Pierce prophesied, *"If the firstfruit is holy, the whole lump will become holy. I am reconnecting you into a place of holiness that this nation has not seen in a hundred years. Let the highway of the Lord begin. And if you will cause that highway to rise up, many will run on this highway of glory. For you, Delaware, have the power to break the spiritual impasse in this land."*

The last section of Route 1, a new highway that covers the majority of Delaware, had just been opened weeks before the meeting. Dutch declared, "A highway of holiness!" There was a shout that rose up out of the people that continued at length.

Chuck prophesied, *"Every city of this state will have a worship gathering in days ahead, and it will re-create the move of My anointing throughout this land. You'll have a three-day prayer blitz across this state where you are praying strategically as one, from city to city, and then you will begin to go like a procession from city to city to worship."*

We had a three-day prayer blitz through all 60 incorporated cities during the fall of 2003. In 2004, we started worship gatherings in cities. On May 22, 2004, we had a one-day procession of worship through the entire length of the state with public worship in three counties. On July 20, 2004, we had a gathering at the capital, Dover, where just under a thousand gathered to worship—Catholic, Methodist, Baptist, Pentecostal, Charismatic, Hispanic, African-American, and Caucasian— seniors, adults, youth, and children. The spirit of worship melted the churches together.

It was prophesied that Delaware would connect with her godly past, leave passivity, and rise up in her position as firstborn; Delaware would move as a forerunner with apostolic authority to pave the way for this nation, breaking its spiritual impasse. Delaware has not been the same since the 50-State Tour. Delaware is rising up with the firstfruits anointing.

Prayer Points[54]

During the 50-State Tour, Delaware received tremendous spiritual identity as the firstfruits state. Delaware is to be holy unto God. Out of that identity flows the destiny of our state. If the firstfruits are holy, the whole lump will become holy. Pray that Delaware would rise up and stand in its spiritual identity and purpose as the firstfruits state.

Delaware was the first to ratify the Constitution. Delaware is given first place in national parades and presidential inaugurations. Dutch Sheets said, "When you were the first to sign a legal document, it gave you rights in the spirit in this nation. You have enough authority to break the impasse. You need to lead the parade of breakthrough! You need to lead the inauguration of the new." Pray that Delaware would rise up to lead the parade of the breakthrough!

Chuck Pierce declared, "*The firstfruits is the Lord's, and the anointing to secure the firstfruits is now upon us. We've been commissioned to secure the firstfruits, and when we secure the firstfruits, the whole lump will become holy. Now say this, 'The whole lump called USA will become holy.'*"

> Chuck went on to say: "And the Lord would say to you, 'This is the time that I'm rising you up to cross over. This is the time that I am sending you forth. This is the time that I'm releasing My sound through the cities of this state. For I'm going to pour My glory on this state. You'll have a three-day prayer blitz across this state where you are praying strategically as one, from city to city, and then you will begin to go like a procession from city to city to worship. I called My people to pray three days before they could see the way the ark was going. Pray three days, and you will move with My glory in these lands. And your home will be unlocked, your people will be unlocked, and this land and this nation will come under My authority again.'"

We have had the three-day prayer blitz. We are planning our time of worship to be completed by the end of May 2004. Pray that God would unlock the worship strategy initiative for Delaware. Pray for the release of His sound through the cities.

During the first meeting of Delaware's 50-State Tour, there were 100 ministries represented. This was an unprecedented and tremendous response from Delaware. The level of anointing was absolutely powerful. Yet that night the enemy visited Chuck Pierce and said, "I'm keeping this gate in place, because if you unlock this gate, you're going to unlock Philadelphia. Then you're going to restore the government. Then the government of this land will experience revival like never before and you'll move forward." We have experienced the force behind these words spoken by the enemy. It is critical that you stand with us for the spiritual breakthrough that we need. Pray that our efforts would not be hindered any more by the enemy. We have experienced this already. Declare that the gate in Delaware is unlocked (see Ephesians 6:12-13)! Pray that Delaware would take on the whole armor of God for this battle; for the God of peace will soon crush satan underneath our feet (see Romans 16:20).

> "If you will rise up, I am hovering over you in such a way that a new birth will be conceived for this nation. But to conceive this new birth, you must reconnect into what I have destined as the firstfruits of this land. And the firstfruits are Mine; and if the firstfruit is holy, the whole lump will become holy. I am reconnecting you into a place of holiness that this nation has not seen in a hundred years. And by 2005, holiness will be known, the power of My holiness, for I am holy. It will be known that I AM visited Delaware. Your garment has grown dirty and dingy over this state, but I have come here tonight to say I am going to remove that garment that is like death. And where death has come and visited this particular state

and produced a shroud to this nation, I say I am removing that death garment." (Prophesied by Chuck D. Pierce.)

Declare that God is reconnecting us into a place of holiness. Pray that our garments would be unsoiled and holy. Pray that the garment of death would be removed. Pray for the visitation of I AM to Delaware. Speak that the breath of God will enter the dry bones of Delaware and that they would make a mighty army. (Note: Every member of the first settlement in Lewes, Delaware, was killed and every building burnt. The first original settlement is literally a graveyard today.)

Dutch Sheets spoke a prophetic message on Ezekiel's dry bones hearing the Word of the Lord.

"I prophesy to the state of Delaware, to hear the word of the Lord; receive the coming together that is happening in the Spirit right now. I command the bones of Delaware to rise up from your dry, dusty places, from your wilderness graves, and I command you to rise up right now, and allow the Spirit of God to join you and to bring you together. Now I prophesy to the state of Delaware, and I say, 'Receive the wind of Heaven, receive the breath of God that is coming to you, to give you life and make you an army.'"

Brief Delaware History[55]

Delaware's history is a long and proud one. Early explorations of our coastline were made by the Spaniards and Portuguese in the sixteenth century, by Henry Hudson in 1609 under the auspices of the Dutch, by Samuel Argall in 1610, by Cornelius May in 1613, and by Cornelius Hendricksen in 1614. During a storm, Argall was blown off course and sailed into a strange bay, which he named in honor of his governor. It is doubtful that Lord De La Warr ever saw, or explored the bay, river and state which today bears his name. In 1631, 11 years after the landing of the English pilgrims at Plymouth, Massachusetts, the first white settlement was made on Delaware soil. A group of Dutchmen formed a trading company headed by Captain David Pietersen de Vries for the purpose of enriching themselves from the New World. The expedition of about 30 individuals sailed from the town of Hoorn under the leadership of Captain Peter Heyes in the ship De Walvis (The Whale). Their settlement, called Swaanendael, meaning valley of swans, was located near the present town of Lewes on the west bank of the Lewes Creek, today the Lewes and Rehoboth Canal.

Arriving in the New World in 1632 to visit the colony, Captain de Vries found the settlers had been killed and their building burned by the Indians. The settlement is commemorated by the Zwaanendael Museum in Lewes.

No further attempts at colonization were made on Delaware soil until 1638, when the Swedes established their colony in present Wilmington, which was not only the first permanent settlement in Delaware, but in the whole Delaware River Valley and North America. The first expedition, consisting of two ships, Kalmar Nyckel (Key of Kalmar) and Vogel Grip (Griffen), under the leadership of Peter Minuit, landed about March 29. The location of the first Swedish settlement was at "The Rocks," on the Christina River, near the foot of Seventh Street. A fort was built called Fort Christina after the young queen of Sweden, and the river was likewise named for her.

The most important Swedish governor was Colonel Johan Printz, who ruled the colony under Swedish law for ten years, from 1643 to 1653. He was succeeded by Johan Rising, who upon his arrival in 1654, seized the Dutch post, Fort Casmir, which the governor of the Colony of New Netherlands had built in 1651, on the site of the present town of New Castle.

Rising governed the Swedish Colony from his headquarters at Fort Christina until the autumn of 1655, when Peter Stuyvesant came from New Amsterdam with a Dutch fleet, subjugated the Swedish forts, and established the authority of the Colony of New Netherland throughout the area formerly controlled by the Colony of New Sweden. This marked the end of Swedish rule in Delaware, but the cultural, social, and religious influence of these Swedish settlers has had a lasting effect upon the cultural life of the people in this area and upon subsequent westward migrations of many generations. Old Swedes (Holy Trinity) Church built by the Swedes at Wilmington in 1698 was supplied by the Mother Church with missionaries until after the Revolution. It is one of the oldest Protestant Churches in North America. Fort Christina State Park in Wilmington, with the fine monument created by the noted sculptor, Carl Milles, and presented by the people of Sweden, perpetuates the memory of these first settlers and preserves "The Rocks" where they first landed.

Following the seizure of the colony of New Sweden, the Dutch restored the name of Fort Casmir and made it the principal settlement of the Zuidt or South River as contrasted with the North or Hudson River. In a short time, the area within the fort was not large enough to accommodate all the settlers so that a town, named New Amstel (now New Castle), was laid out.

The year 1681 marked the granting of the Province of Pennsylvania to William Penn by King Charles II and the arrival of Penn's agents on the Delaware River. They soon reported to the proprietor that the new province would be landlocked if the colonies on either side of the Delaware River or Bay were hostile. As a result of Penn's petition to the Crown for the land on the west side of the Delaware River and

Bay below his province, the Duke of York in March 1682 conveyed, by deeds and leases now exhibited by the Delaware State Archives in the Hall of Records at Dover, the land included in the Counties of New Castle, Saint Jones, and Deale. On October 27 of the same year, William Penn landed in America first at New Castle and there took possession from the duke of York's agents as Proprietor of the Lower Counties. On this occasion, the colonists subscribed an oath of allegiance to the new proprietor, and the first general assembly was held in the colony. The following year the three Lower Counties were annexed to the Province of Pennsylvania as territories with full privileges under Penn's famous "Frame of Government."

Also in this year, the counties of Saint Jones and Deale were renamed Kent and Sussex Counties respectively. After 1682, a long dispute ensued between William Penn and Lord Baltimore of the Province of Maryland as to the exact dominion controlled by Penn on the lower Delaware.

The dispute continued between the heirs of Baltimore and Penn until almost the end of the colonial period. In 1776 at the time of the Declaration of Independence, Delaware not only declared itself free from the British Empire, but also established a state government entirely separate from Pennsylvania. Delaware's boundaries were surveyed in 1763-68 by the noted English scientists, Charles Mason and Jeremiah Dixon.

With the advent of the Revolution nearly 4,000 men enlisted for service from the small state. The colonial wars had built up the militia system and supplied a number of capable officers who led the troops of Delaware in all the principal engagements from the battle of Long Island to the siege of Yorktown. The only Revolutionary engagement fought on Delaware soil was the battle of Cooch's Bridge, near Newark, on September 3, 1777.

An important stimulus to the recovery of the state's economy after the war was the invention of 1785 by Oliver Evans of Newport, Delaware, of automatic [flour] milling machinery, revolutionizing the industry.

In the following year, John Dickinson of Delaware presided over the Annapolis Convention, which called for the Federal Constitutional Convention that met in Philadelphia the next year. When the new Constitution was submitted to the states for ratification, Delaware was the first of the thirteen original states to ratify the Constitution of the United States. This unanimous ratification took place in a convention at Dover on December 7, 1787, whereby Delaware became "The First State" of the new Federal Union. Proud of this heritage, Delawareans continue to honor the traditions which made them the First State to ratify the United States Constitution, the document that continues to protect our nation's justice, strength, and liberty.

DISTRICT OF COLUMBIA[56]

District of Columbia: Named after Christopher Columbus
Motto: *Justitia omnibus* (Justice for all)
50-State Tour: The Ruler or Seat of Authority, October 6-7, 2003 and May 4-5, 2004

October 2002

The Spirit of the Lord initiated the call to visit every state when I (Chuck Pierce) was flying into Washington, DC, in October 2002. Likewise, the Lord also told Dutch Sheets, while he was flying into Washington, DC, for the meetings, to go to all 50 states. The Lord began to speak several other things to me. He said: *"Pray for 17 days.*

Declare that the victory plan and strategy is secured. *If you have My covenant desire in your heart, you will go forth in victory."*

There were four issues that I believe caused the Lord to speak to me regarding these 17 days of corporate, focused prayer:

1. President Bush and the Cabinet needed to gain clear wisdom, timing, and direction for the war ahead.
2. Pastor Dutch Sheets, who was with me, received a tremendous burden for the judicial system.
3. The sniper who was randomly and rampantly bringing havoc in the DC, Virginia, Maryland area needed to be found. The Lord said if we would pray for 17 days and declare victory, the sniper would be found.
4. A manifestation of a new level of provision for us to move God's covenant plans forward in the future was necessary.

Things began to move greatly during those 17 days. We were so thankful that the one who was being used by the enemy to kill and rob life and bring terror in that area was found at the end of the 17-day period. This showed us that God was doing something in His people by bringing us into a new place of *corporate prayer*. There are some battles that will be won only through our uniting in corporate prayer in this nation. The power of unity releases an anointing, and the anointing breaks the yoke. We grieve over the loss of human life that occurred, but rejoice that God has stopped the hand of the enemy.

May 2004

We returned to Washington, DC, for the National Day of Prayer Conference that helped pave the way for the National Day of Prayer in May

2004. This served as our 50-State Tour meeting for Washington, DC. On the morning of May 5, I shared from Psalm 18. Verses 7-12 say:

> *Then the earth shook and trembled; the foundations of the hills also quaked and were shaken, because He was angry. Smoke went up from His nostrils, and devouring fire from His mouth; coals were kindled by it. He bowed the heavens also, and came down with darkness under His feet. And He rode upon a cherub, and flew; He flew upon the wings of the wind. He made darkness His secret place; His canopy around Him was dark waters and thick clouds of the skies. From the brightness before Him, His thick clouds passed with hailstones and coals of fire.*

The Lord told me to lead the people in asking for hailstones to fall on Capitol Hill to verify His word. Dutch Sheets then began to prophesy, "There is going to be a confrontation in Washington, DC, this week. There is going to be a clash of Ahab, Jezebel, Baal, and Asherah. There is going to be a clash of those with My Spirit. Then we are going to find out who is God."

> I then began to prophesy: "For this is your time of connecting. For you have been plowing and plowing and plowing, but now this is a time to plant and root. I am beginning to 'root in' that which will 'sprout forth' at the time of harvest by the end of September. Root now, root now, root now so you will begin to spring forth and begin to sprout in a new way by the time of harvest! Watch that which is working at night, for at night the seeds are being stolen. This is a time that you will

stand for 21 days from 12:00 to 3:00 at night and you will say that you will protect that which is being planted."

I actually began to see a window forming at the end of August into September (2004). I continued prophesying,

"Protect, protect, protect that which is being planted in the Spirit *now* so that the darkness and the watchers in the night cannot uproot that which I am putting in now. You will overthrow that force from the outside that will uproot. So root now, protect, and watch the sprout occur. Do not be confused by that which will be flying through the air throughout the summer months of this particular city. For it will be like vultures in combat over this city. But they will not be able to remove this word. Even though the locust would come to devour you, I will restore. I have a restorative plan to not allow the locust to eat the crop where the seeds are being planted now. My restorative plan is being planted deep. Do not let the deceiver remove My restorative plan. Plant deep now! You will have victory, so you will have victory over those locust."

That same day hail covered the city!

Brief Washington, DC, History[57]

The District of Columbia—identical with the City of Washington—is the capital of the United States. It is located between Virginia and Maryland on the Potomac River. The district is named after Columbus.

When European settlers first visited the area that is now Washington, DC, Piscataway Native Americans lived in the area. During the late 1600s, many of the Native Americans moved west and white farmers and plantation owners settled the new colony of Virginia. In 1749, Alexandria was established as the first town in the area.

The United States of America won its independence in 1783, at the end of the Revolutionary War. Several different cities served as the national capital until the late 1700s. Congress then wished the nation's capital to be permanent. Disagreements rose as to which state it would be a part of. In 1790, Alexander Hamilton proposed a solution that established the new permanent capital on federal land rather than in a state. President George Washington, raised in the Potomac area, was chosen to pick the site. Both Maryland and Virginia gave up land along the Potomac River that became the District of Columbia, established in 1791.

District of Columbia history actually began in 1790 when the United States Constitution was adopted on September 15, 1787. Article 1, Section 8, Clause 17, included language authorizing the establishment of a federal district. This district was not to exceed 10 miles square, under the exclusive legislative authority of Congress. On July 16, 1790, Congress authorized President George Washington to choose a permanent site for the capital city and, on December 1, 1800, the capital was moved from Philadelphia to an area along the Potomac River. The census of 1800 showed that the new capital had a population of 14,103. Congress directed selection of a new capital site, 100 [square miles], along the Potomac. When the site was determined, it included 30.75 [square miles] on the Virginia side of the river. In 1846, however, Congress returned that area to Virginia, leaving the 68.25 [square miles] ceded by Maryland in 1788. The seat of government was transferred from Philadelphia to Washington on [December] 1, 1800, and President John Adams became the first resident in the White House.

The city was planned and partly laid out by [Major] Pierre Charles L'Enfant, a French engineer. This work was perfected and completed by [Major] Andrew Ellicott and Benjamin Banneker, a freeborn black man who was an astronomer and mathematician. In 1814, during the War of 1812, a British force burned the capital including the White House.

District residents won the right to vote in a presidential election on March 29, 1961, to elect a board of education in 1968 and, in 1970, to elect a non-voting delegate to the House of Representatives. In 1973, Congress approved a bill that provided District residents with an elected form of government with limited home rule authority; as a result, District residents voted for a mayor and a council for the first time in more than 100 years. District residents accepted the home rule charter by referendum vote in 1974. Congress delegated to the District government the authority, functions and powers of a state, with a very important exception: Congress retains control over the District's revenue and expenditures by annually reviewing the entire District government budget. In addition, Congress has repeatedly prohibited the District from imposing a non-resident income tax....

On [August] 22, 1978, Congress passed a proposed constitutional amendment to give Washington, DC, voting representation in the Congress. The amendment had to be ratified by at least 38 state legislatures within seven years to become effective. It died in 1985. A petition asking for the district's admission to the Union as the 51st state was filed in Congress on [September] 9, 1983, and new statehood bills were introduced in 1993. The district is continuing this drive for statehood....

As the federal government continues to grow steadily, so does the population of Washington. The city's population reached a peak of

800,000 in 1950 and then declined as the suburb population began to increase dramatically.

Between 1950 and 1980, the metropolitan area grew faster than that of any other large city, increasing from 1.5 million to more than 3 million.

The federal government and tourism are the mainstays of the city's economy, and many unions, business, professional, and nonprofit organizations are headquartered there. Among the city's many educational institutions are the Catholic University of America, Georgetown University, Howard University, and Gallaudet University. Cultural attractions include the National Gallery of Art, the Smithsonian Institution, the John F. Kennedy Center for the Performing Arts, and the Folger Shakespeare Library.

In 1963, Washingtonians were given the right to vote for the President of the United States. In 1970, they were given the right to elect a representative to Congress. Finally, in 1973 Congress gave Washingtonians the right to elect local officials for the first time in 100 years. Recently, some residents have wanted to make the District of Columbia the 51st state. However, Congress denied the request. In 1997, Congress appointed a control board to oversee efforts in solving growing city problems such as street repair and school expansion.

On [September] 11, 2001, terrorists attacked the United States. It began that morning, as two hijacked airplanes crashed into the World Trade Center Towers in New York. Later that morning, at 9:45 a.m., hijacked American Airlines Flight 77 crashed into the Pentagon. The capital was placed on emergency alert. Congressional leaders were taken away in hiding, all federal offices, national monuments, and streets were cleared of people. This event began a war on terrorism within the United States and the world, that continues today.

FLORIDA

Florida: Spanish meaning "flowery"
Statehood: March 3, 1845 (27th state)
Motto: In God We Trust
Familiar Name: The Sunshine State
50-State Tour: First for Revival; The Forerunner State, February 14-15, 2003

Florida is a forerunner state—forerunning in the purposes of God, forerunning in revival, forerunning in destiny—for the nation.

Florida is an apostolic state with a governmental mantle to shift and change the nation. The 22nd floor of the State Capitol Building in Tallahassee is an Isaiah 22:22 floor, from where the Church of Florida is to pray and govern the state.

Prophetic Word for Florida[58]

> "You have been halted between two opinions. But the halt has ended this night. Will My people rise up and move forward to the next level of conflict? I have come with a sword to break the religious war over this state. There is a shaking in Lakeland. A new anointing is about to come. From that place where opinions of man have been released, the opinions are now stopping. Watch, for I am doing a new thing. In the midst of Lakeland, My waters will spread across this state." (Prophesied by Chuck D. Pierce.)

Diane Buker, our USSPN State Coordinator for Florida as well as our USSPN Regional Coordinator for the Southeast, next began to prophesy about the warrior mantle on the state of Florida.

> "Look to Me! I have gone to war. I have released power for war. I have released power in war. I have already won. I have restrained Myself in the past. But now I say war, war, war!"
>
> I continued, "For I came as a fragrance in this state in the past, and you received the wind and fragrance at that time. My scent and wind went across the land, but this has shifted from the state. There is a new smell that is coming in your midst that will break off death of the last season that aligned against My Spirit. Let the new smell arise, and from this fragrance many will be converted." (Prophesied by Chuck D. Pierce.)

Florida will be a state of transformation. Some of these principles include:

1. You must change the atmosphere over your territory.
2. Optimize resources and reorganize for prosperity in the midst of war.
3. "Suddenlies" will occur in 2003.
4. Know how to "take" or be "overtaken."

One of the closing prophetic words dealt with specific cities.

> "I put the mantle on you, used by Me for the sake of the nation. I am setting you on a 14-month course so deliverance breaks forth, and the aroma of deliverance permeates

> the nation. There is a war mantle on you. Stand in the place of victory. Break down the structures that oppose you. Line upon line. A gift I have thrown to you and this nation for war." (Prophesied by Chuck D. Pierce.)

We specifically prophesied about Tampa and the hidden terrorist cell group working there. I declared that this must be found out so dirty bombs could be uncovered and workings of darkness would be exposed. I also prophesied about Jacksonville and the Pensacola region. I saw a double hit on the Miami area from Key West and the Caribbean Islands.

In less than a week, we received our first report from Tampa, the very first city I mentioned. On February 20, 2003, four U.S. residents were charged in a 50-count indictment with supporting, financing, and relaying messages for a violent Palestinian terrorist group blamed for deaths of more than 100 people in and around Israel. This indictment was returned by a federal grand jury in Tampa. Three of the four U.S. residents were *arrested in Tampa*. Those arrested were described as setting up a terrorist cell at the University of South Florida.

Then on February 24, 2003, we learned that a gun, ammunition, and a grenade were found in a state office building in Tampa. Both of these reports came only days after our time in Florida! We must continue to pray for this state, and declare that every hidden cell and terrorist activity in Tampa, Jacksonville, the Pensacola region, and Miami will be uncovered and apprehended.

Brief Florida History[59]

Archaeological evidence suggests that Native Americans have lived in Florida for thousands of years. Some early Native populations included the Calusa, Tesquesta, Ais, Timucua, Apalachee, Tocobaga, and the Matecumbe. An example of Timucua life reads as follows: "The Timucuans practiced a rigid feudal system. The absolute rulers were the cacique and his council of noblemen. Their chief ally was the shaman, or medicine man, who performed all necessary rituals. Large burial mounds and temple mounds for sacrifice to the sun god showed the impact religion had on their daily lives" according to M.C. Bob Leonard, Professor of History, Hillsborough Community College, Tampa, Florida. Due to the climate and natural resources, the people developed civilizations of some complexity.

The first known Spanish explorer to arrive in Florida was Ponce de Leon in 1513. He was exploring in an attempt to find the elusive Fountain of Youth. When he arrived in Florida, he named it La Florida, to honor the Spanish Easter celebration.

French Protestants (Huguenots) founded a colony in 1564 and later built a fort on the Saint Johns River. The Spanish king, however, sent forces to remove the French influence from Florida and was successful in doing so. In 1565 Pedro Menendez de Aviles came from Spain, founded Saint Augustine, and removed the French from the area. Saint Augustine became, "the first permanent European settlement in what is now the United States."

For two centuries the Spanish tried to change the native way of life in Florida. Meanwhile, the French moved into western Florida and the British into the north. The French and British began fighting in the mid-1700s. Spain joined with the French. Havana, Cuba, was taken by the British in 1762. In the following year, Spain exchanged Florida for Havana.

During the American Revolutionary War, Spain advanced on Florida and by 1783 had regained control. It became a place of refuge for prisoners, slaves, and Indians.

Shortly after the War of 1812, the Adams-Onis Treaty was signed, which transferred control of Florida from Spain to the United States in 1819.

Settlers from the U.S. began to move into Florida. The Seminole Indians lived on some of the best land, however. The government asked them to relocate to the other side of the Mississippi River. Some did; others did not. Those who remained were defeated in the Second Seminole War. After the third war, many were relocated again. Those who refused to move went into the swamps for refuge.

Florida prepared to enter the Union in 1839. However, since it intended to come in as a slave state, it was not admitted until 1845. The Congress, at that time, was endeavoring to maintain a balance of power between the slave and free states. The year after Florida was admitted, Iowa came in as a free state.

On January 10, 1861, after the election of President Lincoln, Florida seceded. Being a slave state, it felt threatened by Lincoln. As the nation broke out in civil war, the Union gained control over most of the coastal areas in Florida while the Confederate forces governed the interior. From the interior, Confederate forces received food supplies.

In 1868 the Florida legislature "ratified the 14th Amendment to the Constitution of the United States, guaranteeing civil rights, and Florida was readmitted to the Union."

Through the end of the century, Florida began to advance. Phosphate deposits were found, swamps were drained, railroad lines were laid, groves of citrus fruit were planted, and people migrated from the north.

During the 1900s, hundreds of thousands of people moved into Florida. Many came to speculate on land. As the country entered into World War II, all sorts of defensive bases were located in Florida. After the war, a space center was developed at Cape Canaveral.

The 1960s saw an influx of Cubans fleeing the dictatorship that consumed Cuba. It was also the time when segregation of public schools was determined to be illegal by the Supreme Court. Florida began to desegregate its public schools. (Its constitution previously had upheld the policy of segregation.)

Over two decades, from 1970 to 1990, the population of Florida increased over 70 percent.

Florida was the decisive state in the 2000 elections.

GEORGIA

Georgia: Named after George II of England
Statehood: January 2, 1788 (4th state)
Motto: Wisdom, Justice, Moderation
Familiar Name: The Peach State
50-State Tour: A Governmental Gate, July 11-12, 2003

"Georgia is one of My gates; it is a governmental gate."

Between 1,000-1,500 people from across the state participated during the two days (some attending both sessions, some only one). To our best recollection, this was the first statewide event for the purpose of intentionally receiving God's specific word and vision for our state. Pastors, leaders, intercessors, worshipers, hungry hearts all came together across denominational, racial, geographic, and economic lines to seek the Lord and to receive from Him through His servants. We followed the Lord's instructions to receive His servants from region to region, and to serve one another, just because each one is the Lord's disciple and He promised that we would receive a blessing that could not be taken from us (see Matthew 10:40-42). We obeyed and are believing for the fulfillment of His promises.

Key Words Released for Georgia

We are to be *gatekeepers*—watching and praying to open gates to the Lord and close them to the enemy. Georgia is to be an opened *portal*—a place of revelation, fresh worship, and restoration; where healing of racial divisions and strife take place; where the womb will no longer be hostile to new life (both naturally and spiritually); where new ministries will not just be conceived but brought to full-term maturity; where new sounds of worship will come forth.

G-8 Summit Coming to Georgia, June 8-10, 2004

At Georgia's 50-State Tour, July 11-12, 2003, Chuck Pierce prophesied on Friday night:

> "I will bring a high-level summit of government officials into this city [state]. Before they come in, My Church will be ruling and reigning in such a way that when they come in, what I'm saying from Heaven will penetrate into them. I say, there is an orchestration of events that are coming, and you will see a high-level summit meeting in the midst of this state; and I will say to you, I will change the course of the way that the nations are aligned from this place."

Dutch Sheets continued, "Church's destiny—governmental breakthrough—summits—destinies of nations shaped in Georgia—nations are coming to Georgia. Sound of Heaven, come to Georgia. It's a shout of a King. The King is among them. He roars out of Zion—out of Georgia. Let every leader hear the sound of Heaven over state, church, and schools."

In a Saturday morning Atlanta newspaper following this declaration, the headline read: "Sea Island may play host to G-8 summit." By Tuesday, July 15, it was official, with Wednesday's headline reading: "Ga. Lands 8-Nation Summit." This set us on a journey to prepare the Church in this state to "be ruling and reigning in such a way that when they come in, what I'm [the Lord] saying from Heaven will penetrate into them."

By God's grace, the G-8 Prayer Initiative was formed, working with the Institute for Global Affairs, culminating in ten days of powerful worship and intercession as the Church gathered to rule and reign. Leaders from around the world joined with the Church in Georgia to cover the region—from Sea Island where the Summit was actually held, to Savannah where the protestors were to gather, to Atlanta, the governmental seat of the state. Many times throughout our days together there were documented occurrences of God having us praying ahead of events that later were reported through the news media.

This experience shifted us into a new dimension of authority and understanding of what it means to rule and reign with the Lord over the state and over specific assignments.

> It was prophesied, "Before this state can take ownership, there has to be a removal of hostility between nations and ethnic groups. There is a release from the bondage that is in the bloodshed in this state in past oppressions that have been linked with slavery, domination, and ruler-ship." (Prophesied by Chuck D. Pierce.)

We have conducted an initiative across metro-Atlanta of six sites identified as locations of covenant-breaking and bloodshed. Each site was visited; sins confessed; demonic structures uprooted; and God's grace of reconciliation, restoration, recovery, and revival released. We declared a release of His covenant-keeping power to cause a reverse of violence and bloodshed to be manifested.

Statewide Solemn Assembly, April 24, 2004

We gathered in the center of the state (Macon) to deal with specific issues of sin that were keeping us from being able to enter into the place of authority and grace that the Lord wanted to release. We dealt with pride, issues of the religious spirit/deception/rebellion, the political spirit (political corruption included), injustice, greed, and idolatry. We had a great day of dealing with these issues in a significant manner. Specifically, each issue was dealt with by an assigned team who did a tremendous job supporting the issues with research, biblical foundations, and strategic intercession.

Development of Strategies to Open and Close Gates Across the State

In Savannah, prior to the G-8 Summit, the pastors of the city gathered to go to each of the city's gates and declare them closed to the enemy and opened to the Lord. One specific answer was the extremely low turnout of protestors for the G-8 Summit. Although 10,000 to 50,000 were expected, only 350 arrived; and these were divided between Savannah and Brunswick/Saint Simon's area.[60]

Brief Georgia History[61]

Early Exploration and Conflicting Claims

The Creek and Cherokee inhabited the Georgia area when Hernando De Soto and his expedition passed through the region circa 1540. The Spanish later established missions and garrisons on the Sea Islands. In 1663, Charles II of England made a grant of land that included Georgia to the eight proprietors of Carolina. However, Spain claimed the whole eastern half of the present United States and protested the grant. The English ignored the protest, and the English-Spanish contest for the territory between Charleston (SC) and Saint Augustine (FL) continued intermittently for almost a century. England became interested in settling Georgia as a buffer colony to protect South Carolina from Spanish invasion from the south.

Oglethorpe's Colony

In June, 1732, the English philanthropist James E. Oglethorpe received a charter from George II (for whom the colony was named) to settle the colony of Georgia and form a board of trustees to manage it. Oglethorpe planned to settle Georgia as a refuge for debtors in England. The first colonists, led by Oglethorpe, reached the mouth of the Savannah River in [February] 1733. On a bluff [roughly 18 miles or 29 kilometers] upstream, the colonists laid out the first town, Savannah. In 1739 war broke out between Spain and England. Fighting occurred in Georgia, and in 1742, near Fort Frederica on Saint Simons Island, Oglethorpe defeated the Spanish in the battle of Bloody Marsh, thereby effectively ending Spain's claim to the land [North] of the Saint Marys River.

Georgia's early settlers included English, Welsh, Scots Highlanders, Germans, Italians, Piedmontese, and Swiss. Jews, Catholics, and settlers from other American colonies were at first barred. Immigrants fell generally into two groups: charity settlers, who were financed by the trustees, and adventurers, who paid their own way and came to receive the best land grants. The trustees had hoped that the colony would produce silk to send back to England, and early colonists were required to plant a specific number of mulberry trees for the cultivation of silkworms. The scheme, however, came to nothing. At first slavery was prohibited, but this and other restrictions impeded the colony's growth, and by the time Georgia became a royal colony in 1754, most of the restrictions had been abolished.

Georgia flourished as a royal colony. It fitted well into the British mercantile system, exporting rice, indigo, deerskins, lumber, naval stores, beef, and pork to England and buying there the manufactured articles it needed. Georgia's citizens were slower to resent those acts of the crown that exasperated the other colonies, but by June, 1775, Georgian patriots had begun to organize, and the following month delegates were elected to the Second Continental Congress. Georgia's colonists were about equally divided into Loyalists and patriots during the American Revolution, but the patriots, exposed to Loyalist Florida on the south and Native American tribes on the west, fared badly. In [December] 1778, the British captured Savannah, and by the end of 1779 they held every important town in Georgia.

Statehood

After American independence had been won, Georgia was the first Southern state to ratify (1788) the Constitution. Georgia came into conflict with the federal government over states' rights when the U.S. Supreme Court ruled, in *Chisholm v. Georgia* (1793), that an individual could sue a state, a decision equally distasteful to other states as well as to Georgia. (This decision was later nullified by the Eleventh Amendment to the U.S. Constitution.)

Further difficulties with the federal government stemmed from the related issues of the removal of Native Americans and land speculation centering around the Yazoo land fraud. In the midst of the Yazoo controversy, Georgia ceded (1802) its western lands to the United States in return for $1,250,000 and a pledge that the Native Americans would be removed from Georgia lands. By 1826 the Creek had yielded their lands, but in 1827, the Cherokee set themselves up as an independent nation. The U.S. Supreme Court held (1832) that the state had no jurisdiction over the Cherokee, but President Jackson declined to support the Chief Justice, and in 1838 the Cherokee were forced to migrate west to government land in present day Oklahoma. The path of their journey is known as the Trail of Tears.

Cotton and the Confederacy

With the invention of the cotton gin (1793) by Eli Whitney, Georgia began to prosper as a cotton-growing state. Cotton was grown under the plantation system with labor supplied by slaves. By the 1840s a textile industry was established in the state. Although Georgia was committed to slavery before the Civil War, state leaders opposed secession. However, successive defeats on the national scene, culminating in the election of Lincoln as president, fostered separatist sentiment in the state.

On [January] 19, 1861, Georgia seceded from the Union and shortly afterward joined the Confederacy. The coast was soon blockaded by the Union navy, and in [April] 1862, Fort Pulaski (which had been seized by the state in [January] 1861) was recaptured by Union forces. Georgia became a major Civil War battlefield when, in 1864,

Union [General] W.T. Sherman launched his successful Atlanta campaign. On [November] 15, 1864, Sherman set fire to Atlanta, and his subsequent march through Georgia to the sea, culminating in the fall [in December] of Savannah, left in its path a scene of great destruction.

The Long Aftermath of the Civil War

During Reconstruction, Georgia at first refused to ratify the Fourteenth Amendment and was consequently placed under military rule. During the period of military rule Rufus B. Bullock, a radical Republican, was elected governor. Corruption prevailed during Bullock's administration (1868-71), but after the legislature approved the Fifteenth Amendment (the Thirteenth and Fourteenth having been ratified earlier), Georgia was readmitted (1870) to the Union, and Bullock resigned. Georgia's Democratic party has dominated the state's politics since the end of Reconstruction.

The textile industry recovered from the effects of the war and was expanding by the 1880s. Atlanta, which had succeeded Milledgeville as the capital in 1868, grew into a thriving industrial city, largely due to its importance as the center of an expanding regional railroad network.

The effect of the war on agriculture—which had formerly been dependent on slave labor—was more serious. The breakup of large plantations resulted in the rise of tenant farming and sharecropping, systems often accompanied by poverty and abuse. After World War I agriculture suffered further setbacks as the boll weevil caused great destruction to cotton crops and the soil became exhausted through erosion and overuse. A farm depression began in Georgia long before the general depression of the 1930s. The state weathered the depression, but its subsequent history was marked by political and racial conflict.

The Struggle for Racial Equality

In 1941, [Governor] Eugene Talmadge caused nationwide commotion by discharging three educators in the state university system alleged to have advocated racial equality in the schools. The state university system lost its accreditation for a time as a result of Talmadge's action. Talmadge was defeated in the 1942 Democratic primary by Ellis G. Arnall.

Under Arnall's administration, Georgia became the first state to grant the vote to 18-year-olds, and in 1946 (on the strength of a U.S. Supreme Court decision) blacks voted for the first time in the Georgia Democratic primary. Among Arnall's other administrative acts was the adoption of a new constitution in [August] 1945. The 1945 constitution, which, in amended form, is still in effect in the state, contained a provision for Georgia's notorious county-unit system. This system for nominating state officials in Democratic primaries led to the political control of urban areas by sparsely populated rural areas.

The integration of public schools, following the 1954 Supreme Court decision, was strenuously opposed by many Georgians. However, in 1961 the legislature abandoned a "massive resistance" policy, and Georgia became the first state in the deep South to proceed with integration without a major curtailment of its public school system. Racial tensions persisted, however, and in May, 1970, racial disorder broke out in Augusta.

Georgia's county-unit system (held constitutional by the Supreme Court in [April] 1950) was abolished by federal court order in 1962. In 1972, the Georgian Andrew Young became the first African American elected to the U.S. Congress; he later became mayor of Atlanta. Jimmy Carter, a Democrat and the 39th president of the United States (1977-81), had been governor of Georgia from 1971 to 1975; his administration brought attention to the state, whose urban centers, especially Atlanta, were beginning to experience rapid growth. Today, roughly one half of the jobs in Georgia are in the Atlanta metropolitan area, which is sprawling into formerly rural districts, highlighting the cultural and economic gaps between Georgia's rural and urban areas.

HAWAII

Hawaii: "Homeland"
Statehood: August 21, 1959 (50th state)
Motto: *Ua Mau Ke Ea O Ka Aina I Ka Pono* (The Life of the Land Is Perpetuated in Righteousness)
Familiar Name: The Aloha State
50-State Tour: The Pentecost Harvest State (May 28-29, 2004)

Our 50-State Tour occurred during Pentecost. Hawaii was the first state to experience total revival. We decreed it would happen again.

Spiritual History of Hawaii[62]

Prayer points from 50-State Tour:

* *Pray*...for a greater level of unity within the Body of Christ across denominational lines, from the pastors to the members of each church. Our adversary has perpetrated much division through deceptive means.
* *Pray*...for a greater sensitivity to the leading of the Holy Spirit in leaders of the Body of Christ.

- *Pray*...for our Governor, Linda Lingle, that she would have the support of Congress to accomplish what God has led her to accomplish. She is the first woman Governor of Hawaii and the first Republican Governor in 40 years. Also, pray for righteousness to prevail throughout the halls of state government. *Pray against* the "good ole boy" network mentality.

- *Pray*...for the safety of all military bases, personnel, and family in Hawaii. The very first U.S. military base (Fort Shafter) was established in Hawaii in 1907.

- *Pray*...for the economy of Hawaii—that it continues its strong positive rebound after the destruction of 9/11.

- *Pray*... that the stronghold of drug abuse is completely uncovered and dismantled in Hawaii. It is now at epidemic proportions in users and dealers to the extent that the main objective of the Lieutenant Governor, Duke Aiona, is to break the strongholds of drug abuse in Hawaii. Lieutenant Governor Aiona is a Christian man. Pray God gives him and his team wisdom. *Pray for the deliverance and salvation of all drug users and dealers.*

- *Pray*...for the police departments on each island. Pray that deceptive spirits would be exposed and pray against the spirit of temptation. *Pray* that police officers would overcome them and stand in holiness and integrity.

- *Pray*...for the church as it is on the threshold of a major revival. Pray that the Lord will raise up more laborers to reel in the harvest of souls.

- *Pray*...for the well of revival from many years ago that sprung up in Hilo, Hawaii (with one of the largest churches in the world at around 10,000) to be re-dug with intercession, evangelism, and establishment of churches throughout the state. At that time it was established, about 96 percent of Hawaiians received Jesus Christ as Savior. Today, it is believed that Hawaii is less than 5 percent Christian.

- ★ *Pray*...for God to bring into spiritual alignment the areas of media, government, social services, education, and sports. These five areas affect most areas of life.
- ★ *Pray*...for a paradigm shift from an emphasis on going to the beach on Sunday to an emphasis on going to church on Sunday. *Pray* that the father of the home would take the lead in this area of family life.
- ★ *Pray*...against the spirit of domestic violence. It has been reported that Hawaii is one of the top five states in the nation for domestic violence.

Brief Hawaiian History[63]

Early Settlers and Explorers

The first known settlers of the Hawaiian Islands were Polynesian voyagers (the date of final migration is believed to be circa 750). The islands were first visited by Europeans in 1778 by the English explorer Captain James Cook, who named them the Sandwich Islands for the English Earl of Sandwich. At that time the islands were under the rule of warring native kings.

The Rule of Kamehameha I

In 1810, Kamehameha I…became the sole sovereign of all the islands, and, in the peace that followed, agriculture and commerce were promoted. As a result of Kamehameha's hospitality, American traders were able to exploit the islands' sandalwood, which was much valued in China at the time. Trade with China reached its height during this period. However, the period of Kamehameha's rule was also one of decline. Europeans and Americans brought with them devastating infectious diseases, and over the years the native population was greatly reduced. The adoption of Western ways—trading for profit, using firearms, and drinking liquor—contributed to the decline of native cultural tradition. This period also marked the breakdown of the traditional Hawaiian religion, with its belief in idols and human sacrifice; years of religious unrest followed.

Influence of the Missionaries

When missionaries arrived in 1820 they found a less idyllic Hawaii than the one Captain Cook had discovered.

Kamehameha III, who ruled from 1825 until his death in 1854, relied on the missionaries for advice and allowed them to preach Christianity. The missionaries established schools, developed the Hawaiian alphabet, and used it for translating the Bible into Hawaiian. In 1839, Kamehameha III issued a guarantee of religious freedom, and the following year a constitutional monarchy was established. From 1842 to 1854 an American, G.P. Judd, held the post of prime minister, and under his influence many reforms were carried out. In the following decades commercial ties between Hawaii and the United States increased.

Development of the Sugar Industry

In 1848 the islands' feudal land system was abolished, making private ownership possible and thereby encouraging capital investment in the land. By this time the sugar industry, which had been introduced in the 1830s, was well established. Hawaiian sugar gained a favored position in U.S. markets under a reciprocity treaty made with the United States in 1875. The treaty was renewed in 1884 but not ratified. Ratification came in 1887 when an amendment was added giving the United States exclusive right to establish a naval base at Pearl Harbor. The amount of sugar exported to the United States increased greatly, and American businessmen began to invest in the Hawaiian sugar industry. Along with the Hawaiians in the industry, they came to exert powerful influence over the islands' economy and government, a dominance that was to last until World War II.

The Overthrow of Queen Liliuokalani and Annexation

Toward the end of the 19th [century], agitation for constitutional reform in Hawaii led to the overthrow (1893) of Queen Liliuokalani, who had ruled since 1891. A provisional government was established and John L. Stevens, the U.S. minister to Hawaii, proclaimed the country a U.S. protectorate. President Grover Cleveland, however, refused to annex Hawaii since most Hawaiians did not support a revolution; the Hawaiians and Americans in the sugar industry had encouraged the overthrow of the monarchy to serve their business needs.

The United States tried to bring about the restoration of Queen Liliuokalani, but the provisional government on the islands refused to give up power and instead established (1894) a republic with Sanford B. Dole as president. Cleveland's successor, President William McKinley, favored annexation, which was finally accomplished in 1898. In 1900 the islands were made a territory, with Dole as governor. In this period, Hawaii's pineapple industry expanded as pineapples were first grown for canning purposes. In 1937 statehood for Hawaii was proposed and refused by the U.S. Congress—the territory's mixed population and distance from the U.S. mainland were among the obstacles.

World War II and Statehood

On [December] 7, 1941, Japanese aircraft made a surprise attack on Pearl Harbor, plunging the United States into World War II. During the war the Hawaiian Islands were the chief Pacific base for U.S. forces and were under martial law (December 7, 1941–March 1943).

The postwar years ushered in important economic and social developments. There was a dramatic expansion of labor unionism, marked by major strikes in 1946, 1949, and 1958. The International Longshoremen's and Warehousemen's Union organized the waterfront, sugar, and pineapple workers. The tourist trade, which had grown to major proportions in the 1930s, expanded further with postwar advances in air travel and with further investment and development. The building boom brought about new construction of luxury hotels and housing developments; Hawaii is home to one of the world's most expensively built resort, the Hyatt Regency Waikola, which cost $360 million to construct.

After having sought statehood for many decades, Hawaii was finally admitted to the union on [August] 21, 1959; although it was thought at first to be solidly Republican, the state has long been a Democratic stronghold. Movements for a return of some sort of native sovereignty have been periodically active.

In [September] 1992, the island of Kauai was devastated by Hurricane Iniki, the strongest hurricane to hit the islands in the century.

Hawaii, which had enjoyed sustained economic and population growth since the end of World War II, saw both slow in the 1990s, as tourism, the sugar industry, military spending, and Japanese investment in the islands (particularly important in the 1980s) declined.

IDAHO[64]

Idaho: Shoshone meaning "Sun coming down mountain"
Statehood: July 3, 1890 (43rd state)
Motto: *Esto Perpetua* (May it Last Forever)
Familiar Name: The Gem State
50-State Tour: The Treasure State (Isaiah 45), February 15-16, 2004

Prayer points from 50-State Tour:

- *Pray* for the Lord to unlock and uncover spiritual and natural treasure that God has kept hidden until now in the "Gem" state.
- *Pray* that this unlocked treasure would be used to affect the nation for the cause of Jesus Christ.
- *Pray* for God to unlock revelation.
- *Pray* for a spirit of purity to be released in Idaho, especially that others would see a purity in our Christian walk.
- *Pray* for the strength and grace needed to "cross over" into the reward that God has for us.
- *Pray* for hidden treasures to come forth.

- ⭐ *Pray* for recognition of any wrong alignments that could break the anointing.
- ⭐ *Pray* for new revelation of the intimacy of worship.
- ⭐ *Pray* for the spirit of joy to be released.
- ⭐ *Pray* for a Cyrus anointing to come upon the Church to subdue nations, open doors, and finance restoration.

Brief Idaho History[65]

Early Explorers and Fur Traders

Probably the first non-natives to enter the area that is now Idaho were members of the Lewis and Clark expedition in 1805. They were not far ahead of the fur traders who came to the region shortly thereafter. A Canadian, David Thompson of the North West Company, established the first trading post in Idaho in 1809. The next year traders from Saint Louis penetrated the mountains, and Andrew Henry of the Missouri Fur Company established a post near present-day Rexburg, the first American trading post established in the area.

In this period the fortunes of the Idaho region were wrapped up with those of the Columbia River region, and the area encompassed by what is now the state of Idaho was part of Oregon country, held jointly by the United States and Great Britain from 1818 to 1846. Fur traders in an expedition sent out by John Jacob Astor came to the Snake River region to trap for furs after having established (1811) a trading post at Astoria on the Columbia River. In 1821 two British trading companies operating in the Idaho region, the North West Company and the Hudson's Bay Company, were joined together as the Hudson's Bay Company which, after 1824, came into competition with American mountain men also trapping in the area. By the 1840s the two groups had severely depleted the region's fur supply.

Gold, Settlement, and Resistance

In 1846 the United States gained sole claim to Oregon country south of the 49th parallel by the Oregon Treaty with Great Britain. The area was established as a territory in 1848. Idaho still had no permanent settlement when Oregon Territory became a state in 1859 and the eastern part of Idaho was added to Washington Territory. A Mormon outpost founded at Franklin in 1860 is considered the first permanent settlement, but it was not until the discovery of gold that settlers poured into Idaho.

Gold was discovered on the Clearwater River in 1860, on the Salmon in 1861, in the Boise River basin in 1862, and gold and silver were found in the Owyhee River country in 1863. The usual rush of settlers followed, along with the spectacular but ephemeral growth of towns. Most of these settlements are only ghost towns now, but the many settlers who poured in during the gold rush—mainly from Washington, Oregon, and California, with smaller numbers from the east—formed a population large enough to demand new government administration, and Idaho Territory was set up in 1863.

Native Americans, mostly Kootenai, Nez Percé, Western Shoshone, Bannock, Coeur d'Alene, and Pend d'Oreille, became upset by the incursion of settlers and some resisted violently. The federal government had subdued many of these groups by 1858, placing them on reservations. The Bannock were defeated in 1863 and again in 1878. In 1876-1877 the Nez Percé, led by Chief Joseph, made their heroic but unsuccessful attempt to flee to Canada while being pursued by U.S. troops.

Development and Disputes

A new mining boom started in 1882 with the discovery of gold in the Coeur d'Alene, and although the gold strike ended in disappointment, it prefaced the discovery there of some of the richest silver mines in the world. Coeur d'Alene and Kellogg became notable mining centers, and the Bunker Hill and Sullivan (a lead mine) became extremely famous mines. Severe labor troubles in the mines at the end of the century led to political uprisings. Frank Steunenberg, who as governor had used federal troops to put down the uprisings, was assassinated in 1905. The trial of William Haywood and others accused of involvement in the murder drew national attention and marked the beginning of the long career of William E. Borah (who had prosecuted the mine leaders) as an outstanding Republican party leader in the state and nation.

The late 19th [century] also witnessed the growth of cattle and sheep ranching, along with the strife that developed between the two groups of ranchers over grazing areas. The coming of the railroads (notably the Northern Pacific) through Idaho in the 1880s and 90s brought new settlers and aided in the founding of such cities as Idaho Falls, Pocatello, and American Falls.

Putting Water and the Atom to Work

Expanding Idaho farming led to private irrigation projects. Some of these aroused public opposition, which led to establishment of state irrigation districts under the Carey Land Act of 1894. The Reclamation Act of 1902 brought direct federal aid. Notable among public reclamation works are the Boise and Minidoka projects. Both public and private, these have also helped to increase the development of Idaho's enormous hydroelectric potential. Further private hydroelectric projects along the Snake River were put into operation between 1959 and 1968.

In 1949 the Atomic Energy Commission built the National Reactor Testing Station in [Southeast] Idaho. Now known as the Idaho National Engineering Laboratory, the facility in 1955 provided energy for nearby Arco, the first American town to be lighted by electricity from a nuclear power plant.

Idaho suffered during the recession of the early 1980s but rebounded later in the decade by attracting new business, including high-technology firms. The growth of the winter sports industry has helped make Idaho a leading tourist state. These improvements in its economy made Idaho one of the nation's fastest-growing states in population between 1990 and 2000.

ILLINOIS

Illinois: Algonquian meaning "man"
Statehood: December 3, 1818 (21st state)
Motto: State Sovereignty, National Union
Familiar Name: The Prairie State
50-State Tour: The Apostolic State, August 26-27, 2003

> To Apostle John Eckhardt and to the state of Illinois: "For 13 years you have built your house—the house I said to build. You've done it. It has been a long 13 years. You have been getting it in order. I'm about to visit you in Chicago a second time....I'm about to visit Illinois a second time. You will be a prototype for the states. You'll begin to build what it takes to house My glory. There will be six weeks of rearranging. You will have an order and an anointing to put things in order.

> Many will come to this state to be a part of that glory. The glory will not only be in the house, but without this house. From this state My glory shall proceed forth as a wheel that shall turn this nation. I am doing a work of connecting within regions of this state. There is grace, grace for this connecting. This connecting is necessary to be released into this new anointing." (Prophesied by Chuck D. Pierce.)

Pastor Dutch shared this very pointed word: *"Illinois is My apostolic state."* As such, Illinois will be a prototype state. Pastor Dutch mentioned five key points:

1. For Illinois to move fully to the apostolic anointing, it will have to *transition* to another level of strength, understanding, and maturity. The apostolic governing order must go to another level.

2. Illinois must move forward to *another level of connecting*, networking, and joining one another. Illinois must go to another level of networking the state. Leaders, intercessors, warriors, and pastors have to transition across barriers, bodies, streams, and across racial and denominational lines. One of the things that satan will try to do is bring disconnection as this is one of the greatest strengths of the apostolic anointing.

> "Because Illinois is apostolic, many local expressions of My Spirit—local churches, ministries streams— many of them are very well connected, but they have not gone to the next level of the apostolic and been able to connect properly

> outside of their own realm, outside of their own church. And so some would look at this state and say, 'No, no, no—this is not true. There's good connection here; there's good apostolic order.' And the Lord would say to that, 'Yes, there is good connection, and there is apostolic order.'"

"But the Lord is going to take it to a level now that goes outside of the local expressions....You're not only going to have that [connectedness] in your local expressions, but eight of you are going to get together. The Spirit of the Lord said, *'Eight of you are going to come together.'* But I say to you, not only are the eight going to come together, but the eight are going to multiply again and 64 and then 180 or whatever. They are going to come together until there is a new connecting in the state of Illinois that takes the apostolic anointing to a higher level. And it's going to extend the authority of God over the battlefield on this state in a way that it hasn't been connected before. And you're going to begin to see the armies of God prevail in ways that they have never prevailed before. Demons are going to be disempowered in a new way. Breakthroughs are going to come. Deliverance is going to come. People are going to be set free. On the battlefield there's going to come a turning of the tide because the apostolic order goes to another level of connection.... The Lord says, *'The grace is coming on the place, the grace is coming on the place. The grace to come together is coming on this place. For I say, you've been here and you've been there, but I'm giving you the grace to come on the place and the supernatural abundance of an alignment is falling in this region. I say, let it begin and watch things change,'* saith the Lord....

"We decree there is a connecting of the Body of Christ coming in the state of Illinois going to another level. God is snapping things into alignment. He's healing dislocation and broken places and snapping them back. He's mending the nets so He can bring a great harvest to the state of Illinois. The Lord says, *'I'm going to have a net that will not fail this time. I'm going to have a net that can hold the harvest. I'm going to have a net that won't let one fish out, and you'll be able to say of those you've given to Me, not one has been lost except the son of perdition that the Scriptures might be fulfilled.'* I'm telling you that you're going to go to another level of getting fish, keeping fish, mentoring fish, discipling fish because you're going to have healthy nets."

1. Referring to John 7:37-39, there will be a new release of revelation and a new release of understanding. God has another phase of understanding and revelation: dreams, visits, and insights from Scriptures; angelic visitations; a new level of prophetic, word of wisdom, word of knowledge, discernment of spirits, etc.—also, another level of the glory. The greatest revelation right now that God wants to begin to unfold on you is that God is inside of you. He wants you to be God-is-inside-of-you minded everywhere you go....The state of Illinois will be known as the place where the river of God dwells.

2. If we move into this new level of anointing, there is absolutely another level of harvest coming. You will move out

of Acts chapter 5 (addition) to Acts chapter 6 (multiplication). This year, the Feast of Tabernacles marks something in the Spirit. This year it will begin.

3. Referring back to John chapter 7, from out of your belly, the word *koilia* means "womb" or the "matrix"— the matrix of the spirit, meaning where something originates or is birthed. God will have an apostolic people who know how to birth things, to originate things, to plant the seed of God, the prophetic word of God into the atmosphere, and cause their region to be pregnant with God's words... out from their matrix something is going to flow and it's called the river of life.

4. Illinois is a Horeb place. Mount Horeb is the same as Mount Sinai. These were used interchangeably in Scripture. Moses went up and received the laws, the government, there; the patterns or plans of God were given there. The Lord said Illinois is His apostolic state. It is a place of government, a place where plans are given. Illinois is a prototype for what God wants to do in the rest of the nation, consistent with being a Horeb. Prototypes are apostolic. Horeb is a place where the timings of God are understood more clearly. Moses had to wait for God's timing to be revealed. He went to Horeb when he left Egypt. It was there on Horeb that he waited for God's perfect timing to be revealed to him for leading God's people out of Egypt. It is also a place of waiting, as Joshua waited there 33 days for Moses to come out from the presence of God.

5. In Second Kings chapter 18, Hezekiah destroyed Nehustan (the serpent on the pole that became an idol).

> "I want to come and break the Nehustans in your life, the tradition. I will deal with religion and with religious form in this state. I am shaking the established churches and ministries in the region. I am going to demand change. Ask for My mercy for them, but do not ask for mercy for the structure. Ask for restoration of heart. I am going to shake them so that which is pure can survive," said the Lord. (Prophesied by Dutch Sheets.)

Brief Illinois History[66]

Early Inhabitants and European Exploration

At the end of the 18th [century] the Illinois, Sac, Fox, and other Native American groups were living in the river forests, where many centuries before them the prehistoric Mound Builders had dwelt. French explorers and missionaries came to the region early. Father Marquette and Louis Jolliet, on their return from a trip down the Mississippi, paddled up the Illinois River in 1673, and two years later Marquette returned to establish a mission in the Illinois country.

In 1679 the French explorer Robert Cavelier, sieur de La Salle, went from Lake Michigan to the Illinois, where he founded (1680) Fort Creve Coeur and with his lieutenant, Henri de Tonti, completed (1682–83) Fort Saint Louis on Starved Rock cliff. French occupation of the area was sparse, but the settlements of Cahokia and Kaskaskia achieved a minor importance in the 18th [century], and the area was valued for fur trading.

By the Treaty of Paris of 1763, ending the French and Indian Wars, France ceded all of the Illinois country to Great Britain. However, the British did not take possession until resistance, led by the Ottawa chief,

Pontiac, was quelled (1766). In the American Revolution, George Rogers Clark and his expedition captured (1778) the British posts of Cahokia and Kaskaskia before going on to take Vincennes. The Illinois region was an integral part of the Old Northwest that came within U.S. boundaries by the 1783 Treaty of Paris ending the American Revolution. Under the Ordinance of 1787 the area became the Northwest Territory. Made part of Indiana Territory in 1800, Illinois became a separate territory in 1809.

Statehood and Settlement

The fur trade was still flourishing throughout most of Illinois when it became a state in 1818, but already settlers were pouring down the Ohio River by flatboat and barge and across the Genesee wagon road. In 1820 the capital was moved from Kaskaskia to Vandalia. The Black Hawk War (1832) practically ended the tenure of the Native Americans in Illinois and drove them [west] of the Mississippi. In the 1830s there was heavy and uncontrolled land speculation. Mob fury broke out with the murder (1837) of the abolitionist Elijah P. Lovejoy at Alton and in the lynching (1844) of the Mormon leader Joseph Smith and his brother Hyrum at Carthage.

Industrialization and Abraham Lincoln

Industrial development came with the opening of an agricultural implements factory by Cyrus H. McCormick at Chicago in 1847 and the building of the railroads in the 1850s. During this period the career of Abraham Lincoln began. In the state legislature, Lincoln and his colleagues from Sangamon co. had worked hard and successfully to bring the capital to Springfield in 1839. As Illinois moved toward a wider role in the country's affairs, Lincoln and another Illinois lawyer, Stephen A. Douglas, won national attention with their debates on the slavery issue in the senatorial race of 1858. In 1861, Lincoln became president and fought to preserve the Union in the face of the South's secession. During the Civil War, Illinois supported the Union, but there was much proslavery sentiment in the southern part of the state.

By the 1860s industry was well established, and many immigrants from Europe had already settled in the state, foreshadowing the influx still to come. Immediately after the Civil War, industry expanded to tremendous proportions, and the Illinois legislature, by setting aside acreage for stockyards, prepared the way for the development of the meatpacking industry. Economic development had outrun the construction of facilities, and Chicago was a mass of flimsy wooden structures when the fire of 1871 destroyed most of the city.

Discontent and the Rise of the Labor Movement

In the latter part of the 19th [century] farmers in the state revolted against exorbitant freight rates, tariff discrimination, and the high price of manufactured goods. Illinois farmers enthusiastically joined the Granger movement. Laborers in factories, railroads, and mines also became restive, and from 1870 to 1900 Illinois was the scene of such violent labor incidents as the Haymarket Square riot of 1886 and the Pullman strike of 1894.

In the 20th [century] labor conditions improved, but violent labor disputes persisted, notably the massacre at Herrin in 1922 during a coal-miners' strike and the bloody riot during a steel strike at Chicago in 1937. State politics became divided by the conflicting forces of farmers, laborers, and corporations, and opposing political machines came into being downstate and upstate.

Diversification and Change

In 1937 new oil fields were discovered in southern Illinois, further enhancing the state's industrial development. During World War II the nation's first controlled nuclear reaction was accomplished at the [University] of Chicago, paving the way for development of nuclear weapons during the war. The war also spurred the further growth of the Chicago metropolitan area, and in the postwar period thousands of African Americans from the rural south came seeking industrial work.

Adlai E. Stevenson, governor of Illinois from 1949 to 1953, achieved national prominence in winning the Democratic presidential nomination in 1952 and 1956. Also during the 1950s the "gateway amendment" to the Illinois constitution simplified the state's constitutional amendment process. In 1970, Illinois adopted a new state constitution that, among other reforms, banned discrimination in employment and housing.

Southern Illinois experienced population declines in the 1950s and '60s as farms in the south became more mechanized, providing fewer jobs in the area. The area was hard hit again in the 1980s as farm prices fell and farm machinery, the major industrial product of southern Illinois, was no longer in high demand. The northern portion of the state saw a major decline in manufacturing in the 1970s and '80s, which was partially offset by an increase in the service and trade industry and Chicago's continued strength as a financial center.

INDIANA

Indiana: Land of the Indians
Statehood: December 11, 1816 (19th state)
Motto: The Crossroads of America
Familiar Name: The Hoosier State
50-State Tour: The First-Strike State, July 15-16, 2003

Words, Prayers, and Declarations from the 50-State Tour in Indiana[67]

> Indiana, God is dreaming about you! (Will Ford III)
>
> Jim Chosa heard the song of the desire of God for Indiana... "Oh, Indiana...if you only knew...if you only understood what I have placed in the land, the deposits that I have spoken and released by My Word—the seed of the Word that is in the heart of our nation in Indiana." (Prophesied by Jim Chosa.)
>
> How you set the course for your life this year is how the next five years [are] going to follow, and how we as a nation set the course this year is how the next five years will follow. So we are in the critical time to determine which way we go right now, and we are in the Crossroads state; the Crossroads state is the place you want to take the right turn...so we are at just a key place, a key time...this is where we start refining our course for the future (Chuck D. Pierce).
>
> There has been an inability to go all the way. I keep hearing...short circuits. It is almost like you get to the 6th day,

the 6th time on the 7th day, and *something happens to disrupt things, and it short circuits, and God has to start over*. He is trying to tell you to go all the way to the fullness of time. *Are there some new beginnings for America that are...to begin in Indiana?* Maybe Indiana is supposed to be a coat of many colors. Maybe you are a key to some things that have to do with healing a nation, some kind of liberty thing that God wants to bring to Indiana some sort of deliverance movement or mantle...coming to you... maybe there is a liberty in the spirit that would translate... freedom for believers, but mass deliverance, jubilee, the captive letting go of something that has to come forth *out of INDIANA FIRST IN THE SENSE OF DELIVERANCE OR FREEDOM OR JUBILEE OR LIBERTY;* maybe...a fullness of liberty, fullness of redemption. There is something to do with *firsts.* **First strikes** that have to do with this state that are first for the nation. This is a forerunning state in the sense of covenant, asking people to move into a higher level of covenant. First Strike—Jericho, the place the Captain shows up...the First Strike of the Captain. Maybe the Son is saying... "*I want to be a First-Strike Captain in Indiana*." Maybe He is going to lead you into some victories...to initiate ...revivals for the rest of the nation. I am just going to tell you right now, they are...it is coming! First-Strike places have to do with miraculous profession, the supernatural element of the Lord that comes and begins to multiply. It must have to do with some sort of multiplying of harvest. Maybe there is a First Fruits movement of harvest coming here. Maybe where God is about to *strike first* is this younger generation, and the revival in the college campuses...is going to start right here in Indiana. I had a vision of Him beginning to bring His Spirit to college campuses in America and high schools...I saw the *fire of God* going from place to place, and I saw very clearly **Notre Dame**...I don't want to limit it...I saw a move of God's Spirit literally overwhelm the universities...it was a *first strike*. I saw this coming with such ferocity...It was fire...It was fearsome and fierce and wonderful all at once. It was the fire of cleansing...It was a fire of trials...it was a holiness movement...I saw incredible miracles...this began a rolling move of fire that could not be stopped...I asked, "Lord...is it going to begin in Indiana or is this going to be one of the "*First strike*" states. *First strike people have to be people who insist on heavenly strategy*! (Prophesied by Dutch Sheets.)

I heard the Lord saying right now, "*State of Indiana, move farther into a prophetic mantle.*" You are going to understand how the prophets are being diverted. Let the anointing come into Indiana. May the church be anointed in a new way. Let the gifts of God flow in Indiana. Indiana, next year, find your three gathering places, to connect with the three Feasts of the Lord... Passover, Pentecost, and Rosh Hashanah. I saw a 36-month cycle ahead of you to move into all God has for you here in Indiana and it must start now. If you will start now, you will see a great manifestation of HARVEST. You will have tremendous conflicts...but the evangelistic gift will be restored in Indiana...you'll be sending out from Indiana throughout the world. You are an army in Indiana... filled with God's presence, God's love....You are going to be cohesive enough that you move in this state so you change the atmosphere of the state. Understand these are key times. Understand them and move forward and liberate the harvest field of Indiana. (Prophesied by Chuck D. Pierce.)

...Christian Native American Pow-wows going all over the nation...they were beating the drums...breaking the power of abortion off the nation. And a voice broke through the clouds and said, "*Native Americans must lead this, African-Americans must claim this. White Americans must lead this.*"... all of us must lead this, but the Lord pointed (out) that black America must claim this issue.... The revelation...was that we have to walk in each other's shoes in order to buy back the fruit of the womb...it is a fruit that is a hot issue...to buy back the life of the unborn to release justice. (Prophesied by Dutch Sheets.)

I have just shifted an authority in this nation, and I have come to this State to shift this authority. I have come to this state to make the "First Strike," so say now, "Black America will go forth on their path in this land...that which would resist and swarm against them...I am now giving them the ability to walk on the Fire that is coming on the path of this nation. I am imparting to them the authority to walk...before you on the path that is about to grow hot in this land." (Prophesied by Chuck D. Pierce.)

There are some new beginnings for America that are supposed to begin in Indiana. Maybe He is going to lead you into some victories...that are going to initiate some revivals for the rest of the nation. Maybe where God is about to *strike first* is this younger generation and the revival in the college campuses...is going to start right here in Indiana. I saw the Fire of God going from place to place and I saw very clearly Notre

Dame...I don't want to limit it to just one place because I saw a move of God's Holy Spirit literally overwhelm the universities, and it was...a *first strike*! They would gather for days in prayer and fasting. I saw incredible miracles...and word would spread like in Acts 3...this began a rolling move of fire that could not be stopped. ...I keep asking myself, "Lord, ...is it going to begin in Indiana...is this going to be one of the *first strike* States." (Prophesied by Dutch Sheets.)

I want you to understand how to come into a place of worship new and fresh throughout this state so that you can overthrow thrones of iniquity and bind the strongman that keeps holding back the spoils that I have for you.... You are at a crossroads right now, you are either going to be found wanting or you are not going to come into what God has for you and make a shift this time and not go back. Either the Church will continue to rise up and pray for the structures of society, that they start operating in justice in this particular state, or you will have anti-hate groups. ...Then I saw secret societies that are so entrenched in this state. May the Church be anointed in a new way. (Prophesied by Chuck D. Pierce.)

Brief Indiana History[68]

From the Mound Builders to Tippecanoe

The Mound Builders were Indiana's earliest known inhabitants, and the remains of their culture have been found along Indiana's rivers and bottomlands. The region was first explored by Europeans, notably the French, in the late 17th [century]. The leading French explorer was Robert Cavelier, sieur de La Salle, who came to the area in 1679. At the time of exploration, the area was occupied mainly by Native American groups of the Miami, Delaware, and Potawatamie descents. Vincennes, the first permanent settlement, was fortified in 1732, but for the first half of the 1700s, most of the settlers in the area were Jesuit missionaries or fur traders.

By the Treaty of Paris of 1763 ending the French and Indian Wars, Indiana, then part of the area known as the Old Northwest, passed from French to British control. Along with the rest of the Old Northwest, Indiana was united with Canada under the Quebec Act of 1774 (see Intolerable Acts). During the American Revolution an expedition led by George Rogers Clark captured, lost, and then recaptured Vincennes from the British. By the Treaty of Paris of 1783 ending the Revolutionary War, Great Britain ceded the Old Northwest to the United States.

Indiana was still largely unsettled when the Northwest Territory, of which it formed a part, was established in 1787. Native Americans in the territory resisted settlement, but [General] Anthony Wayne's victory at Fallen Timbers in 1794 effectively ended Native American resistance in the Old Northwest. U.S. forces led by [General] William Henry Harrison also defeated the Native American forces in the battle of Tippecanoe (1811) in the Wabash country.

Indiana Territory and Statehood

In 1800, Indiana Territory was formed and included the states of Indiana, Illinois, and Wisconsin, and parts of Michigan and Minnesota. Vincennes was made the capital, which in 1813 was moved to Corydon. A constitutional convention met in 1816, and Indiana achieved statehood. Jonathan Jennings, an opponent of slavery, was elected governor. Indianapolis was laid out as the state capital, and the executive moved there in 1824-1825.

Indiana was the site of several experimental communities in the early 19th [century], notably the Rappite (1815) and Owenite (1825) settlements at New Harmony. In the 1840s the Wabash and Erie Canal opened between Lafayette and Toledo, Ohio, giving Indiana a water route via Lake Erie to eastern markets. Also in the 1840s the state's first railroad line was completed between Indianapolis and Madison. The Hoosier spirit of simplicity and forthrightness that developed during Indiana's early years of statehood figured in the writings of Edward Eggleston in *The Hoosier Schoolmaster* and was represented in much later days by James Whitcomb Riley, George Ade, Gene Stratton Porter, and also in the nostalgic lyric by Paul Dresser (brother of Indiana-born novelist Theodore Dreiser) for the song "On the Banks of the Wabash, Far Away."

The Civil War and Its Aftermath

The Civil War brought great changes in the state. In the elections of 1860, Indiana voted for Lincoln, who had spent his boyhood in the Hoosier state. Although there was some proslavery sentiment in Indiana, represented by the Knights of the Golden Circle, Oliver P. Morton, governor during the war, held the state unswervingly to the Union cause even after constitutional government broke down in 1862. General John Hunt Morgan led a Confederate raid into Indiana in 1863, but otherwise little action occurred in the state.

Manufacturing, which had been stimulated in Indiana by the needs of the war, developed rapidly after the war. Factories sprang up, and the old rustic pattern was broken. However, Indiana's farmers continued to be an important force in the state, and in the hard times following the Panic of 1873 indebted farmers expressed their discontent by supporting the Granger movement and later the Greenback party in 1876 and the Populist party in the 1890s.

Industrialization and the Labor Movement

Industrial development came to the Calumet region along Indiana's Lake Michigan shoreline in the late 19th [century]. Marshy wastelands were drained and transformed into an area supporting a complex of factories and oil refineries. As the 19th [century] drew to a close, industry continued to expand and the growing numbers of industrial workers in the state sought to organize through labor unions. Eugene V. Debs, one of the great early labor leaders, was from Indiana, and the labor movement at Gary in the Calumet area figured prominently in the nationwide steel strike just after World War I. Indiana was an early leader in the production of automobiles. Before Detroit took control of the industry in the 1920s, Indiana boasted over 300 automobile companies.

Indiana society in the first half of the 20th [century] has been described in a number of studies and books. The classic sociological study by Robert S. Lynd and Helen M. Lynd of an American manufacturing town, *Middletown* (1929), was based on data from Muncie, [Indiana]. Midwestern life and American boyhood were portrayed realistically, and often with humor and optimism, in the novels of Booth Tarkington. Another Indiana author, Theodore Dreiser, wrote more generally of American society in a changing age. In the 1930s and 1940s, Wendell Willkie and Ernie Pyle, both natives of Indiana, became nationally prominent figures in politics and journalism, respectively.

Although Indiana in the latter half of the 19th [century] was regarded as a "swing state" electorally, it has generally been conservative throughout the 1900s. Republican J. Danforth "Dan" Quayle, elected to the U.S. Senate in 1980 and 1986, was elected vice president of the United States in 1988. From the 1980s through the mid-1990s, the northern industrial portion of the state experienced a period of significant decline, along with the rest of the midwestern "rust belt." However, the area around Indianapolis experienced significant growth with a diversified economy.

IOWA

Iowa: Sioux meaning "Beautiful Land"
Statehood: December 28, 1846 (29th state)
Motto: Our Liberties We Prize and Our Rights We Will Maintain
Familiar Name: The Hawkeye State
50-State Tour: The Corn State—Supply and Release, October 27-28, 2003

Revelation of God's Stored National Supply in the Cornfields[69]

I (Chuck D. Pierce) gave a prophetic word on September 16, 2001. One of the things that I do is watch after the words that the Lord has spoken. This word talked about *"emptying the pockets of this nation,"* and how He was going to be *"bringing us to a place of humility as a nation."* And then He said, ***"Don't fear** the emptying of the pockets of our nation, because I have supply that I will release once the pockets are empty. I have stored supplies for such a time as this within the cornfields of the nation."* So, right then, I began to pray for the states that are known for growing our nation's corn supply.

The Lord also said, *"The corn belt states are going to rise up and learn a new way of releasing."* When God speaks prophetically, it's for a time ahead. So I knew those were the states that, at a certain point in time,

He would look to for the release of the supply that our nation needed for the future. I also believe that when God speaks prophetically, and then brings you to the place that He's been speaking about, that prophetic word takes action, and there will be a changing or shifting time when you get there.

The Lord says, *"You will release food. You will release funds. And you will release revelation for times that are ahead."* Now you should be saying, "We, in Iowa will be a revelationary people." So from this meeting forward, we will start seeing *an economic change in our nation.* There will be a shift in the economic system, but it's *a sign for this particular state.* Just as in the days of Joseph, we will start a seven-year season. We'll probably look back at this time frame and see that, as a nation, we began a seven-year economic season, and these corn belt states entered into an anointing of creativity to take resources, multiply them, and release them into this nation in a whole new way.

In Iowa, in the days ahead, you are about to be broken open in a way like never before. A lot of times we don't understand what we are going through until it's time for us to understand it. And that will be very significant this year—how God will start to raise things up through us. You need to say, "We've got resources that are about to be uncovered!" But to do that, you need to get out of unbelief!

> The Lord would say, "***From this state, Babylon will begin to change***. For I will make a supernatural connection from the cornfields to the supply from this state that will change the course of the Church in Iraq. Do not look at the confusion that is going on in that land. For, here in Iowa, you will have a ***supernatural authority to defeat Babylon*** in days ahead."

Vision of Iowa—Four Corners and the Center

While Pastor Dutch was speaking, the Lord showed me the state and lifted me up to show me what the state looked like in the Spirit. And the Lord was saying, *"I'm going to begin to break down that circle of darkness that dwells in the center of this state.... I call you like Ruth at this time, and I would say you would go to the corners and begin to glean. And if you'll glean in the corners, then the center will have to respond."* Now, I believe these words have a literal meaning; you won't be able to see transformation in the center without starting at the corners.

And when the Lord showed me that, He showed me several things:

1. He showed me the southwest corner of the state and said, *"In the southwest corner [there] was going to be a grass-roots movement that would begin to emerge and bring political change into the very center and the very heart of the state."*

2. Then He said that the Church is going to blossom. There is going to be a move of God in the *northwest corner* of the state. The Spirit of God is going to come down, and where it has never blossomed before, all of a sudden, the Church will begin to blossom with revelation. There will be a breakthrough of worship in the northwest corner.

3. Then He showed me the southeast corner and said, *"Much weeping will begin to cause a river to arise and tear down a throne in the southeast corner."* He said, *"There is a throne there that has been erected, but the weeping of My people will cause the throne to decay and fall."* Then He said that there is a kingly anointing rising up in the [eastern portion of the state] that will affect the Middle East.

4. When I looked at the state from the heavens, I saw the *northeast corner* was totally veiled and desolate. There was a blockage of a movement of the Spirit of God. And it was actually causing an influence into the very center or heart of the state. The Lord said, *"I want to lift the veil in the northeast."*

I saw a sword come down into the government. And I saw this sword begin to divide and create confusion. There was confusion in the courts and in the systems of government here. The sword caused the government, where it has always been underneath the veil, to begin to rise up; and a new unity, a new sound, and a new release came into the civil government.

Then the Lord said that there was a drought that was trying to surround the very heart of this state. But from the corners, you would be able to penetrate the heart of the state. Since the drought that was forming would not be able to take hold, there would be such a release. And that what has been released this year, for the cornfields to blossom, will bring a greater release next year.

> The Lord would say to you, "Change is now upon this state. What was, will no longer be. What has been asleep, now will wake up. I will have a people that begin to rise before the sun and make decrees, so that the order that I have for this state will be made. I will have a praying group that rises every morning in the north, south, east, and west corners. They will begin to rise up and make a decree. And from their decree, I will bring to birth My very purpose in this state. And even though you've been submerged under Michigan

and Wisconsin, I say that Iowa is now rising to the attention of this nation."

You started out under the Michigan territory, then under the Wisconsin territory, and then you became Iowa. Well, that's the same way your identity needs to progress—where you really become who you are. You'll see it in the sport arena eventually, where you see Iowa rising up and becoming stronger than Michigan and Wisconsin. This will be a sign to you. I'm not trying to get into sports, but it's something that we see that happens in the earth realm. Remember, we live in Heaven but walk on earth, so we want to notice some things going on here. Finally, Iowa has come into its boundaries of revelation of who we are in the heavenlies.

Brief Iowa History

Marquette and Joliet Find Iowa Lush and Green

In the summer of 1673, French explorers Louis Joliet and Father Jacques Marquette traveled down the Mississippi River past the land that was to become the state of Iowa. The two explorers, along with their five crewmen, stepped ashore near where the Iowa river flowed into the Mississippi. It is believed that the 1673 voyage marked the first time that white people visited the region of Iowa. After surveying the surrounding area, the Frenchmen recorded in their journals that Iowa appeared lush, green, and fertile. For the next 300 years, thousands of white settlers would agree with these early visitors: Iowa was indeed lush and green; moreover, its soil was highly productive. In fact, much of the history of the Hawkeye State is inseparably intertwined with its agricultural productivity. Iowa stands today as one of the leading agricultural states in the nation, a fact foreshadowed by the observation of the early French explorers.[70]

The Indians

Before 1673, however, the region had long been home to many Native Americans. Approximately 17 different Indian tribes had resided here at various times including the Ioway, Sauk, Mesquaki, Sioux, Potawatomi, Oto, and Missouri. The Potawatomi, Oto, and Missouri Indians had sold their land to the federal government by 1830 while the Sauk and Mesquaki remained in the Iowa region until 1845. The Santee Band of the Sioux was the last to negotiate a treaty with the federal government in 1851....

In 1829, the federal government informed the two tribes [Sauk and Mesquaki] that they must leave their villages in western Illinois and move across the Mississippi River into the Iowa region. The federal government claimed ownership of the Illinois land as a result of the Treaty of 1804. The move was made but not without violence. Chief Black [H]awk, a highly-respected Sauk leader, protested the move and in 1832 returned to reclaim the Illinois village of Saukenauk. For the next three months, the Illinois militia pursued Black Hawk and his band of approximately 400 Indians northward along the eastern side of the Mississippi River. The Indians surrendered at the Bad Axe River in Wisconsin, their numbers having dwindled to about 200. This encounter is known as the Black Hawk War. As punishment for their resistance, the federal government required the Sauk and Mesquaki to relinquish some of their land in eastern Iowa. This land, known as the Black Hawk Purchase, constituted a strip 50 miles wide lying along the Mississippi River, stretching from the Missouri border to approximately Fayette and Clayton Counties in Northeastern Iowa....[71]

Iowa's First White Settlers

The first official white settlement in Iowa began in June 1833, in the Black Hawk Purchase. Most of Iowa's first white settlers came from Ohio, Pennsylvania, New York, Indiana, Kentucky, and Virginia. The great majority of newcomers came in family units. Most families had resided in at least one additional state between the time they left their state of birth and the time they arrived in Iowa. Sometimes families had relocated three or four times before they reached Iowa. At the same time, not all settlers remained here; many soon moved on to the Dakotas or other areas in the Great Plains.

Iowa's earliest white settlers soon discovered an environment different from that which they had known back East. Most northeastern and southeastern states were heavily timbered; settlers there had material for building homes, outbuildings, and fences. Moreover, wood also provided ample fuel. Once past the extreme eastern portion of Iowa, settlers quickly discovered that the state was primarily a prairie or tall grass region. Trees grew abundantly in the extreme eastern and southeastern portions, and along rivers and streams, but elsewhere timber was limited....[72]

Statehood, Railroads, and Reform Movements

Iowa became a state in 1846, and Ansel Briggs was elected as the first governor. In 1857 the capital was moved from Iowa City to Des Moines. In that same year the state adopted its second constitution. Iowa prospered greatly with the beginning of railroad construction, and the rivalry between towns to get the lines was so fierce that the grant of big land tracts to railroad companies was curtailed by legislative act in 1857. Two years earlier the state's first railroad line was completed between Davenport and Muscatine along the eastern border. Before and during the Civil War, Iowans, generally owners of small, independent farms, were naturally sympathetic to the antislavery side, and many fought for the Union. The Underground Railroad, which helped many fugitive slaves escape to free states, was active in Iowa, and the abolitionist John Brown made his headquarters there for a time.

Iowa's farmers prospered after the Civil War, but during the hard times that afflicted the country in the 1870s they found themselves burdened with debts. Feeling oppressed by the currency system, corporations, and high railroad and grain-storage rates, many of Iowa's farmers supported, along with other farmers of the West, the Granger movement, the Greenback party, and the Populist party. The reform movements had some success in the state. Granger laws were enacted in 1874 and 1876 regulating railroad rates, but these laws were repealed in 1877 under pressure from the railroad companies. By the end of the 19th [century], times improved, and the agrarian movements declined. Farm units grew larger, and mechanization brought great increases in productivity.[73]

Strong Traditions

Iowans are still widely known for their strong educational systems, both in secondary as well as in higher education. Today, Iowa State University and the University of Iowa continue to be recognized nationally and internationally as outstanding educational institutions. Iowa remains a state composed mostly of farms and small towns, with a limited number of larger cities. Moreover, Iowa is still a place where most people live stable, comfortable lives, where family relationships are strong and where the quality of life is high. In many peoples' minds, Iowa is "middle America." Throughout the years, Iowans have profited from their environment and the result is a progressive people and a bountiful land.[74]

KANSAS[75]

> **Kansas:** Sioux meaning "South-wind People"
> **Statehood:** January 29, 1861 (34th state)
> **Motto:** *Ad Astra per Aspera* (To the Stars Through Adversity)
> **Familiar Name:** The Sunflower State
> **50-State Tour:** The Revival State, October 29-30, 2003

"The Church Arising in the New Day"—the 50-State Tour gathering with Chuck Pierce and Dutch Sheets on October 29-30, 2003—was incredible. There was standing room only at the First Assembly of God in Topeka for the Wednesday evening session and a large crowd on Thursday morning. The worship and banner processional helped to stir up faith and hope as we gathered together. Momentum was building as Chuck and Dutch had just come from Iowa and Nebraska and were now in Kansas.

At the beginning of this year, the Lord gave a burden to Chuck Pierce and Dutch Sheets to go together to all 50 states. As the Regional Coordinator of the Heartland/Central Region (Arkansas, Iowa, Kansas, Missouri, Nebraska, Oklahoma, and Texas), I coordinated the timing for our four states to the north for these leaders (Dutch Sheets and Chuck Pierce) to come during one week (October 27-31, 2003) and was with them during this time. We visited the four state capital cities from Iowa to Nebraska to Kansas to Missouri. Our meetings in Iowa (the 26th state that Chuck and Dutch had visited) began the second half of the total 51 meetings. They believed that being in the "Heartland" was a very significant time, just after the Fall Feasts of the Lord.

In each state, a fresh message and word from the Lord was given. In Kansas it was shared how hope deferred can keep you in unbelief of your inheritance and promise. Jacob believed his son Joseph was dead (which was a lie). When his sons came back from Egypt and said Joseph was alive and ruler of the land, there was still some unbelief. These same sons were the ones who told their father years ago that Joseph was dead. But when the provision (of the Lord) came with a caravan of gifts, horses, and wagons, faith and hope were stirred up again.

In Kansas there is a well of revival, an inheritance that has been capped. At one point, prayers for the uncapping and releasing of this well were brought forth from the center to the state, to the nation(s). The Lord can take each difficult situation and add them together to bring forth a great work (being put in a well + being sold into slavery + being falsely accused + being forgotten in prison = being ruler of Egypt and bringing deliverance to God's people). There have been difficult situations in each generation in this state. They are being added together. May this generation be the one in which they add up to bring deliverance to God's people again. Spring up, ole well...of revival!

At another moment, those in the larger towns cried out and blessed those from the rural communities. Fires of revival were prayed to be released from the bigger cities to flow to the small communities and then to flow back into the bigger cities. We need each other in our state. There was much prayer for the harvest and a celebration of the marriage feast of the Lamb with a covenant/communion meal using grain from this year's wheat harvest. Cries, declarations, and worship went forth. There was a cry for a shifting of governmental authority in our capital city of Topeka and much more.

Brief Kansas History[76]

The year 2004 marked the 150th anniversary of the Kansas Territory. It was on May 30, 1854, that the Kansas-Nebraska act of 1854 was signed, opening up the Kansas and Nebraska Territories for settlement. Numerous Kansas communities are celebrating their sesquicentennials, having been founded in the year 1854.

Prior to 1854, the area of present-day Kansas was known as Indian Territory because of the Indian Removal Act of 1830. This Act pledged that a land west of Missouri and Arkansas, namely Kansas and Oklahoma, would be assigned to the Eastern Tribes. It was here, in what became the Kansas Territory, that many eastern Native American tribes were placed, to be separated from the civilized East, and promised a peaceful existence. A barrier was raised along the Kansas/Missouri border that no white man was to cross, keeping out the encroachment of settlers and protecting the Indians from white men.

Forts were placed along this Kansas-Missouri border to enforce this barrier. Only Indians, military personnel, missionaries, and Indian agents were allowed to live in this area. As the Native Americans came to Kansas, so did many missionaries. Some had been working with the tribes in their old lands and even moved with the tribes. Others established missions as the Indians located to the lands in Kansas.

But, the barrier was unsuccessful and when the land was found to be productive, these tribes were moved again, this time mostly to present-day Oklahoma. After numerous new treaties and land deals were made with the tribes placed in present-day Kansas, the Native Americans moved, or were moved, and the rich land of the Kansas Territory, which included eastern Colorado to the Continental Divide, was opened for settlement.

The settlement of the Kansas Territory was the center of national tensions. The Missouri Compromise of 1820 (revised in 1850) stated that any territories from the Louisiana Purchase above the southern border of Missouri were to be admitted into the Union as free states.

There was a balance of power in Washington, DC, in 1854 with an equal number of proslavery states and free states in the Union. The fear of having two free states (Kansas and Nebraska) join the Union and thus shift the balance of power to the Northern free states is what prompted the Kansas-Nebraska Act of 1854. This Act repealed the Missouri Compromise and proclaimed that each territory had popular sovereignty, allowing a vote of the territorial residents to decide its outcome. The South and pro-slavery Missourians wanted Kansas, on their western border, to be pro-slavery. Northern free-staters, on the other hand, were angry that the promise of the Missouri Compromise of 1820 was broken. Settlers from the North and the South streamed into the Kansas Territory to settle this issue of anti-slavery versus pro-slavery statehood. There was no love lost between these factions.

Camps on each side of the issue were formed, which grew into towns and cities. It was not long before arms were taken up and one group would attack and plunder the other. Pro-slavery strongholds sprang up on the Missouri border and free-stater strongholds sprang up on the Kansas border. Border ruffians from Missouri crossed the line into Kansas and attacked residents who spoke out against slavery. Kansas Jayhawkers also conducted bloody raids into Missouri. It was on this Kansas-Missouri border/barrier that the division between North and South, free and slave, came to its climax, resulting in "Bleeding Kansas," and ultimately ignited the Civil War (April 1861), the year Kansas became the 34th state on January 29, 1861.

As the physical gateway to the West is in Saint Louis, Missouri, the Kansas-Missouri border is the spiritual dividing line of the nation... thus the spiritual gateway to the West.

Kansas had seen bloodshed before. There have been many Indian battles here and also the first known Christian martyr on U.S. soil was in Kansas. In the center of Kansas (Lyons, Kansas) stands an 18-foot-high marble cross in honor of Father Juan de Padilla who was killed by the Quivira Indians in 1542. His name means "bread oven." He traveled to Kansas with Coronado's expedition for the lost cities of gold in 1541. He returned a year later with a small group of priests and servants to Christianize the Indians. When Father Padilla came to this center of the New World, the Cross of Christianity had then reached all four corners of the world.

Bread is very significant to our state. A key redemptive gift of Kansas (the Wheat State) to the nation(s) is being the breadbasket. The average wheat farmer in Kansas grows enough wheat each year to feed over 100 people for one year. The land is very fertile. In the holy place of the temple was the "Bread of His Presence." Grain (wheat) offerings were required of the Lord and pleasing to Him. The Appointed Feasts of the Lord were connected to the harvest of the new grain, new wine, and new oil. The firstfruits of the harvest were given to the Lord. An abundance of new wheat is a symbol of God's provision. "For the bread of God is He who comes down from heaven and gives life to the world" (John 6:33).

The role of Kansas has been a strategic one for the nation(s). It is at the heart of America, being at the exact center. The geographical center of the continental U.S. (lower 48 states) is located just outside of Lebanon, Kansas. For generations, people have journeyed over the Kansas trails.

Kansas has often been a forerunner for the rest of the nation. Bleeding Kansas and the Civil War is one such example. Even today, many companies set up test markets in Kansas to see if their product will be a national success. The temperance movement in Kansas was started (before statehood) by the Independent Order of Good Templars. Kansas was the first state to enact a prohibition amendment to their constitution in 1879. The rest of the nation followed.

There are great wells of revival in this state that need to be redug. On January 1, 1901, the Holy Spirit visited a small group of believers in Topeka. That visitation began the modern-day Pentecostal and Charismatic movements. The modern abbreviation "WWJD" (What would Jesus do?) finds its roots in Rev. Charles Sheldon's book, *In His Steps*. Pastor Sheldon challenged his Topeka congregation to live like Jesus did. Kansans were considered moralizers because of their religious conviction. These convictions led the various communities to provide Christian education. There are still 18 Christian-founded, church-related colleges providing education to the next generation, although some of these schools have lost their way over the years. Many of the state universities in Kansas have Christian college foundations, too. Other schools have stayed the course and are sending out missionaries around the world.

KENTUCKY[77]

Kentucky: Wyandot meaning "Meadowland"
Statehood: June 1, 1792 (15th state)
Motto: United We Stand, Divided We Fall
Familiar Name: The Bluegrass State
50-State Tour: The Trumpet has Sounded—It's Time to Run with the Horses!, April 19-20, 2004

Our 50-State Tour conference theme was "The Trumpet has Sounded— It's Time to Run with the Horses!" The backdrop on the stage (from which we led the meetings) affirmed that theme with a picture of a silver trumpet that appeared to be blowing numerous galloping horses out of the bell as it sounded! Only a couple of weeks before the Kentucky

Derby, we could actually sometimes hear and feel the pounding of horses' hoofs as we were led into incredible times of prophetic worship with Ray Hughes and Selah.

Numerous words were spoken over Kentucky, igniting new passion and zeal in all those who attended. Barbara Yoder opened the meeting with an afternoon leaders' gathering. Some of the things she declared then and in the proceeding meetings were as follows:

- ★ Kentucky is needed for the war over this nation. There will be a warring spirit that will arise from this state that will literally speak to the entire nation.

- ★ Kentucky is on the verge of its biggest change. God is loosing the horses, the runners, and the riders in Kentucky. They will ride and run through this nation once again. There is a breaking out that is going to occur in Kentucky. It is a firstfruit state for revival.

- ★ Abraham Lincoln was born in Kentucky and therefore you have a firstfruit anointing for emancipation proclamation. You were divided then over the issue, but there is going to be an opportunity to redeem the division of past times. Kentucky will set the course for the nation in this.

- ★ Lexington is the stable for the warhorses. From here the horses will be released across the nation. Get ready, I am calling you to war like you cannot imagine!

- ★ God is restoring the prophetic breath in Kentucky, and then Kentucky will restore the breath of the nation. As a sign of the restoration of the prophetic breath, God will begin to cleanse physical disease in the lungs, and there will be supernatural healings of lung cancer in this state.

* God is going to bring a new order to this state, which will cause both the land and the Church to flourish.
* The Lord is loosing a "mongoose" anointing on you and you shall eat the serpent that has held back revival. He is declaring, *"Do not say next year or the following but now, for I am going to swallow the serpent from this state!"*
* A spirit of deliverance shall break out in this state that shall cause freedom to manifest in the entire nation. It is a mantle of deliverance!
* The Lord says, *"I am returning a right mantle of war to the White House from this state, and there will be vindication."*

Chuck Pierce opened the next meeting. Some of the things he declared during the course of the meeting are as follows:

* God is about to do a new thing to unlock the future of Kentucky. This will be a region known for the dismantling of ancient thrones that have been erected.
* A supernatural confession will arise from the government in Kentucky as men attempt to change righteous laws. The outcry and resistance from Kentucky will be seen throughout the nation, and it will cause a remnant from every state to rise up in agreement with Kentucky.
* The governmental anointing in this state will be carried into Washington, DC. Chuck instructed everyone to declare, "From Kentucky to DC!"
* Kentucky, made up of 120 counties, is an "upper room" state!

- ★ God said, *"I am changing the horizon line over this nation, and I am starting here in Kentucky."* Chuck then spoke about a time frame of 15 days, and we later learned that he and Dutch would be in Washington, DC, during that time.

- ★ Worship will be the key in Kentucky to exposing hidden things and causing the enemy to loose his hold. There will be a great and drastic change in Kentucky's atmosphere as a result. As we move into that new dimension, thousands will come and join us in worship.

- ★ The seer anointing will be loosed in Kentucky along with great revelation.

- ★ Chuck declared that on May 1, the day of the Kentucky Derby, the sound of the horses would release the movement of war on earth like never before. There would also be a supernatural release to receive new strength and to move forward. The Lord said that out of Kentucky would come a sound that would cause the nations to come into conflict, but the Bride will rise up and it will be a call of freedom.

Notes From Dutch Sheets

- ★ This meeting is not just about Kentucky; it's about the nation.

- ★ The Lord awakened Dutch at 3:33 a.m. and gave him Ezekiel 33:3, the watchman's charge, for the state of Kentucky. The Lord said there would be a new level of a spirit of wisdom and revelation released to bring us into a higher level of the prophetic.

* Dutch stated Kentucky would become known as the "hearing state" as we move into this new dimension.

* Discerning of spirits will be released to God's people for there is a strong, strong deliverance anointing coming to the state of Kentucky. Once again, he said a strong, strong, strong spirit of deliverance is coming.

* Both a mantle of war and a mantle of worship shall rest on Kentucky unlike anything seen before. It will be a pleasant war because it is born of worship! It will create a new "Great Awakening"!

* A spirit of revelation is coming through many supernatural ways, and divine strategies will be released to gain great victories.

* Universities, schools, and organizations are about to be invaded by God's people, and they will do whatever He says. Signs and wonders will be released even in day cares and elementary schools!

* An unusual mix of wisdom and revelation is going to be released. Do not move out until you have both. Often one will have the wisdom and another the revelation, so we must work together!

* Jeremiah 33:3 was given to Dutch. Kentucky is to experience things it has never seen or heard before! God is laying siege to this state to take back what the enemy has stolen. He is coming with fire because the fire of revival will burn once again.

* Kentucky must learn to hear the "sound" of God so we can both find and go through the gate of revelation. Dutch

warned, "If you don't hear the sound, you won't get the rain, and you won't shift the nation either!"

* Dutch then began to release the sound of war, the sound of waters, the sound of wind, the sound of thunder, the sound of Heaven, etc.

Brief Kentucky History

The name *Kentucky* comes from a Wyandot Indian word that can be translated as "Land of Tomorrow." Once void of any permanent residents, it was considered to be an unoccupied territory. However, Shawnee and Cherokee Native Americans living to the north and south used this land for both hunting and warring expeditions. Some portions of the land were deemed "sacred" as fallen warriors were buried there. As Anglo explorers began to arrive and travel along Kentucky's rivers, a considerable trade business began to develop with the Indians. This became the source of great rivalry between French and British traders, which eventually culminated in the French and Indian War (1754-1763). The Treaty of Paris (1763) had a significant effect on Kentucky history as it opened the door to Anglo colonial expansion beyond the Appalachian highlands through the repeal of political barriers.

Daniel Boone, Kentucky's most famous explorer, first arrived in the spring of 1769. By 1775, the Revolutionary War had broken out, and as a result, settler footholds were secured in the Kentucky backwoods. During this same time the first permanent settlement, Harrod's Town, was established. Shortly thereafter, Boonesborough was founded and a fort was completed in Harrod's Town. In February of 1775, Daniel Boone led a party to blaze a trail from Sycamore Shoals in eastern Tennessee through Cumberland Gap to the south bank of the Kentucky River. In time, this became the Wilderness Road, which provided the means for immigrant travel and expansion. Kentucky's land was rich and full of natural resources and for 200 years the domestic culture and economy revolved around their abundance.

Originally part of Virginia, Kentucky became a "Commonwealth," the 15th state, on June 1, 1792. The government of the Commonwealth of Kentucky was organized in a ceremonial meeting in Lexington on June 4, 1792. (Following our "50-State Tour" event, we learned that the hotel where we met was built on the very site of this first meeting!) Lexington was never intended to become the state capital, and soon after, a committee chose Frankfort due to its central location, available land, building materials, and nearby river. During the decade from 1790-1800, Kentucky experienced phenomenal growth in population, exploding from 73,677 to 220,995.

Kentuckians were negatively impacted by the War of 1812. As a result, by the year 1819, inflation and fiscal irresponsibility left Kentucky in a precarious situation financially. This led to several decades of uncontrolled expansion of local government.

One of the most remarkable segments of Kentucky's history is in the area of religious growth and influence. Lay ministers were among the earliest settlers, and later the state became a "magnet for missionaries." The Baptists came as a "Traveling Church" from Virginia in 1781. Bishop Frances Asbury and a host of Methodist circuit riders crisscrossed the state establishing churches. Roman Catholic missionaries came early to southcentral Kentucky and along the Ohio River. Presbyterians were on hand to exert considerable influence in the framing of the first constitution and the formation of the state.

At the turn of the 19th century, an extraordinary and very influential "religious" movement began during revival meetings along the Muddy and Gasper Rivers in south-central Kentucky. The excitement created there soon spread to Cane Ridge in Bourbon County in August 1801, where crowds of up to 20,000 responded to fervent preaching in a new and demonstrative way! People would come with loaded wagons and stay for days, which coined the new words "camp meeting." Between 1801 and 1840 this revival swept the entire South and became known as the "Second Great Awakening." During 1805, Shaker Missionaries came to Kentucky and established a community in Mercer County adding to the strong influence of faith in the Commonwealth.

Kentucky was deeply divided during the Civil War, and loyalties were split between the Union and Confederate forces. Plantation owners depended on slave labor and thus supported the South. Strong abolitionists, such as Henry Clay, appealed to those opposed to slavery and were supporters of the North. Although the Kentucky legislature decided for the Union cause, approximately 30,000 men fought for the Confederacy. Both the President of the Union, Abraham Lincoln, and the President of the Confederacy, Jefferson Davis, were born in Kentucky. At the beginning of the war, Kentucky was invaded by Confederate forces. Before being driven out, they established a Confederate Capital in Bowling Green, making Kentucky the only state with both a Union and a Confederate capital. During reconstruction, there was much violence directed toward blacks, prompting the Kentucky legislature to pass laws during the 1870s to protect their civil rights.

During the late 18th and early 19th centuries, Kentucky had established an agricultural economy. Corn, barley, hay, hemp, and tobacco were the major agricultural products. Kentucky bourbon began to be manufactured during this time using the corn and barley grown in the fields. Kentucky also became a leading center for breeding thoroughbred horses, which also gave birth to the first Kentucky Derby in 1875. Coal mines in eastern Kentucky led the way toward a more industrial economy as workers migrated to the cities. Two major coal fields presently exist, one in western Kentucky and the other in the Appalachian Mountains in the east. The state's fortunes declined in the 20th century, and Kentucky was particularly hard hit during the Great Depression in the 1930s. Today, the Appalachian region of Kentucky is one of the poorest rural areas in the country.

After World War II, Kentucky began a modernization effort that included an interstate road network. Major thoroughfares now make Kentucky only a day's drive for 70 percent of the United States population. With two major international airports, one in Louisville and the other in northern Kentucky near Cincinnati, Kentucky can easily accommodate travelers from around the world. An international hub for UPS is located at the Louisville Airport. Commerce is also transported by an extensive rail system and via the approximately 1,600 miles of navigable waterways, including the Ohio and Mississippi Rivers that border the state.

Kentucky is called the "Bluegrass State" because of the abundant growth of bluegrass on its rich limestone soil. At times the fields of bluegrass have a bluish-green hue. Our state bird is the cardinal and our state flower the goldenrod. Our motto is "United We Stand, Divided We Fall," and our colors are royal blue and gold. We are made up of 120 counties.

LOUISIANA[78]

Louisiana: Named after Louis XIV of France
Statehood: April 30, 1812 (18th state)
Motto: Union, Justice, and Confidence
Familiar Name: The Pelican State
50-State Tour: The Governmental Mantle State, February 16-17, 2003

The meeting was held in Baton Rouge at Shenandoah Center. We began the meeting by blowing the shofar and taking communion. The Lord then gave the following word:

> "I am beginning to lift the veil dwelling on the state. As it begins to lift, look for spring rain. Spring is coming to this state, and you can expect much rain. I will start the cleansing process in this state not seen in many years. I am coming now in your midst. I will cleanse the government. All the nation will see the cleansing on this state. By November, I will be doing a new thing. Ask Me for the rain. This is a rain of cleansing. The rain in the fall will bring forth a crop of conversions....The death veil will begin to lift. Faith has arisen in My people, and the veil has begun to tear." (Prophesied by Chuck D. Pierce.)

Chuck taught from Second Kings chapter 2 on seeing into a supernatural dimension. "If you see, then you will receive!" This year there is an opening of the heavens which will show us what God has for us. *"I declare that the ceiling over the state and the veil over the state be lifted. I have decreed that My servants are to begin to see in a way they have not seen before."* (Prophesied by Chuck D. Pierce.) It doesn't matter what has covered you in the past or what you've been known for. It's a new, different day. The Lord is ready to rip the veil off, so you see the host of Heaven operating in your midst. This is your year to see. You must see! See the reproach on the government of this state lift and change and take a different course.

> "For you have allowed Me to bring a knife into this state, and I will perform circumcision. I am cutting away what has been held in place and what has influenced and caused you to miss prosperity. I will cut away, and I will establish a new and fresh leadership. Rise up new and fresh in the next 18 months. As they rise, the nation will be affected by this course." (Prophesied by Chuck D. Pierce.)

We made the following declarations over the state:

1. 2003 would be a year of supernatural conversion.
2. 2003 would be a year of supernatural transference.
3. We addressed the besiegement of the enemy in the state.
4. We loosed the gift of faith in this state.
5. We declared that the deadness that had entered the Church because of unbelief would break.
6. We prayed that the enemy would be outwitted in Louisiana.
7. We asked the Holy Spirit to detach the spirit of infirmity from the trauma of the people.
8. We declared that the government of God would shift completely, and immediate change would come to civil government.

9. We declared that blocked doors would open, new influence would arise, and a new release of supply would come into the path of God's people. We shut the door to revelry, and opened the door to glory. And any influence from this state on the nation, arise now!

10. We declared that eyes will open to see new supply; there will be an opening of supply and release, and a transference of wealth into the Kingdom of God. We addressed the spirit of poverty.

11. We declared that the voice of wisdom would arise now, and the rearguard of God would be established, and that Louisiana as a state would be propelled forward into what God has for her.

Dutch Sheets taught on the governmental cities in the Bible and declared that the Louisiana government would arise into a new day! He then declared that the reproach over Louisiana would be lifted, and a wholeness would come into the government of the state. We declared that the Church in Louisiana would be a giant killer. The five governmental cities Dutch discussed were:

1. Gilgal—"rolling" away the reproach of Egypt
2. Shiloh—bringing "wholeness" to the state
3. Shechem—"shoulder"; government
4. Hebron—formerly Kiriath Arba, city of the greatest giant; place from which the giant-slaying spirit can come!
5. Jerusalem—city of wholeness

We declared that Louisiana will come to life and that a desire for righteousness will flood the state. We declared that the river of righteousness would run into the government. We broke a power of barrenness over the state and declared hostility would come off the womb of Louisiana. We then addressed and decreed a cleansing of the hate group issues across the state. The curse of Horace is linked with Freemasonry. We asked the Lord to blind the evil eye linked with this curse and the corruption of gambling so that it would not overtake Louisiana completely. Over the next several months there will be a cleansing occurring so the womb can conceive again. Righteousness is conceived again in the state of Louisiana. That which is coming forth is protected from leviathan and the dragon. The twisted communication spirit is bound against the Righteous One that will rise from this state. The news will report a shift in this Mardi Gras celebration; let darkness overplay its hand.

> Chuck prophesied: "I have brought life and purity [with the two hurricanes]. I brought the wind and the water. This was meant to bring life and purity into the state. But you have resisted life and purity. I will come as a storm that penetrates, known as the storm that broke through and brought change. There will be a breaking and cleansing of hostility. You will see the change manifest or else you will see the sevenfold against you. This is a season of change. If you change, you will cleanse the womb of this nation."

The key phrase used during our 50-State Tour meeting was "governmental mantle," which applies to the spiritual realm as well as the political realm. Since that time, we have concentrated our efforts at legislating in the heavenlies and watching for the changes taking place.

Dutch Sheets emphasized that our moving in our authority would create a release for the entire nation.

In September 2003, Tony Perkins of Louisiana took over the leadership of the Family Research Council in Washington, which was a perfect example of our being able to export righteousness from our state to the nation. We were to transport, pray, and decree shalom into the rest of the nation. We were to provide a place of refuge, wholeness, friendship, intimacy, and fellowship with God. We were said to have a "giant-slaying anointing" and that the government of God has arisen in Louisiana. We were to exhibit covenantal wholeness.

Brief Louisiana History[79]

Early Louisiana

Louisiana has a long and colorful history. The region was possibly visited by Cabeza de Vaca and his fellow survivors of a Spanish expedition of 1528, and it was certainly seen by some of De Soto's men (1541-1542). In 1682, La Salle reached the mouth of the Mississippi and claimed for France all of the land drained by that river and its tributaries, naming it Louisiana after Louis XIV. Europeans did not permanently settle there until 1699, when Pierre le Moyne, sieur d'Iberville, founded a settlement near Biloxi. This settlement became the seat of government for Louisiana, an enormous territory embracing the entire Mississippi drainage basin.

In 1702, Iberville's brother, the sieur de Bienville, was appointed governor and moved the territorial government to Fort Louis on the Mobile River. This colony was later moved (1710) to the present site of Mobile (Alabama), and Mobile became the capital of Louisiana. French missionaries and fur traders explored some of the vast territory, and Natchitoches (the oldest settlement within the present boundaries of the state of Louisiana) grew from a French military and trading post established (circa 1714) to protect the Red River area from the Spanish.

In order to increase the value of the colony, France granted (1712) a monopoly of commercial privileges, which in 1717 passed to a company organized by John Law. The promise of riches under Law's Mississippi Scheme brought many settlers to Louisiana, and a large number of them remained even after his scheme had collapsed. New Orleans was founded in 1718, and in 1723 the capital was transferred there. Large numbers of Africans were brought in as slaves, and the Code Noir, adopted in 1724, provided for the rigid control of their lives and the protection of the whites.

Spanish Louisiana

The last conflict (1754-1763) of the French and Indian Wars was ending disastrously for the French, and in order to keep the entire Louisiana territory from falling into the hands of the British, the French secretly ceded (by the Treaty of Fontainebleau in 1762) the area [west] of the Mississippi and the "Isle of Orleans" to Spain. By the Treaty of Paris (1763), Great Britain gained control of all Louisiana [east] of the Mississippi except the "Isle of Orleans"; these changes were announced in 1764.

The French colonists resisted the new Spanish rule, but were subdued and finally Spanish mercantilistic monopoly of trade was instituted. During the Spanish years agriculture flourished with the cultivation of rice and sugarcane, and New Orleans grew as a major port and trading center. The Spanish government welcomed thousands of Acadians... known there as Cajuns, and they settled what came to be known as the Cajun country. During the American Revolution, New Orleans was a center for Spanish aid to the colonies. After Spain declared war on Great Britain in 1779, Louisiana's governor, Bernardo de Gálvez, became an active ally of the revolutionists, capturing Baton Rouge and Natchez (1779), Mobile (1780), and Pensacola (1781).

After the war Louisiana's control of the great inland trade route, the Mississippi, led to heated controversy with the Americans. In the secret Treaty of San Ildefonso (1800), Napoleon I forced the retrocession of the territory to France. Revelation of this treaty caused profound concern in the United States. President Jefferson attempted to purchase the "Isle of Orleans" from France. To the surprise of the American representatives in France, Napoleon decided to sell all of Louisiana to the United States.

Statehood

The United States took possession in 1803, and in 1804 the territory was divided into two parts. The southern part, which was called the Territory of Orleans, was admitted to the Union in 1812 as the state of Louisiana. Settlement (1819) of the West Florida Controversy gave Louisiana the area between the Mississippi and Pearl rivers, which formerly had been part of Florida. After statehood French and Spanish influence remained, not only in the Creole and Cajun societies but also in the civil law (based on French and Spanish codes) and in the division of the state into parishes rather than counties. In the early years of the 19th [century] the diverse people of Louisiana—the French, the Spanish, the Germans, and Isleños brought by Gálvez from the Canary Islands—united behind Andrew Jackson to defeat (1815) the British at the Battle of New Orleans during the War of 1812. (The battle site is contained in Jean Lafitte National Historical Park and Preserve.)

With settlers pouring in from other Southern states, great sugar and cotton plantations developed rapidly in the fertile lowlands, and the less productive uplands were also settled. The state capital was moved several times, finally to Baton Rouge in 1849. The advent of steam propulsion on the Mississippi (the first steamboat to navigate the river arrived in New Orleans in 1812) was a boon to the state's economy; by 1840, New Orleans was the nation's second largest port. Plantation owners, with their large landholdings and many slaves (more than half the population) dominated politics and largely controlled the state.

The Civil War and its Aftermath

On [January] 26, 1861, Louisiana seceded from the Union and six weeks later joined the Confederacy. The fall of New Orleans to David G. Farragut in 1862 prefaced the detested military occupation under [General] B.F. Butler. Occupied Louisiana was a proving ground for Lincoln's moderate restoration program, but after Lincoln's assassination radical Republicans seized control and Louisiana suffered greatly during Reconstruction. The Ku Klux Klan was particularly active from 1866 to 1871. In the election of 1872 the radical Republican candidate for governor lost but was installed with the help of federal troops. Reconstruction in Louisiana finally ended with the disputed presidential election of 1876, when Louisiana's electoral votes were "traded" to the Republicans (whose candidate was Rutherford B. Hayes) in exchange for the withdrawal of federal troops from the state. Francis R.T. Nicholls, a Democrat, became governor of Louisiana, and white control of the state was reestablished.

Economic recovery was slow. The disrupted plantation system was largely replaced by farm tenancy and sharecropping. The decline of steamboat traffic was offset somewhat by new railroad building and the opening of the Mississippi River for oceangoing vessels from New

Orleans to the sea (a feat accomplished by James B. Eads). Mississippi floods constituted a serious problem, and levee building increased after the flood of 1882; it was only after the disastrous flood of 1927, however, that the federal government undertook a vast control system. The water resources development program encompasses flood control, navigation, drainage, and irrigation.

The pattern of Louisiana's economy was changed by the discovery of oil and natural gas in the early 1900s, and industries began to grow on the basis of cheap fuel and cheap labor. Medical advances helped to curb the yellow-fever epidemics that had periodically disrupted the state.

Huey Long and His Legacy

Industrial growth and the continuing woes of the tenant farmers did not alter control of the state by "Bourbon" Democrats, but in 1928 a virtual revolution occurred when Huey P. Long was elected governor. His almost dictatorial rule, detested by liberals across the nation, brought material progress at the cost of widespread official corruption. Long withstood all outside pressures, including the opposition of President F.D. Roosevelt's administration. After his assassination in 1935 (he had resigned the governorship in 1931 to become a U.S. Senator but had retained control over the state), his political heirs made their peace with the New Deal, and federal funds, withheld during Long's last years, poured into the state.

In 1948, Huey's brother, Earl Long, invoking the memory of his dead brother (still regarded by many as a savior and a martyr), gained the governorship. In addition, Huey's son Russell was elected to the U.S. Senate and served for 38 years until he retired in 1986. In 1956, Earl Long was again elected governor, but his second term was marked by scandal and controversy.

Civil Rights, Disasters, and Diversification

About one third of Louisianans are African American, and their struggle for civil rights has been long and bitter. The move toward integration following the 1954 Supreme Court ruling against racial segregation in public schools was difficult, and continuing resistance to social change is reflected in the careers of David Duke and others.

Hurricanes and flooding are recurrent dangers for the state. In 1965, Hurricane Betsy killed 74 and caused property damage in excess of $1 billion. In 1969, Hurricane Camille was even more destructive, ravaging Louisiana and neighboring states and killing 256 people. In [April] 1973, the Mississippi River rose to its highest level recorded in Louisiana and, with its tributaries, flooded more than 10 [percent] of the state.

Louisiana enjoyed an oil boom in the early 1980s but then suffered following the 1986 collapse of oil prices. The state's unemployment rate rose to the highest in the nation, and economic distress grew. The slump placed a great burden on the tourist industry and led to increased efforts to diversify the economy. The state's recent environmental woes have largely arisen from the fact that natural erosion, oil exploitation, and river control projects have severely degraded its freshwater marshlands, especially in the delta of the Mississippi.

MAINE[80]

> **Maine:** Named after ancient French province
> **Statehood:** March 15, 1820 (23rd state)
> **Motto:** *Dirigo* (I Direct)
> **Familiar Name:** The Pine Tree State
> **50-State Tour:** The East Gate for the King, July 12-13, 2004

We realized that the breaking of the day first comes into our nation's mainland on the coast of Maine. Psalm 24 was a key Scripture, as we welcomed the King of Glory to come through the East Gate. Psalm 110 was another key Scripture. Maine is the "womb of the morning." Prayer will birth revival in this "womb," and the Lord will refresh Maine with His dew. A new day is dawning in this generation (18 to 30 year olds) that is arising in Maine, and they will fight in the day of battle.

Brief Maine History

Maine is the easternmost state in our nation and the first place the sun hits the United States. It is the land of the dawn; and the name of our First Nation People, the Wabanakis, means "the people of the dawn."

Due to its proximity to Europe, it was one of the first places that explorers from the Old World came. Though there is some evidence that Vikings and Celts were here before Columbus, there is much documentation of exploration by the French and English shortly after 1492. Rumors of a city with alabaster walls called Norumbega and the abundance of fish and furs drew men like Cabat and Verrazano here in 1497 and 1524 respectively. Like the space race of the 1960s, political competition of two nations accelerated the pace at which this new world was explored.

From the very beginning, the relationships between the English, the French, and the Wabanakis shaped the history of Maine. The French, with Sieur DeMonts, started an unsuccessful colony on the Saint Croix River in 1604, and in 1605 the English captain George Weymouth placed a cross in Thomaston harbor for the glory of God. Soon after this, the French Jesuits founded a mission on Mt. Desert Island, and the English founded the Popham Colony at the mouth of the Kennebec River in 1607. The Popham Colony failed, and the English destroyed the Jesuit mission in 1613—the beginning of a long conflict over the land.

In 1620, the English started the Plymouth Colony in Massachusetts, and they soon saw Maine as their wilderness territory. A fur outpost was founded in Augusta in 1629 (Cushoc), and in 1642 the first English town in the new world was chartered in what is today York, Maine.

The French established good relationships with the Wabanakis in Maine and eastern Canada, and controlled the land east of Penobscot Bay. The English also wanted the land; and from 1675 to 1763, the French and Indian War was fought here with the Native Americans being caught in the middle. This conflict was finally ended with the treaty of Paris in 1763, when the French lost their holdings in Maine.

Since it belonged to Massachusetts, Maine colonists played an important role in the Revolutionary War. Many went to Boston to fight the British, and the first naval battle of the war was fought in Machias in 1775. That same year, Benedict Arnold was sent by George Washington up through the Maine wilderness, and he tried unsuccessfully to capture Quebec City from the British.

After the 13 colonies defeated the British in 1783, Maine continued its new industry of shipbuilding and by 1860 was producing one-third of our nation's ships. During this time, Maine was granted statehood (1820), and Bangor became the logging capital of the world.

Maine moved into the spotlight again during the Civil War. A lady from Brunswick, Harriet Beecher Stowe, wrote *Uncle Tom's Cabin*, which brought the slavery issue to the forefront for many in the North. A Bowdoin professor, Joshua Chamberlain, led the 20th Maine Regiment at Gettysburg. His brilliant and courageous charge at Little Round Top was a turning point in that great battle.

The late 1800s was a time of great change in Maine. There was great growth in the textile, leather, and paper industries in Maine's cities, which brought a great emigration of French from Quebec. There was also a change in the type of Christianity during this time from strictly Congregational churches, to Baptist and Methodist churches, and finally the Catholic church with the coming of Irish and French emigrants. The English and French had conflicts again, but more so in a cultural way.

The 20th century has brought about a healing of many past wounds. The language and cultural barriers continue to come down, and Maine now expresses itself more in the form of healthy political debate. Many Native Americans still live on three reservations in the state; but a major victory was won in 1980, when the Indian land claims settlement brought new justice and finances to their situation.

Today, Maine remains the most forested state in our nation. Its rugged coastline and mountains still inspire the present generation of explorers from around the world to come and find the beauty of nature in the land of the dawn—the land we call Maine.

MARYLAND[81]

Maryland: Named after Queen Henrietta Maria of England
Statehood: April 28, 1788 (7th state)
Motto: *Fatti Maschii, Parole Femine* (Manly Deeds, Womanly Words)
Familiar Name: The Old Line State
50-State Tour: "I Will Awaken the Seed," March 4-5, 2004

Although great division will come into Maryland, this division will be used to stir things for righteous change. Furthermore, what the Lord stirs in this state will cause the entire nation to be stirred.

We declared that Maryland would be a "state of reversal" and that certain laws would change here that will cause the nation to be changed. Historically, Maryland was a state that "kept the line." Once again, Maryland will be a state where the line is drawn.

Chuck D. Pierce shared, "I saw embers arising in the sky over Maryland," and that the fire of God was dwelling over this state, and that which once was would come back double. He continued by prophesying there is much damned up in Maryland, and that as a sign from the Lord, a physical dam would break in that state.

When Pastor Dutch began to minister, he shared that the Lord said, *"I am going to awaken the seed and open the womb."* There was such a powerful anointing that we actually moved back into worship for the rest of the evening. Interestingly, the charter of this state declares that it is the duty of Maryland to worship. We certainly did that on Thursday evening.

On Friday morning, Chuck taught on the Captain of the Hosts. He then prophesied, *"The Captain of the Hosts will stand in the midst of the state. Maryland is a state that has drawn the line in the past and* [now] *again…in nine months you will see great conflict occurring and My people standing!"*

Brief Maryland History[82]

Exploration and Colonization

Giovanni da Verrazano, an Italian navigator in the service of France, probably visited (1524) the Chesapeake region, which was certainly later explored (1574) by Pedro Menéndez Marqués, governor of Spanish Florida. In 1603 the region was visited by an Englishman, Bartholomew Gilbert, and it was charted (1608) by Captain John Smith.

In 1632, Charles I granted a charter to George Calvert, 1st Baron Baltimore, yielding him feudal rights to the region between lat. 40°N and the Potomac River. Disagreement over the boundaries of the grant led to a long series of border disputes with Virginia that were not resolved until 1930. The states still dispute the use of the Potomac River. The territory was named Maryland in honor of Henrietta Maria, queen consort of Charles I. Before the great seal was affixed to the charter, George Calvert died, but his son Cecilius Calvert, 2d Baron Baltimore, undertook development of the colony as a haven for his persecuted fellow Catholics and also as a source of income. In 1634 the ships *Ark* and *Dove* brought settlers (both Catholic and Protestant) to the Western Shore, and a settlement called Saint Mary's…was set up. During the colonial period the Algonquian-speaking Native Americans withdrew from the area gradually and for the most part peacefully, sparing Maryland the conflicts other colonies experienced.

Religious Conflict and Economic Development

Religious conflict was strong in ensuing years as the Puritans, growing more numerous in the colony and supported by Puritans in England, set out to destroy the religious freedom guaranteed with the founding of the colony. A toleration act (1649) was passed in an attempt to save the Catholic settlers from persecution, but it was repealed (1654) after the Puritans seized control. A brief civil war ensued (1655), from which the Puritans emerged triumphant. Anti-Catholic activity persisted until the 19th cent., when in an unusual reversal of the prevailing pattern many Catholic immigrants came to Baltimore.

In 1694, when the capital was moved from Saint Mary's to Annapolis, those were the only towns in the province, but the next century saw the emergence of commercially oriented Baltimore, which by 1800 had a population of more than 30,000 and a flourishing coastal trade. Tobacco became the basis of the economy by 1730. In 1767 the demarcation of the Mason-Dixon Line ended a long-standing boundary dispute with Pennsylvania.

The Revolution and a New Nation

Economic and religious grievances led Maryland to support the growing colonial agitation against England. At the time of the American Revolution most Marylanders were stalwart patriots and vigorous opponents of the British colonial policy. In 1776 Maryland adopted a declaration of rights and a state constitution and sent soldiers and supplies to aid the war for independence; supposedly the high quality of its regular "troops of the line" earned Maryland its nickname, the Old Line State.

The U.S. Congress, meeting at Annapolis, ratified the Treaty of Paris ending the Revolutionary War in 1783. A party advocating states' rights, in which Luther Martin was prominent, was unsuccessful in opposing ratification of the Constitution, and in 1791 Maryland and Virginia contributed land and money for the new national capital in the District of Columbia.

Industry, already growing in conjunction with renewed commerce, was furthered by the skills of German immigrants. The War of 1812 was marked for Maryland by the British attack of 1814 on Baltimore and the defense of Fort McHenry, immortalized in Francis Scott Key's "Star-Spangled Banner." After the war the state entered a period of great commercial and industrial expansion. This was accelerated by the building of the National Road, which tapped the rich resources of the West; the opening of the Chesapeake and Delaware Canal (1829); and the opening (1830) of the Baltimore & Ohio RR, the first railroad in the United States open for public traffic.

The Coming of the Civil War

Southern ways and sympathies persisted among the plantation owners of Maryland, and as the rift between North and South widened, the state was torn by conflicting interests and the intense internal struggles of the true border state. In 1860 there were 87,000 slaves in Maryland, but industrialists and businessmen had special interests in adhering to the Union, and despite the urgings of Southern sympathizers, made famous in J.R. Randall's song, "Maryland, My Maryland," the state remained in the Union.

At the beginning of the Civil War, President Lincoln suspended habeas corpus and sent troops to Maryland who imprisoned large numbers of secessionists. Nevertheless, Marylanders fought on both sides, and families were often split. General Lee's Army of Northern Virginia invaded Maryland in 1862 and was repulsed by Union forces at Antietam. In 1863, Lee again invaded the North and marched across Maryland on the way to and from Gettysburg. Throughout the war Maryland was the scene of many minor battles and skirmishes.

Industrialization

With the end of the Civil War, industry quickly revived and became a dominant force in Maryland, both economically and politically. Senator Arthur P. Gorman, a Democrat and the president of the Baltimore & Ohio Railroad, ran the controlling political machine from 1869 to 1895, when two-party government was restored. New railroad lines traversed the state, making it more than ever a crossing point between North and South. Labor troubles hit Maryland with the Panic of 1873, and four years later railroad wage disputes resulted in large-scale rioting in Cumberland and Baltimore. During the 20th century, however, Maryland became a leader in labor and other reform legislation. The administrations of governors Austin L. Crowthers (1908-1912) and Albert C. Ritchie (1920-1935) were noted for reform. Ritchie, a Democrat, became nationally known for his efforts to improve the efficiency and economy of state government.

The great influx of people into the state during World War I was repeated and accelerated in World War II as war workers poured into Baltimore, where vital shipbuilding and aircraft plants were in operation. In addition, military and other government employees moved into the area around Washington, DC.

Growth Since World War II

Since World War II, public-works legislation, particularly that concerning roads and other traffic arteries, has brought major changes. The opening of the Chesapeake Bay Bridge in 1952 spurred

significant industrial expansion on the Eastern Shore; a parallel bridge was opened in 1973. The Patapsco River tunnel under Baltimore harbor was completed in 1957, and the Francis Scott Key Bridge (1977), crosses the Patapsco. Other construction projects have included the Baltimore-Washington International Airport, formerly called Friendship International Airport (1950), south of Baltimore, and the Baltimore-Washington Parkway (1954). The state gained a different kind of attention in 1968 when its governor, Spiro T. Agnew was elected vice president.

Maryland experienced tremendous suburban growth in the 1980s, especially in the metropolitan Washington, DC, area. This growth occurred in spite of a decline in government jobs, as service sector employment rose dramatically. Suburban Baltimore grew as well although the city proper lost 6.4 percent of its population during the 1980s. Baltimore undertook major revitalization projects in the 1980s and the early 1990s, including the construction of Oriole Park at Camden Yards, the new home of the Baltimore Orioles baseball team.

Maryland has become increasingly popular as a vacation area—Ocean City is a popular seashore resort, and both sides of Chesapeake Bay are lined with beaches and small fishing towns. The Chesapeake Bay Bridge has brought the culture of the Eastern Shore, formerly quite distinctive, into a more homogeneous unity with that of the rest of the state; the area, however, is still noted for its unique rural beauty and architecture, strongly reminiscent of the English countryside left behind by early settlers.

MASSACHUSETTS[83]

Massachusetts: Indian meaning "large hill place"
Statehood: February 6, 1788 (6th state)
Motto: *Ense petit placidam sub libertate quietem* (By the sword we seek peace, but peace only under liberty)
Familiar Name: The Bay State
50-State Tour: The Mother of Our Nation, July 14-15, 2004

On July 14 and 15, 2004, Dr. Chuck Pierce (Glory of Zion Ministries) and Pastor Dutch Sheets (Dutch Sheets Ministries), came to Boston to deliver their message to our State. They traveled to every state, being led by God, to help align the Body properly and to decree the Lord's redemptive plan for that state. When it was time for God's covenant people to leave Egypt, the Lord brought them out by armies. We are declaring that His Prayer Army arise in each state.

We began by reading Psalm 47 (clap your hands, shout to God with a voice of triumph). The hand clap is like a trumpet sound and is the same word used for driving in a tent peg. So hand claps are like Jael when she drove the tent peg into Cisera's head. When we praise with the hand clap we are breaking the headship of the enemy over our lives. So much has come out of Massachusetts, *but a new sound is coming from Massachusetts.*

> "I have gathered you in this place this night to create a sound of conflict throughout this city and state—releasing that sound of conflict now—even though the enemy has home field advantage—there is a shout of victory that is creating confusion in the enemy's camp that is being released tonight. It only ***appears*** that the enemy of My covenant is winning—there is a roar that is greater than the roar of the devourer,

that is rooted in this particular city [Boston]. That roar is rising; that roar is gaining strength and the other 49 [states] are beginning to roar with you. The call from My house in this city…is extended to this entire nation— and when the call is heard, it will be like the shot heard round the world. For there is a sound of conflict on My covenant that has arisen in this place tonight. The enemy has a voice that will sound loud over the next six months—[he] will shout "treason, treason" from this state, but the shout from My House will cause the shout of treason to fall to the ground. Let the conflict begin! The voice of My people will be heard louder than the voice of the enemy in this state. There is one in this state in your midst that will fall, another that rises up—do not look at falling and rising, but watch My hand begin to move because it will be a sign to this land that I have come to put some down, rise others up to restructure justice in this land." (Prophesied by Chuck D. Pierce.)

Four Points for Massachusetts—How We Move Forward in This Nation

1. We must have full faith.
2. We must enter into the weapons of deliverance—stir them up.
3. We must frustrate the enemy.
4. We must fight for our covenant.

Chuck Pierce shared: The Body of Christ must follow in faith for our provision. The Church is going to have great influence in this state, but first it comes into such great conflict, that we must know how to frustrate the enemy's purpose and also how to hide ourselves when the enemy comes back at us. We must stir up the enemy but the Lord will give us supernatural covering and cause us to walk through Him. Quote what He says about us: "This is who we are!"

Massachusetts has been a state where there are no absolute truths. Do not be afraid. We must be aware of religious and political spirits that will try to align themselves together to frustrate God's purposes (see Mark 3:6—Pharisees and Herodians). It is never just the government; it must have religious backing. Much confusion will come from God—stirring up the enemy so much, but we will walk through it.

> Chuck Pierce prophesied: We must develop watchman strategy in this state where the house is being watched after, and watching after leadership and the House of God (not the state and the city) because of righteous seed in the house that have the seed to dethrone the enemy. The Lord says, "I'm calling My people to watch after My house in this state and to rally My house together so My house is watching and being watched after. If you begin to move in that, I will give you authority to remove a structure that is ruling in this state at a particular place of choice in this state. [You will have] more influence—enough is enough. I'm changing the atmosphere. I'll show you how to follow into the next place of provision when the dry up comes. I'll show you how to have a full faith to move forward so you can win this war."

Know how to sidestep the enemy's confusion and plan and keep moving; break the spirit of defeat off of us. We come back toward the covenant You have established; we work back toward the agreement

You have with us. And anything stopping a fullness of Your covenant blessing from coming in we put on notice; you will be dethroned in Jesus' name.

Pastor Dutch Sheets shared:

* God is coming to bring a Great Awakening to snatch many from hell!
* God is going to break through in Massachusetts and many of His enemies will become His friends.
* God will transform the curses into blessings.

Massachusetts is the mother of our nation—the state that represents the very birth and development of a nation.

Here is a prayer by Chuck D. Pierce:

> Father, just as You're raising up the Boston baseball team, Father, You are breaking a curse off of this city that has... held the city. Word curses that always said that it would be second; it would never move forward; it would never overcome. Father, we say that there is an overcoming anointing penetrating the Massachusetts area and moving through Boston at this time. Father, we thank You that You are beginning to break desolation. We thank You that the river will flow through Boston in a whole new way. The Lord says, "**Go to the river. You watch Me change the waterways. You watch Me change the course of things.**" Father, I want to thank You for what You're doing. Lord,

> I thank You for the anointing You're bringing in there. Lord, I thank You that what the enemy had planned You're going to do the opposite. Lord, I decree right now that a shout of victory will spread all over, all over Boston. Now Father, I thank You for Massachusetts. I thank You for the anointing. Lord, we anoint them with power and authority over death. Lord, we anoint them with healing. Lord, we anoint them to break out of every wilderness spot. We anoint them to pull down the promises. Lord, we anoint them to create new fields that have been closed. Lord, we anoint them to rise above the enemy's land. Lord, we anoint them to come through and pioneer a whole new work. We anoint them for a preaching anointing to move all across Boston. We anoint them for the captives to be set free. Lord, we thank You for the mantle—the Lord says there's going to be a field of healing. Lord, we release that anointing all over Boston, in Jesus' name. Amen.

Other Key Points

Get ready to follow in a new form of provision. The Lord will move in *new way of supply* and provision in Massachusetts. *God will break a poverty mentality off His people in Massachusetts.*

God will show the Church how to follow Him in a new way. When one thing dries up, shift and be willing to go to new environment. Watch what the Lord will do, for many things are drying up in Massachusetts. Elijah had to leave the brook and move to Zeraphath. Do not resist moving, and do not lean on your own understanding in the next three years in Massachusetts for your provision.

Get ready to start moving in a new dimension of *Word of Knowledge*. This gift will be activated in Massachusetts. There are resources in the midst of your state that the Lord will show you supernaturally. Remember, once the widow in Zeraphath overcame self-pity, she and her son were sustained and had plenty for 3.5 years.

A Brief Massachusetts History[84]

When Europeans first explored Massachusetts, about 30,000 Indians from the Algonquian tribes lived in the area. When the Pilgrims arrived in 1620, many had already died of diseases brought to America from the Europeans. Only 7,000 Native Americans remained in Massachusetts at that time.

Englishman John Cabot sighted the coast of Massachusetts in 1498. In 1605, Samuel de Champlain charted maps of the New England coastline. John Smith sailed up the coast of Massachusetts in 1614.

Two main groups came to America in search of religious freedom. In December of 1620, Pilgrims sailed across Cape Cod Bay and settled Plymouth Colony. They suffered greatly their first winter and about half the settlers died. The following year, the Indians taught them how to plant corn and beans. When winter came they had enough food, and better shelter. The Pilgrims celebrated the first Thanksgiving in 1621 and gave thanks to God for delivering them from hardship. Many Pilgrims continued to come in following years.

The second group, the Puritans led by John Winthrop, founded Massachusetts Bay Colony in Boston in 1630. This group established political freedom in 1641 with a document called The Body of Liberties. They allowed only their religious beliefs into the colony.

In 1662, King Philip became chief of the Wampanoag Indian tribe when his father died. He feared the white settlers would overtake Indian land. To protect his people, in 1675 King Philip's War began. Hundreds of people died as settlements and villages were burned. Colonists killed King Philip in 1676 and ended the war.

The French and Indian Wars (1689-1763) brought continued battles on the north and west boundaries of Massachusetts. A peace treaty was signed in the Netherlands in 1713, which allowed considerable growth in the central and western areas of Massachusetts. However, wars broke out again in 1740 until victory for Britain in 1763.

To pay for the wars, Britain placed heavy taxes upon the colonists. The Stamp Act of 1765 led to the phrase "no taxation without representation." British soldiers stationed in Boston killed several colonists while fighting a mob. This became known as the Boston Massacre. The Boston Tea Party in 1773 brought more punishment upon the colonists, but this only unified them. On April 18, 1775, Paul Revere rode across Massachusetts to warn that the British were coming. The next day, colonists fought the opening battle of the Revolutionary War at Lexington.

Much of the early fighting took place in Massachusetts. During March of 1776, Washington drove the British out of Boston with the first major American victory in the war. Most of the fighting then moved south.

Massachusetts ratified the Constitution and became the 6th state of the Union on [February] 6, 1788. They insisted on an amendment of individual rights. The Bill of Rights went into effect in 1791.

With France and Britain at war, President Thomas Jefferson passed the Embargo Act in 1807. This stopped all exports to other countries and forced manufacturing within the United States. The first textile mill in the nation was built in 1814 in Waltham. By 1860, Massachusetts led the nation in production of textiles and shoes.

Many people in Massachusetts led the antislavery movement in the 1830s. The New England Anti-Slavery Society in Boston helped slaves to escape to Canada. Strong support was given to the Union during the Civil War (1861-1865); over 145,000 people served from Massachusetts.

After the war, the textile industry grew and other industries expanded. Many immigrants came to work in factories with poor working conditions. In 1912, workers in Lawrence went on a strike that brought national attention. Working conditions improved after that.

After World War I, many companies moved south from the state. The Great Depression caused many to lose jobs. By 1931, less than half of all workers in Massachusetts had full-time jobs. World War II brought change to the economy in 1939. Huge quantities of war materials were produced in the state's factories. Industries changed to research and electrical equipment production. In 1960, a nuclear power plant started operating in Rowe.

Massachusetts' economy has been improving steadily since the 1970s. Textile production has gone down, but high-technology industries are expanding. The state is one of the top leaders in the nation for military research, education, banking, government assistance and medical care. Tourism is also expanding.

Today, leaders are striving to improve air and water pollution, housing shortages, and racial issues.

MICHIGAN[85]

Michigan: Chippewa meaning "great lake"
Statehood: January 26, 1837 (26th state)
Motto: *Si Quaeris Peninuslam Amoenam, Circumspice* (If You Are Looking for a Beautiful Peninsula, Look Around You)
Familiar Name: The Wolverine State
50-State Tour: A State with a Restored Voice, April 3-5, 2003

Through the 50-State Tour, Michigan's voice as well as its keys were returned so that it could become the "door" in 2004. Already, there has been a major turning in the state, and there are signs of beginning revival. Pontiac, Michigan, is experiencing a beginning of breakthrough in both the churches/pastors and government coming together. That is spilling over into Detroit. There is a breakthrough that has begun in Detroit that will be followed through, which includes the mayor of the city. We have experienced a breakthrough of revelation that released strategy through the 50-State Tour and now are following the strategy through to see transformation begin to occur. What has been happening is miraculous.

What follows is how the "voice" issue emerged at the 50-State Tour meeting. Dutch Sheets was led of the Lord to teach on a people's losing their voice. What Dutch did not know was that a former mayor of Detroit had actually given Saddam Hussein the keys to the city. Thus, the Church in that region lost their voice as the door to another religious structure was opened.

Transcription of Exhortation from Chuck D. Pierce

During the First Night of the 50-State Tour Meeting

Of course, there's a documented article of when the keys of Detroit were given to Saddam Hussein. And I think that's just indicative of what's happened in this area over and over. The keys are always being given away some way—in an inappropriate way. But while we're here, some way or another the spirit has deceived and taken the keys to this region. And once that happens, that is a huge issue. It might just sound like, well, that was just an ignorant thing. It's really not like that. Because when money is exchanged the way that occurred, that is a covenant transaction; and that is a covenant transaction with the enemy that will give right for the spirits to activate that through Detroit, to demise this nation.

My assignment to you is, as you wake up during the night, as we're here these three days, we must ask the Lord how to get these keys back from the enemy, because it gives the enemy legal right to this region. I'm not talking about a person; I'm talking about a spirit. If it doesn't happen through that person, it'll happen through another person. Now hear me, because that has been done here with an exchange of $250,000. A huge door of destruction is now open over our nation, and it's representative of the religious spirit that dwells in this region, that deceives this region to make false alliances and wrong alliances.

These Keys Must Come Back

What our brother [Dutch] is preaching here is a word from the Lord. These keys must come back into the authority of God's apostolic realm, [which] He is allowing to be established now. And then, that gate must be shut now, or else you will see an eruption that comes through this nation that will shake us all. And it's because it has legal right to come in. We also stood in Florida, and we said that thing that will try to come through the keys in Florida will be stopped, and we've already had instances all week of things being stopped that have tried to come through there. Now I'm telling you, it is an open door in this area that will cause this nation to reap great destruction, and the next generation to end up in a demise.

Therefore, we must ask the Lord—and I don't want us to get into any presumption, either, because I don't know how to get the keys back from this demon that was given the keys, too. And so, what we've got to ask the Lord—it's taken a whole military to go over there and try to get the key back. [The Coalition forces were literally surrounding Baghdad, Iraq, at that time and waiting to apprehend Saddam Hussein.] Now hear me, what we're saying here to you—this thing is huge in this region. These three days, and how this shift in atmosphere occurs is going to cause this nation to go in a certain direction. So just lift your hands. I'm going to pray over you.

Now Father, You've gathered us here for a time such as this.... Lord, we declare right now these gates must be shut this weekend some way. Now Lord, we come, and we don't want to come presumptuously; we don't want to say anything yet presumptuously. Lord, we have heard this message tonight. Lord, it is a word from You. And Father, You've got to form in our mouth the very authority from Heaven that will cause the keys to be returned to this region and the gate of hell shut over this region. Now Father, we ask You how to do this.

Lord, We Need These Keys Back

Lord, I'm going to ask for a spirit of revelation. I'm going to ask for a protective shield over everyone in this region. Lord, I'm going to ask

You right now to begin to just come on us, enter into us, in the middle of the night. Lord, just have us say, "Lord, we need these keys back. We need these keys back. We need these keys back in place. We need the gates shut. We need this gate shut in this region." Now Father, I know You have gathered us here. If Gideon could change a whole nation, this group can shut the door and this gate of hell that is open over this nation. So Father, we come and we say, "Here we are. We are Your servants. Lead us forth in the spirit realm to shut this gate that needs to be shut," in Jesus' name."

Just begin to pray with someone next to you. Thank God where there's two touching and agreeing, that which God is wanting to do in Heaven will be done. He wants these keys back in place, and He wants this gate in this region shut, in Jesus' name.

> Father, we thank You this thing is going to turn. We have complete confidence that it will turn these three days, and even that the destruction and the hell that is going on in Iraq we will see a shift occur, in Jesus' name.

All I can do is say give a shout of victory in advance!

Subsequent Remarks from Dutch Sheets

...I know now why the Lord wouldn't go in a different direction tonight, but made me do this message. Now there would be those who would be naïve enough to say that it's a coincidence that we are here for these three days when the troops finally get to Baghdad to take the keys away from him in the natural. He brought us here to do our part, in the spirit, because they can't do it without us. One of several things would happen; either something would just go horribly wrong, and great devastation would happen in the process, or that thing would just go underground for a year or two or three years, and pop up someplace else.

I'm telling you right now, the Lord brought us here for these three days to do our part in the spirit. We're going to take those keys away from that spirit. It's not about a man—Saddam Hussein; it's about the spirit of Babylon. That same spirit that Daniel dealt with, that same spirit that you read about there. This is what this is all about, and this is the place where this nation's in. You can have the keys to America, you can have the key to this region; but I'm telling you, Chuck's right. It wasn't just for this region. It was the nation. Now we're going to do our part. We're going to do the "Battle over Baghdad," as it were. We're going to do our battle. We're going to do our part to get the keys taken back, while they do their part.

This is very fascinating to me, in a very holy way. I don't know how the Lord does this stuff. I'm telling you, I don't know how He does this stuff. You couldn't have put this together; you couldn't have set this up. You can't do that. I mean, you can't have them there marching and the timing of it; and then they get to Baghdad, and we gather here. And there are the keys, and we gave them to Saddam; and they're over there taking them, and we're going to take them in the spirit. You can't set that kind of thing up. You can't do it. *I'm telling you, this is about more than just even blessing on this nation. This is about unlocking the door to the Muslim world. I'm telling you, this is all about unlocking the door.*

Brief Michigan History[86]

Native American Foundations—Council, Resources, and Land Curses

Throughout Michigan's history our people have had the ability to gain, speak and mobilize council. Initially it was Native Americans who used the land for this purpose. Sault Ste. Marie was the council grounds between the eastern portion of Canada and the United States. Along with its ability to council, Michigan's land has great resources, [and it] is a place of innovation and invention that has influenced the nation and world. Our nation's first factory was built by the Native Americans in Alpena, Michigan. It was mainly a thunderbird god factory. They manufactured and traded icon trinkets from Canada to the western United States and south towards to Florida. This set a precedent for religious spirits being linked with manufacturing, to establish it outside of the presence of the Lord as did Cain.

Michigan is surrounded by key waterways and inland trails, which made it a key location for Natives to council and establish trade from our resources. Eventually First Nations people sought to control those resources through war. Over the course of time, conflicts among the First Nations over the land and resources, turning Southeast Michigan into a warring treacherous, murdering territory. Curses were laid upon the people and land to such a degree that we find these curses active today.

French and British Foundations—Military and Government Headquarters

The French and British interest was in land ownership and profiting through resources in the land. Michigan was key because of its waterway access and land trails that proved to be the fastest and most inexpensive way to penetrate the nation (for ownership and profiteering). To gain control of this northern door to our nation, both the French and British established military and government headquarters to give them an advantage in controlling nations and lands around them. Key leaders of both the British and French in the 18-19 century repeated the history of Native Americans through the wrongful shedding of blood (murder), aversion to other cultures, dealing treacherously and deceitfully in trade and in gaining control of the land.

During this era, Detroit earned a place of significance. It became the headquarters or center to the Armed Forces of each nation. It was a place from which each nation directed invasions into the Midwest region of the U.S. By 1805, the Michigan Territory was created. Detroit was designated as the seat of government. Also Detroit was the first city after Washington, DC, to pattern itself after the Masonic layout of a city. In 1837, Michigan was admitted to the Union as the 26th state and Detroit served as our first state capital.

20th Century—Detroit, Ford, Anti-Semitism

In the 20th century, Michigan became a place of invention and innovation which changed the entire nation. Detroit was the birth place and leader of car manufacturing (1908) and became the "Motor City" and automotive capital of the world. In 1941 automobile plants in Detroit area were converted for the production of war materials, helping Michigan become known as the "Arsenal of Democracy."[87] Warren, Michigan (a suburb of Detroit), was the center for the production of tanks for the Armed Forces.

These efforts above were due to Henry Ford, founder of Ford Automotive. Ford, in *US News and World Report*, was called the most influential man in the 20th century.[88] His influence reached beyond car manufacturing to become a major force behind and disseminator of anti-Semitic thought and literature in Michigan as well as the US. He funded the publication and dissemination of anti-Semitic materials in nine languages. His town, Dearborn, Michigan (under Mayor Hubbard's reign), would not allow Jews or Blacks to live within the city limits. He funded Hitler's efforts for a season (until Hitler began to invade Poland); influenced the writing of Hitler's book, *Mein Kampf*. Ford also became a 33rd degree Mason[89] (not by study but by paying to be one) and strongly backed the Masonic order. Ford's actions strengthened the foundation for anti-Semitism in this state.

Ford's actions were treacherous for Jews and Blacks, murderous (in the way that he funded and agreed with the killing of Jews), anti-Semitic, and deceitful. (Dearborn headquarters endorsed Ford Germany supplying Hitler during the war.) It is important to note that Ford's grandson has begun to undo what Ford did by funding such things as the Holocaust Museum in Southfield, [Michigan].

Detroit as of two years ago was the most prejudiced city in the nation.[90] Greater Detroit now has the largest and most concentrated Arab and Islamic population outside the Middle East.[91] Since 9/11 the region has been even more volatile. What occurs in the Mideast strongly affects Detroit through the reaction of Arabic or Islamic people living in Detroit, Dearborn. Detroit experienced the highest population decline in the nation between 2000-2003.[92] It had the highest job-loss rate in the nation in April 2004. It has the highest death rate in the nation[93] among children younger than 18 (68 percent above the national average)[94] and is considered to be the most violent city in the nation.[95]

Conclusion

The state is making progress. The Upper Peninsula is advancing. AGLOW International held a conference there in May 2004 on Native American land. A number of Native Americans attended the conference. We are seeing some breakthrough in reconciling our relationships with Native Americans, partnering with them for this territory.

We have positioned the state apostolically and prophetically to breakthrough in every county, region and major city but two. We are advancing and on the verge of breakthrough in many areas. Great faith and confidence are returning to Michigan.

MINNESOTA[96]

Minnesota: Sioux meaning "sky-colored water"
Statehood: May 11, 1858 (32nd state)
Motto: *L'Etoile du Nord* (The Star of the North)
Familiar Name: The North Star State
50-State Tour: The Threshing Floor State, August 4-5, 2003

An entire book, *The Threshing Floor*, has actually been written to capture our 50-State Tour meeting in Minnesota. With this book, Rick Heeren has created a tremendous prophetic blueprint for how to pray to see a state transformed. This book will become a model for transformation in days ahead. If every state in our nation will "prepare" at the same level that Rick and Minnesota are preparing, then we will see one of the greatest moves of God that our nation has ever known.

Brief Minnesota History[97]

Humans first came to Minnesota during the last ice age, following herds of large game as the glaciers melted. Long before the first Europeans arrived, Indians from as far away as 1,000 miles came to make ceremonial pipes from soft [red] pipestone carved from sacred quarries. The Pipestone National Monument in southwest Minnesota illustrates how these quarries were and still are used.

Five thousand years ago, humans made rock carvings of people, animals, and weapons that can be seen today at Jeffers Petroglyphs in southwest Minnesota. These people also brought to Minnesota the idea of building earth mounds for graves and sacred ceremonies. At one time, there were more than 10,000 of these mounds in Minnesota.

When the first French fur traders, or voyageurs, arrived in the late 1600s, the Dakota (or Sioux) people had lived in Minnesota for many years. They hunted buffalo, fished, planted corn, beans, and squash, and harvested northern beds of wild rice. They lived in warm skin tipis in the winter and had airy bark houses, or wigwams, for the summer. The Anishinabe (or Ojibwe, also Chippewa) people moved into Minnesota from the east. They lived much like the Dakota, but from the French fur traders they obtained metal tools and weapons, cloth, blankets, and ornaments. By 1800, the Anishinabe had taken over the lakes and woods of the north.

In the early 1800s, the U.S. government said it needed more land in this area. The Dakota signed a treaty with the U.S. government for the land where the Minnesota River joins the Mississippi, and, in the 1820s, Fort Snelling was built there. During the years that followed, the Dakota and Anishinabe tribes were forced to sign treaties to relinquish most of Minnesota to the U.S. government. Thousands of new people poured into the region to build farms and cut timber. In 1858, Minnesota became the 32nd state.

By 1862, the Dakota were crowded into a small reservation along the Minnesota River. Times were bad and Indian families went hungry. When the U.S. government broke its promises, some of the Dakota went to war against the white farmers and towns. Many of the Dakota did not join in, but the fighting lasted six weeks; and many people on both sides were killed or fled Minnesota. Afterwards the government forced most of the remaining Dakota to leave Minnesota. The Anishinabe stayed in northern Minnesota, and were not involved in the war.

The Dakota who stayed and those who eventually returned have formed four communities in southern Minnesota. There are seven Anishinabe Indian reservations in northern Minnesota. Many of the Indian people and their families who moved to the cities after World War II have continued to live there. Wherever they live, Minnesota's Indians are maintaining their cultural identities.

Large number of immigrants came to Minnesota beginning in the 1830s to work in lumbering and farming. They were mainly from the eastern United States, Canada, and northern Europe. By 1900, the combined total of Scandinavians from Norway, Sweden, and Denmark outnumbered those from any single country. Later, as cities and new industries grew, people came also from eastern and southern Europe. Finland, Yugoslavia, and Italy sent many workers to Minnesota mines and factories. In 1900, nearly half of all Minnesotans were of German ancestry.

A few people of African descent had come with the early fur traders and soldiers. More moved to Minnesota after the Civil War, living and working mainly in the cities. By the 1920s, many migrant farm workers of Mexican descent had come to the state. In the 1990 census, 53,884

Minnesotans were of Spanish-speaking ancestry. By the 2000 census, that number had grown to 143,382. In the 1980s, Minnesota became home to many Southeast Asian refugees who left Vietnam, Cambodia, and Laos because of the Vietnam War and its aftermath. The biggest of these groups is the Hmong people group from Laos, who now number around 80,000.

MISSISSIPPI[98]

Mississippi: Choctaw meaning "father of waters"
Statehood: December 10, 1817 (20th state)
Motto: *Virtute et Armis* (By Valor and Arms)
Familiar Name: The Magnolia State
50-State Tour: The State in the Valley of Decision, February 17-18, 2003

The meeting of 1,000 people began with incredible worship. Then the following word came forth:

> "You stand at the valley of decision over this nation. I have gathered you to this place. Even when I determined to gather you, I had determined to turn this land at the crossroads. The nation stands at the crossroads. Decisions are being made to set the course I will determine. Agree with Me that only My decisions will be made. Even the waters are in turmoil! Even the waters are in turmoil! I have brought you to this city to determine the course of war of waters. I long to be in authority over waves and seas. Even now the water is being churned and conflict is going forth. You have authority to determine what that course will be and adversity on the waters will not

> bring defeat to My covenant plan." (Prophesied by Chuck D. Pierce.)

The Lord wanted to release the host of Heaven to earth. The shofars were blown, and we declared the host of Heaven was free to enter into the earth realm.

Dutch Sheets had a vision of individual pockets of breakthrough, but there was no ability for these pockets to converge or move into the heavenlies in a united symphony of agreement over the entire state. He declared a convergence of these pockets of light across Mississippi. He also saw an item being unfurled that was being cut to shreds and burned, as well as a tapestry woven over the state becoming a banner of the Lord. He went on to share about the incredible destiny of the state of Mississippi. "If there wasn't some incredible potential and destiny in assignment, the enemy would not have fought so hard to control Mississippi and create the strongholds and structures and things that he has, that has held you back.... Mississippi is at one of the greatest crossroads of any group of people that I have ever ministered to in my life.... This state, your destiny, whether you move on in the Lord, you are so in the balance. It is almost like you are the most complete microcosm in this state of what I see for this nation. This is the determining year—so many things for this nation. But I don't know if I have been in a state yet where I felt the same thing that I can say about the nation—of this being the year that would determine the future.... There is something about this state right now that is very important to the Lord. And the Lord is really raising the bar for Mississippi."

> There is a burning wind coming from Heaven to Mississippi. "I have pronounced judgment and am coming with My holy fire. There is a short opportunity for grace. Don't think I will

be stopped or alter My course; I am coming to do this, and I will not be stopped!" (Prophesied by Chuck D. Pierce.)

Chuck taught on changing your mind and your thinking. Mississippi must see that the old season has ended and they must move into the new. He also saw a tent of worship stretched over the state with ten poles supporting it. The ten poles would be where worship would be key.

> "I am going to raise a center pole in Jackson. I am going to change the covering over you and put My glory over you. Watch the center pole rise and establish ten anchor poles. Call to rise up now. Call to gather. Call to worship Me. Call to come before Me and celebrate....I want to become at home with you in Mississippi.... If you raise the tent, harvest will be under it, and you will see Me sweep this state." (Prophesied by Chuck D. Pierce.)
>
> He also prophesied, "I'm going to break the power over you that keeps you from entering My joy and liberty. I love you and will overtake you. Don't be afraid to align differently and make mistakes, for I will cover your mistakes. You've thought with fear that if you don't do right, then the enemy will gain access. I will set a standard! Change your mind and break the power of superstition, and My glory will invade the land."

The meaning of *Mississippi* is "father of waters." God wants to break the orphan spirit off of Mississippi and raise up the apostolic mantle. *"I visited you in the '60s and '70s to bring forth apostolic mantle, but you shifted and lost this. I am bringing a fathering anointing in this state. The isolation on you will break. From this you will see much fruit come forth."* (Prophesied by Chuck D. Pierce.)

Brief Mississippi History

In the winter of 1540 Hernando de Soto led a large expedition into Mississippi and wintered along the Pontotoc River. In the following spring he reached the Mississippi River, but because he found no gold or silver in the region, Spanish explorers directed their efforts elsewhere.

Nearly 130 years later a small group of French Canadians sailed down the Mississippi River and immediately realized its commercial and strategic importance. In 1699 a French expedition led by Pierre le Moyne d'Iberville established France's claim to the lower Mississippi valley. French settlements were soon established at Fort Maurepas, Mobile, Biloxi, Fort Rosalie, and New Orleans.

Following the French and Indian War in 1763, France ceded its possessions in the lower Mississippi valley, except New Orleans, to Great Britain, which also gained possession of Spanish Florida and divided that territory into two colonies. One of those was West Florida, which included the area between the Apalachicola and Mississippi rivers. Fort Rosalie was renamed Fort Panmure, and the Natchez District was established as a subdivision of West Florida. Natchez flourished during the early 1770s. After the outbreak of the U.S. War of Independence, Spain regained possession of Florida and occupied Natchez. The Treaty of Paris of 1783 fixed the 31st parallel as the boundary between Spanish Florida and the United States, but Spain continued to occupy Natchez until the dispute was settled in 1798.

The original Mississippi Territory, created by the U.S. Congress in 1798, was a strip of land extending about 100 miles north to south and from the Mississippi River to the Chattahoochee on the Georgia border. The territory was increased in 1804 and 1812 to reach from Tennessee to the Gulf of Mexico. In 1817 the western part achieved statehood as Mississippi (the eastern part became the state of Alabama in 1819). Natchez, the first territorial capital, was replaced in 1802 by nearby Washington, which in turn was replaced by Jackson in 1822.[99]

When Mississippi became a State in December of 1817, the Choctaw Indians still retained Federally recognized claims to over three-fourths of the land within the State's boundaries. …The Federal government under President Andrew Jackson, pursuing a policy of Indian removal from lands east of the Mississippi River, pressure the tribe into ceding the last of its lands in the Treaty of Dancing Rabbit Creek in 1830.

This treaty ultimately resulted in the migration of about two-thirds of the Choctaw Tribe to the Oklahoma Territory over the next fifty years…. [By March of 2000,] the Mississippi Band of Choctaw Indians [was] a Federally recognized tribe of 8,400 members, with a small reservation of 29,000 scattered acres in seven communities in East Central Mississippi.[100]

The 1820s and 1830s were marked by the decline of the Jeffersonian Republicans, the ascendancy of the Jacksonian Democrats, as well as the removal of the Indians to Oklahoma. They were the days of steamboats, land speculation, and the growth of a plantation-based cotton economy and a slave population. Slave owning, however, was not common among the small landowners, who became more numerous than the large planters but who had little influence on public affairs for many years.

Sectionalism in both North and South had been growing for some time. Its ill feelings gradually became dominated in both North and South by slavery. In January 1861, a convention adopted an ordinance of secession, and within a year the state was in the midst of war. The people suffered much privation, and the land underwent great devastation; by 1865 the state was in economic ruin.

For 25 years following the Civil War, Mississippi's former slaves and their former owners grappled with the political, social, and economic consequences of emancipation. The white minority could not or would not accept a biracial society based on equality of opportunity. In 1890 the ruling elite adopted a constitution that established a caste system of racial segregation and an economic order that kept blacks in a position of dependency. Mississippians hoped to find economic salvation in the coming of industry and the railroads, but the hope was only partially realized. Emancipation had made the former slaves free to go where they wished, but most remained and eventually were absorbed into the tenant-farming system. The continued economic interdependence of the two races kept intact many of the customs and social systems that had developed before the war.[101]

The "separate, but equal" Jim Crow laws were followed up by the constitution of 1890, effectively disfranchising most of the black population. After the turn of the (20th) century, the Supreme Court began to overturn Jim Crow laws on constitutional grounds. In 1964 the Congress passed the Civil Rights Act, outlawing discrimination and attacking these laws and practices.[102]

MISSOURI[103, 104]

> **Missouri:** Algonquian meaning "canoe haver"
> **Statehood:** August 10, 1821 (24th state)
> **Motto:** Salus populi supreme lex esto (The welfare of the people shall be the supreme law)
> **Familiar Name:** The Show-Me State
> **50-State Tour:** The Show Me Your Glory State, October 30-31, 2003

Last night, you could just feel the presence of God, and Pastor Dutch led us in that. The glory of God is coming to Missouri!

I saw the word "Assemblies." And I really thought—Isaiah 4. Your mind is to aid your spirit. Your mind is not the ruling force of your life. Your mind and your heart and your spirit are interchangeable in the Word of God. But the Holy Spirit dwells in your spirit, and your mind has been given to you to aid the Spirit of God, to help you interpret God's ways—not to rule over the way that you think and what you do.

> "...But I keep going back to the Assemblies [of God]. You've got to hear this. You can end by drinking just what was there, or you can press on in until supernaturally you get what is ahead for you. That's a word to this state and everything in this state. This hasn't been said to any other state. I have no idea why God looks at you like that, but it's very clear that's how He's looking at you. There are certain things that He wants you to review, and what has not been completed He wants completed. But then, He also wants to unlock what's ahead for you.

- ★ "There's something very, very key about the state. It has more rivers than any other state. Declare that we'll have all the rivers of God flowing here!

- ★ "If your destiny is now '*Show me Your Glory*,' this becomes very significant to you. What it says to you is that you are ending a season. You've experienced good, but now you're headed into the next dimension of best. And you will be a model of that best.

- ★ "I actually saw four cities in Missouri transformed. I saw this by the Spirit last night during worship. I am going to tell you that once the glory of God visits them, the whole state will begin to quake under His glory. I don't know enough about Missouri to know where the cities are, but I see them, and they are there" (Chuck D. Pierce).

Then Dutch Sheets went on to say, "You are not going to succeed through past methods and formulas—how you did it before. You are going to have to listen for the sound. Now listen, that's the word for you, Missouri. I'm telling you. That's the word for you. *You are going to have to hear from God and listen.* You don't need the whole state to be doing it. You don't need the majority of Christians to be joining you. You just need whoever shows up. Don't wait for this thing, to where you feel like we've got to get 'X' amount of pastors on board, 'X' amount of churches, 'X' amount of people, and if we don't get it, we can't do it."

> Chuck prophesied, "This is a time that I am coming, I am coming, and I have surprises, and I have releases that I'm bringing to this state. The captives that have been held, this state will be known as one who opened the prison doors....I

> will say to you today, what I do in this state and how I use this state will tingle the ears of this nation. Put your ear to the ground for this will be a group that will run faster than the horses in Missouri. And they will say about Missouri, we didn't even know they have horses, but I am setting a course in Missouri, that will control and open up the gates of this land. My hand is now upon you."

Dutch said, "He (God) said I am going to show the 'show me' state signs and wonders and great miracles. Because when the cloud comes you can't help but have signs and wonders and miracles. And you can't help but have harvest because impregnation, conception, occurs and the seed of life is deposited and something comes forth."

Missouri, help is on the way! God is going to show His glory to the "Show Me" state. The river of God will flow through Missouri bringing signs, wonders, and miracles. God is releasing the "seer" anointing, opening the eyes of Missouri to see prophetically. Four cities will have a release of evangelism that will overtake them: Kansas City, Saint Louis, Jefferson City, and Carthage. Missouri is to have 24 simultaneous worship gatherings that will lift worship in Missouri to a new level. This state will set the captives free. Isaiah 49 declares, "Come out!" "Be free!"

Brief Missouri History

It is believed that the first Europeans to visit Missouri's land were De Soto, Father Jacques Marquette, and Louis Joliet in the 17th century, proceeded by Robert Cavelier, Sieur de La Salle who claimed the area west of the Mississippi for France naming it the Louisiana Territory. The Louisiana Territory was secretly given to Spain, then returned back to France and sold to the U.S. by Napoleon Bonaparte. The seat of government for the territory was in Saint Louis, which was also the departure point for the Lewis and Clark expedition into the Pacific Northwest.

Missouri has been called the "Mother of the West" or the "Gateway to the West" because it was a starting point for much exploration and travel. The Oregon and Santa Fe Trails began in Missouri, as well as the Butterfield Overland Mail route and the Pony Express.

Fur trading and mining were the major activities of Missouri in the earlier years. The business of mining brought the first blacks to Missouri as slaves. Fort Osage was built overlooking the Missouri River and was governed by William Clarke. Many military and trade alliances were made between the white settlers and Indians, particularly with the Osage tribe. As settlement increased in the area, Indians became upset over the loss of their ancient hunting grounds and began raiding frontier settlements.

In 1812, a portion of the Louisiana Territory became the Missouri Territory; and by 1818, Missouri requested to be admitted into the Union. This request caused a nationwide uproar over the issue of slavery, and the bitter debates created further division within the US. In 1820, the Missouri Compromise was passed, allowing Maine in as a free state and Missouri in as a slave state, keeping the ratio between slave and free states equal. It also stipulated that slavery was prohibited in the remainder of the Louisiana Territory north of the southern boundary of Missouri. On August 10, 1821, Missouri was admitted as the 24th state and was at the time the nation's western frontier. Saint Charles was designated as the temporary state capital, until Jefferson City was made the permanent state capital.

In 1831, Joseph Smith and his followers, known as the Mormons or Latter-Day Saints, settled in Independence, Missouri, after being forced to leave two previous states. The growing Mormon population was not well received by other Missourians. In 1838, hostilities escalated into what is known as the "Mormon War." The Mormons were tired of being driven from state to state and county to county and decided to defend themselves with local and legitimate state militia groups.

The governor of Missouri issued his famous Extermination Order to the militia: "The Mormons must be treated as enemies and must be exterminated or driven from the state if necessary for public peace." There were raids, burning of homes and businesses, and rapes; and both sides committed murder. An unprovoked attack at Haun's Mill left 17 Latter-Day Saints men and boys dead. During the winter of 1838, 10,000 Mormons fled Missouri led by Brigham Young. Joseph Smith had been jailed in Missouri, but was allowed to escape and join his followers. Smith reports that this imprisonment provoked further revelations from Heaven and increased his strength.

The well-known Dred Scott case took place in Missouri. Scott was a slave who claimed that he was due his freedom based on the seven years that he had lived in a free state. The case was taken to court in 1846 and went on for over ten years. Based on Missouri law, the Missouri Supreme Court had freed numerous slaves who had traveled and lived in free states, but because of the increasing conflict of the times, they ruled against Scott. The case was taken to the United States Supreme Court, and the resulting decision, in 1857, upheld slavery in U.S. territories that had previously been ruled as non-slavery areas by the Missouri Compromise and denied the legality of black citizenship in America. "Scott's case left America in 'shocks and throes and convulsions' that only the complete eradication of slavery through war could cure."[105]

When the Kansas-Nebraska Act was signed in 1854, it did away with the Missouri Compromise and allowed each state to decide if it would be a slave or free state. The country was afraid of what it would cost either side if Kansas became a free or slave state. Numerous Missourians went into Kansas to try to force Kansas into becoming a slave state. What ensued was a border war. "For five years before the Civil War, residents of the neighboring states of Missouri and Kansas waged their own civil conflict, which was characterized by unremitting and unparalleled brutality. More than anywhere else in the nation, this was truly a civil war—a conflict whose wounds were a long time in healing."[106] Jayhawkers from Kansas and bushwhackers from Missouri led raids on the others' land, homes, business, and families, committing numerous violent atrocities. Between November 1855 and December 1856 alone, 200 died in the conflict.

In August of 1863, Order #11 was issued that called for Bates, Cass, Jackson, and Vernon counties to be made into a wasteland. People were given 15 days to leave the area and then every home, barn, and outbuilding was burned to the ground, and all food appropriated or destroyed. For many years after the Civil War, this area was called the "Burnt District." The order was issued in an attempt to stop bushwhackers from committing crimes, which it did in that area, but they simply moved north to "Little Dixie" and continued their guerilla warfare.

As the Civil War began, "Missouri's allegiance was of vital concern to the Federal government. The state's strategic position; the two rivers, Missouri and Mississippi; its abundant manpower, and natural resources made it imperative that she remain in the Union."[107] Missouri did remain in the Union, but its governor at the time was pro-slavery and created a rebel government that voted to secede. The result was a divided state. Missouri experienced 1,162 skirmishes and battles, had more fighting within its borders than any other state except Virginia, and ranks as the third most fought over state in the nation during the Civil War. By the third year of the war much of Missouri had been burned and depopulated. The Battle at Pea Ridge in Arkansas drove the Confederate army south and determined that Missouri would remain in the Union.

MONTANA[108]

Montana: Latin meaning "mountainous"
Statehood: November 8, 1889 (41st state)
Motto: *Oro y Plata* (Gold and Silver)
Familiar Name: The Treasure State
50-State Tour: The Pure Atmosphere State, April 29-30, 2004

When Dutch and Chuck flew into Billings for the 50-State Tour, they commented that there was a cleanness in the air, a clear atmosphere, a cleanness in the Spirit over Billings and Montana. Dutch prophesied, *"There is something here that is very pure. He is going to do something very unique."* And he began to pray, "Thank You for Your Spirit that is hovering over Montana ready to bring forth wondrous things. Thank You for the shaking that is coming, so glory can come at a new level, so increase can happen in the Spirit. Thank You for the increase that is coming to Montana—increase of anointing, increase of life, increase of revelation, increase of the river, increase of power, increase of breakthrough. I see a breaker anointing over this state, an ability to break through. This people will come into a new awareness of their breaker anointing, that they can indeed be used by You in extraordinary ways, that You have preserved them and kept them and done amazing things in the Spirit; and now is the season for that to be released to create breakthrough not only here, but out from this place. Your people coming together in agreement can shift things across the entire state of Montana [so that it is] launched into another level of God's purpose."

Please pray in agreement with us:

1. That the Lord would continue to purify the hearts of the believers in Montana. (We all know that according to Matthew 5:8 it is the pure—*purified by fire, free from corrupt desire, from sin and guilt*—of heart who will see God.)
2. That the increase in the spiritual and the natural would break forth (Montana has been the 41st state in per capita income in the nation), and come forth as a blessing to the nation and the nations of the world.
3. That just as there has been repentance between tribes, as well as between Indians and whites, that there would be repentance between denominations, and that a strong unity in the Body of Christ would bring people together in prayer to accomplish God's purpose for Montana and for the lives of the individuals here. In the name of Jesus, we bind and break off [remove from] the Body of Christ that independent, self-sufficient spirit that undergirds all of the social structures. We release a dependence on God and a valuing of all genders, races, cultures, and the gifts of the Spirit in others. We declare that we who are called by His name would join together to establish His Kingdom, so that many who are lost will come to Christ. *"That they all may be one, as You, Father, are in Me, and I in You... that they may be made perfect in one, and that the world may know that You have sent Me, and have loved them as You have loved Me"* (John 17:21-23).

Dutch prophesied, "Treasures locked up in this state, both in the natural and in the Spirit, things that God from the beginning decreed for you and put in this state—you're just now coming into it. The everlasting God is about to manifest Himself in Montana. Hidden things that were decreed from the beginning He is about to move you into. The Lord said, 'I'm about to bring into alignment what I decreed about a long time ago for Montana. This is the day and time, I'm about to awaken a part of their destiny.'"

Please pray:

> Lord, let it be *in* Montana, and *with* Montana, according to Your will. Awaken our destiny. We say, manifest Yourself in Montana. Move us into the place in You that You desire. Move us into the plan and purpose You have for us as individuals, and as a state, that we might contribute to Your greater plan for this nation.

Governmental Authority

Pastor Dutch prophesied, "There is a governmental mantle on the state of Montana, a governmental authority here. [There is] a governmental authority that God wants to awaken in the state that you have, that can release something for the nation. You are coming into it now through an alignment that God is doing, that is shifting you into something that

He has hidden for you. The great O-lam-EL says: 'I put it in them and there is a treasure, both in the spirit and the natural, and I am bringing it forth in this hour.' There is wealth that is going to spring out of Montana right now that is going to shock the world—a physical wealth as well as a spiritual."

Please pray in agreement with us:

1. That the Lord would give us His choice for civil governmental leadership.
2. That the foundational, governmental authority and structure in the Church, the Body of Christ, would be established according to God's standard and purpose.
3. That the shifting for alignment that the Lord is doing would be ordered by Him and unhindered by the enemy.

> We call forth the wealth that will spring out of Montana in this season—both the physical and the spiritual. May it produce and yield all the Lord wants for His plans and purposes. We bind the thief that comes to steal, kill, and destroy in the name of Jesus. We declare: "The earth is the Lord's, and the fulness thereof; the world, and they that dwell therein" (Psalm 24:1 KJV).

The River Is Rising

Pastor Dutch declared the word from the Lord: *"Tell them the river is rising. You are moving into a season where, because of the spring thaw [nacal—the winter torrent], everywhere the river goes, everything lives, everything is healed."* John chapter 7 tells us we are the temple of God—flowing out of us, flowing out of our innermost being—womb.

Chuck Pierce prophesied, *"I say, in the waters, there will be a wind and a shout; as they roll into the nation, they will shout '**grace**.' And from this state, the nation will experience a move of my grace, saith the Lord."*

Montana Is a Womb

> Pastor Dutch prophesied, "God says, 'Montana is one of My wombs in this nation.' There is an ability here to birth this river, this force of life that God says is rising. It is in the same way that these rivers initiate here in this state [the Missouri River has its headwaters here], and they are rising. This state is a womb for the river, and it flows out from here naturally. And God says, 'That's a picture of what I'm doing in the Spirit. Montana is a womb for Me and the river of My Spirit to begin to flow to the nation.'"

Please pray and declare in agreement with Dutch's words:

> "The river of Your Holy Spirit is going to be released in the churches of Montana in a new way in the coming days and months. They are going to see a level of it, and they are going to begin to operate in a new level of anointing more

> than they have ever operated in before. There is coming a very unique release of the anointing and flow of the river with manifestations of the river that have not yet been seen, because You have hidden it for now. And I say it is going to be released in them now, and it is going to be the river of God's Spirit in the realm of the Spirit that is even going to begin to expose and release things that have been hidden in her in the natural—resources that are going to be uncovered, released, brought forth in this hour, because You have hidden them for now. And through the force of the river, the very life of God will be coming forth right now, in Jesus' name."

Brief Montana History

The first human inhabitants of what became Montana were nomadic bands. They followed the mammoth, the buffalo, other herd animals, and gathered plants. A number of Indian historians believe their ancestors always inhabited the northern Rocky Mountain region. Most archaeologists, however, maintain that these people crossed the Bering Strait.... Some tribal historians trace their ancestry to the Great Lakes and Hudson Bay regions. They describe rather recent migrations onto the Montana stage. In ancient times, many hunting, gathering societies followed the game along the slopes of the Rocky Mountains, some reaching as far south as South America....

Modern human history of the region that became Montana begins during the seventeenth and eighteenth centuries. According to Michael Malone, et. al., "Indians acquired two of the whites' most valuable possessions—horses and guns—and the Indian cultures were transformed" (Malone, Roeder, Lang, *Montana: A History of Two Centuries*, page 11). With their new mobility, the Salish, or Flatheads, lived in the western valleys, ranging to hunt across the Columbia Plateau, down to the Three Forks area. To the north, the Kutenai people ranged across a broad area including what became the Idaho Panhandle, northwestern Montana, and the Kootenai Valley of southeastern British Columbia.

East of the Rockies lived three separate tribes that made up the Blackfeet Nation. This proud, plains, warrior society probably totaled [15,000] people in 1780. The Blackfeet collided with another proud horse culture, the Shoshoni, ranging north as far as the Three Forks area. Strengthened by smooth-bore guns obtained from the Hudson Bay traders, the Blackfeet drove the Shoshoni south and west....

In the Yellowstone Valley of south-central Montana lived the Crows or Apsaalooke (Large beaked-Bird-People). They were one of the earliest tribal peoples to reach Montana from the east and probably entered the Yellowstone plains just prior to 1600. Through the years, the Blackfeet and the Crows fought over the valuable hunting grounds between the Missouri and Yellowstone Rivers. Their cultural rivalry began in the late 1700s and continues to this day....

All these tribal cultures practiced a pantheistic spirituality, worshipping all sources of life and honoring the interdependence of all elements of creation. They believed the earth was sacred and strove to live in harmony with it.[109]

Fur trappers arrived in Montana hard on the heels of Lewis and Clark (1804-06). Although they tramped all of the state's watersheds, there were only about 150 of them in Montana at any given time. They explored, hunted, trapped, and traded on the Montana stage into the 1860s. These trappers and traders brought a new attitude toward the land, an attitude that has more or less prevailed until today—exploitation....

European and Native trappers depleted the valuable resource of fur-bearing animals. Fur traders explored, mapped, and wrote descriptions of the territory. They brought a commercial relationship and dependency on manufactured goods that changed Native culture forever. They also brought epidemic diseases that devastated some tribes and afflicted all.[110]

With the discovery of gold in the 1860s came the brief, but critical period of placer mining. Gold drew seekers from all over the west and from the eastern population centers. Unlike most fur traders, the gold seekers and the businesspeople who lived off them saw the Indians as obstacles. By 1870, the placer-mining boom had pushed Montana's non-Indian population above 20,000. But many of these "short-timers" left. The lucky ones with their "piles" and the unlucky ones with their empty pokes were gone by the early 1880s.

Territorial boosters, a combination of Civil War influences, and Montana's gold-rush bonanzas influenced Congress to create Montana Territory in 1864. Some of the associated boom-time merchants, farmers, ranchers, and capitalists remained in small Montana communities. These entrepreneurs constantly barraged the federal government to restrict Montana's Indians to reservations, and then lobbied incessantly to reduce the size of these reservations, an attitude that sometimes exists even today.[111]

The next migrants washing into the state started Montana's open-range stock-raising industry (1870-1887). Stock-raising spread white ranchers across the federal domain grasslands and foreshadowed today's high plains cattle ranching and wheat farming industries. Charlie Russell perhaps best depicted that open-range lifestyle. The ranchers' and farmers' Montana became a national industry with the arrival of transcontinental railroads during the 1880s. Physically and psychologically, these lines linked Montana with the nation and led directly to statehood in 1889.[112]

The arrival of the railroads to Montana in the late 19th century also made possible the rise of industrial mining. The Industrial Revolution in Europe and across the Atlantic created a demand for Montana's mineral resources....

The state's industrial boom drew an extremely diverse ethnic population to its towns and cities. Although Montana's tribal peoples suffered mightily under reservation restrictions, other ethnic groups prospered....[113]

Montana's next wave of immigration featured the forest and high-plains homestead boom (1906-1918).

...But the homestead boom "busted" when severe drought swept the state (1917-1923). The drought was compounded by plummeting market prices and banks demanding repayments.[114]

As with the rest of the nation, World War II really shook Montana up! Not only did we send a disproportionate number of our young men and women into the armed forces, but many other Montanans emigrated to the West Coast for high-paying jobs in the war industries. Federal expenditures increased in the state. For example, the Federal government built East Base at Great Falls (later Malmstrom Air Force Base).

After the war, Montana continued to be the site of military readiness. In the 1950s, the government built Glasgow Air Force Base and billeted a strategic bomber squadron there, doubling the size of this small farming community. A defense-minded Pentagon buried two hundred nuclear missile silos in the north central Montana prairie. The nuclear threat of the "cold war" was a stark reality in eastern Montana.[115]

NEBRASKA[116]

Nebraska: Omaha meaning "flat river"
Statehood: March 1, 1867 (37th state)
Motto: Equality Before the Law
Familiar Name: The Cornhusker State
50-State Tour: The Unique State, October 28-29, 2003

During the 50-State Tour to Nebraska, the Lord sovereignly drew together intercessors from across our state. Many previously unknown ones were identified. At least 600 people attended the sessions. The Lord stressed the importance of unity between the rural and urban regions of the state and the need to recognize the rural intercessors. The Lord said He would use Nebraska to surprise His people and bring us to the attention of the nation. (The surprises began at the conference. Most people were very surprised at the number in attendance, and especially at the number from outside the metropolitan areas of Lincoln and Omaha.)

The Lord said that Nebraska would be used in two areas to affect our nation:

1. To tear down false ideology of humanism, intellectualism, and the soul man.
2. To bring supply—food, funds, and revelation for times to come; there will be a Joseph anointing.

We also received an abundant offering, which I believe is a sign of the supply that is to come.

God is setting things in order, rearranging and creating a different order in Nebraska. We need to function first in the spirit, using supernatural giftings, instead of the soul realm. Our "methods" won't work. The Lord said that we have put many things in order in Nebraska, but now He is going to rearrange some things and set a new order. We will be one of seven states that rise up and begin to hold the keys to the future of this land. We will be as Joseph and store up supply. *Pray that Nebraska will be covered with a Joseph anointing and pray for the Josephs to come forth. Pray that we will learn a new way of releasing food, funds, and revelation for times to come, and that we will develop plans for the future.*

We have a unique governmental structure with our nonpartisan, unicameral form of government. We have taken a strong stand against partial birth abortion and have declared that marriage is between one man and one woman. Both are being challenged in the courts, but the people of Nebraska have already made our declarations in the heavenlies as well as in the political arena, and we will continue to stand.

We received strategy from Heaven:

> And the Lord would say, "If you will meet for 21 days, 24 hours of prayer from church to church, meeting throughout this state, that structure that is trying to overshadow this nation will be pushed back. Then I would say to you, if you will begin to meet one night and worship in this state, I will begin to cause the atmosphere of this state to change. I say meet and praise, meet and declare, meet and draw near to Me intimately, but meet and make the right declarations that what I long to do in this land will be done. I say come together, clap, shout, and decree that I am going to change the

course of this land. And from Nebraska it will be changed."
(Prophesied by Chuck D. Pierce.)

Our mandate is for us to ratify, affirm, and establish what God did in our state of Nebraska. We need to continue to proclaim that which was proclaimed, to thank God for doing it and not negate what God has done by continuing to ask Him to do something He has already done. If we continue to ratify and establish what was proclaimed, God will not allow us to fail.

There is an excitement and an expectation in Nebraska that I have not seen before. We have heard the call to our state and we expect to "arise and see the glory of the Lord!"

Brief Nebraska History[117]

Hunters, Explorers, and Fur Traders

Nebraska's soil has been farmed since prehistoric times, but the Native Americans of the plains—notably the Pawnee—devoted themselves more to hunting the buffalo than to farming, since buffalo, as well as the pronghorn antelope and smaller animals, were then abundant in the area. The Spanish explorer Francisco Vásquez de Coronado and his men were the first Europeans to visit the region. They probably passed through Nebraska in 1541.

The French also came and in the 18th century engaged in fur trading, but development began only after the area passed from France to the United States in the Louisiana Purchase of 1803. The Lewis and Clark expedition (1804) and the explorations of Zebulon M. Pike (1806) increased knowledge of the country, but the activities of the fur traders were more immediately valuable in terms of settlement. Manuel Lisa, a fur trader, probably established the first trading post in the Nebraska area in 1813. Bellevue, the first permanent settlement in Nebraska, first developed as a trading post.

Steamboats and Wagon Trains

Steamboating on the Missouri River, initiated in 1819, brought business to the river ports of Omaha and Brownville. The natural highway formed by the Platte valley was used extensively by pioneers going west over the Oregon Trail and also the California Trail and the Mormon Trail. Nebraska settlers made money supplying the wagon trains with fresh mounts and pack animals as well as food.

Nebraska became a territory after passage of the Kansas-Nebraska Act in 1854. The territory, which initially extended from lat. 40°N to the Canadian border, was firmly Northern and Republican in sympathy during the Civil War. In 1863 the territory was reduced to its present-day size by the creation of the territories of Dakota and Colorado. Congress passed an enabling act for statehood in 1864, but the original provision in the state constitution limiting the franchise to whites delayed statehood until 1867.

Railroads, Ranches, and the Growth of Populism

In 1867 the Union Pacific RR was built across the state, and the land boom, already vigorous, became a rush. Farmers settled on free land obtained under the Homestead Act of 1862, and east Nebraska took on a settled look. The population rose from 28,841 in 1860 to 122,993 in 1870. The Pawnee were defeated in 1859, and by 1880 war with the Sioux and other Native American resistance was over. With the coming of the railroads, cow towns, such as Ogallala and Schuyler, were built up as shipping points on overland cattle trails. Buffalo Bill's Wild West Shows opened in Nebraska in 1882.

Farmers had long been staking out homestead claims across the Sand Hills to the high plains, but ranches also prospered in the state. The ranchers, trying to preserve the open range, ruthlessly opposed the encroachment of the farmers, but the persistent farmers won. Many conservationists believe that much of the land that was plowed under should have been left with grass cover to prevent erosion in later dust storms.

Nature was seldom kind to the people of Nebraska. Ranching was especially hard hit by the ruinous cold of the winter of 1880-1881, and farmers were plagued by insect hordes from 1856 to 1875, by prairie fires, and by the recurrent droughts of the 1890s. Many farmers joined the Granger movement in the lean 1870s and the Farmers' Alliances of the 1880s. In the 1890s many beleaguered farmers, faced with ruin and angry at the monopolistic practices of the railroads and the financiers, formed marketing and stock cooperatives and showed their discontent by joining the Populist party. The first national convention of the Populist party was held at Omaha in 1892, and Nebraska's most famous son, William Jennings Bryan, headed the Populist and Democratic tickets in the presidential election of 1896. Populists held the governorship of the state from 1895 to 1901.

Twentieth-Century Changes

Improved conditions in the early 1900s caused Populism to decline in the state, and the return of prosperous days was marked by progressive legislation, the building of highways, and conservation measures. The flush of prosperity, largely caused by the demand for foodstuffs during World War I, was almost feverish. Overexpansion of credits and overconfidence made the depression of the 1920s and '30s all the more disastrous.... Many farmers were left destitute, and many others were able to survive only because of the moratorium on farm debts in 1932. They received federal aid in the desperate years of drought in the 1930s.

Better weather and the huge food demands of World War II renewed prosperity in Nebraska. After the war, efforts continued to make the best use of the water supply, notably in such federal plans as the Missouri River basin project, a vast dam and water-diversion scheme.

Recent attempts to diversify Nebraska's economic base to reduce dependence on meat processing and agriculture have made Lincoln, where state government and the University of Nebraska generate many jobs, a business center, along with Omaha. Among noted Nebraskans have been the pioneer and historian Julius Sterling Morton, who originated Arbor Day, and authors Willa Cather, Mari Sandoz, John G. Neihardt, Loren Eisley, and Wright Morris, all of whom have vividly described the state.

STATE BY STATE

NEVADA[118]

Nevada: Spanish meaning "snow-clad"
Statehood: October 31, 1864 (36th state)
Motto: All for Our Country
Familiar Name: The Silver State
50-State Tour: The Transformation State, April 21-22, 2004

Regarding the state of Nevada, Chuck D. Pierce proclaimed:

> "*I am ready to deal with a bitter root that is in this particular city* [Las Vegas] *that is affecting this state, and that is going to cause, instead of bitterness, a move of healing to spring forth.*" This healing move of God will make national news...it will come to this city and last a full 180 days. This place will be known as a refuge for California. There will be a move of healing like we saw in the 1940s and '50s springing forth in this place, and it will create a great, great stirring in this entire land. So the Lord says, "*Get ready, for healing will spring forth in this desert. I have done some things in the desert. I have hovered by My Spirit. I've been moving...I've been brooding there, and I've been putting seeds in the dry barren place. I bring travail. I bring birth pangs there. I'm releasing My river, and it's going to begin to bring birth pangs so that reproduction is going to start happening in the desert.*"

Nevada, and especially this city [Las Vegas], will be ***transformed***. This will be the state that's known that transformation has come. Transformation comes when you reflect God's glory. You will be known in days ahead for the transformation—the transforming power of God's glory that has visited this city and affected this entire state. And where you've been known for one thing in the past, and you are known for that reproach worldwide, you will be known for putting on another garment! You will radiate. And you will cause not only the enemy to be blinded, but you will cause many to be drawn to that light. Nevada, get ready! Las Vegas, get ready! Reno, get ready! Transformation is coming to this state.

God is going to heal this region. Healing will spring forth in this desert. There is life that is coming to this state that is going to shock the nation. Gifts of healing are coming to Nevada right now, and the working of miracles. There is a level of discerning of spirits that is very unusual that is coming to Nevada that is going to bring a high level of deliverance. You are not going to have to spend hours and days working with people. You will speak the word, and demons will go instantly. There is a high level of deliverance that is coming. Prodigals will come home. I see people being delivered of broken hearts. The Lord says, "*I am going to stop suicides. I am going to transform people and deliver them from the broken place inside of them. I am going to break deception off of them. And they will go to bed in their sin, and they will awaken with revelation and say, 'I want Father back.' They are going to lay down their drugs and lay down other sins.... I am going to heal their bodies from incurable diseases in their sexual organs.... I am going to cleanse them spiritually, and I am going to heal them physically.*"

Regarding the Church, it's not that your ideas get better, and that your methods get better. Rather, the heavenlies get better; the atmosphere changes. Out from this desert there is something that's going to happen that is going to begin to change and shift the government of this land. I prophesy and say over this state that you are an influencing state. We cut off every ungodly well. We say there is now a river of pure revelation flowing in Nevada...and a well-known practitioner of magic will renounce magic and enter the Kingdom of God. What is about to happen here is all about harvest and life; it's about a river bringing life in the sense of harvest to the desert. But so much of this is going to happen through the miraculous.

Dutch Sheets declared:

> I saw an incredible move of the supernatural into this region through the river of God. This move of the river was going to heal, but it was also going to bring ***resurrection life*** and ***salvation***. I saw it bringing life. I saw it bringing this reproductive thing from God. I saw the river flowing out of the womb of the Church. You're pregnant with it. You crossed into it and became pregnant. Then everywhere you took it, life came—the lifegiving, healing power of God. He's coming to a leper state that does not know Him. And God says, "***You know what? I'm not coming because they deserve it. I'm not coming because they've earned it. I'm coming with the river because I love them—just the way they are. And I'm going to bring My life and My healing to them in the desert.***" It's going to lead to a harvest...it is a literal miracle anointing that is coming to this region...to this state...this city...this region...that is going to get the attention of this world.
>
> And I'm telling you right now, it's going to shake things up.... It comes with incredible signs and wonders. It will be said,

"Go to Las Vegas! You can be healed of cancer in Las Vegas. You have terminal disease? Go to Las Vegas. There's life in Reno. Go to Nevada. You can be healed there." This is going to be a place where there will be, more than once, such a power of God that the literal dead will be raised in this state. It will happen in ways that grip people. They will know about it. It won't just be the kind of thing behind the scenes and nobody happens to know about it, where somebody died on a table and they come back to life. I'm talking about ***signs and wonders of an extraordinary magnitude*** are coming to this region. Acts 17-type signs and wonders are coming that are extraordinary miracles, that are going to get the attention of the world.

The Lord says, "I have My own lights. I have My own glitz. I have My own ways to get the attention of the world, and I am coming to draw them to My light. I am coming to draw them to My anointing. They will come to Me. They will come to Me, and they will come to Me for life. I say as you come out, it will be as when Moses first struck the rock. I will strike this city. And then after the strike comes upon this city, you will speak to the city for it is now time for My Church in Nevada to rise up and begin to speak forth that grace that I have. I will bring many here that are broken and wounded, and grace will be delivered to them.... You're going to go to a higher realm of higher level of hearing and seeing and moving by the Spirit. I am coming with the river of My Spirit into the schools. I am going to come in ways that cannot be stopped.... It will come in through the students. Through the miraculous.... A fire is going to begin to burn. It will be a student-led movement. it will disrupt schedules and...meetings. and classrooms."

For Reno

"I am beginning to do a work to reconnect those in that city. There's much division and much confusion, but the reconnect anointing is upon you. Now I'm going to rise the sun over you again, and even now you'll have two or three of My people come into the city that begin to point the way for you. Neither will have the fullness of My plan, for I will begin to raise up and connect three leaders in the cities.... [There will be] intercessory strength...apostolic leadership... prophetic.... [There will be a] major shift in what is going on in governmental structure...[with] a new 18-month plan over that city." (Prophesied by Chuck D. Pierce.)

Again, for Nevada

"There is a redemptive gift on this region for the supernatural and for revelation. We say that the gates of hell are no longer going to hold back God's revelation. The heavens are going to be rent over Las Vegas, over Reno, and over all the other small towns of Nevada. There will be a move over the economic system here— a shift. It will be heard of throughout the whole nation. Something is happening in this region that is going to release billions of dollars for the harvest and for the Kingdom of God. Across the nation, works of God will be funded because something was broken in the heavenlies over Nevada. The watering hole in Las Vegas will be cleansed. The nations will be healed from Nevada...from Las Vegas, because there is a pure river that flows from this place." Amen! So be it! (Declared by Dutch Sheets.)

Brief Nevada History[119]

Early inhabitants lived in rock shelters or caves, and gathered most of their food. People who lived in Lovelock Cave near Lake Lahontan about 3,000 years ago hunted animals with darts rather than bows and arrows. Archaeologists have even found decoy ducks that were used to attract birds.

About 300 BC, people of the Anasazi culture appeared, living in pit houses around the Muddy and Virgin rivers. The Anasazi built their houses with adobe and rocks, mastered pottery and basketry, and may have mined salt. Between about AD 700 and 1100, the Anasazi began raising corn, beans, and squash, and also developed irrigation. Before the migrating Paiutes pushed them out of Nevada, the Anasazi had domesticated dogs and begun growing cotton.

The Great Basin environment forced all native peoples in Nevada to live a nomadic existence as hunter-gatherers. The continuous search for food was the dominant aspect of life in this harsh land, and the native inhabitants of Nevada demonstrated remarkable survival skills. While their material culture was limited, these Native Americans, particularly the Washoe, are known for their excellent basketry. One Washoe woman, called Datsolalee, achieved wide recognition for the intricate designs on the baskets she wove in the late 19th and early 20th centuries.[120]

In the 1770s, several Spanish explorers came near the area of present-day Nevada, but it was not until half a century later that fur traders venturing into the Rocky [Mountains] publicized the region. Jedediah S. Smith came across [southern] Nevada on his way to California in 1827. The following year, Peter Skene Ogden, a Hudson's Bay Company man trading out of the Oregon country, entered [northeast] Nevada. Joseph Walker in 1833-1834 followed the Humboldt [River] and crossed the Sierra Nevada to California.

Later, many wagon trains crossed Nevada on the way to California, especially during and after the gold rush of 1849. Travelers going to California over the Old Spanish Trail also crossed [southern] Nevada, and Las Vegas became a station on the route. Guided by Kit Carson, John C. Frémont had explored much of the state between 1843 and 1845, and his reports gave the federal government its first comprehensive information on the area, which the United States acquired from Mexico in the Mexican War. These accounts may have aided Brigham Young when he was shepherding the Mormons west to build a new home in the mountains and valleys of Utah.

When in 1850 the federal government set up the Utah Territory, almost all of Nevada was included except the southern tip, which was then part of New Mexico.

Non-Mormons had been averse to settling in Mormon-dominated territory, but after gold was found in 1859 non-Mormons did come into the area. A rush from California began and multiplied manyfold as news of the Comstock Lode silver strike spread. Most of the newcomers preferred to consider themselves as still being within California, and a political question was added to the general upheaval. Meanwhile, miners came helter-skelter, raising camps that grew overnight into such booming and raucous places as Virginia City.

Partly to impose order on the lawless, wide-open mining towns, Congress made Nevada into a territory in 1861 as migrant prospectors and settlers poured in. The territory was then enlarged by increasing its eastern boundary by one degree of longitude in 1862. It was rushed into statehood in 1864, with Carson City as its capital. President Lincoln (in order to get more votes to pass the Thirteenth Amendment) had signed the proclamation even though the territory did not actually meet the population requirement for statehood.

In 1866 Nevada acquired its present-day boundaries when the southern tip was added and more eastern land was gained from Utah. Communications with the East, which had been briefly maintained by the Pony Express, were firmly established by the completion of the transcontinental railroad in 1869. The state continued to be dependent on its precious ores, and its fate was affected by new strikes such as the "big bonanza" (1873), which enriched the silver kings, J.W. Mackay and J.G. Fair, and the discoveries of silver deposits at Tonopah (1900), of copper at Ely, and of gold at Goldfield (1902).

Resting on such an undiversified base, the economy was seriously shaken by mining depressions and by fluctuations in the market prices of the minerals. Naturally, the political leaders of Nevada were vociferous in favor of the free coinage of silver. From the 1870s to the 1890s, the people of Nevada were strong supporters of the "cheap money" advocates and were thus linked with the discontented farmers of the Midwest in favoring the Bland-Allison Act and the Sherman Silver Purchase Act (although both were considered insufficient measures). They enthusiastically endorsed the silver program of William Jennings Bryan and the Democrats in 1896, and even after its resounding defeat, they continued to clamor for government purchase and coinage of silver.

In the 20th [century], the federal government has played a major role in Nevada's development. Some federal works, like the Newlands Irrigation Project (1907)—the nation's first federal irrigation project—and the Hoover Dam (completed in 1936), have been generally welcomed. Others have aroused opposition. The Atomic Energy Commission began conducting nuclear tests in Nevada at Frenchman Flat and Yucca Flat in the 1950s. In 1987, the Department of Energy chose Yucca Mountain for the storage of high-level nuclear wastes; the state has continued to fight that decision. Federal activities in general gave impetus to the so-called Sagebrush Rebellion, which demanded that the U.S. government give Nevada lands "back" to Nevadans.

Nevada's population, sparse since the time when the Paiute and other tribes eked out a meager living from the land and animals, increased by more than 1200 [percent] between 1950 and 2000. By far the fastest-growing U.S. state, Nevada is increasingly home to retirees and to workers in new, especially technological, industries.[121]

Las Vegas bills itself as the "Entertainment Capital of the World," and tourism, gaming, and entertainment represent a large portion of the city's revenue. In addition to its renowned casinos, Las Vegas attracts visitors to its outdoor shows, including simulated volcanic eruptions, pirate duels on artificial lakes, and laser cannon displays. Indoor casino shows, with world-famous entertainers, are also popular.[122]

NEW HAMPSHIRE[123]

New Hampshire: Named after Hampshire County, England
Statehood: June 21, 1788 (9th state)
Motto: Live Free or Die
Familiar Name: The Granite State
50-State Tour: The State of Freedom, July 13-14, 2004

Word to New Hampshire Through Chuck D. Pierce:

The word of the Lord to New Hampshire is that our worship will be a prototype of how the nation goes. The atmosphere we create will cause a shift of turning our nation back to God. The army of God in the nation will gather strategy from this state for the battle. We were

the first state to sign the Declaration of Independence. We will be the first state to restore a full covenant with God that will bring the nation back to liberty and freedom again. Because we are first in the nation for our political primary that determines one of the greatest leaders of the world (the President of the United States), we have great influence. We are the Esther state for this nation. We will bring a voice of the uncompromising truth politically and spiritually—a voice that will cause the enemy to know that he will not be able to divert the plan of God. We have a peculiar anointing for breakthrough. Our state will become a refuge for many nations.

God's eye is upon us. We will have great influence. What has been scattered will be gathered. What is dead will come alive and an aroma of our worship will sweep this nation.

Word to New Hampshire Through Dutch Sheets:

The people of New Hampshire are giant killers. We have persistence, tenacity, and a holy stubbornness. We are a hammer state. Our prayer and worship brings an anointing like a hammer that brings blow after blow to bring breakthrough for us. We must take the arrow of the Lord and strike hard! We are a gate state. We reflect the authority of the gatekeepers. We have a very strong governmental anointing. We are a group of called-out spiritual governors and ambassadors. We will build God's legislative people. We have a governmental authority to lock and unlock, to bind and to loose. We have a mantle of governmental influence. We are an ambassadorial state. God is telling us to take the signet ring of authority and that we are going to be used to rearrange the heavens. We will have an atmosphere to overthrow the thrones of iniquity and bring freedom to the covenant of God. We will produce a new sound from Heaven, and God will use us to rearrange the nation.

Gates and government are our calling. Dutch said that the same governmental authority that he carries is on us. Isaiah 33:22 says, *"For the Lord is our judge, the Lord is our lawgiver, the Lord is our king; He will save us."* Our forefathers built our government on this verse. We must sit down and rule with God.

Our state is about to experience a spiritual unity and alignment unlike anything we have ever seen. There is a coming together of leaders. The firstfruits are already here. This will fracture something in the spirit realm and bring the government and glory of God to this state and to the nation.

Religious Background of New Hampshire[124]

Two major religions were born here in New Hampshire. The first and most well-known is Christian Science. The founder of that religion, Mary Baker Eddy, lived in Bow, New Hampshire.

The second major religion is the Seventh Day Adventist. This movement began in Washington, New Hampshire, in 1844. The original building is there today.

Another religious movement that influenced New Hampshire, although not birthed here, was the Shaker Movement. The colony buildings still exist in Canterbury today.

The Great Awakening had an effect on New Hampshire, but surprisingly, 20 years before Jonathan Edwards' revival, New Hampshire had a major earthquake. This put the fear of God in everybody. People put God first and returned to the church in droves—the Congregational church, that is. For over 50 years, the earthquake shook the consciousness of the church-goers and was a reference point to call men to the fear of the Lord.

George Whitfield, the great evangelist, preached his last sermon in Exeter, New Hampshire, among a crowd of 6,000, although he had not been scheduled to speak.

Brief New Hampshire History

Before the Europeans settled in New Hampshire, an estimated 5,000 Native Americans lived there. The tribes belonged to the Algonquian family of Natives. The Indian people fished, hunted, and also tended small farms.

A variety of European explorers came into the area. These included Martin Pring of England in 1603; de Champlain, the French explorer, in 1605; and John Smith from England in 1614.

David Thompson was granted land by the Council for New England in what is now New Hampshire and brought settlers over in 1623. They settled near Rye. Edward Hilton was also granted land and set up a colony in the 1620s called Hilton's Point. Over time, the Council for New England, set up by King James I, granted land to others as well. By the time of King Charles II, 1680, the crown made New Hampshire a separate province with a president.

From 1689 to 1763, the French and Native people fought battles with the English in an attempt to take over the land.

These attempts failed. By 1767, New Hampshire's population numbered 52,700.

The British began passing laws that controlled trade and imposed taxes. In December 1774, Paul Revere traveled to New Hampshire to inform the residents that the British military was increasing its forces in Massachusetts. As a result, one of the first actions of the Revolutionary War took place when a group of people in New Hampshire took military supplies from a fort in New Castle.

When the people of Massachusetts began to fight the British, people from New Hampshire joined them as "minutemen." However, no fighting occurred in New Hampshire at any time during the Revolutionary War.

New Hampshire was the first colony to establish its own government separate from the British and became the ninth state of the Union on June 21, 1788.

From the beginning, agriculture was the main emphasis, but after the Civil War began, this emphasis shifted to industry. Woolen mills, shoe and boot factories, and production plants for machine tools and wood products were constructed. Ship manufacturers began building clipper ships in Portsmouth, and, in fact, the Portsmouth naval yard constructed ships that the Union used during the Civil War. At the completion of the war, additional industry developed, including leather and textiles.

During World War I, warships were built at the Portsmouth Naval facility. During the Second World War, submarines were built and warships repaired there. In 1944, Bretton Woods was the site of the International Monetary Conference. At this conference, representatives of 44 nations set up the International Monetary Fund and the World Bank, both UN agencies.

NEW JERSEY[125]

> **New Jersey:** Named after the island of Jersey
> **Statehood:** December 18, 1787 (3rd state)
> **Motto:** Liberty and Prosperity
> **Familiar name:** The Garden State
> **50-State Tour:** The Watchman State, June 1-2, 2003

The New Jersey 50-State Tour meeting, held in early June, was both life-giving and life-saving. God proved once again that He is speaking to His children today. Chuck Pierce and Dutch Sheets came into our state with a huge mandate, to snap the watchmen back into alignment. The urgency of the hour demands it. We are living in perilous times. New Jersey is a gateway state into our nation. The watchmen need strengthening and equipping, and they need reinforcements added to their ranks.

Dutch began the Monday morning meeting with this word: "Lord, You call it the watchman anointing. It's the watchman equipping; it's the watchman enablement. I'm asking You to put a mantle of prayer for watchman intercession on everyone here, Lord, and those across this state, so that New Jersey can be the 'Watchman State.' New Jersey can be the gate-keeping state. New Jersey can be the state that keeps the serpent out of New Jersey and out of the nation. New Jersey shall say, 'This gate is secure, America. New Jersey is on duty. We're the watchmen there.'"

> Chuck followed with this prophetic word from the Lord: "There are vipers working in Jersey City and Newark. Find those vipers, so the vipers do not become snipers. Look carefully and watch, for I have found a nest, and I am ready to

> break the eggs of that nest so they do not hatch out. I have raised up this time and released this anointing because you must watch and you must watch now. I am calling you into a night watch, and I am saying as you watch in the night, you will see what is wanting to break out and even be harvested in the day. Find the night watches that will be established in this state. Establish the night watches and watch these next two and half months. Watch carefully, for you are playing a major part. If you will gather the state to pray for the first 21 days of August, one county per day, during the fourth watch of the night, I will break the power of the enemy from off of your state."

Immediately, not only did small pockets of intercessors across this state begin night watches in their homes, but in a concerted, ongoing effort from August 1-21, the entire state of New Jersey began "The Fourth Watch of the Night Prayer Initiative." Each of the 21 counties in New Jersey was assigned a 3 a.m. to 6 a.m. watch. Look what the Bible says happens when we watch during that time:

> *And have you ever ordered Morning, "Get up!" told Dawn, "Get to work!" So you could seize Earth like a blanket and shake out the wicked like cockroaches? As the sun brings everything to light, brings out all the colors and shapes, The cover of darkness is snatched from the wicked— they're caught in the very act!* (Job 38:12-15 MSG)

Just yesterday (August 12, 2003), two British men were apprehended in the Newark Airport trying to smuggle in a surface-to-air missile and launcher, with plans to use it on commercial aircraft. These vipers did not become snipers! And, before that, in the month following the 50-State Tour (early July), a hidden group (or nest as Chuck had prophesied) of three young men were caught planning a mass murder rampage in their neighborhood of Oaklyn, New Jersey. They were apprehended while trying to steal a car at three o'clock in the morning, the beginning hour of the fourth watch! Many weapons and ammunitions were found along with the murderous plan. The state officials said they cannot even begin to count the lives that were saved by this sudden find. These vipers did not become snipers!

As we watch in obedience during the early hours of the morning, we are given the power to shake out the wicked from their nests like cockroaches. Hidden things get uncovered and scattered. God moves on our behalf when we obey the strategy He releases to us prophetically in our territories. Moving forward by faith, obediently, causes us to overcome the confederacy of demonic power in our region. Onward to victory!

History tells us that five men from New Jersey signed the Declaration of Independence. *Five* is the number of God's grace. This is a prophetic picture for us today that even at the very birth of our nation, New Jersey was graced to *declare freedom*. Chuck Pierce spoke a word to us at the 50-State Tour meeting that the very ground of New Jersey was crying *freedom*.

New Jersey is also known for its superb militia during the Revolutionary War. This militia was made up of hardworking men and boys who would drop everything at the sound of the trumpet and fight for freedom. Like the men of Nehemiah's time, they were able to both build the wall and wield the sword. The saints of New Jersey are a people who carry within them this awesome DNA. Dutch Sheets called us, "The Watchman State," during the 50-State Tour. He said that we were called to be a prophetic, intercessory army, not only for our state, but for the nation. This history, along with today's prophetic utterances, enables us to stand in faith, declaring God's will and purposes across our region. We are a warring, worshiping militia posted at the wall to both build and watch!

The advance of God's government here is right on time. Our state government is in the worst condition it has been in for many years. Chuck Pierce prophesied during the 50-State Tour assembly that in Trenton, our state capital, a voice of deception has arisen that has caused the city to be blocked off. This blocking off in the spirit is keeping our government from making a full shift toward righteousness. Teachings released in Trenton against territorial warfare have shut down the prophetic and apostolic declarations needed to open the heavens over that city. This needs to be repented of so the block will be removed.

Our former governor, James McGreevy, signed a legislative bill into law that could allow the incubation of human embryos, up to nine month's gestation, within a host mother's uterus. The unborn child can then be "harvested," aborted, and used for scientific experimentation, particularly embryonic stem cell research, which was lobbied for by celebrity Christopher Reeves. This actor's influence, together with the finances from New Jersey's huge drug industry, has moved us into a precarious position. Our state government has entered into a covenant with death. We have sinned. Many of our extremely liberal, agnostic, and spiritually lukewarm governmental leaders have chosen the wrong path, motivated by the spirit of mammon. We will now have to wait to see what the Lord will say on this matter. We are very burdened over this situation.

Chuck Pierce prophesied that vipers wanting to become snipers were resident in Jersey City and Newark. To date, none of the statewide intercessory networks have solid prayer teams in place within these cities.

Brief New Jersey History[126]

New Jersey's first residents were the Lenni Lenape Indians who inhabited the territory...before the first European arrived on its shores. Other tribes, including the Powhatan-Renape, also lived there.

The first European to explore New Jersey was Giovanni de Verrazano, from Florence, Italy, who sailed along the Jersey coast and anchored off Sandy Hook in 1524.

Nearly a century later, in 1609, Henry Hudson arrived and New Netherland, a Dutch colony, was established in 1624 in what was then called "the northeast territory."

In 1638, a Swedish colony settled along the Delaware River and was taken over by the Dutch in 1655. In 1664, the area fell to the British. King Charles II granted domain to his brother James Duke of York, who granted the land between the Delaware and Hudson to Lord John Berkeley and Sir George Carteret. They named the land New Jersey, after the Isle of Jersey, in the English Channel. The land was later sold to Quakers, who divided it into East and West Jersey. In 1702, the rights to both Jerseys were surrendered to the English Crown, who united the inhabitants under a royal governor. The governor of New York also served as the governor of New Jersey until 1738, when Lewis Morris became governor of New Jersey. More than 100 battles took place on New Jersey soil during the Revolutionary War. In 1776, Washington crossed the Delaware and surprised and defeated the Hessian garrison at Trenton. A few days after the new year, he defeated a British force at Princeton. His army spent the winter of that year and the 1779-80 winter in Morristown.

New Jersey was the third state to ratify the U.S. Constitution in 1787 and the first to ratify the Bill of Rights in 1789. Francis Hopkinson, a signer of The Declaration of Independence is credited with designing the first American flag with thirteen stars and stripes. His design was adopted by the Continental Congress on June 14, 1777.

In 1791, Alexander Hamilton selected the Great Falls of the Passaic River as the site of a model factory town. Throughout the 1800s, the state continued to expand economically—roads were built, canals dug and railroads constructed. Rail and steamboat service helped Jersey City, Newark, Paterson, Camden and Trenton become leading industrial areas.

By 1850, New Jersey's population of nearly half a million, and the industries in which most of those people worked, was concentrated in the north. The sparsely populated southern areas remained rural. After the Civil War, industrialization attracted still more workers from the south, along with many thousands of European immigrants. The railroads played a large role in helping the north Jersey lakeland and south Jersey seashore areas expand.

The entire state prospered greatly in the late 1800s. A good part of the state's economic expansion was due to the genius of its inventors—Thomas Edison was one of the most famous—who were responsible for the development of a number of important technological and research areas.

A strong and effective reform movement, which flowered in the early 1900s, brought Woodrow Wilson to power. He was elected governor in 1910 and resigned in 1913 to become President of the U.S. Among the many important social reforms associated with Wilson were a series of welfare acts providing workmen's compensation and protection for laborers, including restrictions on the employment of women and children, as well as a number of important antitrust laws.

During the war, New Jersey's economy expanded still further. The state became the site of important training centers, as well as a major port. Chemicals and munitions were two of its most important and profitable products. As its highway and transportation systems improved, it became one of the most important industrial states in the US.

New Jersey produced an enormous amount of war materiel [sic]. Twenty-five percent of U.S. Navy destroyers were constructed in the state, along with battleships, heavy cruisers and many aircraft engines. More than 500,000 New Jersey residents served in the armed forces.

Today, New Jersey is recognized for its present as well as its past.

One of New Jersey's premier landmarks, the Statue of Liberty, is America's greatest symbol of freedom. The freshly restored Ellis Island was a port to many in search of the American dream. Atlantic City, with its legendary boardwalk and casinos, is a vacation resort renowned worldwide. Four professional sport teams make their homes here: the 1990 National Football League Champion Giants, American Football Conference Jets National Basketball Association Nets, and National Hockey League Devils. Horse racing is a popular spectator sport. And the abundance of flowers, fruits and vegetables has given New Jersey its well-deserved nickname, the Garden State. New Jersey's tourism industry is currently ranked seventh in the United States.

NEW MEXICO[127]

New Mexico: Spaniards' name for "area"
Statehood: January 6, 1912 (47th state)
Motto: *Crescit eundo* (It grows as it goes)
Familiar Name: The Land of Enchantment
50-State Tour: The Supernatural State, January 19-20, 2003

Because New Mexico, Oklahoma, and Arizona have the greatest concentration of Host People in the lower 48 states, we chose to start our tour with those states. Our first 50-State Tour meeting for 2003 was held in Albuquerque, New Mexico. Pastor Jack Webb, our SPN State Coordinator for New Mexico, hosted this gathering at Church on the Rock. Both the sanctuary and overflow room were filled to capacity, with still more standing along the outside wall. People literally came from all across the state to partner with us and cry out for a shift in New Mexico. We felt we were to begin in New Mexico because the oldest recorded civilizations in our nation are in that region. In the past, New Mexico has had a spirit of isolation upon it. So it was so good to see so many come together. The "Land of Enchantment," as this state is known, has a very supernatural atmosphere that actually creates a ceiling against the move of God. The Spirit of God fell, and we declared a Jesus-of-Nazareth, blood-bought, prophetic people arising in New Mexico who would have greater wisdom than the supernatural forces that operate there presently.

As Pastor Dutch began to minister, he declared Isaiah chapter 35 over New Mexico. He declared that the desert will bloom. The following cumulative prophecy came forth.

"The moving of My Spirit is on this land, and the firstfruits of My Spirit will be manifested here. There will be an outbreak of the supernatural, with a firstfruits demonstration of miracles. Welcome My Spirit, for there are many spirits in this land. I am the Revelator. From this day forth, the prophets will be able to sound a clear trumpet in New Mexico. Watch the winds for they are a sign. Don't hide yourself from the wind, but allow the wind to blow away that which has grown dusty. Many who have come into the supernatural but not by My Spirit will now come into My Kingdom. I will bring in the witches and the warlocks, and a great conversion of those that have experienced the supernatural dimension of the enemy. I am getting ready to bring them in and raise up prophets in your midst. Current leaders who stand in My pulpit, will stand to speak, but the spirit of prophecy will come upon them. I am releasing mysteries, strategies, and revelation. Cry out for the leaders of this state to receive the prophetic mantle. New Mexico will surprise the nation! The hidden will be revealed. A supernatural 'something' will happen that will shift the economy of this state. This is a time of springing forth in New Mexico. Have faith for the pueblos for I will invade them with faith. Death and destruction has been in this state, but faith is coming to the pueblos. Invite faith into the pueblos!"

Brief New Mexico History[128]

Both the Mogollon and Anasazi were early people groups who lived in New Mexico. Of the early Native people in North America, the Anasazi was one of the most advanced. Some Anasazi fashioned homes in the cliffs. Others constructed multilevel apartments on the ground. Present-day Pueblo Indians are related to the Anasazi.

Soon after Columbus landed in the New World, the Navajos and Apaches moved into the area. The Comanches and Utes followed.

The first settlement in New Mexico was in 1598. Juan de Onate founded it at Pueblo of San Juan de Los Caballeros. This precedes the founding of Jamestown in 1607 by eight years. In 1609-1610, Santa Fe became the capital of the province making it the "oldest seat of government in the United States."

Roman Catholic missionaries kept the colony from dying in the early days. However, the Native people were compelled to work by the Spaniards. By 1680, the Native people had had enough of taxes and near slavery. Pope, from the San Juan Pueblo, led a revolt that caused the death of 400 Spaniards and drove the rest back into Mexico.

After 12 years of exile, the Spanish returned under the leadership of Diego de Vargas and regained control of the area.

By 1821, New Mexico had become a province of Mexico. In that year, Mexico became an independent nation. It was also the year that the Santa Fe Trail was "opened to bring goods to New Mexico from Missouri" by William Becknell, a black man.

While Mexico ruled, two attempts to take control of the territory were made by two different groups. First, Mexicans and Native people tried. Taos Indians were placed in charge of the area; however, the Mexican government retook control after only a month. Another group that attempted control came in from Texas. The Texans were also defeated by the Mexicans.

Eventually, New Mexico came under the control of the United States in 1848.

During the initial phases of the Civil War, Confederate troops took control of New Mexico. However, by March 1862, the Union had gained control. After the war was underway, Colonel Kit Carson was responsible for forcibly removing the Apaches and Navajo onto reservations.

Other notable individuals in New Mexico during the 1800s were Billy the Kid and Geronimo.

On January 6, 1912, New Mexico became the 47th state in the Union.

The first atomic weapon was produced in Los Alamos, a town in northern New Mexico. The Trinity Site, in southern New Mexico, was the place where the first atomic bomb was exploded. This weapon was then dropped in Japan at two sites, thus ending World War II.

NEW YORK[129]

New York: Named after Duke of York, later James II
Statehood: July 26, 1788 (11th state)
Motto: *Excelsior* (Higher)
Familiar Name: The Empire State
50-State Tour: His Kingdom State, January 15-17, 2004

We began the *New Year* declaring a *New Day* for *New York!* Our 50-State Tour actually spanned three cities—New York City, Albany, and Rochester.

Key themes for New York include:

- ★ "God is looking to see if we will lay down our own agendas and agree to connect with one another, which is His agenda!" (Dutch Sheets at New York City)
- ★ "A statewide call to gather and worship will come forth and a *new* sound will arise." (Chuck D. Pierce at Albany)
- ★ "Sixty houses of revival will spring forth throughout New York State!" (Chuck D. Pierce at Rochester)
- ★ "A prophetic sign will be given during the spring thaw!" (Dutch Sheets at Rochester)
- ★ "Our *Empire State* will become His *Kingdom State!*" (Declared by Joseph Askins in each city of the tour)

The 50-State Tour was a "whirlwind" time that began in Brooklyn, New York, on Thursday evening, January 15, where the greater New York City Body of Christ gathered and received an impartation to shift us from being an Empire State to His Kingdom State! The watchword was "connect," which was repeated at every gathering—that we needed to connect as a whole rather than to continue to operate as separate parts. This doesn't mean that every Christian was going to connect but rather a remnant would connect and God would release authority to the remnant to legislate in the heavenlies. God is going to judge this state of New York by our willingness to come together and worship at different times throughout the year, regardless of the circumstances! It was a blessing to see how many came together in spite of the snow and record cold that hit New York City.

We then gathered on Friday night, January 16, with the Body of Christ in the Capital Region district of Albany where it was even colder than what it was in New York City! And yet the Lord began to release a flaming sword to Chuck and Dutch that released an anointing to govern and legislate from the heavenly realm over governmental structures that have been resisting God's moves, and declare that the gates of New York are open to the King of glory! A sound and call to gather and worship would begin from Albany and then go all across New York State that would set the course for our state for the next four years and also affect our nation. God is going to judge us by our willingness to stop and agree with His call to worship these times. These corporate worship gatherings statewide over this next year will begin to shift our state.

One of the things the Holy Spirit was saying to us on the 21-day prayer focus prior to these gatherings was that we needed to ask to receive an impartation of the "zeal of the Lord of hosts." As we left Albany last night from Light of the World with host, David Digges, and the greater Capital Region Body of Christ, we received an impartation from the Lord that gave us the ability to press on through to Rochester, arriving at 3 a.m. in order to be in position to gather at 10 a.m. Saturday morning, and release what the Lord desired to speak to the Body of Christ in western New York.

On Saturday morning, January 17, in Rochester, the presence of God was so heavy during worship that when Pastor Willie Jock (representing the Mohawk—Keepers of the Eastern Gate— and others of the First Nations people of New York who traveled across New York State with us) came to declare, "The Gates open to the King of Glory," they almost could not stand! Dutch Sheets spoke on "the rain, the fire, and the river of God."

Apostle Ron Domina of Bethel Christian Fellowship, who had set down his own plans for these three days to personally take us *all* by van to the three cities, prophesied that the leadership in New York would lay down their own agendas and answer the call to gather and worship, even if it meant we would have to get in buses and travel to where these statewide gatherings to worship were taking place.

Chuck released a word from the Lord that there would be 60 revival houses throughout New York State that would spring up over this next year, and that we needed to not only hear what the Lord was saying, but enter into what the Lord was doing!

This was the 33rd state that Chuck and Dutch had visited, and the Holy Spirit gave a word for me to declare that the occult power of Free Masonry, of which the highest level is the 33rd degree, would begin to be dismantled; and the effect of free masonry in this nation would begin to be exposed even as in the day of the revival fires that were spread through the ministry of Charles G. Finney.

Brief New York History[130]

Of all the various groups of Native Americans in the northeastern United States and southeastern Canada, none is more famous than the six nations that comprise the Iroquois Confederacy that were located in what is now New York State. Formed around 1570, the confederacy, or Iroquois League was originally comprised of five tribes. Starting from east to west, they were the Mohawks, Oneidas, Onondagas, Cayugas, and the Senecas. In the early 1700s, the sixth tribe, the Tuscaroras migrated from North Carolina to the border regions between New York and Pennsylvania and united with the original five tribes into one cohesive alliance.

Known amongst themselves as the "Hodinoshone," or "People of the Long House," the Iroquois League dominated all its neighbors, *drawing strength from its unity*. From earliest times, a wampum belt fashioned in a pattern that has become known as "Hiawatha's Belt" symbolized the unity of the Iroquois. Wampum, it should be mentioned, was a trading currency based upon small shells tied together into strings or entire picture tableaus.[131]

Verrazano visited New York harbor in 1524, and Henry Hudson first explored the Hudson River in 1609. The Dutch settled here permanently in 1624 and for 40 years they ruled over the colony of New Netherlands. It was conquered by the English in 1664 and was then named New York in honor of the Duke of York. Existing as a colony of Great Britain for over a century, New York declared its independence on July 9, 1776, becoming one of the original 13 states of the Federal Union. The next year, on April 20, 1777, New York's first constitution was adopted.

In many ways, New York State was the principal battleground of the *Revolutionary War*. Approximately one-third of the skirmishes and engagements of the war were fought on New York soil. The Battle of Saratoga, the most decisive battle of the Revolutionary War, was the turning point of the Revolution leading to the French alliance and thus to eventual victory. New York City, long occupied by British troops, was evacuated on November 25, 1783. There, on December 4 at Fraunces Tavern, General George Washington bade farewell to his officers. Today New York is home to the U.S. Army Academy at West Point.

The first government of New York State grew out of the Revolution. The State Convention that drew up the Constitution created a Council of Safety, which governed for a time and set the new government in motion. In June 1777, while the war was going on, an election for the first governor took place. Two of the candidates, Philip Schuyler and George Clinton, were generals in the field. Two others, Colonel John Jay and General John Morin Scott, were respectively leaders of the aristocratic and democratic groups in the Convention. On July 9, George Clinton was declared elected and he was inaugurated as Governor at

Kingston, July 30, 1777. The capital of the state was officially moved to Albany in January 1797.

Alexander Hamilton was a leader in the revolutionary movement, which ended in the development of the Federal Constitution (which drew some of its outlay from the document of the 1st Nations Iroquois Confederacy), and he was active in its ratification. New York City became the first capital of the new nation, where President George Washington was inaugurated on April 30, 1789.

In following years, New York's economic and industrial growth made appropriate the title "The Empire State," an expression possibly originated by George Washington in 1784. According to a PBS special the name came from being called the "GREAT SOUTHERN EMPIRE OF THE NORTH" when New York refused to go against the Southern Confederacy until Fort Sumter was attacked, because they feared the loss of revenue from the trading of goods harvested or made in the southern states by slaves. Also, the construction of the "North River Steamboat," the first successful steam-propelled vessel, began a new era in transportation.

The Erie Canal, completed in 1825, greatly enhanced the importance of the port of New York and caused populous towns and cities to spring up across the state. The Barge Canal replaced the Erie Canal in 1918; and the system of waterways was further expanded by the construction of the Saint Lawrence Seaway.[132]

New York has been the seedbed of many Christian awakenings and revivals, including the Fulton Street Prayer Meetings, which preceded the Finney revivals. Through the anointed preaching of Charles Grandison Finney, the upstate New York area from the Mohawk Valley to Rochester, New York, became known as the "Burned Over District." This was due to the numerous "Fires of Revival" that swept through this region. It is recorded that at the height of the Finney revivals in Rochester, 95 percent of the citizens were born again. Also with the Fulton Street Prayer Meetings that preceded the Finney revivals New York has been the birthplace of several moves of the Holy Spirit.

At the same time, New York State has also been the seedbed of many *unholy* awakenings. It is where Joseph Smith was visited by the (dark) angel Moroni and was given another gospel that birthed the Mormon religion (just outside of Rochester, New York). It is also worth noting that the Seneca Indian Prophet Handsome Lake was also visited by three (dark) angels and shown another religion (known as the code of Handsome Lake). Joseph Smith's father was a translator at the signing of the peace treaty between the United States and the Seneca Nation, of which Handsome Lake was a participant (just outside of Rochester, New York). The Fox sisters of Hayesville, New York (also just outside of Rochester), were responsible for the outpouring of spiritism, which swept upstate New York in the mid1800s, and there are many modern-day mediums that continue this practice in Lilydale, New York (which is south of Buffalo).

Overland transportation grew rapidly from a system of turnpikes established in the early 1880s to the modern-day Governor Thomas E. Dewey New York State Thruway. By 1853, railroads that had started as short lines in 1831 crossed the state in systems like the Erie and New York Central.

During the nineteenth century, America became a haven for many of the oppressed people of Europe, and New York City became the "melting pot." The Statue of Liberty (dedicated in 1886 in the harbor), with its famous inscription, "Give me your tired, your poor, your huddled masses yearning to breathe free," was the first symbol of America's mission.

The international character of New York City, the principal port for overseas commerce, and later for transcontinental and international airways has been further enhanced by becoming the home of the United Nations, capital of the free world.[133]

In addition, in Flushing Meadow Park, Queens, New York, Israel received her charter to be a member nation of the United Nations, thus New York has played a part in seeing biblical prophecy fulfilled.

As one of the wealthiest states, New York made tremendous strides in industry and commerce. The New York Stock Exchange, founded in 1792, has become the center of world finance. Diversified and rich natural resources, together with unmatched facilities for transport, produced a phenomenal growth in [manufacturing] and industry. Research and inventive genius have been extensive, especially in the field of electronics, power and the peaceful and productive use of atomic energy.

New York City also became a leading national center for art, music and literature, as exemplified by the Metropolitan Museum of Art, The Metropolitan Opera Company, and large publishing houses.

The state has supplied more than its share of national leaders, beginning with Alexander Hamilton, the first secretary of the treasury; and John Jay, the first chief justice. Aaron Burr and George Clinton served as vice presidents. Martin Van Buren, Chester A. Arthur and Grover Cleveland went from New York politics to the presidency. In the 1900s, Theodore Roosevelt and Franklin D. Roosevelt achieved the presidency; and Nelson Rockefeller served as vice president. Governors Charles E. Hughes, Alfred E. Smith, and Thomas E. Dewey all were candidates for the presidency.[134]

With the major role that New York has played, and continues to have, in the affairs of the nation, the world, and the Church—not to mention the large Jewish population—it is little wonder that when terrorists wanted to strike a blow against our nation, they chose New York as one of their first targets, not realizing the unifying effect it would have on our nation, much of the world, and the Church.

NORTH CAROLINA[135]

> **North Carolina:** Named after Charles II of England
> **Statehood:** November 21, 1789 (12th state)
> **Motto:** *Esse quam videri* (To be rather than to seem)
> **Familiar Name:** The Tarheel State
> **50-State Tour:** Shifting Into a Release of Wealth, March 28-29, 2003

> The heavens were churning over the state of North Carolina, and an interesting prophetic word came forward during the 50-State Tour meeting: *"In September, you will see great rain. In the months from April to September there will be great rearrangement and breakthrough, with a release coming to the Body of Christ."* (Prophesied by Chuck D. Pierce.)

There was also a declaration that *North Carolina must make a shift into the new.* To *shift* is to change position or direction. The prophet declared, "Now hear me, some of you must shift out of the old position that you are in and into the new place. You must shift from one direction into another direction, or exchange or replace something with something that is better. *It is time to make a shift!*" (Chuck D. Pierce)

Please agree with us in Jesus' name that as we pray over the following issues a shift will occur, from the old, into the new!

- *Pray* that the churches will rise up and put on the spirit of purity—because blessed are the pure in heart for they shall see God—so that we may see revival break forth as it did in the Book of Acts.
- *Pray* against the spirit of antichrist that is trying to remove all mentions of God from public places, such as the removal of "One Nation Under God" in our courtrooms.
- *Pray* that the favor of God and man would come upon the believers according to Luke 2:52.
- *Pray* for reconciliation of the Native American population in North Carolina, of whom many are still under a spirit of heaviness manifesting in rejection, sorrow, sadness, hopelessness, gluttony, depression, and suicide. Pray that they will receive the spirit of joy, because the joy of the Lord is our strength.
- *Pray* for exposure and dismantling of Freemasonry, Knights of Pythias, New Age groups, and Wicca, and that the demonic gate holding back the river of life from flowing in and through the lives of these people will be opened; pray that the spirit of blindness would be removed from their hearts and minds to hear and receive the gospel of Jesus Christ.
- *Pray* that God will redeem the land and restore the firstfruits of harvest naturally and spiritually causing miracles with signs and wonders to manifest on earth.
- *Pray* that God will open up the flow of living waters we read of in Ezekiel chapter 47.
- *Pray* that we as believers will protect what comes in and goes out of the eye gates, ear gates, and mouth gates.

- ★ *Pray* that God will cleanse and heal our lands, because they have been defiled by injustices, the sin of greed, and sins of our forefathers.
- ★ *Pray* that the spirit of perversion would be broken off our government and that leaders will be accountable in their words and character.
- ★ *Pray* that God will restore the ancient paths of North Carolina and that we will rise up and guard it with the flaming sword.
- ★ *Pray* for reconciliation among the blacks and whites of North Carolina and that we will love one another as Christ commanded.

Brief Post Civil War North Carolina History

The farm, whether of ten acres or ten thousand, was the basic unit of economic production and social organization in antebellum North Carolina. The Tar Heel town, whether port city or backcountry village, was intrinsically tied to agriculture.[136]

Though North Carolina was spared the worst ravages of the Civil War, few would have predicted in 1870 that [North Carolina] would, within fifty years become the most industrialized state in the South. Hamlets such as Durham and Winston…would in the decades ahead become centers of industry.

…A rushing stream and a willing workforce opened the way for the creation of mill villages in the countryside wherever the capital could be collected. The value of goods manufactured in North Carolina was less than $10 million in 1870. It was almost $1 billion by 1920.[137]

The terms of life were altered by 1870. Not only did emancipation of the slaves change the relationship between black and white, planter and freedman, but the Civil War expanded horizons and shook old [mind-sets]. Over 100,000 North Carolinians had left their localities, traveled hundreds of miles from home, and seen a wider part of the world. Women had managed farms and plantations while their men were away. Though most Tar Heels returned to rebuild after the war, deprivation created new opportunities. More and more farmers would plant crops for market. Others were ready to go beyond the plow and the plantation to take their chances with factories and the life of commerce.[138]

Though the folkways of country life persisted into the twentieth century, rural North Carolina was also transformed. Emancipation set the stage for the emergence of tenancy and sharecropping as the predominant labor system for the black farmers of the state. The coming of the railroads and the growth of commercial centers opened the way for thousands of white and black farmers to shift from subsistence agriculture to a concentration on the growth of cash crops. Greatest was the expansion of the tobacco crop of the state, which, by the turn of the century, surpassed 100 million pounds. By 1920, North Carolina tobacco filled many of the nation's cigarettes and pipes.

For black North Carolinians, the half-century after 1870 was a time of new freedom, new striving, and new setbacks. Enfranchised through federal law by the 1870s and politically active for three decades thereafter, they saw their voting and civil rights systematically revoked by state legislation after 1900. Widely employed as skilled artisans in North Carolina towns through the 1890s, they found their opportunities increasingly restricted and confined after the turn of the century. Throughout the uncertain years between legal emancipation, legal segregation, and amidst the adversity intensified by disfranchisement and formal passage of Jim Crow laws, blacks built communities, churches, colleges, and business enterprises.[139]

Black North Carolinians, despite violence and disenfranchisement, built the churches, colleges, and businesses that prepared the next generation to reclaim its rights. By 1920, North Carolina was a state transformed.[140]

NORTH DAKOTA[141]

North Dakota: Sioux meaning "allies"
Statehood: November 2, 1889 (39th state)
Motto: Liberty and Union, Now and Forever; One and Inseparable
Familiar Name: The Sioux State
50-State Tour: The Faith and New Wineskin State, June 27-28, 2004

Chuck Pierce's Prophetic Message to North Dakota

When you thresh the mountains, you get a plain. The Spirit of God said to me, *"The people of North Dakota are going to rise up with faith in such a way that they are going to unite in such a way. They are going to become a new sharp, threshing instrument, in such a way that the mountains of the past will not be able to stop them in the future. And they will have a voice of decree that will cause every mountain that has stopped the move of God to begin to fall and the mountains will become as a plain."* As the mountains become as a plain in the Northern plains, the glory of God will visit this Northern Plains state and then it will flood down south.

I saw that here in the Northern Plains, here in North Dakota, you are actually the northern state that represents the circle of life. The Lord said,

> *"Tell them the things not fulfilled in the past in My destiny; I am going to start working in a way in their midst [so] that a supernatural fulfillment of My promise and destiny is going to come into the state. That which has been disconnected in the past, that which has been broken down in the past, right at the time for spiritual breakthrough, this will be a year that I will deal with the covenant-breaking spirit in this land and what has caused covenant breaking in the past. I am going to give you authority over what has broken My circle of destiny in this state. No longer will it be able to break.* **Unity is coming upon this state!***"*

* *Pray* for a new level of unity that will cause us to rise up in faith and become a new sharp, threshing instrument.

Hope deferred from the generations since the early 1800s must be broken out of the land, and sorrow must be broken out of the land. God says to North Dakota, *"Joy will be seen in this land!"* Joy comes when covenant is restored. I believe when we hear the report that there is a new joy flooding across the land of North Dakota, we will know that our nation has taken a shift in His covenant blessing. Though you feel like you are isolated, thinking, "What influence could I have?" you are going to be known for some of the greatest influence that our nation has seen.

* *Declare* that joy will overtake the people and land of North Dakota.

North Dakota is heading into a windy season. But this windy season will be different from any other windy season. This windy season is going to be stirring up a fragrance of destiny that has never fully come into the atmosphere. As the wind blows naturally over the next six months, it will be a spiritual sign to you that that which God has planted, He is unlocking. And by unlocking it here in the north, the fragrance of the Spirit of God in North Dakota will begin to blow south into the rest of this nation so that the fragrance of God's purpose for this land will be fully in synch.

It was prophesied about this land that it would probably have the most glorious future. I don't believe that was a wrong prophecy. I believe you have a glorious future! I believe you have resources in North Dakota that will sustain our nation. I believe there is influence in this land that will sustain our nation.

- ★ *Ask* for the wind to come and begin to blow the fragrance of the Spirit of God south into the rest of the nation.

North Dakota is entering into a fruitful season. You have been travailing and travailing and travailing. Now, start calling forth the fruit. Once the wind blows, then the fruit will come. The Lord says there is going to be a great fruitful harvest in this state. Get ready for it.

- ★ *Call forth* the physical and spiritual fruit of North Dakota and declare it will be brought into the storehouse of the Lord.

There is a new thing going on in North Dakota. I have waited to really find the state that I could really say that I see the new thing. Who would have thought it would be North Dakota? God said, "*You wait! I am going to do a new thing in that state that will become a model, a pattern, that will be a successful thing that others will be able to see. Don't look with your eyes. Don't judge by what you know, for I have chosen North Dakota for a new thing."* I thought it was really interesting. I would have chosen Texas for a new thing if I had been the Lord, and I actually like Michigan a lot. But God said, *"In North Dakota, I am going to do a new thing. I am moving."*

> ★ *Ask* God for things to begin to stir in North Dakota. When we are asking God, He will begin to do it.

> The Lord says, "It is time for the people in North Dakota to know that they are becoming a new wineskin." He said, "You will bring the wineskin and you will present the wineskin and you will declare from this time forward, a structure that is new. Something that is fresh. Something that is of greater quality than has been seen before in this nation will begin to form in North Dakota. I will begin to do a work in the Church in North Dakota that is going to be one that will [be a] model to this entire nation."
>
> The Lord is saying, "I want to preserve everything because this is a different place, still virginal in its aspect and identity. I want to preserve what has gone before, but the only way I can preserve what has gone before in the history of the spiritual life of this state, is to do something new now. And if you allow Me to do something new now, what has gone before will synergize with it, and then you will move forward and unlock the treasure that is in this state for this hour.... I will do something in this state that represents the territorial wineskin that I am attempting to present to My people. I will

require from North Dakota a connection and a relationship that represents what the Spirit is saying to the Church in the entire territory. I will deal with the circle or the plain called North Dakota, and I will produce a new wineskin from that plain. *This is a new wineskin state....* I say an apostolic, prophetic anointing is coming upon you. I declare North Dakota a new wineskin of this land!"

★ *Join* with us in declaring the Lord's word that North Dakota is a new wineskin state!

A Portion from Dutch Sheets' Prophetic Message

I just heard the Lord say, *"I am going to heal North Dakota."* **There are signs and wonders coming. He is going to heal relationships.** What I felt was that there is just a general sense God is coming to heal, including a healing of the land. I see an atmosphere of healing that is going to begin to just hover over the state of North Dakota, and it is going to heal people. I heard the Lord say, *"I want to heal this state."* That's *really big*, by the way! This is far greater than somebody getting up and saying your crops are going to do better this year. If there is a spirit of healing that really begins to flow through this state, I just want you to know, it is going to affect everything—absolutely everything. It is going to affect the weather patterns; it's going to affect the crops; it will affect the animals; it will affect your churches; it will affect your kids; it will affect your grandparents; it will affect everything. It will release healing of relationships. It will release signs and wonders. This will affect *everything.* And I believe it is coming. I believe. I am just going to say this one more time: **There is an atmosphere; there is an atmosphere** *of healing that is going to be released.* The very anointing of healing is going to hover over this state.

* *Declare* that an atmosphere of healing will hover over North Dakota, and that signs, wonders, and miraculous healings will begin to manifest.

Brief North Dakota History[142]

Prior to the 1800s Native Americans were living in the land. Some of these tribes were the Arikara, Hidatsa, and the Mandan. According to the *North Dakota Centennial Blue Book,* these tribes led a sedentary lifestyle. Their homes were earth lodges. Each tribe was engaged in farming and hunting. Their communities were trading centers when the fur trading business began to grow. In contrast, the Dakota, Assiniboine, and Cheyenne led a more nomadic life that was significantly changed when the horse was introduced on the Plains. These tribes depended on the bison to sustain their nomadic lifestyle.

Rene Robert Cavelier, Sieur de La Salle, came into the area in 1682 and claimed large portions of what is now North Dakota for France. He laid claim to the land below Hudson Bay and property drained by the Mississippi River Basin. France gave up the claim to the Hudson Bay area in 1713, handing it over to the British. By 1738 a Frenchman named La Verendrye came into the area near Bismarck. He was the person who first explored the area.

North Dakota was included in the land that the United States purchased from France in the Louisiana Purchase of 1803. The next year President Jefferson sent Lewis and Clark on the famous, "Voyage of Discovery." By October 1804, they were in North Dakota and had built Fort Mandan near the present-day city of Stanton.

In the year that the Civil War began, 1861, Congress designated this area the Dakota Territory. It included much more than North and South Dakota; it also included large sections of present-day Wyoming and Montana. Two years later, settlers were allowed to homestead. It was slow going, however, as transportation was poor and fear of Indian uprisings was great. However, in about 1875, large wheat farms began to be established, which turned out to be profitable for the owners.

The population centers in the territory were far apart. Consequently, the people asked Congress to split the territory, which it agreed to do. Congress set the borders between the north and south in February 1889. By November, North Dakota was accepted into the Union as the 39th state and South Dakota as the 40th.

In the early 1900s, outside interests owned businesses and influenced state politics. Farmers disliked this. Douglas Munski and Jerome D. Tweton explain the situation in this way:

In 1915, the Nonpartisan League was founded in North Dakota. This Organization supported the farmers. It called for state ownership of grain elevators, flour mills, packing houses, and cold-storage plants. It also wanted banks in farming areas that would grant loans at cost. Thousands of farmers joined the league.[143]

A governor was elected in 1916 that supported the League's position, and he began to institute changes. Farming issues continue to play an important role in the state.

OHIO[144]

Ohio: Indian meaning "great"
Statehood: March 1, 1803 (17 state)
Motto: With God, All Things Are Possible
Familiar Name: The Buckeye State
50-State Tour: The State That Swings the Sword, October 2-3, 2003

The following is a summary of prophetic words from our 50-State Tour gathering in Middletown, Ohio, on October 2 and 3, 2003. This was a powerful prophetic gathering! Chuck D. Pierce, Dutch Sheets, and Barbara Yoder were the leaders in prophetic ministry.

- Ohio is a swing state to lift the nation back into place.
- God is going to catch the state up quickly. There will be war in the heavenly realms.
- Ohio is a sign post. Suddenly, things will change. Ohio will come from the back of the pack to the front.
- It is time for Ohio to pick up the sword to overcome and break the religious spiritual stronghold over us. The prophetic breaker anointing will be a battering ram to shift the state.
- Apostolic order will come into place. Our nation depends upon the movement of God in our state.
- Fire to purify is coming. Much iniquity is to be dealt with. A radical Church in Ohio is being birthed.
- A great buzzing has started.
- Columbus must receive a pioneer anointing.

* Cincinnati will be volatile.
* Cleveland, revival is at the door.
* Eagles again will fly as the bird of war.
* A new thing is birthed.
* Lack of personal breakthroughs have hindered Ohio. Transitions are coming from unbelief, idols, fear, and complacency.
* A great restructuring to the enemy's camp is happening. Confusion is being brought to the enemy. Ancient seeds of darkness are about to be undone.
* The distrust that was birthed 25 years ago is being healed. Again, the heart of the father and the heart of the children will turn to each other. There will be supernatural reconciliation.
* Dayton will come to a new weightiness! There will be a breaking of false covenants and a building of new covenants. As the Wright brothers flew from Dayton, so a repair between brothers will bring a flying. The free masonry spirit root in Dayton will be taken by the axe.
* Ohio will go through the process of *travail, conception, birth, refinement,* and finally, to *restoration* of our joy. We will run with the horses! Surprises will happen. A new sense of order is coming in the state.
* Iniquitous patterns are broken! We will be in our places.
* In the 2004 national election, Ohio will become a deciding force. There will be a breakthrough in revelation of God's word. Energy from Heaven will be released. The revelatory sword of the Lord is going to do surgery on the state of

Ohio. The outcome of the presidential election is going to be somehow determined by what takes place in Ohio!

Brief Ohio History[145]

In prehistoric times, Ohio was inhabited by the Mound Builders. Before the arrival of Europeans, [eastern] Ohio was the scene of warfare between the Iroquois and the Erie, which resulted in the extermination of the Erie. In addition to the Iroquois, other Native American tribes soon prominent in the region were the Miami, the Shawnee, and the Ottawa.

La Salle began his explorations of the Ohio valley in 1669 and claimed the entire area for France. The Ohio River became a magnet for fur traders and land seekers, and the British, attempting to move in, hotly contested the French claims. Rivalry for control of the forks of the Ohio River led to the outbreak (1754) of the last of the French and Indian Wars. The defeat of the French gave the land to the British, but British possession was disturbed by Pontiac's Rebellion. The British government issued a proclamation in 1763 forbidding settlement [west] of the Appalachian [Mountains]. Then in 1774, with the Quebec Act, the British placed the region between the Ohio River and the Great Lakes within the boundaries of Canada. The colonists' resentment over these acts contributed to the discontent that led to the American Revolution, during which military operations were conducted in the Ohio country.

Ohio was part of the vast area ceded to the United States by the Treaty of Paris 1783. Conflicting claims to land in that area made by Connecticut, Massachusetts, and Virginia were settled by relinquishment of almost all of the claims and the organization of the Old Northwest by the Ordinance of 1787. Ohio was the first region developed under the provisions of that ordinance, with the activities of the Ohio Company of Associates promoted by Rufus Putnam and Manasseh Cutler. Marietta, founded in 1788, was the first permanent American settlement in the Old Northwest.

In the years that followed, various land companies were formed, and settlers poured in from the East, either down the Ohio on flatboats and barges, or across the mountains by wagon—their numbers varying with conditions, but steadily expanding the area's population. The Native Americans, supported by the British, resisted American settlement. They successfully opposed campaigns led by Josiah Harmar and Arthur Saint Clair but were decisively defeated by Anthony Wayne in the battle of Fallen Timbers (1794). The British thereafter (1796) withdrew their outposts from the Northwest under the terms of Jay's Treaty, and the area was pacified. Ohio became a territory in 1799. General Saint Clair, as the first governor, ruled in an arbitrary fashion that made Ohioans for many years afterward distrustful of all government. In 1802 a state convention drafted a constitution, and in 1803 Ohio entered the Union, with Chillicothe as its capital. Columbus became the permanent capital in 1816.

In the War of 1812 the Americans lost many of the early battles of the war that took place in the Old Northwest, and their military frontier was pushed back to the Ohio River. Two British attacks on Ohio soil were successfully resisted: one against Fort Meigs at the mouth of the Maumee River and the other against Fort Stephenson on the Sandusky. The area was further secured by Oliver Hazard Perry's naval victory on Lake Erie near Put-in-Bay, Ohio, and William Henry Harrison's victory in the battle of the Thames on Canadian soil.

After the war, Ohio's growth was spurred by the building of the Erie Canal, other canals, and toll roads. The National Road was a vital settlement and commercial artery. Settlement of the Western

Reserve by New Englanders (especially those from Connecticut) gives [northeast] Ohio a decidedly New England cultural landscape. Ohio's society of small farmers exported their produce down the Ohio and the Mississippi rivers to Saint Louis and New Orleans. In 1837, Ohio won a territorial struggle with Michigan usually called the Toledo War. The Loan Law, adopted in the Panic of 1837, encouraged railroad and industrial development. Railroads gradually succeeded canals, preparing the way for the industrial expansion that followed the Civil War.

Most Ohioans were sympathetic with the Union in the Civil War, and many Ohioans served in the Union army. Native sons such as Joshua R. Giddings, Salmon P. Chase, and Edwin M. Stanton had long been prominent opponents of slavery. Nevertheless, the Peace Democrats, the Knights of the Golden Circle, and the Copperheads were very active; Clement L. Vallandigham drew many votes in the gubernatorial election of 1863. Ohio was the scene of the northernmost penetration of Confederate forces in the war—the famous raid (1863) of John Hunt Morgan, which terrorized the people of the countryside until Morgan and most of his men were finally captured in the southeast corner of the state.

After the Civil War, industrial development grew rapidly when shipments of ore from the upper Great Lakes region increased and the development of the petroleum industry in [northeast] Ohio shifted the center of economic activity from the banks of the Ohio River to the shores of Lake Erie, particularly around Cleveland. Immigrants began to swell the population, and huge fortunes were made....

Floods in the many rivers flowing to the Ohio and in the Ohio River itself have long been a problem; a devastating flood in 1913 led to the establishment of the Miami valley conservation project. Continuing long-term state and federal projects have improved locks and dams along the entire length of the Ohio and its major tributaries, for navigation as well as flood control purposes.

Both farms and industries in Ohio were hard hit by the Great Depression that began in 1929. In the 1930s, the state was wracked by major strikes such as the sit-down strikes in Akron (1935-1936) and the so-called Little Steel strike (1937). World War II brought great prosperity to Ohio, but labor strife later resumed, as in the steel strikes of 1949 and 1959. Political unrest also affected the state in the protests of the 1960s and most violently in 1970 when four students were killed by national guardsmen who fired on a group of Vietnam War protesters at Kent State [University].

Ohio's economy went into massive decline in the 1970s and '80s as the automobile, steel, and coal industries virtually collapsed, causing unemployment to soar. Akron, once world famous as a rubber center, stopped manufacturing rubber products altogether by the mid1980s. During this period, the state's northern industrial centers were especially hard hit and lost much of their population. Since then, Ohio has concentrated on diversifying its economy, largely through expansion of the service sector. The state became an important center for the healthcare industry with the opening of the Cleveland Clinic. Industrial research is also important, with Nela Park near Cleveland and Battelle Memorial Institute in Columbus among the more notable research centers; there are also still important rubber research laboratories in Akron.

OKLAHOMA[146]

Oklahoma: Choctaw meaning "red people" or "red man"
Statehood: November 16, 1907 (46th state)
Motto: *Labor Omnia Vincit* (Work Conquers All)
Familiar Name: The Sooner State
50-State Tour: The Open Heaven State, January 20-21, 2003

From our 50-State Tour meeting in New Mexico, we traveled on to Oklahoma City, Oklahoma. I was trying to rest on the flight from Dallas to Oklahoma, and I opened my eyes and looked out the window (which I never do since I don't sit by the window). I looked down on the ground and actually saw a dove imprinted in the ground. It looked like it was outlined with fire with liquid glory in the middle.

> I heard the Lord say, "I AM present in this state. I AM redeeming this ground. I AM moving. I AM here. Honor Me because I am in the midst of these people and will change the course [of the] nation. This is a day of your visitation. Visit the tribes for I will be visiting the tribes. Go to all tribes that even exist in this state and take to them a gift that says I AM in your midst and I AM coming to visit and invade and restore and reconstruct them. Visit each one this year, and in your visiting I will visit and the glory that I have will flood this land."
>
> To the apostolic leadership of Concerts of Prayer in Oklahoma: "This is a time of gathering. Because I have marked this land, gather one of every tribe into this place. And as you gather them in, I will restore My mind with My people, and they will go forth from this place and carry My glory across this land."

> To the gatekeeper of Norman, Oklahoma, Bill Sanchez, where the University of Oklahoma is: "Go to that campus gate and declare that I will interrupt it this year for I am in this land. I will interrupt the sports events. I will interrupt everything that is going on for I will interrupt and invade the campuses, and it will be seen in the nation."
>
> To some of you who have been striving to break in and see prosperity come: "I am in the land. I am cutting forth a way. And where you could not enter in, in the past, you will enter in, in this season."
>
> For the religious structures of this city (I actually saw Nazarene, Pentecostal Holiness, those headquarters groups): "Tell them the glory is in this land, and I will invade what they stand for!"

John Benefiel, our SPN State Coordinator for Oklahoma, coordinated our gathering as part of the Oklahoma Concert of Prayer. Once again, both the sanctuary and overflow rooms were full, with many people standing along the back wall. Dutch ministered the first night and was very excited about the message that the Lord had given him coming from Denver—that we had reached the fullness of time, that the Lord had declared the land holy, and that we are now moving into a season of multiplication.

He had never spoken anything like this. I can't tell you how the glory and God's presence came into this place. There is no way to describe it. The Native people were overwhelmed, wailing and crying. Dutch began to encourage us to think of the door of Heaven being opened vertically, not horizontally, and to move through the gate of covenant to receive revelation. I then taught on the keys for prosperity, and how to optimize resources and reorganize for prosperity in the midst of war.

On Tuesday, January 21, I saw a picture while we were worshiping. I saw many people in the river, but some were actually caught between two rocks. The people had gotten in the river but couldn't go farther downstream. As a matter of fact, the Lord will put us in the river, and as He carries us down the river, He eventually lands us into a place where we begin to catch a fire for His purposes. For some people, it wasn't that our head was under water. It's as if we were caught and trapped, and didn't know how to move forward into the new things and into the Spirit of God the way He wanted to release and move us into a whole new dimension. It was as if the Lord said, "You are resisting the current instead of just getting real still; you're fighting to get loose." The Lord says, "Stand still until I begin to get you through this narrow place and take you on into a whole new dimension of My Spirit of seeing and victory. So just for a moment, stand still with your arms straight up and surrender to Him, and with those arms straight up, notice that He will begin to loose you to move on."

I released the following word: *"The River is flowing from the throne room. Many have heard My voice and have come into My presence. Many have heard what I would like to do for them. But on their way back to accomplish My purposes in the earth realm, the enemy has blocked their way. I'm going to remove those rocks out of My river of revelation, and what you saw I will accomplish."* I declared a loosing, I declared a release, and I declared movement. I thanked the Lord that He has a people ready to move in a new way. I declared we would move past those confinements that have been around us and that would keep us from moving forward. I went on to say, "Some of you have been in very hard places this past year, and it's as if you haven't quite allowed the Spirit of God to do the work of that hard circumstance. So right now, just surrender yourself new and fresh."

The prophetic word continued,

"This is a new day of gathering. And I see My people and I see from Heaven that which has stopped you. I see that which you have strived with. I see that which has attempted to wound you and stop you from moving forward. But it's a new day of gathering, and it is I that is beginning to gather in a new way. I have future prosperity and in this season of gathering it is My season. Therefore I will teach you to gather. So you must move forward into a place and a mind for gathering. For it is that mind of gathering that will draw in the resources for the future.

"This is the day of covenant and this is the day of release. And though you have not understood the multiplication factors, I will teach you now to multiply for it is My day of gathering. I am moving you forward. Even now there will be an ending of the old way of gathering; you will see that ending in this state. And then there will be a release. My people would go forward in a way like never before to snatch away those that the enemy has captured. In this day of gathering you know your enemy. Some have resisted knowing the enemy; therefore, the enemy has taken the spoils. Know your enemy this day. Know your enemy this day; stand still and watch Me give you revelation of that which has confined you.

"Know your enemy for you have settled for normality instead of settling for multiplication. Know your enemy and you will take the enemies' spoils back. For this, My day of gathering, I will enter through the door of the enemy, and it is you that I will enter through.... I am sending you in through the door the enemy has held shut. It will now open. Stand still so that you know how to move quickly; take the enemies' spoils, and advance My Kingdom in this earth.

"The last season of Saul is ending this year. Many of you have not mourned properly over the Sauls of the past. But this will be a year that you will see the ending of Saul structures that have held back the move of My Spirit. Mourn over that which did not come to completion, and then I will release an anointing to complete and bring forth the fullness of what I have for you. Look and even see now...this did not happen, and this did not happen, and this did not happen. When you see clearly and you see the blockage of those that didn't have a heart for My glory, I will remove that blockage, and then I will give you the plan of completion. Mourn first, then rejoice, for completion is coming."

Brief Oklahoma History[147]

Oklahoma is a Choctaw word meaning "red people" or "red man." The territory was inhabited by Native American tribes when Coronado, the first European, arrived in 1541. In the 16th and 17th centuries, French traders visited. Part of the 1803 Louisiana Purchase, Oklahoma was established as Indian Territory but was not given territorial government. It became home to the "Five Civilized Tribes"—Cherokee, Choctaw, Chickasaw, Creek, and Seminole—after the forced removal of Indians from the eastern US, 1828-1846, otherwise known as the "Trail of Tears." The land was also inhabited by Cheyenne, Comanche, Osage, and many other Plains Tribes. As settlers pressed west, conflicts arose between Natives and settlers throughout the west, and Oklahoma was no exception. A tragic result was a massacre of some 200 Cheyenne women and children in western Oklahoma. John Sipes, Southern Cheyenne historian, gives the account of the massacre at Washita:

On November 27, 1868, Custer and the Seventh Cavalry charged into a Cheyenne village on the Washita River in Indian Territory. The result was a massacre of children, women and elders of the tribe and the total destruction of their camp by burning. The horses owned by the Cheyenne were slaughtered. He surrounded the camp and at dawn... he attacked the sleeping camp. This camp was headed by Chief Black Kettle, had no wolves (scouts) out to guard the sleeping village and the sleeping village was unaware of the attack and slaughter of the people that was to happen. What followed was a massacre of the people from the pregnant Cheyenne women being cut open at the womb and babies left on the frozen ground dead with their mothers. Women, children and elders alike were shot down as at a turkey shoot. Custer took 52 captives back to Camp Supply...as prisoners of war. Thus this needless massacre just four years almost to the date later from the Sand Creek Massacre and to the very same bands and families nearly wiped out this extended kinships of families that had survived the Sand Creek Massacre in 1864 in southeastern Colorado.[148]

By the 1880s Congress passed laws opening Oklahoma Territory for settlement. This was accomplished by runs and lottery starting on April 22, 1889. Some people, anxious to claim the choice lands first, earned the title "sooners" because they entered the land illegally prior to the official opening. The promise of free land opened the floodgates for people from all over the nation to clamor for the coveted 160-acre plots. It drew those who were sincere in their desire to start fresh in a new land, but it also attracted those with hearts filled with greed, murder, lust for power, prostitution, gambling, etc. This flood of people caused great chaos, resulting in land ownership disputes and divisions. However, the greatest loss took place against the Native Americans who were cheated out of their land by the breaking of over 400 treaties made by the U.S. government.

The broken covenants with the Natives and their bloodshed have defiled the land in Oklahoma. Contributing to further defilement of the land is Freemasonry. Many of the founders of the territory, political leaders, and city fathers were Freemasons. Many of the founding churches in Oklahoma have members who were also Freemasons. This syncretism of Christianity and Freemasonry has harmed the effectiveness of the church, resulting in the "buckle of the Bible belt" being cinched up with spirits of religion and lack of unity. This syncretism has also been an inhibition against the emergence and recognition of the fivefold ministry. Freemasonry has become the seedbed for all other forms of occult practices by Natives and non-Natives. This idolatry has created another layer of defilement in the land.

Many Christian leaders believe that the Oklahoma City bombing in 1995 resulted from the open doors that were created by the culmination of these iniquities.

OREGON[149]

> **Oregon:** Algonquian meaning "beautiful water"
> **Statehood:** February 14, 1859 (33rd state)
> **Motto:** She Flies With Her Own Wings
> **Familiar Name:** The Beaver State
> **50-State Tour:** The State to Throw Jezebel From the Wall, December 16-17, 2003

Oregon has become a state where spiritual intercessors abound and even prophets are beginning to notice, increase in number, and come from faraway places to further decree that Oregon is the state whose people protect the prophets. This used to be the state where one might say, "Why do none of the prophets ever come here?" Now, just a few years later, we are hearing from others, "Why do all the prophets go to Oregon instead of our state?"

As prophesied by several prophets recently, including Todd Bentley, Kim Clement, Dutch Sheets, and Chuck Pierce, we are called to take out "Jezebel," which will facilitate revival around the globe. During the 50-State Tour meeting, Chuck Pierce and Dutch Sheets declared that Oregon will have (or has) the authority to see the Jezebel spirit torn down over the entire nation. As a result, what we pray for and prophesy and decree from this state (along with other states, of course, but there is a special anointing in this state) will help to determine much of what happens in revival nationwide and worldwide.

Because the prophets have told us that we, in Oregon, have been assigned the task of taking out the spirit of Jezebel (which kills the prophets, among other things), we must pray that prophets will flock here in larger numbers to defy the prophets of Baal and the spirit of Jezebel, and throw that spirit down—not as an act of the flesh but by the blood of Jesus. Pray that no one will try to take on Jezebel alone (which is not safe to do unless he or she is called and anointed by God to do so), but corporately, in larger and larger corporate gatherings to stand, in unity, against that which stands against God and His servants and friends, the prophets.

Brief Oregon History[150]

Early Exploration and Fur Trading

Initial European interest in the region was aroused by the search for the Northwest Passage. Spanish seamen skirted the Pacific coast from the 16th to the 18th [century], hoping to claim the area. The English may first have arrived in the person of Sir Francis Drake, who sailed along the coast in 1579, possibly as far as Oregon.

Two centuries later, in 1778, [Captain] James Cook, seeking the award of £20,000 for the discovery of the Northwest Passage, charted some of the coastline. By this time the Russians were pushing southward from posts in Alaska and the British fur companies were exploring the West. Oregon's furs promised to become an important factor in the rapidly expanding China trade, and the Oregon coast was soon active with the vessels of several nations engaged in fur trade with the Native Americans. British captains, among them John Meares and George Vancouver, made the coastal area known, but it was an American, Robert Gray, who first sailed up the Columbia River (1792), thus establishing U.S. claim to the areas that it drained.

Canadian traders of the North West Company were approaching the Columbia River country when the overland Lewis and Clark expedition arrived in 1805. David Thompson was already making his way to the lower river when John Jacob Astor's agents (in the Pacific Fur

Company) founded Astoria, the first permanent settlement in the Oregon country. In the War of 1812 the post was sold (1813) to the North West Company, but in 1818 a treaty provided for 10 years of joint rights for the United States and Great Britain in Oregon (i.e., the whole Columbia River area). This agreement was later extended. The North West Company merged with the Hudson's Bay Company in 1821, and soon the region was dominated by John McLoughlin at Fort Vancouver.

Settlement and Statehood

In 1842 and 1843 enormous wagon trains began the "great migration" westward over the Oregon Trail. Trouble between the settlers and the British followed. The Americans set out to form their own government, and demanded the British be removed from the whole of the Columbia River country up to lat. 54°40' N; one of the slogans of the 1844 election was "Fifty-four forty or fight." War with Britain was a threat momentarily, but diplomacy prevailed. In 1846 the boundary was set at the line of lat. 49°N, but disagreements over the interpretation of the 1846 treaty were not successfully arbitrated until 1872....

Two years later the Oregon Territory was created, embracing the area [west] of the Rockies from the 42d to the 49th parallel. The area was reduced with the creation of the Washington Territory in 1853, and Oregon became a state in 1859 with a constitution that prohibited slaveholding but also forbade free blacks from entering the state. Although the California gold rush caused a temporary exodus of settlers, it also brought a new market for Oregon's goods, and the Oregon gold strike that followed attracted some permanent settlement to the eastern hills and valleys.

Wheat farming prospered and in 1867-68 a surplus crop was shipped to England—the beginning of Oregon's great wheat export trade. Cattle and sheep were driven up from California to graze on the tallgrass of the semiarid plateaus, and soon cattle barons, such as Henry Miller, acquired huge herds. They dominated the industry until the late 19th [century], when sheepmen and homesteaders succeeded in reducing the cattle range. The 1850s, '60s, and '70s were plagued by Native American uprisings, but by 1880 troubles with the Native American were over, and the next few decades brought increasing settlement and internal improvements.

Railroads and Industrialization

During the 1880s, and largely under the management of Henry Villard of the Northern Pacific RR, transcontinental rail lines were completed to the coast and down the Willamette Valley into California, bringing new trade and stimulating the beginnings of manufacture. Lumbering, which had long been important, became a leading industry. Seemingly overnight logging camps and sawmills were built in the western foothills. The huge stands of Douglas fir and cedar brought fortunes to the lumbering kings, but the threat to natural resources led ultimately to the creation of national forests.

By the time of the Lewis and Clark Centennial Exposition at Portland in 1905, less than 50 years after statehood had been gained, the frontier era had passed. Most of the feuding on the eastern plateaus was over, and cattle and sheep grazed peacefully on fenced-in ranges. In spring the Willamette Valley was abloom with fruit blossoms, and the river cities were busy with trade and industry.

Reform Movements and Environmental Issues

Oregon has been a leader in social, environmental, and political reforms. It was the first state, for example, to institute initiative, referendum,

and recall; to ease the laws governing the use of marijuana; and to initiate a ban against nonrecyclable containers. Several issues have sharply divided conservatives and liberals; one of the most important has been the question of minority groups. In the 1880s the influx of Chinese threatened the labor market and brought violent anti-Chinese sentiment, and in the 20th [century] there was opposition to the Japanese. Feeling against minorities has never been statewide, however, and large groups have vigorously opposed it.

In the 1930s one of the most disputed issues was the question of whether the development of power should be public or private. Today, however, it is widely recognized that the federal power and irrigation projects have had a profoundly positive effect on the economy of the entire Pacific Northwest. Many acres have been opened to irrigated farming, and the tremendous industrial expansion of World War II was to a large extent dependent on Bonneville power.

Environmental issues have dominated Oregon politics since the 1970s. Controversy arose in the late 1980s over the spotted owl, which has become endangered as old-growth forest has been cut down. Restrictions on logging on public lands were initiated in 1991, and attempts to establish forest policies acceptable to both environmentalists and the timber industry bogged down as other species were also shown to be in danger. There also is concern that the state's numerous hydroelectric dams are disrupting the migratory cycle of Pacific salmon.

PENNSYLVANIA[151]

Pennsylvania: Named for founder William Penn and *"sylvania,"* Latin for "woods"
Statehood: December 12, 1787 (2nd state)
Motto: Virtue, Liberty, and Independence
Familiar Name: The Keystone State
50-State Tour: The First Shall Be Last—A Governmental Shift State, August 2-3, 2004.

"Dutch and I finished our meeting in Pennsylvania last night. *Mission accomplished!* The Lord had ordered our steps to end with Pennsylvania, the 'Keystone State.' The keystone is the stone at the top of an arch that holds everything together. We declared that the synergy from the other 49 states would connect with the meeting last night held in one of the darkest parts of America in downtown Philadelphia. We decreed that God would reconnect, revive, and restore His plan for our nation. We were in Saint Mark's Episcopal Church. This facility once had 2,500 members in the early 1900s, but had dwindled down to 17. The meeting was packed with over 1,000 last night. What a picture of revival. We also decreed that the government was on *His* shoulders. We declared that His government was the absolute government over our nation and that every other civil government would align with His purpose. Watch for great shakings ahead" (Chuck D. Pierce, August 4, 2004).

We had wonderful attendance at each of the meetings: about 1,000 each in Camp Hill and Philadelphia, and 400 at the daytime meeting in York. Wonderful worship teams led us into the presence of God and provided an atmosphere for the prophetic and teaching.

Much of Dutch's teaching related to governmental authority. He said, "God is government!" God rules. Therefore, whatever He decrees will become reality. Therefore, we must get snapped into the place that God has for us, get to know God well, find out what He wants to do, and decree it. Jesus said, "As in Heaven, so on earth."

The prophetic word indicates that Pennsylvania is truly the Keystone State. A keystone is the block that holds all the other blocks of an arch in place. The prophetic sense is that Pennsylvania will play a role in helping the nation come into alignment spiritually and that we will set the pace in governmental praying and declaration. The indication is that the greater agreement that we come into in our prayers, the greater the power in prayer.

It was also prophesied that the next 90 days are crucial. God will do something (not specified) if we seek Him in the next 90 days. Chuck mentioned that worship will be a big part of this and that there will be a "grass roots movement." He said there would eventually be seven key centers for worship that will cut off the head of the enemy in the state.

Brief Pennsylvania History[152]

It would be impossible to understand the beginnings and potential of the state of Pennsylvania without an understanding of its founder William Penn. William Penn came alive in Jesus in England at a time when King James persecuted anyone who did not conform to the Church of England. However, Penn's passion for the Lord did not allow him to live the life of comfort that could have been his. Instead of living the life of a courtier, he spent much time in prison, persecuted for his faith in the Lord.

Because of the persecution that Penn received, he dreamed of a place "where men and women could serve God freely without hindrance." Penn formally petitioned the crown for a land grant in the New World.

King Charles II granted Penn's request so that he could personally be freed from a debt that he owed Penn's father.

William Penn had high hopes that his settlement, known as Pennsylvania, would have an impact upon the entire nation. He wrote to his friend Robert Turner, "...My God who has given it [Pennsylvania] me through many difficulties, will, I believe bless and make it the *seed of a nation*"[153] (emphasis mine). He indicated how he believed this would happen in a letter to another friend, James Harrison. He told Harrison that he desired "that an example may be set up to the nations: there may be room there...for such an *holy experiment*"[154] (emphasis mine). His desire was that men live in holiness, which would include living in covenant with God and in covenant with men. He desired to see men live by laws that they would write but knew that this would only work as they lived under submission to God.

Fields says, "The platform created by William Penn was a grand opportunity for this land's own indigenous people and every other ethnic group that came to America to know God, not through manipulation, but through a righteousness that so firmly confessed the value of all men."[155] He concludes that it worked. A continuation of the love and holiness of Penn would have resulted in a demonstration to the world of how differing peoples could have lived in love and mutual trust that would have provoked the world to the kind of jealousy that God intended when He established a people in the land of Canaan (see Deuteronomy 4:5-9).

Penn's work provides a seed for the nation in another important manner. The fourth revision of the constitution for Pennsylvania, "The Charter of Privileges," served as an outline for the Constitution of the United States.

Unfortunately, the climate began to change after the death of William Penn. Instead of seeking to coexist in mutual respect and love, those who came after Penn began to push out the Natives. This eventually led to unjust treatment of the Natives. The many injustices are illustrated by the following. First there was "The Walking Purchase." The Europeans were to take the amount of land that a man could walk in a day and a half. Instead of using an average man to walk, they used the kind of men we would consider athletes in our day. Instead of walking 30 miles, these "ringers" ran 66 miles. The Albany Treaty was another such debacle where one tribes' claim to land was given over to others even though there was not proper representation of the Natives in Pennsylvania at the treaty signing. These and many other injustices alienated the Natives from the British.

Over the early years of Pennsylvania's history, she has shown herself to be the seed of the nation in other ways. The signing of the Declaration of Independence took place in Philadelphia; Washington's famous prayer took place at Valley Forge, just a few miles from Philadelphia; and York, Pennsylvania, became the nation's first capital.

The early history of the state clearly shows that Pennsylvania has a role in planting seed. Unfortunately, as we have already seen, this seed has not always been pure seed.

Early in the process, we see the contamination of the seed with leaders of the Masonic order—such as Pennsylvania's own Benjamin Franklin. As a result the holy seed of the gospel began to be mixed with the esoteric philosophies of freemasonry. Today, the lodge itself lists many Blue Lodges in the State. The result is that thousands, some serving in leadership in the church, have made pacts with other gods. In addition, other aspects of witchcraft including Powwow and Wicca have and still do hold sway over many in the state.

In addition, no history of Pennsylvania would be complete without some discussion of the Battle of Gettysburg. This battle took place over three days in 1863 with the participation of 97,000 Union and 75,000 Confederate soldiers. When the battle was over, 51,000 had lost their lives, ranking Gettysburg as the deadliest battle on U.S. soil. Today, people continue to see apparitions of ghosts in Gettysburg and many coffee shops draw in customers with storytellers sharing the macabre stories of ghosts on the battlefield.

Over the years, Pennsylvania has been plagued with injustice and racism. In the 1960s, the city of York, Pennsylvania, became a hotbed for black/white hatred. Just a few years ago, two trials for murders on each side of this issue captured the nation attention. Other hate groups such as the KKK have set up residence in Pennsylvania. It seems that because of the way satan has perverted things in the state, the Lord desires for Pennsylvania to be the state of brotherly love (just as the name Philadelphia means "city of brotherly love").

RHODE ISLAND[156]

Rhode Island: Roodt Eylandt meaning "red island" for its red clay
Statehood: May 29, 1790 (13th state)
Motto: Hope
Familiar Name: Little Rhody
50-State Tour: The Miracle State, July 19-20, 2004

Key themes from the 50-State Tour for Rhode Island:

★ A sweeping move for repentance will come to Rhode Island that will cause miracles to happen across the state.

- ★ God is bringing a message of hope by the demonstration of signs and wonders.
- ★ This is the year to break a spirit of infirmity.
- ★ An anointing for awakening is being released in Rhode Island.
- ★ The government of Rhode Island will see that God is present in the state.

Rhode Island Prayer Focus[157]

The current spiritual condition of Rhode Island: There is a demonic assignment to "weaken male leadership"—fathers, pastors, Christian and unbelieving men alike, spiritual sons of the state, and also apostolic authority. This assignment is a Jezebel spirit aimed at authority. It attacks the man by way of fear, passivity, religiosity, immorality, self-sufficiency, physical affliction, and natural distraction that causes spiritual blindness, all of which culminates in hardhearted spiritual apathy. However, God answers prayer.

Prayer for the State's Spiritual Leaders

1. *Pray for leadership energy.* Pray for church leaders to have the Holy Spirit active and continually resident in their personal devotion life as well as in their churches. Pray for a "personal revival" for each of them, and for their passions to be stirred to raise up an army of Spirit-filled people to heal a nation.

2. *Pray for a hedge of protection for the spiritual leaders of this state* that will protect them from divorce, control,

witchcraft, independence, addictions, accusations, criticism of each other, and a lack of care for one another.

3. *Bind the weaknesses of the independent spirit*, evidenced by self-sufficiency, isolationism, small-mindedness, and division. Declare that obedience is better than sacrifice over the spiritual leaders of the state.

4. *Loose the strength of the independent spirit*—that which is necessary to pioneer and chart out new truths, new territory for the Kingdom, revelation of what it truly means to be apostolic in the region, and fearlessness in Christ in confronting the "giants." Pray for new initiatives to impact the cities and the state, leading them toward righteousness.

5. *Pray that the pastors will not fall prey to a passive leadership style.*

6. *Loose unity*, peace to oust confusion, spiritual discernment, pastoral friendship, and love...*the greatest of these is* **love**!

Church and State Prayer Requests

1. Pray that the intercessory prayer coordinators from differing "streams" and cities would come together at the Rhode Island State House.

2. Pray that the state officials will be open to receiving prayer and the establishment of a prayer room in the State Capitol Building.

Governmental Prayer Requests

1. Pray that our civic officials will give their hearts to Christ and be transformed.
2. Pray that God's mercy will triumph over judgment for the residents and voters of the city of Providence.
3. Pray that civil union measures and same-sex marriage bills will not be accepted or ratified by the Rhode Island courts or voters.
4. Pray that Christians will run for public office as well as lobby and pray for legislation that would expand foundational Judeo-Christian beliefs and morality into the areas of education, the judicial, the economy, the many levels of government, the media, medicine and medical practices, and marriage and families. Pray that these changes would flow through every gateway into our every city and community in the state of Rhode Island.

Brief Rhode Island History[158]

Early Exploration and Colonization

The region of Rhode Island was probably visited (1524) by Verrazano, and in 1614 the area was explored by the Dutchman Adriaen Block. Roger Williams, banished (1635) from the Massachusetts Bay colony, established in 1636 the first settlement in the area at Providence on land purchased from Native Americans of the Narragansett tribe. In 1638, Puritan exiles bought the island of Aquidneck (now Rhode Island) from the Narragansetts. There they established the settlement of Portsmouth (1638). Because of factional differences, Newport was founded (1639) on the southwest side of the island, but the two towns later combined governments (1640-1647).

Another settlement, Warwick, was made on the western shore of Narragansett Bay in 1642.

In order to thwart claims made to the area by the Massachusetts Bay and Plymouth colonies, Williams, through influential friends, secured (1644) a parliamentary patent under which the four towns drew up a code of civil law and organized (1647) a government. The liberal charter granted (1663) by Charles II of England ensured the colony's survival, although boundary difficulties with Massachusetts and Connecticut continued well into the 18th [century].

The early settlers were mostly of English stock. Many were drawn to the colony by the guarantee of religious freedom, a cardinal principle with Williams, confirmed in the patent of 1644 and reaffirmed by the royal charter of 1663. Jews settled in Newport in the first year of Williams' presidency (1654), and Quakers followed in large numbers. All the early settlers owned land that, following Williams' practice, was bought from the Native Americans. Fishing and trade supplemented the living won from the soil. Moreover, livestock from the Narragansett county (South County), especially the famous Narragansett pacers, figured largely in the early commerce, which developed rapidly in the late 17th [century].

Because of the colony's religious freedom, it was viewed with mixed loathing and fear by the more powerful neighboring colonies and was never admitted to the New England Confederation. However, it bore its share of the devastation caused by King Philip's War in 1675-76. Between 1750 and 1770 there was bitter strife between Providence and Newport over control of the colony.

The Coming of Revolution

Until the American Revolution, Newport was the commercial center of the colony, thriving especially on the triangular trade in rum, slaves, and molasses. Rhode Island, like other colonies, objected to British mercantilist policies and consistently violated the Molasses Act of 1733 and the Navigation Acts. Narragansett Bay became a notorious haven for smugglers, and the British revenue cutter Gaspee was burned (1772) by patriots in protest against the enforcement of revenue laws.

After the start of the American Revolution, Rhode Island militia under Nathanael Greene joined (1775) the Continental Army at Cambridge, and on May 4, 1776, the province renounced its allegiance to George III. British forces occupied parts of Rhode Island from 1776 to 1779, when they withdrew before the arrival of the French fleet. The Revolution won, Rhode Island, jealous of its independence, refused to sanction a national import duty; it therefore deprived the Continental Congress of a major source of revenue and became one of the state's responsible for the failure of the Articles of Confederation. Rhode Island did not send delegates to the Constitutional Convention at Philadelphia and resisted ratifying the Constitution until the federal government threatened to sever commercial relations with the state; even then, ratification passed (1790) by only two votes.

Industrialization

The post-Revolutionary era brought bankruptcy and currency difficulties. Shipping, which continued to be a major factor in the state's economy until the first quarter of the 19th [century], was hard hit by Jefferson's Embargo Act of 1807 and by the competition from larger ports such as New York and Boston. However, this post-Revolutionary period also marked the beginning of Rhode Island's industrial greatness.

Samuel Slater built the first successful American cotton-textile mill at Pawtucket in 1790. An abundance of water power led to the rapid development of manufacturing, in which merchants and shipping magnates invested their capital.

With the growth of industry the towns increased in population, and Providence surpassed Newport as the commercial center of the state. Since suffrage had long been restricted to freeholders, Rhode Island's increased urbanization resulted in the disenfranchisement of most townspeople. Frustrated in repeated attempts to amend the constitution, many Rhode Islanders joined Thomas Wilson Dorr in forcibly establishing an illegal state government in Providence in 1842. Dorr's Rebellion, though abortive, resulted in the adoption of a new constitution (1842) extending suffrage; however, the property qualification was not abolished until 1888. Antislavery sentiment was strong in Rhode Island, and the state firmly supported the Union in the Civil War.

Mill Towns, Discontent, and a Changing Economy

Until well into the 20th [century] Rhode Island's political and economic life was dominated by mill owners. (Nelson W. Aldrich was a power in the nation as well as the state.) The small mill towns, with their company houses and company stores and their large numbers of foreign-born residents, were important elements in the social fabric. English, Irish, and Scottish settlers had begun arriving in large numbers in the first half of the 19th [century]; French Canadian immigration commenced around the time of the Civil War; at the end of the 19th [century] and the beginning of the 20th there was a large influx of Poles, Italians, and Portuguese. Politically, Rhode Island was generally controlled by Republicans until the 1930s, when the Democrats' insistence on reapportionment of representation (which tended to favor small towns over urban areas) helped bring their party into power.

Sporadic labor troubles in the 19th [century] had little effect on the state's economy. However, after World War I there was a long textile strike, centered in the Blackstone valley; this, together with the gradual removal of the mills to the South—the source of the cotton supply where labor was cheaper—led to a continuing decline in the cotton-textile industry. Nevertheless, the manufacture of textile products is still carried on in the state today and new industries such as high-technology electronics have been introduced. Since the 1970s the overall shift in the state's economy has been away from manufacturing altogether and toward the service sector. This shift has coincided with major suburban growth.

SOUTH CAROLINA[159]

> **South Carolina:** Named after Charles II and Charles II of England
> **Statehood:** May 23, 1788 (8th state)
> **Motto:** *Animis Opibusque Parati* (Prepared in Mind and Deed)
> **Familiar Name:** The Palmetto State
> **50-State Tour:** The State That Reversed the Curse, July 10-11, 2003

Dutch Sheets shared:

> The Lord has told me to remind you of your corporality. The Lord says, "I am creating a window of opportunity for South Carolina. This is ***another*** window of opportunity." In South Carolina, there is a cycle of getting to a certain place—and within a certain closeness of proximity of revival, or breakthrough, or of turning some things, breaking some strongholds—and getting to a place in the Spirit that would

really radically shift this state. There is a cycle (that I saw in the Spirit) of getting to a certain point and stopping, losing the opportunity—getting to a certain point, again losing the opportunity. The Lord says, "This time I want them to break through all the way and have My Body go through the window. *This is very much a grace thing.* I am alerting you that you have come to another window here. *Now I am going to show you how to go through it."*

Proverbs 29:18 says, "Where there is no vision, the people perish." In Hebrew chazown is the word "vision." The word really means a revelation, a prophetic revelation. Haggai 2 says, "It is time!" It really is time for South Carolina to move forward. Now is the time to agree that it is time for South Carolina! South Carolina has more than once rebuilt the walls, but they have never had the gates and doors in place. South Carolina is going to have to have a corporate mindset. You are moving into a season where it is going to be very critical that you begin to think now more big-picture corporality than just for your own vision. You are going to have to become intentional about thinking whole, corporate, what God is saying to us as a state...rise to a little bit higher level for a season.

There is a stronghold of division; there is a stronghold cloaked in a very subtle way hidden in this state because of some of the roots in this state. There is a very subtle thing—not animosity—not warring going on between brothers and sisters—that is rooted in a weak understanding of what the Lord wants to do. You are going to see a completion of the breaking through of racism—denominationalism, sectarianism—even in the government of this state. You will see people begin to come together, work together, and lay down divisive things that are not even in the context of churches and Christianity. You are going to see political leaders that at one time warred against one another, bury the hatchet, and they will begin to come together. "I am trying to fracture something that is centuries old," says the Lord, "and it is going to permeate every area of this culture and society."

Chuck Pierce began to declare:

> The spirit of isolation will break in the atmosphere of this state. We declare a shield of faith now forming. And the Lord would say, "There is a crisis at hand. There is a crisis at hand in the land, and I have brought you together to shut a door. Not only will you go through a window, but you are called at this time to shut the door. Have I not even directed the President of this land to go across the earth to declare that this is a time for slavery and its power to be broken.
>
> "Because of the entryway into this state, I will give you as a people an opportunity to shut the door to domination of races in this land. You will shut a door that has been there, and this is a time that you will…rise up in crisis, and you will begin to even move in a new way. You will not *secede* this time, but I am calling you to *lead*. Begin to lead in a new way. Even the identity over this state, I am ready to change. I am ready to make a shift, for you are seen in one way, but I am going to cause you to be seen in another way."
>
> Lord, we declare whatever turn this state took in 1987, which shifted it away from Your ultimate purpose, bring us back to that place and accelerate us forward. Whatever occurred in

1867 that was so devastating when there was an opportunity to turn right, we say, Lord, this is a time for a turning back to the full purpose of God.

And the Lord said, "I can create and I can change things in a day. This is a time of leadership in this state that will cause a nation to begin to quake. It is very important the shift in leadership, governmentally that is going on in this state. A wind is coming as a sign. Watch for the strong wind that comes across this state this season. And when you hear the sound of the wind in the myrtle bush or at Myrtle Beach," saith the Lord—"When you hear the sound of the wind and the wind is heard about, as it comes across Myrtle Beach, that signifies that change has come. ***Rise up and enter in!***"

Dutch Sheets continued:

> We can change things in the Spirit through breakthrough. We can change the atmosphere, and change will begin to manifest in every area of society. But if you try to implement these things without breakthrough in the Spirit, you just repeat cycles of frustration and fruitlessness. I'm hearing the word "cycle"...*past.* ***Disconnect*** and ***reconnect.***

God doesn't just ignore our history—He heals history. Get disconnected from our past sins and wounds, or we will repeat the cycle. Disconnect through repentance, through forgiveness. Establish proper alignment so the next generation of South Carolina will get life instead of another cycle of death, racism, hatred, infirmities coming through occultish things. Align, arrange properly, equip in Ephesians 4 to be useful. God has never needed a majority to bring change.

Chuck Pierce declared:

> There is a strategy right now for something to come out of this state, to try to bring division throughout this entire nation. There's a domination that is trying to rise up in this state to say, "But we're good and we're doing good right now" so you never enter into the best of what God has for you. Government influence is arising in this state that is going to begin to say, "Now wait a minute, we're not going to pull out." The Lord says, "There are two states in this nation that have strategies of secession within them to violate the independence that I am trying to bring to the land—South Carolina and Texas! There's a strategy, that if it is not broken now, you'll see it manifest in the next five years; and there will be an uprising that comes that creates the same confusion [as secession] throughout this land, plus seven times worse!"
>
> The enemy has paved the way for the waterway coming into Charleston to be used by the enemy. This is an entry point for the enemy to come into this land to oppress this entire nation. And the Lord said to me, "You tell them to go down to every major coast city and hold a worship gathering and a prayer and intercession gathering, and decree that a shield of change is coming across and around this state. You tell them to go to the twelve most populous cities of this state and hold a worship, apostolic, prophetic, intercessory gathering and decree that the heavens will change and the administration of God will be secured in this state. If you make the shift now, true liberty will be flowing in South Carolina. That shot is just ricocheting back and forth throughout this entire nation, just waiting to create the same chaos. The shot originated here.

You release an anointing in this state to bring such change that that shot is neutralized, or else we'll see division in this land like we have never known in the next five years." The Lord says, "Snap back in place your prophetic destiny, your leadership destiny. Instead of moving out of time and moving in a way with the enemy to produce chaos, you're going to move with Me and liberty will come from South Carolina."

Dutch Sheets then decreed:

> This is so critical for the Lord to do this. Fire the shot in the Spirit now and let it be a holy fire—it will be a holy shot. A major portion of the root of the sectarian spirit in this nation is coming from South Carolina. This state is a major root of this whole system of division and strife and bigotry—in the church and gender and anti-Semitism and all that stuff.
>
> Leadership of this state: Come out of your old wineskins. Let God snap you into place and position you in your position as a gatekeeper and a doorkeeper. Pray for understanding how to do it, for revelation.
>
> Diane Buker (Member of USSPN National Apostolic Council) decreed: The very thing that the enemy used, to use you, South Carolina, as a breech, the Lord is using now to build a siege mound around you, to enable you to break through. You are a battle axe in the hand of the Lord!

Brief South Carolina History[160]

The Spanish established the colony of Santa Elena in South Carolina in 1566. They also marked this land with cruelty and abuse. The brutality of the conquistadors led to the demise of the tribe that preceded the Cherokee, Creek, and Yemassee in South Carolina.

Charles Town, named after King Charles II (and later renamed Charleston in 1783), was an English proprietary colony founded in the year 1670. Of the Carolina's eight proprietors, only one took an interest in the Charles Town colony—Anthony Ashley Cooper. A godly man, Lord Ashley had a holy vision in which social equality and justice among all races and classes was the goal. He sought to develop a free society in which anyone could increase and abound socially, economically, politically, and spiritually. The original community blueprint for Charles Town envisioned a divine destiny and a heavenly calling—the Holy City! The spiritual vision of Charles Town being a "Holy City" could have stamped the entire colony with godly, Christian values. Tragically, many of the early settlers were seasoned English colonists from the Barbados who introduced and promoted the institution of slavery. Greed and the accumulation of wealth and power were their values. By 1690 rice cultivation, which required a large labor force, became the primary source of wealth. Charles Town was then and continues today to be a hedonistic city—drinking, partying, gambling, sexual promiscuity, and pleasure seeking. God's divine plan and holy vision has been thwarted up until now.

Division has always marked the state physically, politically, and economically. The territory comprising what is now South and North Carolina was originally named Carolina in honor of King Charles I. In 1710, the land of Carolina was divided into North Carolina and South Carolina. The boundary remained disputed until 1815. The prosperity of the coastal area made South Carolina the wealthiest colony in British North America. Before the American Revolution, Charleston had inventoried wealth more than six times that of Philadelphia, and maintained business ties to England. In stark contrast, poor immigrants slowly settled the wild backwoods. Many were Scots-Irish Presbyterians who had tasted persecution under British rule in their homeland. They settled in uninhabited land, not knowing these were favorite hunting grounds of the Cherokee nation. War with the Cherokee ended in 1755 with a treaty ceding the up-country of South Carolina to the whites.

Political power was held by the wealthy ruling class in Charleston, but they did not extend justice to the backwoods. Vigilante groups called Regulators were formed to create law and order, but they also became lawless. The capital city, Columbia, eventually moved to the geographic center of the state.

The battles of Kings Mountain and Cowpens are considered by many historians to be the turning points in the American Revolution. But the price was high. South Carolina had more dead, more wounded, and more widows than any American colony. More Revolutionary War battles were fought in South Carolina than any other state. Presbyterian pastors in the backwoods crystallized opposition to England. The American Revolution in South Carolina became a civil war, neighbor against neighbor. Covenant-breaking and betrayal defiled the land. Unhealed, our state was fertile soil for another conflict—the Civil War.

On December 20, 1860, Charleston, South Carolina, became the first state to pass the ordinance of Secession and secede from the Union. On April 12, 1861, the first shots of the Civil War were fired in Charleston. The Civil War and its aftermath were devastating for the state. We lost nearly one-fifth of the white male population, and the economy was shattered. General Sherman marched through South Carolina, burning and looting with vengeance. The reconstruction period that followed the war was marked by general economic, social, and political upheaval.

"Today huge economic challenges face our state, with the textile industry moving overseas and manufacturing plants closing their doors. Unemployment is a crisis issue in some cities. The state lottery deepens the poverty of the poor. Sectarianism and racism still challenge the status of citizens in South Carolina based on gender, ethnicity, and religion."[161]

In 2005, a gentile people await God's holy plan for the future of South Carolina.

Historical Root Issues

As a native South Carolinian who loves our state and people, I submit my spiritual mapping analysis of our history. The root issue throughout our history was and is pride. The fruit of our pride has been the release of a spirit of rebellion. A key historical focus is the original Preamble to our South Carolina Constitution. The significant thing is what is missing. There is no wording about thanksgiving for or submission to Almighty God. Forty-three states have their state firmly grounded and protected by these or similar words in their state constitutions:

We the people of _____, grateful to Almighty God, do ordain and establish...

Five other states at least recognize there is a supreme ruler of the universe. South Carolina is one of two states with no recognition of Almighty God and His authority and providence of blessing. Individually and corporately, South Carolina has walked in illegitimate authority. One of the fruits has been freedom for the religious spirit to divide the Church in South Carolina. Our rebellion has led to many abuses such as racism, sexism, domestic violence, murder, substance abuse, and social oppression. Repenting individually and corporately (identificational repentance) for this pride and rebellion and walking humbly under God's authority is bringing healing to South Carolina.

South Carolina Prophetic Prayer Declaration[162]

"It's time for a new corporate identity." The Lord has caused our iniquity to pass from us, and He has clothed us with rich apparel (see Zechariah 3). Just like Joshua was given clean garments and a clean turban—new mind-set and new authority—we declare that it is so with South Carolina. Jesus has stepped into South Carolina's history, and He has become the glory and lifter of her head. The harlot's "evil" conscience is being cleansed (see Hebrews 10:22), and she is beginning to identify with Jesus the Bridegroom. Her message is His message—the Spirit and the Bride say, "Come." Jesus the Bridegroom is carrying His Bride across the threshold to a place of intimacy and authority. South Carolina has been forgiven much. South Carolina will love much! *Instead of secession, South Carolina is called to intercession*—doing whatever He says—weeping yet rejoicing because His judgments will remove everything that hinders His love. We in South Carolina bow down to the "Worthy One"— we bow down to the Lamb. We "curtsie" and bow in honor, no longer bent over in shame as the harlot. He has washed us. He has redeemed us. He had betrothed us to Himself in righteousness. The Spirit and the Bride in South Carolina say, "Come." Jesus, the Bridegroom is carrying us where we cannot go alone—across the threshold—through the door—a new corporate bridal company in South Carolina that follows the Lamb wherever He goes.

SOUTH DAKOTA[163]

South Dakota: Sioux meaning "allies"
Statehood: November 2, 1889 (40th state)
Motto: Under God the People Rule
Familiar Name: The Coyote State
50-State Tour: The Stronghold State, June 28-29, 2004

Clearly, now, the Spirit is stirring here and something quite spiritually significant is underway. God is going to use this state very strategically to take down national strongholds. In the Fall of 2003, we nearly became the first state in the union to outlaw abortion. Chuck D. Pierce has noted that there is a strength resident here to take on a national stronghold: *"If we don't get breakthrough in South Dakota, we don't get the nation. There is a strongman here, and there is a stronghold here; but it is supposed to be a key place for the nation. And if we don't get this dealt with, we don't get revival in America."*

My sense is that we are in a crescendo season here. In music, the crescendo is the majestic and harmonious swelling of sound and intensity that fills a room with a surge of ordered power. Regionally, in the spiritual realm, God seems to be strategically placing leaders across our state as seasoned "conductors" who know how to give expression to the welling emotion in the "score." The key men and women of God are now rising up and standing before this orchestra of saints and calling forth the fullness of sound before the throne of the Father. God is after a harmony here—one of our state slogans is *"the land of infinite variety."* God is using all flavors of Christians to join the "chorus" of the coming Kingdom in South Dakota.

One of the fruits of the 50-State Tour was the declaration that South Dakota will become a very conspicuous place, a "conspicuous high place of God on earth"; a "conspicuous stronghold of the Lord Jesus." "There are giants in this land, but God is going to transform this region that is belittled, trodden down, and disparaged, and make it a Hebron—a place of friendship with God" (Dutch Sheets). We are going to be conspicuous because of the presence of the Lord.

It was noted that "Dakota" means friendship—north and south friendship. God is giving us a new name and identity. Psalm 88:12, Job 11:21, and Isaiah 62:4 stand out to us at this time—a land of forgetfulness, a land of oblivion, a land of gloom and deep shadow, of deep night and disorder. But then comes Isaiah 62:4: *"You will no longer be called desolate, forsaken, or forgotten. You will be called Beulah." Beulah* means "married to the land" or "the land is married"; and that speaks of great covenant. Verse 12 says, *"You will be called sought after."* So the Lord gives the land a new name, and I think the Lord is going to give us a new name. We are not a wasteland. We're not even farmland; we're not even Indian land. We're not even heartland. But I would suggest to you that because of what God is doing, this is north and south friendship. Do you know what "friendship" is? Friendship is a covenant joining together.

Pray for the establishment of sacred covenants in South Dakota, for the networking of networks already here, for strategic partnerships to form, for the restoration of covenant relationships with Native Americans here.

To again quote from the 50-State Tour meeting: "One of the most defining voices in our land comes out of this state. Now that is amazing, that South Dakota has that much influence in a nation; and yet that voice serves as a prophetic voice into our nation—whether it is right or whether it is wrong. Because you see, it is your call as a state. And that is why you are always going to see coming out of South Dakota an expression of truth....You are going to always have great influence because God has put that anointing on this particular state. So you are going to have to learn how to express yourself the way that God would have you express yourself, because you will have influence. It is amazing that South Dakota, one of the least populous states in our nation, has one of the greatest voices in our nation" (Chuck D. Pierce).

This becomes even more significant when you recall the extremely tight Senate race held in South Dakota in 2004 that had great national impact—where John Thune defeated Tom Daschle (who was, at that time, the Senate Minority Leader).

> "I say, there will be three cities in this state that will experience a great move of My Spirit, and from the move of My Spirit, it will be seen and heard throughout this entire land." (Prophesied by Chuck D. Pierce.)

Pray for these pockets of revival to break out in our cities. Pray for the planting of house churches in every community, on every reservation.

> "I would say to you, not any would have thought I would have watched after South Dakota; but I say, My eye is upon you and from this place the nation will begin to be legislated." (Prophesied by Chuck D. Pierce.)

There is something here that has to happen that is going to release the nation. Or, there is a destiny here that God is about to bring forth that is for the nation; and if we don't get it here, the nation can't go into what the Lord wants.

Pray that we are increasingly in a place of usefulness to God for His purposes nationally—that we'd move out into a place of strategic national influence.

> "It is time, in this region; it is time to rock the boat a little bit. You're not going to see this broken unless you're willing to get out of the box and let the Lord begin to do some things that are of a supernatural nature..." (Chuck D. Pierce).

Pray that the spirit of religion here will be exposed, disarmed, and bound. Pray for a number of key leaders and churches in key places to break out and join God in reaching this region.

> "If you won't do what I just said, then at least have some churchwide, regular prayer and worship meetings, where all you do is turn into the prophetic anointing and begin to decree the word of the Lord over your city, your people, your region. If you will begin...then by all means take it outside the doors of your church and go to these places that we are talking about and do this. If you will do that, you will begin to see things change immediately. It is time. If you do not heed this word, this stronghold will increase, and you will miss the time of your visitation. Now I am telling you by the Spirit of God, that is both a promise and a warning" (Chuck D. Pierce).

Worship-warfare events are now being planned and will be taking place over the course of this next year. During Labor Day 2004, over 240,000 people gathered at the fairgrounds in Sioux Falls, South Dakota, for the LifeLight Outdoor Music Festival. The heavens literally opened (with rain) near the end of the Sunday morning worship gathering of over 30,000 made up of believers from 50 supporting churches. God gave us a rainbow! Approximately 6,500 accepted Jesus as their Lord and Savior during LifeLight 2004. Who would have thought that one of the largest Christian music festivals in the U.S. is now being held in South Dakota!

Brief South Dakota History[164]

Early Inhabitants, European Exploration, and Fur Trading

At the time of European exploration, South Dakota was inhabited by Native Americans of the agricultural Arikara and the nomadic Sioux (Dakota). By the 1830s the Sioux had driven the Arikara from the area. Part of the region that is now South Dakota was explored in the mid-18th [century] by sons of the sieur de la Vérendrye. The United States acquired the region as part of the Louisiana Purchase, and it was partially explored by Lewis and Clark in their Missouri River expedition of 1804-1806. Later explorers became well acquainted with the warlike Sioux, who continued to dominate the region from the period of the fur trade until to the middle of the 19th [century]. Individual traders from the time of Pierre Dorion in the late 18th [century] made the region their home, and the posts founded by Pierre Chouteau and the American Fur Company were the first bases for settlement. (Fort Pierre was established in 1817.)

Settlement

It was not until land speculators and farmers moved westward from Minnesota and Iowa in the 1850s that any significant settlements developed in South Dakota. Two land companies were established at

Sioux Falls in 1856, and in 1859 Yankton, Bon Homme, and Vermillion were laid out. A treaty with the Sioux opened the land between the Big Sioux and the Missouri, and in 1861 Dakota Territory was established, embracing not only present-day North and South Dakota but also [eastern] Wyoming and [eastern] Montana. Yankton was the capital. Settlers were discouraged by droughts, conflicts with the Native Americans, and plagues of locusts; however, by the time the railroad pushed to Yankton in 1872, the region had received the first of the European immigrants who later came in great numbers, contributing significant German, Scandinavian, and Russian elements to the Dakotas.

Gold Fever and the End of Sioux Resistance

Rumors of gold in the Black Hills, confirmed by a military expedition led by George A. Custer in 1874, excited national interest, and wealth seekers began to pour into the area. However, much of the Black Hills region had been granted (1868) to the Sioux by treaty, and when they refused to sell either mining rights or the reservation itself, warfare again broke out. The defeat (1876) of Custer and his men by Sitting Bull, Crazy Horse, and Gall in the battle of the Little Bighorn (in what is now Montana) did not prevent the whites from gradually acquiring more and more Native American land, including the gold-lined Black Hills.

The near extinction of the buffalo herds, Sitting Bull's death (1890) at the hands of army-trained Native American police, and the subsequent massacre of Big Foot's band at Wounded Knee Creek were among the factors leading to the permanent end of Native American resistance in South Dakota. Tribal organization was weakened by the Dawes Act of 1887. Although the Indian Reorganization Act of 1934 attempted to restore tribal ownership of repurchased lands, younger generations have moved to the cities in increasing numbers. During the

1870s the gold fever mounted; Deadwood had its day of gaudy glory, Wild Bill Hickok and Calamity Jane created frontier legends, and the town of Lead began its long, productive history.

The Dakota Land Boom, Statehood, and Agrarian Reform

Although gold did not make the fortune of South Dakota, it laid the foundation by stimulating cattle ranching—herds of cattle were first brought to the grasslands of [western] South Dakota partly to supply food for the miners. Settlement in the east also increased and the period from 1878 to 1886, following the resumption of railroad building after the financial depression earlier in the decade, was the time of the great Dakota land boom, when the region's population increased threefold.

Agitation for statehood developed; in 1888 the Republican party adopted the statehood movement as a campaign issue, and in 1889 Congress passed an enabling act. The Dakotas were separated; South Dakota became a state with Pierre as capital. Disasters, however, rocked its security. The unusually severe winter of 1886-1887 had destroyed huge herds of cattle in the west, ruining the great bonanza ranches and promoting among the ranchers the trend—dominant ever since—of having smaller herds with provisions for winter shelter and feeding. Cattle grazed on public land and were rounded up only for branding and shipment to market.

Recurrent droughts added to the difficulties of the farmers, who sought economic relief in the cooperative ventures of the Farmers' Alliance and political influence in the Populist party, which won a resounding victory in 1896. Initiative and referendum were adopted (1898; South Dakota was the first state to adopt them) and other progressive measures of the day were enacted. However, prosperity resumed, and with it South Dakota quickly returned to political conservatism and the Republican party.

Railroads, Droughts, and the Great Depression

The extension of railroads (particularly the Milwaukee, which was the only transcontinental line passing through South Dakota) encouraged further expansion of agriculture, but new droughts (especially that of 1910-1911) brought a brief period of emigration. Many new farmsteads were abandoned, and a turn toward political radicalism developed. The Progressive party, led by Peter Norbeck (governor 1917-1921) and operating as a branch of the Republican party, revived the attempts of Populist reform programs to regulate railroad rates and raise assessments of corporate property. The Progressives also entered into experiments in state ownership of business.

Prosperity-depression cycles again affected the state after the boom of World War I. The combination of droughts and the Great Depression brought widespread calamities in the late 1920s and early 1930s, and the state's population declined by 50,000 between 1930 and 1940. Vigorous relief measures were instituted under the New Deal, and higher farm prices during World War II and the ensuing years brought a new era of hopefulness.

Postwar Changes

The 1950s began a period of Democratic strength in state politics. George McGovern was elected to the House of Representatives in 1956 and to the Senate in 1962, 1968, and 1974. In 1972 McGovern ran unsuccessfully for president. In 1973 a militant Native American group occupied a courthouse at Wounded Knee and the resulting gun battle with federal marshals heightened the long-time Native American resentment of the U.S. government over the issue of broken treaties.

In the postwar period the adoption of improved farming techniques resulted in a steady increase in agricultural and livestock production. This was accompanied, however, by the consolidation of small farms into large units and the displacement of many small farmers. Irrigation projects, extension of hydroelectric power, and protective measures against wind and water erosion have been implemented, avoiding the threat of new disasters. In 1981 a major New York bank relocated its credit-card operations to Sioux Falls, marking the beginning of the state's shift toward service, finance, and trade industries that, in turn, has resulted in significant economic growth. Some casino gambling was legalized in 1989 and tourism continues to be one of the state's top sources of income.

TENNESSEE[165]

Tennessee: Name of Cherokee village
Statehood: June 1, 1796 (16th state)
Motto: Agriculture and Commerce (Tennessee—America at Its Best)
Familiar Name: The Volunteer State
50-State Tour: A State Receiving God's Covenant Blessing, March 27-28, 2003

> "God is saying for this region that He wants to release a new level of governmental authority and it's a word for this state. God wants you to go to another level of governmental authority. 'I want you to realize I have given you the authority in this

> nation to decree, to bind, to loose, to close doors and open doors.' The Lord is saying, 'Go to another level of governmental authority. This is the Volunteer State, the Psalm 110 State. I will take this state *to a new level of power and strength and functioning as a volunteer army of God*. A new warring spirit is breaking forth in the state of Tennessee, and you will step into that mantle again.'" (Prophesied by Dutch Sheets.)

Renewed Covenant and Curse Broken

Dutch began to speak on how the Lord showed him on the plane flight to Tennessee that a curse relative to Israel had been removed off the state. On Monday, March 24, 2003 (just three days earlier), at the Capitol, the Lieutenant Governor of Tennessee publicly formalized the resolution passed by Tennessee that the state would support Israel! This is the word of the Lord for this state! (Dutch had no idea.) That night God gave Tennessee its reward! Dutch continued, "Tennessee, I'm telling you, it's a new day for you. You did something in natural government this week that did something in the Spirit, and it broke decades-long or probably a 100-150 year-old curse. God said, *'Because of your allegiance and alignment with Israel here, I moved you from curse to covenant blessings.'* That's just the word of the Lord. It's a fact. It's just the truth. The word volunteer means a freewill offering. They had to volunteer, to feel it in their heart. The Lord said, *'I'm going to take this state to a new level of serving.'"*

> Chuck D. Pierce prophesied, "Because of broken covenants in this state, especially with the Native American people—because of that, there has been a curse that has worked in this state of Tennessee. Because this state and people in this state

have aligned themselves with the nation of Israel and chose to bless My people and covenant with them, I am reversing the curse of the broken covenant, and I am bringing them into a new blessing of covenantal release. And this is the hour that I am going to begin to release the fruit of the covenant because they have covenanted with My people. It's reversing the old and bringing the new! ***I'm going to break a curse off this land. I'm going to break a curse and renew a covenant with this state.***"

Declaration by Chuck D. Pierce

"There is a new order rising in this house tonight. There is a convergence of the promises of God for many generations. There is a new order that is being released through this pure language. All that has occurred here tonight is a revelation of the new order, the revelation of a people of a pure language, the connectedness, the flow, the regeneration of a new generation, a priesthood after the order of Melchizedek. There will not be a vying or contending for this.... He is bringing order into the house, an order into the priesthood...the curse has been reversed.... There is a new level of set-apart, true, holy faith through this pure language that will be expressed in worship and in prophetic declaration and the communion of the saints as we commune with one another. It is going to be with a pure language, and there shall be a blessing released. There is a blessing being released and declared in the heavens tonight. All these things would be impossible to have planned or computed. It is God in the midst of this week of war. There is a sound rising up in the opposite spirit. Embrace it and carry it and declare it in your region. For this should not be a fire in one region. There are fires on the borders; there are fires in the corners. There are fires in the center.... He is bringing out those He has hidden for many times to bring them forth now. '*And this state shall be on fire from the corners, from the borders and in the center. It shall be on fire and in one accord with a pure language. I'm ready to answer the prayers that have been prayed in this place for a level of unity and the coming together of the Body of Christ in this region. And I am going to bring it to a new level of unity.*'"

Brief Tennessee History[166]

Early History

Western Tennessee abounds with artifacts of the prehistoric Mound Builders, who were the earliest inhabitants of the area. Cherokee, Chickasaw, Shawnee, and Creek were in the region when it was first visited by a European expedition under De Soto in 1540. French explorers came down the Mississippi River, claiming both sides for France, and circa 1682 La Salle built Fort Prudhomme, possibly on the site of present-day Memphis. The French established additional trading posts in the area, but they suffered continual harassment from the Chickasaw.

Meanwhile, English fur traders and long hunters (frontiersmen who spent long periods hunting in this area) came over the mountains from the Carolinas and Virginia, prevailed over the Cherokee, and made ineffectual the French claims to the area, which in any event was lost (1763) by the French in the French and Indian Wars.

The first permanent settlement was made (1769) in the Watauga River valley of eastern Tennessee by Virginians; they were soon joined by North Carolinians, including perhaps a few refugees of the Regulator movement. In 1772 these hardy settlers living beyond the frontier formed the Watauga Association, the first attempt at government in

Tennessee, and in 1777, at their request, North Carolina organized those settlements into Washington co.; Jonesboro, the county seat and oldest town in Tennessee, was founded two years later.

The American Revolution and Statehood

In the American Revolution, John Sevier was among the notable Tennesseans who served with distinction. When, after the war, North Carolina ceded its western lands to the federal government, the eastern Tennessee settlers, incensed at being transferred without their consent, formed a short-lived independent government (1784–1788) under Sevier.... The cession was reenacted in 1789, and in 1790 the federal government created the Territory of the United States South of the River Ohio (Southwest Territory), with William Blount as governor. This act disposed of various schemes to place the area under the control of Spanish Louisiana. In 1796 Tennessee, with substantially its present boundaries, was admitted to the Union as a slave state, with its capital at Knoxville. It was the first state to be carved out of national territory.

Tennessee's constitution, which provided for universal male suffrage (that is, including free blacks), was described by Thomas Jefferson as "the least imperfect and most republican" of any state. Armed with land grants awarded for service in the American Revolution, veterans and speculators (who had acquired the grants from veterans, sometimes fraudulently) swarmed in from the Carolinas, Virginia, Pennsylvania, and even from New England via such overland routes as the Wilderness Road and Cumberland Gap. Others poled keelboats from the Ohio up the Cumberland and Tennessee rivers.

The Early Nineteenth Century

For the most part a rough and ready people, numbering over 100,000 by 1800, the settlers of Tennessee were nevertheless strongly influenced by the Great Revival, a wave of religious hysteria that swept the state that year. The virtues and vices of their strongly egalitarian society were exemplified by Andrew Jackson, who was prominent in the faction-ridden politics of Tennessee. By 1829 when Jackson became president, the state was prospering. The first steamboat had reached Nashville in 1819, the year in which Memphis, soon to become the metropolis of a fast-growing cotton kingdom, was platted.

Internal improvement projects—canals and then railroads—were pushed, and a new, smaller wave of immigrants (predominantly Irish and German) arrived after the Cherokee and the Chickasaw were banished West in the late 1830s. Insatiable land hunger, the spirit of adventure, and personal considerations carried many white Tennesseans beyond the state; among them were Governor Samuel Houston and David Crockett, both of whom had been conspicuous in the fight for Texan independence. A decade later the response of Tennessee to the request for volunteers to fight in the Mexican War was so overwhelming that it has since been known as the Volunteer State. Tennessee's James K. Polk, a Jackson protégé, was the president of the United States during that war.

The Civil War and Reconstruction

Although slaves were numerous in western Tennessee, and to a lesser extent in Middle Tennessee, and free blacks were subjected to a series of discriminatory regulations, the state was pro-Union; it voted in the presidential election of 1860 for its own John Bell, candidate of the moderate Constitutional Union party. Secession was rejected in a popular referendum on [February] 9, 1861. However, after the firing on Fort Sumter and Lincoln's call for troops, the pro-Confederate element, led by Governor Isham G. Harris, canvassed the state, and on June 8, 1861, a second referendum approved secession by a two-thirds majority. The one third opposed represented mainly eastern Tennessee, where slavery was a negligible factor and where Andrew Johnson (then U.S. Senator) and William G. Brownlow had strengthened the natural Union loyalties of the people.

In the Civil War Tennessee was, after Virginia, the biggest and bloodiest battleground. The rivers served as Union invasion routes. Nashville was occupied by General D.C. Buell in [February] 1862, after the victories of General Ulysses S. Grant on the lower Tennessee and Cumberland rivers (see Fort Henry and Fort Donelson). In April one of the bloodiest battles of the war was fought near the Mississippi state line [the battle of Shiloh], and Memphis fell to a Union fleet in June. Confederate General Braxton Bragg, defeated at Perryville, [Kentucky] in [October] 1862, retreated further in [January] 1863, after the battle of Murfreesboro, and Grant, successful in the Vicksburg campaign, completely routed him ([November] 1863) in the Chattanooga campaign.

The Confederates did manage to hold on to Knoxville until [September] 1863, and their cavalry, particularly the forces of General N.B. Forrest and General J.H. Morgan, remained active. An army under General J.B. Hood made a last desperate attempt to regain the state late in 1864 but was defeated at Franklin [November 30] and annihilated at Nashville [December 15-16] by federal troops under G.H. Thomas. The Union military government that had been set up under Andrew Johnson in 1862 was succeeded in [April] 1865, by a civil government headed by Brownlow. An amendment to the state constitution of 1834 freed the slaves, and, with exConfederates disfranchised and radical Republicans in control, the state was readmitted to the Union in [March] 1866.

As the first Confederate state to be readmitted, Tennessee was spared the worst aspects of Congressional Reconstruction, but the postwar years were nonetheless bitter. The organization formed largely to reestablish "white supremacy" in the South, the Ku Klux Klan, was founded (1866) in Tennessee, at Pulaski. The situation improved after Brownlow left (1869) the governorship for the U.S. Senate, to which the state also returned (1875) Andrew Johnson in vindication of his record as Lincoln's successor in the presidency. Brownlow's successor, Governor De Witt C. Senter, although nominally a Republican, encouraged the calling of a new state constitutional convention. In 1870 the delegates drew up a constitution that rejected the reforms of the radical Republicans; African-American suffrage was limited by means of the poll tax and former Confederates were reenfranchised.

Industrialization, Prohibition, and the Scopes Trial

Economically, the farm-tenancy system, which had replaced the plantation system, brought much misery; industry, however, made advances after the Civil War. The iron and steelworks of eastern Tennessee were unable to meet the competition of Birmingham, [Alabama], but coal mining continued and textile production increased. The use of convict labor in the mines precipitated the state's first major labor disturbance (1891-1892), but not until 1936 was the convict-leasing system abolished.

A statewide Prohibition bill (not repealed until 1939) was passed over a governor's veto in 1909, and this question so divided the Democratic party that in 1910 a Republican was elected governor for the first time since 1880. In World War I the thousands of Tennessean volunteers in the U.S. armed forces included Sergeant Alvin C. York, who became one of the nation's most highly publicized heroes. In 1925 the state attracted international attention with the famous Scopes trial at Dayton. The fact that the state law banning the teaching of evolution was not repealed until 1967 is indicative of the strong role that Protestant fundamentalism played in the lives of many Tennesseans. Its further influence was reflected in the passing of a 1973 bill prohibiting the teaching of evolution as a fact rather than a theory.

The TVA and an Expanded Economy

One of the most important events in Tennessee since the Civil War was the establishment of the Tennessee Valley Authority (TVA) in 1933. Although opposed by private power companies, the TVA succeeded in providing hydroelectric power cheaply and in abundance, bringing modern comforts to thousands. Over the years its programs expanded and were supplemented by other projects for water-resources development. Most important, the TVA was chiefly responsible for the basic change in the state's economy from agriculture to industry and for the significant growth and diversification of industry, especially during and after World War II. The TVA also came to be associated with atomic energy, for it provides the power for Oak Ridge, one of the sources of production of the constituents for the first atomic bombs.

Since the late 1970s there has been significant growth in the service, trade, and finance sectors of the state economy and Tennessee has been very aggressive in attracting new industry. Many of the firms that have been setting up new factories and distribution centers in Tennessee come from America's northern industrial states and from Japan.

TEXAS

Texas: Indian meaning "friend"
Statehood: December 29, 1845 (28th state)
Motto: Friendship
Familiar Name: The Lone Star State
50-State Tour: The Prophetic State, December 8-9, 2003

You can reread the Texas report in Chapter 4. *The results of this meeting were heard worldwide.*

Troops from the 4th Infantry went in and found Saddam Hussein three days after the meeting! Even though many were praying around the world, I believe it took a corporate gathering to express God's purpose on earth.

Brief Texas History[167]

Spanish Exploration and Colonization

The region that is now Texas was early known to the Spanish, who were, however, slow to settle there. Cabeza de Vaca, shipwrecked off the coast in 1528, wandered through the area in the 1530s, and Coronado probably crossed the northwest section in 1541. De Soto died before reaching Texas, but his men continued west, crossing the Red River in 1542. The first Spanish settlement was made (1682) at Ysleta on the site of present day El Paso by refugees from the area that is now New Mexico after the Pueblo revolt of 1680. Several missions were established in the area; but the Comanche, Apache, and other Native American tribes resented their encroachment, and the settlements did not flourish.

A French expedition led by La Salle penetrated [east] Texas in 1685 after failing to locate the mouth of the Mississippi. This incursion, though brief, stirred the Spanish to establish missions to hold the area. The first mission, founded in 1690 near the Neches, was named Francisco de los Tejas after the so-called *tejas* [friends] Native Americans. This is also the origin of the state's name. In general, however, Spanish attempts to gain wealth from the wild region and to convert the indigenous population were unsuccessful, and in most places occupation was desultory.

American Expeditions and Settlement

By the early 19th [century], Americans were covetously eyeing Texas, especially after the Louisiana Purchase (1803) had extended the U.S. border to that fertile wilderness. Attempts to free Texas from Spanish rule were made in the expeditions of the adventurers Gutiérrez and Magee (1812-1813) and James Long (1819). In 1821 Moses Austin secured a colonization grant from the Spanish authorities in San Antonio. He died from the rigors of his return trip from that distant outpost, but his son, Stephen F. Austin, had the grant confirmed and in [December] 1821, led 300 families across the Sabine River to the region between the Brazos and Colorado rivers, where they established the first American settlement in Texas. Austin is known as the father of Texas.

The newly independent government of Mexico, pleased with Austin's prospering colony, readily offered grants to other American promoters and even gave huge land tracts to individual settlers. Americans from all over the Union, but particularly from the South, poured into Texas, and within a decade a considerable number of settlements had been established at Brazoria, Washington-on-the-Brazos, San Felipe de Austin, Anahuac, and Gonzales. The Americans easily avoided Mexican requirements that all settlers be Roman Catholic.

By 1830 the Americans outnumbered the Mexican settlers by more than three to one and had formed their own society. The Mexican government became understandably concerned. Its sporadic attempts to tighten control over Texas had been hampered by its own political instability, but in 1830 measures were taken to stop the influx of Americans. Troops were sent to police the border, close the seaports, occupy the towns, and levy taxes on imported goods. The troops were withdrawn in 1832, when Mexico was again in political upheaval, but the Texans, alarmed and hoping to achieve a greater measure of self-government, petitioned Mexico for separate statehood (Texas was then part of Coahuila). When Austin presented the petition in Mexico City, Antonio López de Santa Anna had become military dictator. Austin was arrested and imprisoned for eighteen months, and Texas was regarrisoned.

Independence from Mexico

The Texas Revolution broke out (1835) in Gonzales when the Mexicans attempted to disarm the Americans and were routed. The American settlers then drove all the Mexican troops from Texas, overwhelming each command in surprise attacks. At a convention called at Washington-on-the-Brazos, Texas declared its independence ([March] 2, 1836). A constitution was adopted and David Burnet was named interim president.

The arrival of Santa Anna with a large army that sought to crush the rebellion resulted in the famous defense of the Alamo and the massacre of several hundred Texans captured at Goliad. Santa Anna then divided his huge force to cover as much territory as possible. The small Texas army, commanded by Samuel Houston, protected their rear, retreating strategically until Houston finally maneuvered Santa Anna into a cul-de-sac formed by heavy rains and flooding bayous, near the site of present-day Houston. In the battle of San Jacinto ([April] 21, 1836), Houston surprised the larger Mexican force and scored a resounding victory. Santa Anna was captured and compelled to recognize the independence of Texas.

The Texas Republic and U.S. Annexation

Texans sought annexation to the United States, but antislavery forces in the United States vehemently opposed the admission of another slave state, and Texas remained an independent republic under its Lone Star flag for almost 10 years. The Texas constitution was closely modeled after that of the United States, but slaveholding was expressly recognized. Houston, the hero of the Texas Revolution, was the leading figure of the Republic, serving twice as president....

Southerners pressed hard for the admission of Texas, the intrigues of British and French diplomats in Texas aroused U.S. concern, and expansionist policies began to gain popular support. President Tyler narrowly pushed the admission of Texas through Congress shortly before the expiration of his term; Texas formally accepted annexation in July, 1845. This act was the immediate cause of the Mexican War. After [General] Zachary Taylor defeated the Mexicans at Palo Alto and Resaca de la Palma, the Mexican forces retreated back across the Rio Grande.

Civil War and Reconstruction

...During the Civil War, Texas was the only Confederate state not overrun by Union troops. Remaining relatively prosperous, it liberally contributed men and provisions to the Southern cause.

Reconstruction brought great lawlessness, aggravated by the appearance of roving desperadoes. Radical Republicans, carpetbaggers, and scalawags controlled the government for several years, during which time they managed to lay the foundations for better road and school systems. Texas was readmitted to the Union in [March] 1870, after ratifying the Thirteenth, Fourteenth, and Fifteenth amendments. Although Texas was not as racially embittered as the Deep South, the Ku Klux Klan and its methods flourished for a time as a means of opposing the policies of the radical Republicans....

Oil, Industrialization, and World Wars

The transformation of Texas into a partly urban and industrial society was greatly hastened by the uncovering of the state's tremendous oil deposits. The discovery in 1901 of the spectacular Spindletop oil field near Beaumont dwarfed previous finds in Texas, but Spindletop itself was later surpassed as oil was discovered in nearly every part of Texas. Texas industry developed rapidly during the early years of the 20th [century], but conditions worsened for the tenant farmers, who by 1910 made up the majority of cultivators. Discontented tenants were largely responsible for the election of James Ferguson as governor.

World War I had a somewhat liberating effect on African-American Texans, but the reappearance of the Ku Klux Klan after the war helped to enforce "white supremacy." The economic boom of the 1920s was accompanied by further industrialization. The Great Depression of the 1930s, while severe, was less serious than in most states; the chemical and oil industries in particular continued to grow (the East Texas Oil Field was discovered in 1930).

The significance of the petrochemical and natural gas industries increased during World War II, when the aircraft industry also rose to prominence and the establishment of military bases throughout Texas greatly contributed to the state's economy....

Industry in the Late Twentieth Century

In the 1960s, Texas began to develop its technology industries as oil became less easy to exploit—even though soaring oil prices in the 1970s caused the energy industry to boom. Since then, the state has become a preferred location for the headquarters of large corporations from airlines and retail chains to telecommunications and chemical companies. High technology industries have boomed since the 1980s, especially in the Dallas–Fort Worth, Houston, and Austin areas. The state's economy proved still vulnerable to the fluctuations of the energy industry in the mid-1980s, however, when falling oil prices resulted in massive layoffs, hurting the state's real estate market and in turn precipitating the failure of hundreds of savings and loans in the state.

Texas has, however, continued to grow, becoming the second most populous state in the nation. Its population increased by nearly 23 [percent] between 1990 and 2000, and its economy slowly recovered in the 1990s. Its political influence has grown commensurately, and since the 1960s three sons (or adopted sons) of Texas have been president of the nation: Lyndon Johnson, George Herbert Walker Bush, and George Walker Bush.

UTAH[168]

Utah: Navajo meaning "upper" or named after the Ute tribe
Statehood: January 4, 1896 (45th state)
Motto: Industry
Familiar Name: The Beehive State
50-State Tour: The Worship State, February 16-17, 2004

Chuck Pierce prophesied to Utah on February 16, 2004, that a different sound would come from Utah that would begin to penetrate through the entire nation. He prophesied it would be an "unlocking sound," "the sound of harvest" coming to Utah. He gave us direction to begin having corporate worship services where we "ascend in worship and descend in warfare." He prophesied that these worship services would start with a one-hour time of worship, and progress to two hours, three hours, etc., until we are able to engage in a 12-hour corporate worship event. This strategic worship would release this sound coming forth and break through the veil. Several churches have responded by having focused worship times on a regular basis. However, it has been difficult to coordinate these worship experiences among the churches.

Please pray that the Lord would remove the barriers keeping us from having unified corporate citywide and statewide worship events.

There are four areas that are critical for spiritual breakthrough in our state. They are the redemptive purposes God has given to this land: *prophetic blessing, evangelistic blessing, the restoration of women,* and *prosperity.*

Prophetic blessing: We believe God intended Utah to be a place of training and freedom for prophets and for those seeking the prophetic gifts to equip them to be a blessing to others by bringing the fresh word of God. Satan has used numerous false prophets here through the presidency of the Church of Jesus Christ of the Latter-Day Saints (LDS). Most notably, Joseph Smith was used in false prophecy to veil this land's people with mind control.

Evangelistic blessing: We believe God intended Utah to be a life-giving and prosperous place for the discipleship and commissioning of believers called to evangelism and missions. Satan has used this land's resources and people for the massive export of LDS missionaries.

Restoration of women: We believe God intended Utah to be a place of restoration for women. This restoration would release women in the full potential of their giftings and allow them to operate in those giftings according to the authority the Lord has given them. Satan has used dominance and mind control to oppress the women in this region.

Prosperity: We believe God intended the Great Basin region to be a fertile land with a large body of *fresh* water (Ancient Lake Bonneville) that will produce prosperity in the land and its inhabitants. This prosperity is intended not just for the blessing of the people who live in Utah, but it is also to bless people beyond the boundaries of this state through our generosity. Satan has used a poverty spirit and dominance to rob the people of this land of the prosperity God intended.

Blessings

- ✯ We are blessed with an anointing to produce prophets and a prophetic people.
- ✯ We are blessed with a call to release women into their proper place in the Body of Christ.
- ✯ We are blessed with prosperity that will abound in many forms.

- ★ We are blessed with having a true, evangelistic army.
- ★ We are to be a house of prayer filled with the "rhema" word of God that will enable us to walk in the "kairos" timing of God.
- ★ There is building an establishing (apostolic) anointing to begin new things that will spread throughout the Kingdom.
- ★ We live on good ground that will allow the planted things of God to grow—much like a rain forest.
- ★ We are blessed with a pioneer anointing to start new things.

The Battles We Face

- ★ Seductive and divisive spirits, designed to draw us away from the truth and keep us from revelation.
- ★ Masonic and Mormon foundations in fertility cult spirits; oppression of women and the demonic exaltation of men.
- ★ Barrenness and untapped productivity in women— held in check by demonic forces and curses pronounced over them on a daily basis.
- ★ Being strong and courageous—to challenge and undo the works of the enemy and the ignorance of believers who cannot see.

Please pray that we will walk joyfully in the blessings God has given us, and walk victoriously through the battles!

An Issue of Injustice That Must Be Redeemed

Redeeming the status of women in our state is of critical importance. Because LDS doctrine teaches that a woman's "exaltation" and security in the afterlife is determined by her marriage, her worthiness, and her participation in very Masonic-like rituals performed in the temple, LDS women are under intense pressure to perform as wives and mothers. The LDS church is a patriarchal religion, and only men can hold the priesthood. Women are entirely dependent on men, as only men, specifically husbands, can administrate the proper ordinances for "exaltation." A woman, for example, is not allowed into the higher levels of Heaven unless her husband calls her by a secret name given her at the temple marriage ceremony.

Women in Utah continually strive to be "worthy" and "strive for exaltation." "At almost twice the national average, Utah leads the nation in prescriptions for anti-depressants. Researchers felt the explanation is the state's dominant Mormon culture, which demands much of its people, especially women."[169]

Please pray that women in Utah will be assured of their status before God, and that the status of women in the natural will be restored.

Brief Utah History[170]

At historic contact, Native American groups living in Utah included the Ute, Southern Paiute, Navajo, Goshute, and Northern and Eastern Shoshone. The Ute, Paiute, Goshute, and Shoshone speak different but related languages from a family known as the Numic Language Family; the Navajo speak a language that is in the Athapaskan Language Family....

The Ute once lived over much of Utah and all of western Colorado. In historic times, they ranged well onto the great plains of eastern

Colorado, into Nebraska and south into New Mexico. In historic times, there were at least 11 different bands of the Ute Tribe. Each band claimed its own territory but membership in a band was fluid.... During the late 1800s, the Ute lost most of their lands and were restricted to reservations in southern Colorado and northeastern Utah.[171]

The word Utah is of Native American origin. According to one source, Utah is named after the Ute tribe, but another states that Utah is the Navajo word for "upper." Either way, Brigham Young announced, "This is the place!" when he led the first Mormon settlers into Salt Lake Valley in 1847, a year before the U.S. acquired the territory from Mexico. There, after a thousand-mile trek to escape persecution, members of the Mormon Church established the first permanent white settlement in Utah. At that time, the area was sparsely populated with Paiutes, Shoshones, and Navajos. Pioneering in irrigation, the well-organized Mormons brought water from the Wasatch Mountains to cultivate the rich, arid valley and soon built thriving farms—with the help of seagulls that, in 1848, miraculously appeared to destroy swarms of crickets and save the crops. The valley settlement became the center of the Mormon's expanding community, and modern Salt Lake City, with its Tabernacle and shrines, remains the center of the state of Utah and of Mormon culture today.

Utah Territory had a tumultuous and prolonged history. From the time the Territory was established, the Mormon practice of polygamy caused friction with the federal government. In 1857, it led to the Utah War, in which the U.S. Army did little more than occupy the area. The Army's discovery of valuable ore deposits and the completion of the railroad brought others to the Territory, but the Mormons' struggle with the federal government continued. Congress passed anti-polygamy laws and imprisoned thousands. Finally, in 1890, the church renounced polygamy; in 1896 the way was open for Utah to join the Union as the 45th state, after 46 years as a territory.

Still dominated by Mormon culture, modern Utah has developed manufacturing to more than match its extensive farming—raising cattle, poultry, and field crops. Mining (copper, oil, iron, coal, and uranium), copper and petroleum refining, guided missile construction, and steel making are principal industries. Near Provo is the largest steel plant in the west. Best known of Mormon achievements is the Mormon Tabernacle in Salt Lake City and its distinguished Tabernacle Choir.

VERMONT[172]

Vermont: French meaning "green mountain"
Statehood: March 4, 1791 (14th state)
Motto: Freedom and Unity
Familiar Name: The Green Mountain State
50-State Tour: The Passover State and The Sleeping Beauty State, April 5-6, 2004

Chuck D. Pierce prophesied: "I would say to you, I have chosen this state at this time of Passover. And I would say that My blood in this state will begin to arise. I have chosen you as the 'Passover State.' And I am causing My blood that has been hemorrhaging in My Bride to stop this night. And I say your doorposts will change and families will experience My deliverance."

Summary of Directives from the 50-State Tour for Vermont

1. The Lord would say to Vermont, "*This is a time that I am calling you to* **ask Me for the MORE**. *Even though I have come and have visited you in the past—now I would say to you, cry out and watch Me begin to come in a way that you are not expecting from Me.... For I say now is the time of reversal for the state of Vermont.*" (Prophesied by Chuck D. Pierce.)

2. "...When we were singing about 'turning the night to day,' I felt it is time for Vermont to experience *spring* in the spirit....You've got to change your mentality, and it is time to enter into that next phase of your inheritance.... Spring is also the time for kings to go to war.... *It's time for Vermont to go to war for your inheritance*" (Chuck D. Pierce).

3. "Now it is the time for our nation to hear a different sound out of Vermont. It's time for a major reversal where you are not known as the one crying to leave God's covenant plan but the one [who] is declaring [that] the covenant plan of God has come to earth" (Chuck D. Pierce).

4. And God would say, "*I have a people that's coming away. I have a people that's stopping up the holes in their wall. I have a people that's finding the little foxes. I have a people that's protecting the vine and the revelation that I have in this state. I have a people rising up.... Receive the new season of resurrection in this state.*"

5. "*The beauty of holiness I have rested on this state...the light of your inner radiance has dwindled. Even now I am ready to move and cause that holiness to shine forth. You are known as*

*the Sleeping Beauty of this nation and I would say to this state, it is time for that sleeping beauty to wake up. You have kicked against the pricks, and you have been pricked; and even poison has caused you to go to sleep. I will even go back 16 years and remove poison that entered this state. I will even go back 12 years; and when I began to visit to renew you, I was attempting to awaken you. And even though you were renewed in measure, your inner radiance has now dwindled again. So **I am calling forth the leaders and the princes of this state to rise up and begin to stand together and decree into the atmosphere together. And that which has been encompassed by thorns will begin to break.... It is time to rise up and allow Me to move. It is time to stand together. It is time to shout into the atmosphere AWAKE, and as you shout, healing will begin to fall in your midst.***" (Prophesied by Chuck D. Pierce.) Dutch Sheets had prophesied earlier that "Awakening days are here!"

6. "What we want to do is remove anything in our prayer life [that is out of order or lacking in any way] as we stand, as we go, as we make decree, as the Church gets established in a new way, as we move forward" (Dutch Sheets).

7. "You are saying, '*You are going to wake it up.*' You are saying, '*It's Sleeping Beauty.*' But You are also saying, '*The Church has to rise up to contend with the things that are trying to put it to sleep.*'" (Prophesied by Dutch Sheets.)

8. "He wants us to respond to Him out of time so we reflect what He longs to be doing in time on earth" (Dutch Sheets). While God is trying to present something to us of new revelation, He also orchestrates circumstance into our path to demonstrate that revelation.

9. "...That's what He [God] is saying here to Vermont—*'Make room! I'm ready to come in a new way. Make room from...your past, the renewal. Make room for Me to do something you've not seen before.'*" (Prophesied by Dutch Sheets.)

10. Keys to how we get into the next dimension (given by Chuck D. Pierce):

* You must know the Holy Spirit.
* You must understand the times we are living in.
* You must enter into a new level of faith.
* You must understand the authority structure that you are part of.
* You must understand your connections.
* You must be willing to worship and sacrifice in a new way.
* You need to determine the ceilings in your atmosphere that are pressing down on you.

1. You need to learn how to "cross over" for yourself, for your home, for your church, and for your nation. (Declared by Dutch Sheets.)

2. "...We have to learn how to focus our attention more on the unseen than what we see around us.... Corinthians says that's the way we're supposed to walk—not by the seen but the unseen" (Dutch Sheets). This directive is specifically relating to legislating in the heavenlies and changing the atmosphere around us through our voice, decrees, and prophetic declarations.

3. "Vermont is going to have to get the word of the Lord, find out what He's saying, and begin to decree over this state what God is saying about this state. Some of you could change your church, your house, your business, if over the next few weeks you went in there every day and you took 20-30 minutes—an hour—and you begin to decree the word of the Lord in that building and over that vision and over that congregation.... If you do enough decreeing/prophesying together, you [will] change this state" (Dutch Sheets).

4. "There is going to be a prophesying machine, a prophesying Body of Christ in the state of Vermont—that every day they are going to begin to decree that Word of the Lord. They're going to write out these prophecies; they're going to take the Scriptures that have been spoken over them. And every day, prayer groups all over this state are going to begin to decree that there is something different now in Vermont, that Vermont is experiencing awakening, that awakening days are here! ...When they drive down the street, they are going to turn off their radios, and they are going to begin to prophesy to neighborhoods and communities and schools and homes and churches" (Dutch Sheets).

5. "...The wind that you spoke of is going to begin to blow. The wind tunnel is coming; the force of God is coming to break religious structures and religious slumber" (Chuck D. Pierce). We feel it is time for the Church of Vermont to "Call for the Wind" to come to our state. Chuck Pierce called for the Wind of Pentecost to come in the closing session of our 50-State Tour.

6. "Rise up and go to each city and cry awake. For I say if you will cry and decree that each city will awake, there will be a movement of My Spirit that surprises each church in each city." (Prophesied by Chuck D. Pierce.)

Brief Vermont History[173]

French Vermont

The first European known to have entered the area that is now Vermont was Samuel de Champlain, who, after beginning the colonization of Quebec, journeyed south with a Huron war party in 1609 to the beautiful lake to which he gave his name. The French did not attempt any permanent settlement until 1666, when they built a fort and a shrine to Ste Anne on the Isle La Motte in Lake Champlain. However, this and later French settlements were abandoned, and until well into the 18th [century] the region was something of a no-man's-land.

Benning Wentworth and the New Hampshire Grants

Fort Dummer, built (1724) by the English near the site of Brattleboro, is considered the first permanent settlement in what is now Vermont. However, Vermont's history may be said to have really begun in 1741, when Benning Wentworth became royal governor of New Hampshire. According to his commission New Hampshire extended west across the Merrimack River until it met "with our [i.e., the king's] other Governments." Since the English crown had never publicly proclaimed the eastern limits of the colony of New York, this vague description bred considerable confusion.

Wentworth, assuming that New York's modified boundary with Connecticut and Massachusetts (20 mi/32 km E of the Hudson River) would be extended even farther north, made (1749) the first of the New Hampshire Grants—the township called Bennington—to a group that included his relatives and friends. However, New York claimed that its boundary extended as far east as the Connecticut River, and Governor George Clinton of New York (father of Sir Henry Clinton) promptly informed Governor Wentworth that he had no authority to make such a grant.

Wentworth thereupon suggested that the dispute between New York and New Hampshire over control of Vermont be referred to the crown. The outbreak of the last of the French and Indian Wars in 1754 briefly suspended interest in the area, but after the British captured Ticonderoga and Crown Point in 1759, Wentworth resumed granting land in the area of present Vermont.

In 1764 the British authorities upheld New York's territorial claim to Vermont. New York immediately tried to assert its jurisdiction—Wentworth's grants were declared void, and new grants (for the same lands) were issued by the New York authorities. Those who held their lands from New Hampshire resisted, and a hot controversy, long in the making, now exploded. New York and New Hampshire land speculators had the most at stake, with the New Hampshire grantees, first on the scene, having the advantage. Regional pride among the New England settlers played a large part in creating resistance to New York authority. Chief among the leaders of this resistance was Ethan Allen, who organized the Green Mountain Boys. New York courts were forcibly broken up, and armed violence was directed against New Yorkers until the outbreak of the American Revolution in 1775, when the British became the major threat and common enemy.

The American Revolution and Independent Vermont

At the beginning of the Revolution, Ethan Allen and the Green Mountain Boys captured Ticonderoga, and Seth Warner took Crown Point. In [January] 1777, Vermont (as its citizens were soon calling the region) proclaimed itself an independent state at a meeting in the town of Westminster. Chiefly because of the opposition of New York, the Continental Congress refused to recognize Vermont as the 14th colony or state. The convention that met at Windsor in July reaffirmed Vermont's independent status and adopted a constitution, notable especially because it was the first in the United States to provide for universal male suffrage. Thomas Chittenden was elected the first governor.

The Green Mountain Boys under Seth Warner and John Stark made an important contribution to the American cause with their victory at Bennington in [August] 1777.... Later, Ethan Allen and his brother Ira Allen, acting on their own, entered into devious negotiations with British agents, possibly with the intent of annexing Vermont to Canada. The talks were inconclusive and ended when the Americans finally triumphed at Yorktown in 1781. For ten years Vermont remained an independent state, performing all the offices of a sovereign government (such as coining money, setting up post offices, naturalizing new citizens, and appointing ambassadors) and gradually becoming more and more independent.

Statehood, at Last

Not until 1791, after many delays and misunderstandings and, most important, after the dispute with New York was finally adjusted (1790) by payment of $30,000, did Vermont enter the Union. It was the first state to be admitted after the adoption of the Constitution by the 13 original states. In the next two decades Vermont had the greatest population increase in its history, from 85,425 in 1790 to 217,895 in 1810. As in the earlier days, most of the settlers migrated from [southern] New England, and, since the more desirable lands in the river valleys were soon taken, many of them settled in the less hospitable hills.

Although the Embargo Act of 1807 aided the development of many small manufacturing establishments, it was bitterly opposed in Vermont for its disruption of the profitable trade with Canada. The War of 1812 was unpopular in Vermont as it was in the rest of New England, and during the war extensive smuggling across the Canadian border was carried on. Vermont was threatened by British invasion from Canada until U.S. troops, under Thomas Macdonough, won (1814) the battle on Lake Champlain.

At this early period in its history, Vermont, lacking an aristocracy of wealth, was the most democratic state in New England. Jeffersonian Democrats held control for most of the first quarter of the 19th [century]. Beginning in the 1820s political and social life in Vermont was considerably affected by the activities of those opposed to Freemasonry, and in the presidential election of 1832 Vermont was the only state carried by William Wirt, candidate of the Anti-Masonic party. Anti-Masonry agitation was soon succeeded by even more vigorous efforts in behalf of another cause—the one against slavery.

The Mexican and Civil Wars

In the Mexican War, which it viewed as having been undertaken solely to increase slave territory, Vermont was very apathetic. However, no Northern state was more energetic in support of the Union cause in the Civil War, and Vermonters strongly favored Lincoln over Vermont-born Stephen Douglas. One of the most bizarre incidents of the war was the Confederate raid (1864) on Saint Albans, a town which, after the war, also figured in the equally bizarre attempt of the Fenians to invade Canada in the cause of Irish independence.

The Changing Economy of Vermont

The economy of the state, meanwhile, was in the midst of a series of sharp dislocations. The rise of manufacturing in towns and villages during the early 19th [century] had created a demand for foodstuffs for the nonfarming population. Consequently, commercial farming began to crowd out the subsistence farming that had predominated since the mid-18th [century]. Grain and beef cattle became the chief market produce, but when the rapidly expanding West began to supply these commodities more cheaply and when wool textile mills began to spring up in [southern] New England, Vermont turned to sheep raising.

After the Civil War, however, the sheep industry, unable to withstand the competition from the American West as well as from Australian, and South American wool, began to diminish. The rural population declined as many farmers migrated westward or turned to the apparently easier life of the cities, and abandoned farms became a common sight. The transition to dairy farming in the 20 years following the war staved off a permanent decline in Vermont's agricultural pursuits.

Since the 1960s, Vermont's economy has grown significantly with booms in the tourist industry and in exurban homebuilding and with the attraction of high-technology firms to the Burlington area. In recent years, prosperity has to some degree conflicted with concern for environmental issues. Nonetheless, the state has been active in attempts to preserve its natural beauty, enacting very strict laws regarding industrial pollution and the conservation of natural resources.

VIRGINIA[174]

Virginia: Named after Elizabeth I, Virgin Queen of England
Statehood: June 25, 1788 (10th state)
Motto: *Sic Semper Tyrannis* (Thus Always to Tyrants)
Familiar Name: The Old Dominion
50-State Tour: The Covenant Root State, March 5-6, 2004

Our 50-State Tour meeting for Virginia was held in Hampton. This was probably one of the most historical gatherings of all the 50-State meetings. The hand of God sovereignly orchestrated a reconciliation between Blacks and Whites. We called the state our "Covenant Root State" and dealt with root issues that prevent God's covenant plan for our nation from coming forth. I taught on covenant from Genesis chapter 15, where God promised Abraham that His people would be held in bondage in a different nation for 400 years. Interestingly, Hampton, Virginia, is the place where the first slave was brought into America, and the 400th anniversary of the Jamestown settlement will be held April 29, 2007.

God is about to bring a great release in this nation to those of African descent. The leadership in Black America is about to arise with great revelation from God. From Virginia, a curse will be broken off our nation. The covenant plan of God will be released in our nation in unexpected ways over the next three years.

Redemptive Purpose and Prayer Focus for Virginia[175]

I believe that a primary redemptive purpose for the state of Virginia is that of governance, or the art of godly governing.

1. *Pray* that the Church will maximize the outreach and media opportunities during the *Jamestown 2007* celebration.
2. *Pray* against the spirits of crime, murder, and death over our cities. *Pray* for transformation in all Virginia cities. *Pray* that the Church will arise to its place in affecting the community.
3. *Pray* for holiness and godliness among youth and for godly education.
4. *Pray* that the sanctity of marriage will be protected in our state and that we will not go the way of other states.
5. *Pull down/immobilize* forces of witchcraft over the region. Also, pull down spirits of division within the house of God.
6. *Pray* that ungodly politicians and judges at every level be removed and replaced with those who will govern in accordance with God's Word.
7. *Pray* for the protection of our troops. Also *pray* that nothing evil will attach itself to them—spiritual, chemical, biological, etc.—and that they will be brought back to their homes. *Pray* that their families/marriages will remain intact. (This is in light of the fact that after soldiers returned from Afghanistan, several murdered their wives.)

Brief Virginia History[176]

When Spanish explorers entered the Virginia region in 1570, several Indian tribes inhabited the area. Missionaries built a settlement along the York River, but were killed only a few months later. English explorers also arrived in the late 1580s, but their expedition failed due to lack of supplies.

Colonization

The history of America is closely tied to that of Virginia, particularly during the Colonial period. After the failure of several attempts by Sir Humphrey Gilbert and Sir Walter Raleigh to plant a settlement in Virginia and after Gilbert's death, Raleigh in 1606 transferred his interests to the Virginia Company of London. The first settlers, 144 in number, left England in December of that year in the "Susan Constant," the "Godspeed," and the "Discovery" and arrived at Jamestown on May 13, 1607. The colony was kept alive during the first years mainly through the efforts of Captain John Smith, who secured food, made peace with the Indians, explored the country, wrote the first published book on Virginia (*A True Relation*, London, 1608), and drew a map of Virginia remarkable for its accuracy. After Smith left in 1609 the colonists experienced a year of great suffering—the "starving time."

Jamestown, founded in 1607, was the first permanent English settlement in North America which was reorganized and almost absolute control over the colony was placed in the hands of the governor. The first governor was Sir Thomas West, Lord De la Warr, whose arrival in 1610 saved the colony from being abandoned as a hopeless venture. Attempts to set up industries such as glassmaking, shipbuilding, and the production of naval stores failed. In 1622 there occurred an Indian massacre, followed by a siege of the plague.

Yet the colony survived. Settlements spread beyond Jamestown. A head right system was established for land. The New World's first English women and Africans came to Jamestown in 1619, the year and place where the Western Hemisphere's first representative legislature met. Virginia was the largest, most populous and prosperous of the original 13 colonies.

Royal Rule

In 1624 the English government revoked the charter of the Virginia Company and organized in Virginia its first royal colony. During the century and a half that followed, the two outstanding factors in the colony's history were the northern and western expansion of the population and a growing political maturity that produced a strong representative lower house in the Assembly, an able group of leaders, and a spirit of independence.

The first serious attempts to explore the TransAllegheny region were made during Sir William Berkeley's administrations (1641-1652; 1660-1677). The Indian massacre of 1644, in which at least 500 colonists perished, delayed exploration, but trading routes soon led from the sites of Richmond and Petersburg to the Indians in the southwest.

Virginians remained loyal to Charles I during his struggle with Parliament, but in 1652 parliamentary commissioners with an overwhelming force assumed control of the colony. During the eight years of rule by Parliament, life in Virginia changed but little.

Berkeley's second administration was marked by difficulties: the establishment of proprietorships in Virginia, human and cattle plagues, wars, hurricanes, oppressive trade laws, threats from the Indians, who resented English encroachment, and, among the people, widespread discontent and growing distrust of those who governed the colony.

The climax came when the Indians, made desperate by English encroachment, began to war on the colonists. When in 1676 the people found Berkeley unable or, as they believed, unwilling to protect them, they chose young Nathaniel Bacon as their leader, compelled the governor to give him a commission, followed him against the Indians, and forced reforms through the assembly. When the governor threatened to use military force against them, Bacon and his men defied him. On the death of Bacon, however, Berkeley soon ended the struggle with a series of hangings that shocked the home government and brought his recall. From the end of Bacon's rebellion to the revolution of 1688 in England, Englishmen in Virginia, like their kinsmen in England, struggled to lessen the royal prerogative represented in the colony by a succession of autocratic governors.

During the remainder of the colonial period, Virginia generally had able and conscientious governors. But conflicts inevitably arose when the mother country failed to realize the growing independence of the colony and refused, in such matters as the use of veto, trade regulations, and taxation, to keep the promise of early charters that Virginians would "enjoy all liberties, franchises and immunities…to all intents and purposes as if they had been abiding and borne within this our realm of England."

Presbyterians gained a strong foothold in Virginia during the 1730s and 1740s and organized Hanover presbytery, and in the 1750s the Separate Baptists from New England entered the colony. Both denominations increased rapidly.

During the quarter-century before the Revolution, as Virginia grew in strength and political maturity, its House of Burgesses became increasingly active in opposing the royal prerogative in matters as the veto of the colony's laws, the Proclamation of 1763 restricting westward expansion, and taxes imposed by Parliament. Before 1776 leaders such as Richard Bland and Jefferson were formulating the constitutional and ethical bases for revolt, Patrick Henry was becoming an orator, and Washington was acquiring military and political experience.

Virginia in 1763 had an estimated total population of 121,022, almost evenly divided between whites and slaves. The population was increasing rapidly. The great planters were building substantial homes; the homes of lesser farmers were neat and well built.

Revolutionary Period

Virginians took the lead in the constitutional crises preceding the Revolutionary War. They passed the Stamp Act resolutions of 1765; started in 1769 the boycott of British goods in order to cause the repeal of the Townshend Acts; revived in 1773 the Committee of Correspondence of 1759 and brought about an intercolonial committee; called the first Continental Congress in 1774 and furnished its president, Peyton Randolph; set up a Revolutionary Committee of Safety and armed for defense in 1775; called on Congress on May 15, 1776, to declare independence; furnished the author, Thomas Jefferson, of the Declaration of Independence; and provided the leader of the Revolutionary Army, George Washington. The May 1776 convention, in addition to proposing that Congress declare independence, form a union, and make foreign alliances, also set up a commonwealth and chose Patrick Henry as its first governor. Meanwhile, in 1775, Governor John Dunmore, fearful of the volunteer riflemen gathering in Williamsburg, had fled to the safety of the British fleet. On November 7 he declared martial law and waged war against Virginia until forced to leave the following July.

In 1778 George Rogers Clark led an army of Virginia and Kentucky riflemen in the conquest of the Northwest Territory; his campaign ended the Indian menace. At Yorktown on [October] 19, 1781, British forces under General Charles Cornwallis surrendered to the combined French and American forces serving under the command of General George Washington.

Virginia moved its capital from Williamsburg to Richmond in 1780. Previously, it had set up 19 counties in the west (1776-1782), abolished its African slave trade (1778), and reformed its code of laws (1779). The British captured Portsmouth (q.v.) in October 1780. In January 1781 Benedict Arnold took Richmond and set up headquarters at

Portsmouth. Cornwallis brought his army into Virginia from the south that spring, and Jefferson, governor of the state, with inadequate forces, was unable to stop him. Cornwallis, after marching through Richmond, Williamsburg (near which, at Green Spring, he was attacked by Lafayette), and Portsmouth, came to Yorktown and fortified the place. There, trapped by the American and French armies under Washington and Rochambeau and by French naval forces under the comte de Grasse, he was forced to surrender on [October] 19, 1781. This practically ended the war.

Post-Revolutionary Period

For almost half a century after the Revolution, Virginia, impoverished by two wars and finding its soil depleted as a result of tobacco growing, suffered economically, and Virginians migrated to the west, northwest, and southwest. But the foundations for future progress were being laid.

Virginia began an efficient system of chartered banks in 1804. The state undertook, or aided in the building of roads, canals, and railroads, and Virginians began direct trade with Europe and South America. By 1860 Virginia was the leading manufacturing state in the South. A state university and several colleges had been founded before 1850, public schools were being established by local option in 1846, and numerous private schools were flourishing. The constitution of 1851 provided white manhood suffrage, popular election of many officials (including the governor), and ended sectional inequalities in representation.

Slavery, however, remained an unsolved evil. In January 1832, after Nat Turner's slave insurrection in Southampton the previous year, the Virginia Assembly tried in vain to find a solution; and Abolitionists' indiscriminate abuse almost silenced native reformers.

Civil War and Reconstruction

In 1861 Virginia seceded from the Union. Richmond became the capital of the Confederacy, and Virginia was a battleground throughout the war that followed. In 1863 the state lost one-third of its territory to form West Virginia.

More major battles of the American Civil War were fought in Virginia from 1861 through 1865 than in any other state. Today, one-third of America's most important Civil War battlefields are in Virginia, and most are open to the public. In 1867 Congress placed the South under military rule, Virginia being Military District No. 1, with General John M. Schofield in command.

Under the Reconstruction acts most Virginians with any experience in government were disfranchised. A constitutional convention drew up a new constitution, which included articles that would have excluded thousands of whites from voting and disqualified almost every native white citizen from holding office. A committee of nine citizens headed by Alexander H.H. Stuart, however, secured permission from the federal authorities to vote separately on these articles and they were rejected by the voters. The remainder of the constitution, including manhood suffrage, was adopted (1869), and Congress readmitted the state to the Union on [January] 26, 1870.

Virginia escaped much of the punishment that Reconstruction inflicted on other states, but it had lost thousands of its young men and had been devastated by invading armies, its banks, had been closed, its labor force demoralized, and its territory occupied by its former enemy.

The Democratic Party was revived in 1883. Virginia adopted a new constitution in 1902.

20th Century

In 1926 Harry F. Byrd became governor of Virginia and within four years had revolutionized the governmental machinery. During the first 60 days of his administration, the General Assembly instituted a remarkable group of reforms through statutes or constitutional amendment. The years after World War I found the state's prosperity increasing as agriculture was diversified, manufacturing grew in importance in the economy, and the tourist business became a major enterprise.

The depression of the 1930s was less severe in Virginia than in many other states. Employment continued at a high rate after the war, with continued growth in the nonagricultural sector, including government, and agricultural production became more diversified....

Virginia continues to maintain a strong diversified economy. Industrial growth has expanded into many areas such as chemical, clothing, and computers.

Eight states were also formed in whole or in part from Virginia, including Wisconsin, Michigan, Illinois, Indiana, Ohio, West Virginia, Kentucky, and Pennsylvania. The state is called the "Mother of Presidents" because eight U.S. Presidents were born there. Virginia has produced more U.S. presidents than any other state: George Washington, Thomas Jefferson, James Madison, James Monroe, William Henry Harrison, John Tyler, Zachary Taylor, and Woodrow Wilson.

WASHINGTON[177]

Washington: Named after George Washington
Statehood: November 11, 1889 (42nd state)
Motto: *Al-Ki* (By and By)
Familiar Name: The Evergreen State
50-State Tour: The Whirlwind State, December 14-15, 2003

> Chuck Pierce prophesied: "There is a great harvest in the midst of this state, and I am putting an urgency and a passion in My people. For the sound that has come forth this night will now flood this state and permeate My people, and they will not be able to shut their mouth, but boldly proclaim the good news. Salvation will flood the state of Washington.... This is My year to start moving on the pastors; and either they'll respond to My visitation, or I'll remove them."

Dutch Sheets shared: "Chuck called me early this morning He said, 'I have a word. I don't know anything about it, but I just keep hearing this word. The word is *"overshadow"'* ....If God is saying 'overshadow,' then He is about to bring forth something. And He is going to hover until it happens and releases seeds. He is going to release a deposit of life and bring forth. As I was meditating on this, I began to see a picture. It is a very unique picture, and it was just a very short vision the Lord gave me. I saw a puzzle, but the puzzle was not put together. It was just pieces of a puzzle that were just sort of haphazardly laying on the table, like you would when you were going to put it together, but it was not in any kind of shape yet.

"I heard the Lord say, *'I am coming to bring order to the Church in Washington.'* Now, I don't even pretend to know all that that means, and I know very little about how the Church functions and where you are in your progression in the state of Washington. But I know what I heard. I heard Him say: *'I am coming to bring order, and I am going to be taking the pieces of the puzzle and putting them into my arrangement so that there is a new release of life in the state of Washington.'*

"Then I saw something very interesting. I saw a whirlwind come and the puzzle pieces were picked up off of the table, and they began to fly around in a circle just like in a whirlwind. It was not a hand that took them one at a time; it was a whirlwind.... I saw the whirlwind, but out of the whirlwind pieces began to fly out of there one at a time. By the time it finished, there was this puzzle. I did not see what the puzzle looked like. It was just there. God said, *'I am going to bring a whirlwind.'*

"I don't know if it is Pentecost wind or judgment wind or both, but I want to tell you that if you are a believer, you are part of the Church. Then I want you to know that the whirlwind is not coming to destroy you— whatever it looks like. What I saw was that it was of God, and it picked these pieces up because there was disarray and there was not order.... What I could see— that there was a spirit of confusion over the state of Washington. It was like you as an individual could hear from God, and you know individual ministries that could hear from God. It wasn't that everybody was in total disorientation and out of God's will and order. But in general, in the heavenlies, there was just something there that was able to send confusion. And the Church just could not get aligned, and people could not get properly aligned. And visions would get off track at times, but more than that, there was this chaos.

"I don't know anything about this state, but it seems like the enemy has an ease of defiling revelation. Maybe occult deception is an easy thing for the enemy in this region. I don't know a thing about

Washington, but...I saw Him pick up the pieces of the puzzle and then begin to deposit them. And when He finished, it was all in order. It was all right.

"I see these puzzle pieces right now. I see this same conglomeration of things flying around. I see them as words. They are not puzzle pieces that I see right now; they are words. I see confusion and just curses—words and all this garbage in the atmosphere. God says, *'I am going to bring My word and My voice is going to come forth, and it is going to bring order.'* I would say to you that this is a whirlwind of judgment and blessing. It is a whirlwind that is meant to deal with the disorder and some of the things over this region that are not good. But in God's profound way when He dealt with satan and brought judgment, He was also bringing life.

"Here is what I feel the Lord is saying to Washington state: There has been addition; there will be addition. You are in the final phases of addition. If you hear the word of the Lord, Washington, and you do what God is saying to you now, you are about to transition at some point in the near future into an exponential growth that moves into multiplication of harvest....

"There is coming something into the established religious community in this state that when this whirlwind takes place—a voice of reason is going to come, and there will be some in the established religious community that you would have thought would have resisted the Spirit of God [but who will then change]...the whirlwind will clear up the confusion and the deception.

"There is going to come a revelation to some in established churches that we would not think would be open to the Spirit of God, and some of those leaders are going to back up and become open to what He is saying. Some will harden their hearts all the more; but some are going to turn, be saved, filled with the Spirit of God, get on fire, and be transformed. I tell you it is coming. It is going to come through the whirlwind.... There is going to be a shaking in denominations and streams over this because voices are going to rise up that God is dealing with. And they are going to say, 'Wait a minute. I don't talk against this stuff anymore. I don't want to fight this anymore. In fact, I am open to this now.' You are going to see a real dividing line in the spirit that is coming."

Chuck Pierce then declared: "Foursquare—God's going to shake it up. I decree from Washington State that in the next several months... there will be a great shaking in the Foursquare Church. Leadership will change. What is hidden will be exposed! Signs and wonders. We loose signs and wonders. There is a very destructive wind to religion that is going to be removed in Washington State. Even now there is coming a season, and we are moving into it now, where for a while do not be surprised when it looks a little bit less orderly and more chaotic than it even does now. Because God is coming to bring such a whirlwind and rearranging that for a season it is going to feel very disjointed. Now just hear that word because that is to keep you from panic. That is to keep you from unbelief and to moving back into your own understanding on this and trying to take control.

> "The Lord says to you, 'Do not be alarmed when that happens to you. Anchor yourself to your faith in Me and understand that I am doing something which is going to dislodge, which is going to stir things up and rearrange; and there will be a lack of comfort for a season. But do not be deceived by this; and do not fall prey to that which would want you to step in and take over and take control; and do what you know in your own understanding. I say to you, in that season, wait on

Me. Wait on Me and see if I don't rearrange things in a way that really answers the cry of your heart and causes to come forth what you have tried to bring forth and have not been able to do. I say to you, watch Me, by the power of My Spirit, cause it to land in supernatural arrangement.'"

Chuck also shared: "I hear the Lord saying that worship is going to be very significant and important in this season. 'You must give to Me extended seasons of worship. You must take meetings where all you do is worship Me. You must have special meetings that are designed just to worship Me. In your own devotion and prayer life, you must transition into a season where there are prolonged periods of worship and praise because this is going to do something in you that you do not understand or are aware of. This is going to lubricate you and make you pliable and soft, because as You exalt Me and as you exalt what I am saying and as you speak My praise and My worship over your life, there is going to be a soaking of My presence. It will happen when you don't even understand the how or why or don't even know it is happening, and you are going to be changed in a very subtle, and yet very profound way during these seasons of great worship. This is important to you at this moment. Praise is going to break things in the Spirit. Praise is going to free things. Praise is going to enthrone Me in situations. You will see Me move where you did not even ask Me to move.'

"The Lord says, 'I will come into situations that are wrong, and you didn't even know they were wrong. I will move into strife.'"

Dutch continued: "I see God saying, 'I want to come and properly align you to things in your past, properly align you with history, disconnect you from things that are not right that have caused things to be moved off of the foundation and bones to be set improperly. And you've grown. But when you stop and look back at it, it has grown crooked, or it is not square, not right. And the more that is built on that improper foundation, the more out of alignment it is going to get. If you will listen to Me, I am going to bring a spirit of revelation to you right now. And I am going to adjust you and cause you to properly connect past and future, and the result of that is going to be a release of the glory of God. There are ways of thinking, there are even relationships in your past that I am going to disconnect you from. There are those that need to be separated; there are those that I am going to connect you to for your future. And I am going to reach back into your past, and I am going to begin to adjust things in your history that are not right. I am going to even heal the land in ways, because of defilement that has come to this region. I am going to come and move into past situations that have caused fractures, and there has never been a proper healing or alignment of that. I am going to come to bring a holy adjustment. I am going to connect you with those from the past that you need to be connected to. I am going to connect movements of the past.'

"Just as God says that He is going to connect Foursquare with roots, God says, 'I am going to properly connect some of you to giftings and anointings and inheritances that belong to you that you do not know of and are not aware of and things that you thought were dead; I am going to connect you to inheritances—things that you need to be moving in that have grown stagnant. I am going to move you back onto the foundation that aligns you properly. So there will be a connection of the old and the new.'"

Chuck D. Pierce prophesied: "The cloud that has been on this state—I am creating a wind to blow that cloud away, but then I will come in and overshadow you new and fresh. Watch the wind blow. Watch the March winds blow, for even then that cloud which has rested down, which has brought a fogginess of what I am doing in this state, will begin to blow away. But then a new cloud of My anointing is coming upon you. You will be hidden in a way for a season. But then you will rise up; and I will send you forth; and deliverance will break out and sweep this state."

Dutch continued with his message on "overshadowing": "The Lord says, *'I am about to overshadow you and kick you out of the nest.'* That is not a bad thing; that is a good thing. You are going to fly like you have never flown before. You are going to come into a season where—like the eagle rises up to its destiny and ability to soar. That is what God is trying to do with you, Washington. That is what this wind, these changes, are all about. God is saying, *'I am going to make you fly, make you move into your destiny. I am going to make you—I am going to hover over you, and I am not going to take no for an answer. You are going to get there.'*

"What God is saying is, 'I want fruit, Washington....You are ready to break this canopy, this thing that is over your state. You have come a long way, and now I am going to finish what I started. I am going to break you through all the way. I am going to rearrange this thing with the whirlwind; and when you come out of it, you are going to fly like an eagle. And you are going to receive those promises that have been lying there dormant and you thought were dead. I am going to bring the loved ones in. I am going to bring the prodigals home. I am going to build the vision that I gave to you. I am going to fulfill the promise that sat there for twenty years because you let it die—because you didn't think it was from God anymore—but it was. I am going to stir that up in you. I am going to accomplish every thing I have spoken to you.'

"Listen, this is the word of the Lord over you right now. He is going to connect you with the old. There is coming a fertility to the state of Washington. There is coming a fruitfulness to the state of Washington. There is coming a resurrection of promises to the state of Washington. There is coming a rebirth of promise. There is coming a reconnecting to the old—but God's way, God's time, God's season. There is something coming that God is saying, *'I am going to resurrect every thing I have promised you, and I am going to give you the Isaac I told you I was going to give you.'*"

Chuck D. Pierce prophesied: "Thank God for these eagles that are coming! The Lord says, 'I am coming to the reservations of this state, and I am going to loose the eagles that have been captured on those reservations. They are going to rise up.' The Lord says, 'There will be a surrounding of the Space Needle with the eagles of God in this region, and I say from that, the explosion of the revelation will begin to move on this state. Wait for proper alignment. But in days ahead, the reservations will be released in a new way, and it will be a sign. And then as you come around the Space Needle, the course of the atmosphere of this state will fully change, and My anointing will flood the entire state!'"

Brief Washington History[178]

Before the coming of the Europeans, the Native American peoples inhabiting what is now the state of Washington included the Nez Perce, Spokane, Yakima, Cayues, Okanogan, Walla Walla, and Colville in the interior, and the Nooksak, Chinook, Nisqually, Clallam, Makah, Quinault and Puyallup in the coastal area.

Exploration and Settlement

...The first American[s] interested in the Pacific Northwest were merchants who came from Boston as early as the 1780s. The Lewis and Clark expedition (1804-1806) stimulated public interest, and in 1811 John Jacob Astor established a fur-trading post—Astoria—near the mouth of the Columbia River and a fort at the mouth of the Okanogan River. In 1818, the U.S. and Britain agreed to a ten-year period of joint occupancy of the Oregon County.

Territorial Status and Statehood

In 1846 the present US-Canadian boundary was established, and Washington became part of the United States territory of Oregon two years later. When it was separated from Oregon in 1853, the new territory contained fewer than 4000 inhabitants and stretched from the Pacific Ocean to the crest of the Rocky Mountains. The first territorial governor, Isaac I. Stevens, moved quickly to extinguish Native American title to the land and to improve transportation, the two keys to rapid settlement and economic development. The treaties negotiated by Stevens in 1854-1855 were an attempt to defuse tensions between natives and settlers, but for various reasons the treaty structure quickly deteriorated, and intermittent warfare took place between 1855 and 1858....

Completion of the Northern Pacific (1868) and Great Northern (1893) rail lines boosted Washington's economy, and statehood in 1889 brought political stability, beginning a period of rapid growth that lasted through [World War I]. During that time the population increased from 75,000 to 1.2 million. Wheat growing and cattle raising in eastern Washington and lumbering and fishing in the western portions of the state were the main economic activities. The Boeing Airplane Company, founded during [World War I], became the largest private employer in the state during and after [World War II]. Lack of diversification led to a series of boom-and-bust periods....

By the mid-20th century, agriculture had made dramatic gains. Construction of huge dams provided irrigation and flood control, as well as cheap electric power, and led to the development of inland ports and increased river shipping. As the gateway to Alaska, Washington had been moving away from dependence on federal contracts and has encouraged new industries to develop and process Alaskan resources. During the 1960s, 1970s, and the 1980s the population increased rapidly—especially in the Seattle and Puget Sound areas. State authorities tried to encourage industrial growth while protecting the environment.

The Character of the State

Washington's reputation as a maverick state with citizens who tend toward radicalism in politics and social attitudes springs from its agrarian populist tradition and onetime strong radical labor movement. Both influenced the adoption of the initiative, referendum and recall, the open primary, and workers' compensation and consumer protection laws. Perhaps the most pervasive elements determining the character of the state, however, have been the relative homogeneity of its population, a relaxed pace of life, and a philosophy of harmony with the natural environment. Many citizens have enjoyed Washington's status as an isolated corner of the nation. This isolation was reflected in national politics, in which the state had little impact until after World War II, when Warren G. Magnusen, who represented Washington in the U.S. Senate from 1945 to 1981, and Henry M. Jackson, who served in the Senate from 1953 until his death, acquired considerable influence in health, consumer affairs, foreign policy, and defense.

WEST VIRGINIA[179]

West Virginia: Named after Elizabeth I, Virgin Queen of England
Statehood: June 20, 1863 (35th state)
Motto: *Montani Semper Liberi* (Mountaineers Are Always Free)
Familiar Name: The Mountain State
50-State Tour: The Breakthrough State, July 18-19, 2004

Chuck Pierce taught on the "Four Phases of Transformation" from Ezekiel chapter 37.

1. *Prophesy to the bones!* The sound comes forth of a new order.
2. *Prophesy again!* We must persevere with revelation, for hope deferred makes the heart sick.
3. *Prophesy again!* Spirits of death that have infiltrated life cycles must be addressed. Things that have never been opened must be opened! Chuck said that he believes this is where we are as a state.
4. *Performance Stage!* "*I will put My Spirit within you!*" As we are entering this stage, we are on the verge of the performance of God's word.

Dutch Sheets declared, "West Virginia, you are poised for a breakthrough—*but you must push! You are very close to some wonderful things.*"

Pastor Dutch encouraged us to seek out the deep wells of the past. We must connect synergistically with the covenantal strength of our forefathers. (We must also break some elements that are evil.) He spoke to us rhetorically, "Can something from our past come into the present and give us victory?"

This spoke to us of our Celtic heritage and the ancient missionaries who arrived in our land almost 1,000 years before the Columbian era and left their prophetic witness carved into the firmament of our land, awaiting the dawning of the time of awakening. Every year, for almost 1,500 years, at the Winter Solstice, a shaft of light from the rising sun peeks through a crevice in a rock on a mountainside in Wyoming County, West Virginia, and illuminates from left to right a petroglyph of what has come to be called "America's First Christmas Card." It reads, translated from the ancient Celtic language of Ogham: "At the time of sunrise, a ray grazes the notch on the left side on Christmas Day, the first season of the year, the season of the blessed advent of the Savior Lord Christ. Behold He is born of Mary, a woman." The prayers of those ancients long for their full realization in the hearts of the people of this land.

Pastor Dutch told us that we have come to an appointed time! Boundaries have been set in the predetermined plan of God. Time is catching up to the Lord's decrees. West Virginia, you have caught up with some decrees. Now is the time! But there must be a response of faith, for hope deferred will block the appropriate response—there must be a repositioning. We must defeat a religious spirit that has brought with it a spirit of unbelief.

Brief West Virginia History[180]

Early Inhabitants and European Settlement

The Mound Builders were the earliest known inhabitants. When the first Europeans arrived, however, the region was for the most part unpopulated, serving as a common hunting ground (and therefore a battleground) for the settlers and Native Americans. This part of Virginia, which later became West Virginia, was penetrated by explorers and fur traders as early as the 1670s. It was cut off from the eastern regions by rugged mountains and remained uninhabited for more than a century after Virginia had thriving colonies.

What is now the Eastern Panhandle attracted the first settlers. They were Germans and Scotch-Irish, and they came not over the Blue Ridge [Mountains] from Virginia but rather down the valleys from Pennsylvania. German families established (circa1730) a settlement on the Potomac and named it Mecklenburg; now called Shepherdstown, it is the oldest town in the state. Homes sprang up along the rivers, but the formidable Allegheny Plateau barrier was not crossed until after the British government, concerned about French claims to the Ohio valley, granted (1749) the Ohio Company large tracts of land in the transAllegheny region.

Settlers began laboriously making their way over the mountains, and they eventually came into conflict with the French; this conflict was the direct cause of the French and Indian War (1754–1763). During the war, most settlers fled the area. They returned after the English captured Fort Duquesne in 1758 and broke the French hold on the Ohio valley. Great numbers poured back over the mountains, ignoring the British proclamation of 1763, which, in the hopes of avoiding conflict with the Native Americans, forbade settlement [west] of the Alleghenies.

The Native Americans resented this encroachment on their hunting grounds, and their hostility was fed by the often unjust treatment they received at the hands of settlers. The brutal murder of the family of chief James Logan provoked a series of attacks that resulted in Lord Dunmore's War…in which the Native Americans were decisively defeated (Oct. 10, 1774).

The American Revolution

During the American Revolution the area was invaded three times by British-led Native American forces. After the American conquest of the Northwest by an army (consisting mostly of western Virginians) under George Rogers Clark, the British and Native American threat to the area was virtually removed. Western Virginians overwhelmingly supported ratification of the U.S. Constitution; they wanted a strong federal government that would quell further conflict with the Native Americans and that would enrich commerce along the Ohio, a river of central importance to their economic life.

Growth and Estrangement from Eastern Virginia

Population growth and prosperity were spurred by the opening of the Mississippi River with the Louisiana Purchase in 1803, by the resulting expansion and improvement of river-borne commerce, and by the completion (1818) of the National Road at Wheeling. The area became an increasingly important part of Virginia, but the predominance of small farms and the almost total absence of slavery were already contributing to a sense of estrangement from the eastern part of the state.

Virginia was politically dominated by the wealthy tidewater planters, who were overrepresented in the state legislature because slaves were counted in apportioning representation. As a result the western

Virginians suffered from inequitable taxation, and their demands for internal improvements and public education were not met. A new Virginia constitution, ratified in 1830, brought no reforms, but another charter (1851) effected a compromise by which representation in the lower house was based on white population and under which universal white male suffrage was granted. It was not enough; tidewater domination of the state legislature continued, and the two sections were being pulled further apart by economic differences—western Virginia was becoming an industrialized coal and steel center—and by the increasing prominence of the slavery issue.

Civil War and the Creation of West Virginia

At the outset of the Civil War the northwestern counties of Virginia overwhelmingly opposed the state's ordinance of secession (Apr. 17, 1861). Unable to halt Virginia's secession from the Union, westerners in the state were quick to take advantage of a long-awaited opportunity for their own separation from Virginia. Protected by federal troops, delegates representing most of Virginia's western counties met at Wheeling on June 11, 1861, and nullified the Virginia ordinance of secession, declared the offices of the state government at Richmond to be vacated, and formed the "restored government" of Virginia, with Francis H. Pierpont as governor.

Creation of a new state was overwhelmingly approved in the referendum of [October] 24, and in November another convention at Wheeling began to draft the state constitution that was approved in [April] 1862. President Lincoln proclaimed (Apr. 20, 1863) admission of a new state, West Virginia, to be effective 60 days thence, and on June 20, 1863, Arthur I. Boreman was inaugurated as its first governor. Pierpont and his "restored government" of Virginia had, of course, consented to the formation of the new state, thereby technically fulfilling the requirement in the U.S. Constitution that a state consent to its own division. Pierpont continued to act as governor of occupied Virginia throughout the war.

Meanwhile, the Confederates had failed to hold on to the region militarily; Union forces, under the command of General George B. McClellan and then under General William S. Rosecrans, were victorious in battles at Philippi (June 3, 1861), Rich [Mountain] (July 11), Corrick's Ford (July 13), and Carnifax Ferry (Sept. 10). General Robert E. Lee's attempt to rally the Confederate forces ended in defeat at Cheat [Mountain] (Sept. 12-13), and a year later Rosecrans's victory at Gauley Bridge extended Union control to the lower Kanawha valley.

The Confederates made no serious endeavor to recover the territory [west] of the Allegheny Front, although guerrilla attacks persisted throughout the war. The strategically important Eastern Panhandle, on the other hand, was the scene of continual fighting; not originally a part of West Virginia, it had been quickly annexed (1863) because it contained the Baltimore and Ohio [Railroad]. (West Virginia's possession of this area was confirmed by the U.S. Supreme Court in 1871.) Of the many West Virginians who remained loyal to the old state, Virginia, the most notable was General Thomas J. (Stonewall) Jackson; his only sister, however, was a staunch Union supporter. Such a division in allegiance was common in many families, and these divisions affected West Virginia's politics for several decades after the war.

Postwar Political Changes and the Hatfield-McCoy Feud

Slavery was abolished in 1865, but it was not until 1872 that the state allowed African Americans to vote and to hold public office. In 1866 Radical Republicans disenfranchised all persons who had aided the Confederacy, but after the Democrats came to power (which they held for 25 years thereafter), this act was annulled (1871) by the Flick Amendment.

In 1885 the capital, which had been shuttled back and forth between Wheeling and Charleston, became fixed at Charleston. Three years earlier, along the border region between West Virginia and Kentucky, there had begun the now famous Hatfield-McCoy feud, which was to encompass many killings and embroil the governors of the two states in lengthy and heated controversy. The blood of West Virginia Hatfields and Kentucky McCoys was shed until 1896.

Industrial Expansion and the Labor Movement

Of great significance to West Virginia was the state's industrial expansion in the late 19th [century]. Based on rich resources and supported by the immigration of Southern blacks and northern laborers, industrialization marked a change from the largely self-sufficient economy of local communities to one of dependence on industry's profits and labor's wages. West Virginia's great chemical industry was founded during World War I when German chemicals could no longer be imported, and it was greatly expanded during World War II.

Both wars also brought unprecedented boom periods to the mines and the steel mills. The state's rapid industrialization, however, was long accompanied by serious labor problems. This was especially true in the coal mines, where wages were low and working conditions dangerous. Unionization was bitterly resisted by mine owners, and strikes throughout the latter part of the 19th [century] and the first third of the 20th [century] were often marked by serious and extended violence, particularly in 1912-1913 and in 1920-1921.

The Great Depression in 1930 intensified difficulties, but reform measures under the New Deal finally assured the miners their right to organize; membership in the United Mine Workers of America soared, and by 1937 labor leaders enjoyed tremendous political power in the state. During the 1950s economic weakness in the coal industry, combined with the mechanization and automation that enabled mines to operate at top efficiency with far fewer employees, were the chief factors in bringing about the highest unemployment rate in the country and a major exodus of the state's population—down 7.2 percent from 1950 to 1960 and another 6.2 percent from 1960 to 1970.

Late Twentieth-Century Developments

Economic conditions improved during the 1960s, as federal aid poured into the state (in part owing to the rise to power in the U.S. Senate of Robert C. Byrd), and massive efforts were made to attract new industry. Since the 1960s the ravages of surface mining have been a major political issue; recently, the practice of leveling mountains and filling creeks with slag has come under fire. In the 1970s, West Virginia's coal-based economy flourished as energy prices rose dramatically; but in the 1980s energy prices fell and employment in the mines rapidly declined as West Virginia suffered through one of the worst economic periods in its history. By 1983 the state's unemployment rate had risen to 21 percent as its manufacturing base also slumped. West Virginia's population declined 8 percent from 1980 to 1990. It rose slightly from 1990 to 2000, as a modest recovery based largely on foreign investment and further development of the tourist industry took place, but the state still ranked last in U.S. housing construction.

WISCONSIN[181]

Wisconsin: Chippewa meaning "gathering of the waters"
Statehood: May 29, 1848 (30th state)
Motto: Forward
Familiar Name: The Badger State
50-State Tour: The River State, August 22-23, 2003

50-State Tour Excerpts

A Word from Chuck D. Pierce

This is a new season in Wisconsin. Each state has a destiny. We are to hear this destiny and begin to move in it. We are to see the relationship of Wisconsin with the nation. Each state will be judged on how they worship and how they protect the generation coming up.

1. There is a strong religious spirit linked with Freemasonry. There is a covenant agreement through this spirit to stop the appropriation of the blood of Jesus in Wisconsin.

2. God desires to bring forth something new. We are called to be a shield of defense to this land, and if we move forward, it will expose the plans of the enemy.

3. There is a fountain in place in Wisconsin, but it is corked up. When the cork is removed, there will be 12 faucet-like flowing streams coming out of the fountain. There will be a new administration by the end of September [2003]. Get your boats ready. Water is going to flow across this state!

A Word from Dutch Sheets

Unless every state fills their part of God's plan, the nation will be hurt. God says, *"Wisconsin is My River State."* God is trying to release the river. Satan tries to stop what God is doing and comes with the opposite of what God wants to do. Satan brings in a religious spirit to stop God's river from flowing. When God's river starts to flow, it will undo the religious spirit. In the Church, there is a spirit of unbelief that says, "God cannot change things suddenly." A shift in the heavenlies brings a change on earth.

Revelation 22:1-3 (NIV) says: *"Then the angel showed me the river of that water of life, as clear as crystal, flowing from the throne of God and of the Lamb down the middle of the great street of the city. On each side of the river stood the tree of life, bearing twelve crops of fruit, yielding its fruit every month. And the leaves of the tree are for the healing of the nations. No longer will there be any curse. The throne of God and of the Lamb will be in the city, and His servants will serve Him."*

Twelve kinds of fruit (12 fountains) bring healing for the nations. The river of life and the river of living water are the same.... Deep water carries it to the nations and shallow water is the river of refreshing.... The River comes from the throne room, watering the trees and bringing healing to the nations.... This river is supposed to flow out of the Church.

John 7:37 (NIV) says, *"On the last and greatest day of the Feast, Jesus stood and said in a loud voice, 'If anyone is thirsty, let him come to Me and drink.'"* The "Feast" spoken of in John is the Feast of Tabernacles, also called the Feast of Ingathering or the Feast of Illumination. It was the harvest season and candles were lit all over the city. God wants to bring a fresh flow of revelation for the people of Wisconsin through dreams, visions, and the prophetic. *Light* is coming! Intellect stops the free flow of revelation. The River frees it.

Prophetic Directive from Chuck Pierce

In the fall of 1986, God brought an opportunity to this state through His Holy Spirit but the Spirit was quenched. We need to find that place and worship there to unquench the Spirit.

Dutch Sheets Prophesies

A wave of the miraculous is coming to Wisconsin, and a harvest with many fish! But there is a spirit of unbelief rooted in the religious spirit. Choose to take God outside the walls of the Church and break the religious spirit. Out of your "womb" will flow rivers of water. The womb is a place of birthing, reproduction. Wisconsin has the opportunity to be one of the firstfruit states of harvest for the nation. God will begin to move from the center of Wisconsin—to the east, then south, then north, and then west.

A Final Word from Chuck Pierce

The ruling spirit over Wisconsin is intellectualism. First, bind the strong man (see Matthew 12:29). The principle presented is that if you can divide something, then you can conquer it. When an apostle and a prophet are in place, you can address the strongholds. Satan hates the fivefold ministry and its order. Intercessors are the foundation. We bind the strongman through revelation, and we use revelation in worship. Wisconsin needs the prophetic gift.

Brief Wisconsin History[182]

French Fur Trading and the Influx of Eastern Tribes

The Great Lakes offered an easy access from Canada to the region that is now Wisconsin, and the Frenchman Jean Nicolet arrived at the site of Green Bay in 1634 in search of fur pelts and the Northwest Passage. He was followed by other traders and missionaries, among them Radisson and Groseilliers; Marquette and Joliet, who discovered the upper Mississippi; and Aco and Hennepin, from the party of La Salle.

Meanwhile the spread of settlers in the East was bringing the Ottawa, the Huron, and other Native American tribes into Wisconsin, where they in turn displaced the older inhabitants, the Winnebago, the Kickapoo, and others. Similarly, the Ojibwa drove their kinsmen the Sioux westward from Wisconsin. Only the Menominee remained relatively settled.

Nicolas Perrot helped (1667) establish Green Bay as the center of the Wisconsin fur trade, and in 1686 he formally claimed all the region for France. The fur trade flourished despite the 50-year war between the Fox and the French, and the historic Fox-Wisconsin portage was used by generations of traders from Green Bay and Prairie du Chien in their search for beaver and other furs.

British-American Struggles

Like all of New France, Wisconsin fell to the British with the end of the French and Indian Wars (1763). British traders mingled with the French and eventually gained the bulk of the fur trade. The British hold continued even after the end of the American Revolution, when the Old Northwest formally passed (1783) to the United States and was made (1787) a part of the Northwest Territory. After Jay's Treaty

(1794), northwestern strongholds were turned over to the Americans, but the British continued to dominate the fur trade from the Canadian border. In the War of 1812 Wisconsin again fell into British hands. It was only with the Treaty of Ghent...that effective U.S. territorial control began and that the American Fur Company gained control of much of the fur trade.

Settlement and Native American Resistance

Present-day Wisconsin was transferred from Illinois Territory to Michigan Territory in 1818. By then the fur trade was diminishing, but the lead mines in [southwestern] Wisconsin had long been active, and booming lead prices in the 1820s brought the first large rush of settlers. The region's great agricultural potential was also apparent, and after 1825 a considerable number of easterners began arriving via the new Erie Canal and the Great Lakes. They settled in the Milwaukee area and along the waterways. The U.S. army preserved order from key forts established at Green Bay (1816), Prairie du Chien (1816), and Portage (1828) and built bridges, trails, and roads throughout the region. The hostility of the Native Americans toward the incursions of aggressive settlers culminated in the Black Hawk War (1832). This revolt, brutally crushed, was the last Native American resistance of serious consequence in the area.

Territorial Status and Early Statehood

In 1836, Wisconsin was made a territory, and the legislators chose a compromise site for the capital, midway between the Milwaukee and western centers of population; thus the city of Madison was founded. By 1840 population in the territory had risen above 130,000, but the people, fearing higher taxes and stronger government, rejected propositions for statehood four times. In addition, politicians were at first unwilling to yield Wisconsin claims to a strip of land around Chicago and to what is now the Upper Peninsula of Michigan. However, hopes that statehood would bring improved communications and prosperity became dominant; the claims were yielded, and Wisconsin achieved statehood in 1848. The state constitution provided protection for indebted farmers, limited the establishment of banks, and granted liberal suffrage. These measures and the state's rich soil attracted immigrants from Europe.

The influx of Germans to Wisconsin was especially heavy, and some parts of the state assumed the tidy semi-German look that has persisted along with an astonishing survival of the German language. Liberal leaders, like Carl Schurz, came after the failure of the Revolution of 1848 in Germany and added to the intellectual development of the state. Contributions were also made, then and later, by Irish, Scandinavians, Germans who had previously emigrated to the Volga region of Russia, and Poles.

The state's development was not always smooth. Although the state constitution provided for a system of free public schools, the principle was implemented only slowly. Similarly, the [University] of Wisconsin (chartered 1848) was slow to assume importance. After a referendum (1852) ended the state constitutional ban on banking, farmers and many others mortgaged their property to buy railroad stocks, only to suffer distress when the state's railways went bankrupt in the Panic of 1857.

Late Nineteenth Century Political and Economic Developments

Wisconsin was steadily antislavery; the Free-Soil party gained a large following in the state (although the party's homestead plank and economic program were the major attractions). Wisconsin abolitionists played an important part in the formation of the Republican party. In the Civil War Wisconsin quickly rallied to the Union. Copperheads were few, but many War Democrats opposed the abridgment of civil liberties and other aspects of the war effort, and some of the German immigrants, who had left Germany because they opposed compulsory military service, opposed even voluntary war service.

The boom times brought by the war mitigated discontent, and economic and social growth was rapid during the 1860s and after. Railroads and other means of communication linked Wisconsin closely to the East. The meatpacking and brewing industries of Milwaukee began to assume importance in the 1860s. Wheat was briefly dominant especially in [southern] Wisconsin, but was superseded in the 1870s as states further west became wheat producers and Wisconsin shifted to more diversified farming. Its great dairy industry developed, spurred by an influx of skilled dairy farmers from New York and Scandinavia and by the efforts of the Wisconsin Dairymen's Association (est. 1872). In these years the great pine forests of [northern] Wisconsin began to be greatly exploited, and in the 1870s lumbering became the state's most important industry. Oshkosh and La Crosse flourished. With lumbering came large paper and wood products industries, and the opening of iron mines in Minnesota and Michigan promoted the [northern] Great Lake ports and increased industrial opportunities.

Although hard hit in the panics of 1873 and 1898, Wisconsin was generally prosperous in the late 19th [century], and the reform-minded Granger movement and Populist party received less support than in other Midwestern states. A trend toward liberal political views was stimulated in Wisconsin by socialist thought, which was introduced early. Socialism, in a pragmatic and reformist rather than a doctrinaire form, dominated Milwaukee politics for many years and gave the city efficient government, particularly under the leadership of Victor Berger and Daniel Hoan. Stemming from a different source was the reform spirit of specialized and advanced Wisconsin farmers, who recognized the need for a more viable political and economic framework.

Robert La Follette and the Progressive Movement

In the early 20th [century], reform sentiment blossomed in the Progressive movement, under the tutelage of the Republican leader, Robert M. La Follette. This pragmatic attempt to achieve good effective government for all and to limit the excessive power of the few resulted in a direct primary law (1903), in legislation to regulate railroads and industry, in pure food acts, in high civil service standards, and in efforts toward cooperative nonpartisan action to solve labor problems. An important adjunct of progressivism was the "Wisconsin idea"—that of linking the facilities and brainpower of the [University] of Wisconsin to progressive experiments and legislation. The plan owed much to Charles McCarthy and to the support of university president Charles Van Hise, and it brought such diverse benefits as the spread of scientific agricultural methods and the many labor and other bills drafted by Professor John R. Commons.

The progressive movement was temporarily halted by World War I. La Follette, some Socialists, and many German-Americans were critical of U.S. involvement in that war, but they were a distinct minority. Wisconsin was generally prosperous in the 1920s; industrialization made rapid strides, reforestation of the once great but now exhausted timberland was stimulated by state legislation, and the dairying industry continued to grow.

Wisconsin was alone in voting for its native son, La Follette, when he ran for president on the Progressive party ticket in 1924, and in the state his policies continued to be carried forward by his sons Robert M. La Follette Jr., and Philip La Follette. Wisconsin's pioneer old-age pension act (1925) and its unemployment compensation act (1931) served as models for national social security a few years later. The Great Depression of the 1930s struck particularly hard in industrialized Milwaukee, but some relief was provided by the New Deal, and in addition Gov. Philip La Follette attempted, in his "little new deal," to improve agricultural marketing, promote electrification, and enforce fair labor practices.

World War II to the Present

During World War II, Wisconsin's shipbuilding industry flourished, and in the prosperous postwar era, urbanization and industrial growth continued; even in the nationwide slump of the late 1980s, the state's manufacturing sector proved resilient. Wisconsin politics continued to resonate on the national scene. U.S. Senator Joseph McCarthy aroused controversy with his unsubstantiated anti-Communist campaign of the 1950s, but "McCarthyism" was balanced by other political strains in the state; thus Milwaukee, in the same period, again elected a Socialist mayor, and the Democratic party, long no match for Republican or Progressive forces, has gained strength in state elections since the late 1950s. In the 1990s the state was a pioneer in welfare reform.

WYOMING[183]

> **Wyoming:** Delaware meaning "end of the plains"
> **Statehood:** July 10, 1890 (44th state)
> **Motto:** Equal Rights
> **Familiar Name:** The Equality State
> **50-State Tour:** The Deliverance State, April 28-29, 2004

The Lord released the following word to Wyoming at our 50-State Tour through Chuck Pierce and Dutch Sheets:

> The voice of the Lord will be heard across the state of Wyoming. The prophetic word of the Lord will ascend over this state. And the word of the Lord will rain on Wyoming. It will bring release. It will bring breakthrough. It's going to heal the broken hearts; it's going to set the captive free. We just say this is the favorable year of the Lord. It is the year of the Lord's favor. It is the year that the gospel will be preached to the poor; that the downtrodden will be ministered to and released; the oppressed will go free. We decree change is coming. Favor is coming to Wyoming. We decree that fire is coming to the Church—outpouring, renewal, life, victory, renewed hope, and vision.
>
> The Lord says, "*I need for the people, My people in Wyoming to know that they have a loud voice in the Spirit—that they have significance.*" The Lord says it is in the corporate sense. He wanted you to know that your size of population is not significant in the Spirit, but your voice is, and that you carry as much weight in the Spirit as any other state or any other city any place in the nation. What He wants to do through

you, through your intercession and your voice in the Spirit, is very significant. The Lord wants you to shift over to a spiritual realm and see that where you don't have much of a voice really in the natural—He just kept saying to me, "***You have a great voice in the Spirit. And when you pray, and when you decree things, you have as much as a voice as any place else in this nation.***" And sometimes, just to show that it's all about Him, the Lord will do more through a smaller group of people than He will through the majority.

God is saying, "I'm giving you a sword. I'm bringing you in unity. You will overthrow thrones of iniquity. This territory will be a place of habitation of My Spirit. Many will come in to this territory. And the voice of God will be heard here." (Prophesied by Dutch Sheets.)

A Ministry of Deliverance

The Lord has spoken to Wyoming repeatedly about its gifting to be a place of the ministry of restoration and healing, to be a place of renewal to the leaders, both secular and spiritual, of the world. Many retreat here to experience renewal. Leaders from across the world, including kings and presidents, come here for peace.

Dutch Sheets declared:

> Deliverance is coming to this state. Iniquities are being broken. People are being released from bondage. Eyes are being opened; scales and veils— scales are falling off; veils are being lifted. Deception is being broken. Every age group is about to receive a visitation, an outpouring by the Spirit of God. Nothing can stop it. Nothing can stop it. Signs and wonders

> are coming to Wyoming; miracles are coming. Deliverance is coming. Breakthrough is coming. The voice of the Lord will be heard across the state of Wyoming. The prophetic word of the Lord will ascend over this state. And the word of the Lord will rain on Wyoming. It will bring release. It will bring breakthrough. It's going to heal the broken hearts; it's going to set the captive free. We say this is the favorable year of the Lord. It is the year of the Lord's favor. It is the year that the gospel will be preached to the poor, that the downtrodden will be ministered to and released; the oppressed will go free. We decree change is coming. Favor is coming to Wyoming. We decree that fire is coming to the Church. Outpouring, renewal, life, victory, renewed hope, and vision. Father, in Jesus' name, thank You for Wyoming. You love Wyoming. You love the Church of Wyoming. You love the sinners. You came to save Wyoming. Thank You, Lord, for the spirit of deliverance. I know I keep coming back to that, but it's coming. There is an anointing. There is a spirit of deliverance. Captives are going to be set free across Wyoming. Break off any hope deferred, any discouragement, any lethargy, any cynicism.

Pray for both the deliverance of Wyoming's Church and the power of the Church to fully minister the deliverance that God has called her to.

Brief Wyoming History[184]

European Claims

Portions of what is now Wyoming were at one time claimed by Spain, France, and England. The acquisition of the territory by the United

States was completed through five major annexations—the Louisiana Purchase in 1803, the Treaty of 1819 with Spain, cession by the Republic of Texas in 1836 and partition from Texas after it was annexed in 1845, the Treaty of Guadalupe Hidalgo (1848) after the Mexican War, and the international agreement (1846) with Great Britain concerning the Columbia River country.

The Fur Trade and Westward Migration

The early development of Wyoming was closely linked with the fur trade and the great westward migrations. French trappers and explorers may have reached the area in the middle to late 18th [century], but the first authentic accounts of the region were provided by John Colter, who, trapped in the Wyoming mountains for several years, returned to Saint Louis in 1810 with fantastic accounts of the steaming geysers and great canyons of the Yellowstone. Colter returned west, and other fur traders made their way into Wyoming. The overland party on its way to found Astoria on the Columbia River went through Teton Pass in 1811. The following year Robert Stuart, returning from Astoria, crossed South Pass and followed much of the route that was to become the Oregon Trail.

Only the hardiest and most self-sufficient could survive the Native American attacks and the rugged isolation of the country. With the expeditions of William H. Ashley, the mountain men entered the country, and some of the most famous of those early explorers—Thomas Fitzpatrick, James Bridger, and Jedediah S. Smith—crossed and recrossed the land. Attracted by the fur trade, Captain B.L.E. de Bonneville organized a sizable expedition, and his were the first wagons to go (1832) through South Pass. The first permanent trading post was Fort William (1834), famous under its later name, Fort Laramie. In 1843 Fort Bridger (now in a state park) was built. The area also aroused the interest of John C. Frémont, who made an expedition in 1842. By the 1840s the route west through Wyoming was in steady use by caravans headed toward Oregon, and the fur-trading posts became stations on the Oregon Trail.

As the fur trade declined, many former trappers and mountaineers settled along the trail, furnishing horses and other supplies to the migrants and purchasing debilitated stock to be put to pasture and sold the following year. Mormons trekking to Utah (Brigham Young led the first party in 1847) and Forty-Niners rushing to the gold fields of California joined the many thousands traversing the mountain passes of Wyoming. A number of Mormons settled for a time in [western] Wyoming. The death of Mormon pioneers in a blizzard (1856) and the thousands of graves along the Oregon Trail give an indication of the toll taken by disease, starvation, attacks by Native Americans, and winter snows. Despite the hardships, telegraph stations (1861) and stagecoach and freight lines were established, and in 1860-1861 pony express riders crossed Wyoming on their route between Saint Joseph, Missouri, and Sacramento, California.

Native American Hostilities and Increased Settlement

Native Americans hostile to encroachment in the early 1860s forced the rerouting of stagecoaches to the south, along the Overland Trail. Displaced from their former homes in the east and west, and waging internecine warfare for control of the rich buffalo ranges, the tribes feared further encroachment by the settlers on their hunting grounds, especially after the opening (1864) of the Bozeman Trail. Treaties were made and broken by both sides, and wars with the Sioux persisted, particularly in the Powder River valley.

Meanwhile, [southern] Wyoming was relatively free of attacks, and a gold rush, stimulated by the discoveries at South Pass (1867), brought the first heavy influx of settlers to that region; the flow was increased by the uncovering of vast coal deposits in [southwest] Wyoming. Probably the greatest stimulus to settlement was the completion (1868) of the Wyoming sector of the Union Pacific Railroad. Towns, including Cheyenne, sprang up beside the tracks, and trade thrived on the demands of the road crews and the new settlers.

Territorial Status and Economic Development

In 1868 the region became the Territory of Wyoming, with Cheyenne as its capital. Wyoming pioneered in political equality when, in 1869, the first territorial legislature granted the vote to women. The territory continued to advance economically as huge herds of cattle were driven up over the Texas or Long Trail. Native American resistance had been suppressed by the late 1870s. The Arapaho were placed on the Wind River Reservation with their former enemies, the Shoshone, and cattlemen safely moved their herds to grasslands throughout Wyoming.

After the complete opening of rangelands, cattle rustling became so common that the authorities could not control it, and juries grew fearful of returning just verdicts against criminals. The Wyoming Stock Growers Association was organized in 1873 to protect cattle owners, and members frequently formed vigilante groups to administer their own justice. The struggle reached its height in the Johnson county cattle war of 1892. Lawlessness was also exemplified by the Hole-in-the-Wall gang, which broadened its activities to include bank and train robberies as well as cattle theft.

Gradually, vast areas were fenced in and winter pastures were established. The influx of sheep in the late 1890s, however, brought new violence. Cattlemen made frantic efforts to exclude the sheep from close grazing on the precious grasslands. Homesteaders were also unwelcome, and many left when they realized that the country was unsuited for small acreage cultivation. Nonetheless, population increase was steady, advancing from about 9,000 in 1870 to over 90,000 in 1900. With expanding population came other kinds of development: eager frontiersmen rapidly (and somewhat chaotically) established schools, and in 1887 the [University] of Wyoming was founded.

Statehood and Progressive Legislation

Statehood was achieved in 1890, and in keeping with its frontier ideals, Wyoming adopted a liberal state constitution that included the secret ballot. The Carey Act of 1894, providing for the reclamation and settlement of land, stimulated further agrarian development and, in addition, pointed out the need for conservation and efficient use of water. The establishment of national parks protected timberlands and extensive grazing areas, and water power was harnessed to furnish electricity for farms and industries.

In politics, the Progressive movement found numerous adherents in Wyoming; in 1915, after one of the most bitter fights in the state's history, Progressive forces triumphed over the railroad and related interests with the establishment of a state utilities commission. A worker's compensation law was passed in 1915, and also in that year the legislature authorized the [University] of Wyoming to accept federal grants for agricultural experiments and demonstrations. Thus were begun the state's outstanding and widespread services for agrarian improvement. In 1924 Wyoming became the first state to elect a woman governor, Nellie Tayloe Ross.

The Energy Industry and Agriculture in the Twentieth Century

By the mid-1920s the state ranked fourth in the nation in the production of crude oil, but the valuable finds at Teapot Dome are probably remembered best as the symbol of corruption in the administration of President Warren Harding. Under the New Deal, Wyoming was well served by national soil conservation programs, which benefited dry farmers who had extended operations into semiarid regions and had suffered severely in the drought years beginning in the late 1920s. The cooperative movement in agriculture also gained ground in this period and has since grown.

One of the most important events in the state since World War II was the discovery of uranium. New oil finds also helped to offset economic losses resulting from a disastrous four-year-long drought in the 1950s. The decade from the early 1970s to the early 1980s was a boom period for Wyoming as high energy prices boosted the state's coal, oil, and natural gas industries. By the mid-1980s, however, energy prices were falling and the economy was hurt by its lack of diversity. Wyoming also has suffered from the injurious environmental effects of the energy industry, and pollution has become a serious problem in some mining towns. Although its population rose by almost 9 percent between 1990 and 2000, the state is still the least populous in the nation.

– 11 –

DECLARATIONS *and* DECREES *for the* NATION

We decree that the United States of America has reconnected to its covenant roots and has proceeded into a God-ordained season of reset.

We decree that we are in days of change and angel armies are activated to assist with His purpose, His prophesied promise of U-Turns, Turnarounds, and Boomerang Strategies, and hell will not stop this.

We decree a glorious remnant is arising. This remnant will mobilize angel armies with their decrees, utilizing Isaiah 55:11 (MSG) declaring that *"the words that come out of my mouth will not come back empty-handed. They'll do the work I sent them to do, they'll complete the assignment I gave them."*

We decree we are in days of awakening and revival. We align with Heaven today and ask for an acceleration of anointing and outpourings, assisted by angel armies of revival.

We decree America will be saved, and we stand for all nations to participate as well. We decree it is time.

We decree no more delay. Revival come.

We decree dry bones will live. A new breath is entering God's people and resurrection life will cause them to come together and stand as a great army.

We decree *re-vive-all* angels will refresh us for this season and, indeed, He will revive all.

We decree that angels are stirring the waters and healings and miracles are accelerating.

We decree harvest is now—prodigals returning, brand-new converts, and a prophesied word for a billion-soul harvest is manifesting.

We decree angels will assist, according to Matthew 13:39, "...*The harvest is the end of the age, and the reapers are the angels.*" So be it, in the name of Jesus.

We decree that when the King comes in, everything changes. WE EXPECT GOD to reign over our lives, our nation.

We decree justice will prevail over injustice. As the Ekklesia, we rise up and use our voice and our authority to declare that demon principalities, powers, mights, and dominions will be shaken down from their influence because a glorious Church prevails.

We decree evil decrees will not prevail in our nation. Powers of darkness will come down and thrones of iniquity will not stand.

We decree the battle is the Lord's, and He does not lie. The Baal stronghold over our nation is bound and the Naphtali

generation is coming forth and will make a stand against societal and cultural sins (Deuteronomy 27:13).

We decree a new backbone in Your Ekklesia, Lord, and a rising up of strong, vital, and courageous ones who will not back down. We decree every confinement is broken off and we release angels to assist in the advance of Your Kingdom.

We decree God's promise—break up, break out, and breakthrough—we will run with our Breaker (Micah 2:13).

We decree our prayers are hitting the mark and we will pass over into new levels. We decree an anointing to prevail is being released.

We decree doors to new areas, opportunities, places, and lands are opening, and He is making a way through. Pass over and possess!

We decree we are raising the bar today, receiving fresh, fresh vision and increased anointing.

We decree You are pouring out a new Pentecost that will be greater than the outpouring in the book of Acts. We decree You are enabling us to function in a Holy Spirit-planned purpose for the decades to come, for Your glory.

We decree the barren places will become fruitful.

We decree the arrow of the Lord's deliverance has been released from Heaven, and we will experience fresh anointing and outpourings of Holy Spirit, as well as increased angel activity.

We decree ancient wells to open. We decree capped wells of evangelism—open!

We decree new roads, inroads, mantles, vision, and new harvest, in the name of Jesus.

We decree this is the era when the Ekklesia sits on the throne of their regions and influences the natural realms of earth through the spiritual Kingdom.

We declare a move of God has begun and cannot be stopped.

We decree a breaking of hope deferred and replaced with supernatural hope and strength.

We decree the sound of an abundance of rain and revival that affects every generation.

We decree America Shall Be Saved.

We decree that angels are assisting fivefold ministries to overcome darkness in their regions.

We decree the Kingdom of Christ Jesus is growing and expanding its influence in all 50 states.

We declare God is doing new things, and now they will spring forth.

We decree the Church will rise and be the salt and light Jesus said it would be.

We decree promises, faith decrees, dreams, and visions of Holy Spirit are activating in our nation.

We decree those who have sat in great darkness will now live in great light.

We decree angels of breakthrough are working with the heirs of God to break oppression from the land and release freedom.

We decree the angel gate of Heaven is open over this nation and angel armies are aligning us with our covenants with God.

We decree the greatest days are not in our past—they are in our present and in our future.

We decree supernatural recovery is coming for all lost inheritance.

We decree every promise God has made will grow and produce its fruit.

We decree no weapons formed against us will prosper. Our God will anoint us to defeat them.

We decree the gifts of Holy Spirit will function at higher levels than the Church has ever seen before, assisting in harvest evangelism.

We decree the true Ekklesia is moving from glory to glory to glory.

We decree the assignments in prophetic words will accelerate to fullness and not one will return empty.

We decree waves of Kingdom revival will surge around the world, and hell cannot stop it.

We decree rebel government will be purged from the land, and God will raise up leaders who have His heart.

We decree evil ones are being dethroned, displaced, and removed. We decree the world will see a mighty, bold, New Testament Church in this era, and it begins with me.

We decree favor, favor, favor—open doors that are orchestrated by Holy Spirit, and angel armies accompanying us to achieve decrees that have been planned by You. We decree there are more with us than against us; and by the power of Your Spirit and in Your name, we win.

We decree Holy Spirit is bringing order into the disorder of this world, and an innumerable number of angels are activating to assist us.

We decree the Ekklesia will now deploy and the roots of hell will wither and die, scatter and shatter. We decree God's calvary, the chariots of fire, will assist us to win great victories.

We decree the release of government angels to assist the Ekklesia to reign with Christ.

We decree the arrow of the Lord's deliverance will hit the mark.

ENDNOTES

1. Some would call what I experienced a "vision." I would agree but use the phrase "mental picture" because it is often what a vision is. I was not in some sort of trance when this occurred, but simply began to see in my mind a scene, which I knew was not originating with my imagination, but was from God. This is often the case when people refer to a "vision" from God.

2. Jack Canfield and Mark Victor Hansen, *A Third Serving of Chicken Soup for the Soul* (Deer Field Beach, FL: Health Communications, Inc., 1996), 12.

3. A more complete account of this can be read in C. Peter Wagner, ed., Destiny of a Nation (Colorado Springs, CO: Wagner Publication, 2001), 74-76, including portions of the alert that was sent.

4. I realize that there are sincere believers who would disagree with me. For one thing, it is clear that certain minorities, especially in the United States, feel their cause is much safer in the hands of Democrats. I respect that position and I understand the passion behind it in the hearts of many brothers and sisters. Nevertheless, in this particular historic moment, I simply believe it was absolutely imperative that God have someone as our president who is very open to Him and who walks in righteousness. To me, the entire ordeal was never about Republican or Democrat.

5. C. Peter Wagner, ed., *Destiny of a Nation* (Colorado Springs, CO: Wagner Publications, 2001), 80-84.

6   William J. Federer, *America's God and Country, Encyclopedia of Quotations* (St. Louis, MO: Amerisearch, Inc., 2000), 384-385. Abraham Lincoln, June 1863, in a discourse with a college President, just weeks before the Battle of Gettysburg, July 1-3, 1863. William J. Johnson, *Abraham Lincoln, The Christian* (New York: The Abington Press, 1913), 109-110. Peter Marshall and David Manuel, *The Glory of America* (Blooming, MN: Garborg's Heart 'N Home, Inc., 1991), 4.26.

7   Dutch Sheets, *Intercessory Prayer* (Ventura, CA: Regal Books, 1996), 37.

8   Ibid., 37.

9   Ibid., 50.

10 Ibid., 32.

11 Chuck D. Pierce and Rebecca Wagner Sytsema, The Best Is Yet Ahead (Colorado Springs, CO: Wagner Publications, 2001), 14.

12 Ray Summers, Quickverse Bible Dictionary.

13 C. Peter Wagner, ed., *Destiny of a Nation*, 97.

14 Chuck D. Pierce with John Dickson, The Worship Warrior (Ventura, CA: Regal Books, 2002), 243.

15 Chuck D. Pierce and Rebecca Wagner Sytsema, The Future War of the Church (Ventura, CA: Regal Books, 2001), 66-67.

16 Chuck D. Pierce with John Dickson, The Worship Warrior, 244-245.

17 Joanna Gaines's Facebook page; https://www.facebook.com/JoannaStevensGaines/?fref=nf; accessed March 15, 2017.

18 Chuck D. Pierce and Rebecca Wagner Sytsema, Possessing Your Inheritance (Ventura, CA: Regal Books, 1999), 98.

19 Chuck D. Pierce with John Dickson, The Worship Warrior, 199-202.

20 Ibid., 141-142.

21 Chuck D. Pierce and Rebecca Wagner Sytsema, *The Best Is Yet Ahead*, 34-36.

22 Chuck D. Pierce and Robert Heidler, Restoring Your Shield of Faith (Ventura, CA: Regal Books, 2004), 163-164.

23 Spiros Zodhiates, Hebrew-Greek Key Word Study Bible, New American Standard Bible (Chattanooga, TN: AMG Publishers, 1977), 1846.

24 When we speak of this stronghold of Islam, we are not speaking of the Muslim people. We are referring to the religion itself, which we believe to be born of deception. The Scriptures teach that there is no other way to God but through Jesus Christ (see John 14:6).

25 Spiros Zodhiates, Hebrew-Greek Key Word Study Bible, New American Standard Bible, 1756.

26 Ibid., 1170.

27 Ibid., 1287.

28 Dutch Sheets, *God's Timing for Your Life* (Ventura, CA: Regal Books, 2001), 16-17.

29 Arthur Burk, *Relentless Generational Blessings* (2004).

30 Dutch Sheets, *God's Timing for Your Life,* 26-27.

31 Ibid., 33.

32 Chuck D. Pierce and Robert Heidler, Restoring Your Shield of Faith, 165-166.

33 Bill Yount, "I Saw Angels Turning Cartwheels Over the Nation's Capitol, Shouting… 'WE ARE ON A HOLY ROLL!'" See www.billyount.com, November 27, 2004.

34 Spiros Zodhiates, *The Hebrew-Greek Key Word Study Bible, New American Standard Bible,* 1710.

35 Ibid., 1712.

36 The quote and seven defining aspects of the *ekklesia* are taken from Colin Brown, *The New International Dictionary of New Testament Theology,* vol. 3 (Grand Rapids, MI: Zondervan Pub. House, 1975). The comments on each point are the author's.

37 Gustav Gilbert, *The Constitutional Antiquities of Sparta and Athens* (Chicago: Argonaut, 1968), 137-138, 167-168, 265-310.

38 "The Church, the Ekklesia," His Holy Church, March 18, 2015, http://www.hisholychurch.net/ekklesia.php; accessed September 28, 2023.

39 Joseph Mattera, "God, Politics & the Kingdom of God," Mattera Ministries International, May 13, 2016, Ecclesia, http://josephmattera.org/god-politics-the-kingdom-of-god/; accessed September 28, 2023.

40 Submitted by John Buhler, USSPN State Apostolic Coordinator for Alabama. Other sources include: Microsoft Encarta Reference Library, and Alabama Department of Archives and History; https://www.archives.state.al.us/.

41 Submitted by Stina Rhoades (Valdez, AK) and Bea Johnson (Albuquerque, NM). Other sources include: Patrick F. Fitzgerald and Claus M. Naske, *World Book Encyclopedia:* Alaska (Vol. 1, A) (Chicago, IL: World Book, Inc., 2004) and the following website: http://xroads.virginia.edu/~CAP/BARTLETT/49state.html; accessed September 28, 2023.

42 Submitted by Chuck D. Pierce.

43 Submitted by Donna Nelesen, ARISE (Arizona Researchers for Intercession and Strategic Evangelism). Other sources include:

ENDNOTES

Todd W. Bostwick, "Hohokam Rock Art, Astronomy, and Religion." *Glyphs,* Newsletter of the Arizona Archaeological and Historical Society, February 1998.

Thomas Edwin Farish, *History of Arizona,* Vol. I (San Francisco, CA: The Filmer Brothers Electrotype Company, 1915).

Thomas Edwin Farish, *History of Arizona,* Vol. II (San Francisco, CA: The Filmer Brothers Electrotype Company, 1915).

Odie B. Faulk, *Arizona, A Short History* (Norman, OK: University of Oklahoma Press, 1970).

Morris Goldwater, *History of Masonry in Prescott,* Unpublished manuscript, (Prescott, AZ: Prescott Public Library files).

"Hohokam Religion"; www.cudenver-edu/stc-link/hohokam/TEMPLE.htm; accessed May 1, 1999.Melissa Keane and A.E. (Gene) Rogge and Sharon K. Bauer, "Cornerstones of the Faith: The First Eight Congregations in Phoenix and the Archaeology of the First Presbyterian Church Site," *Pueblo Grande Museum Occasional Papers No. 2* (Phoenix, AZ: City of Phoenix, 1998), 73.

Richard W. Kimball, "History Revealed on Naming Prescott," *The Prescott Courier,* March 8, 1993, Prescott, AZ, page 8B.

Bradford Luckingham, *Phoenix: The History of the Southwestern Metropolis* (Tucson, AZ: The University of Arizona Press, 1989).

Peter Pilles Jr., *The Southern Sinagua Plateau,* Vol. 53, No. 1 (Flagstaff, AZ: Museum of Northern Arizona, 1983), 8.

Jay J. Wagoner, *Early Arizona: Prehistory to Civil War* (Tucson, AZ: The University of Arizona Press, 1989).

Jay J. Wagoner, *Arizona Territory, 1863-1912: A Political History* (Tucson, AZ: The University of Arizona Press, 1970).

Robert J. Winters, *The Valley of the Son—Fulfilling Christ's Redemptive Purpose for Greater Phoenix in the 21st Century* (Glendale, AZ: Restoration International Ministries and Publications, Inc., 2000).

Robert Woznicki, *The History of Arizona* (Tempe, AZ: Woznicki Publications, 1999).

44 Submitted by Dr. Jay D. and LaNeé Morse, USSPN State Apostolic Coordinators for Arkansas, and Lisa Lyons, USSPN State Mobilizing Coordinator for Arkansas.

45 Submitted by Dr. Jay D. and LaNeé Morse, Arkansas Apostolic Coordinators, and Lisa Lyons, Arkansas Mobilizing Coordinator.

46 Taken from portions of the California 50-State Tour meeting transcript.

47 Submitted by Jean Steffenson, USSPN State Apostolic Coordinator for Colorado.

48 Submitted by Jean Steffenson, USSPN State Apostolic Coordinator for Colorado.

49 Quoted from "History of Colorado." *The Columbia Electronic Encyclopedia,* 6th ed; http://www.encyclopedia.com/html/section/colorado_history.asp; accessed December 30, 2004.

50 Submitted by Barbara LaChance, USSPN State Apostolic Coordinator for Connecticut.

51 Submitted by Nick Uva, associate pastor of Harvest Time Church, Greenwich, Connecticut. Other sources include:

Connecticut State Register and Manual, published annually by Office of the Connecticut State Secretary of the StateConnecticut State Register and Manual; Connecticut State Register and Manual. Web reference: "The Fundamental Orders of Connecticut," *American Historical Documents, 1000-1904, Harvard Classics Series,* Vol. 43 (New York: P.F. Collier & Son. Co.,

1909-1914; Bartleby.com, 2001); http://www.bartleby.com/43/; accessed October 2, 2023."The Scarlet Standard, No. 2," *The Connecticut Society of the Sons of the American Revolution,* August 1997.Robert Asher, *Connecticut Inventors.* Bruce Fraser, *Connecticut 1763-1818.*Paul Gomme and Peter Rupert; "Per Capita Income Growth and Disparity in the United States, 1929-

ENDNOTES

2003"; www.clevelandfed.org/Research/Com2004/0815.pdf; accessed October 2, 2023.

52. The Foxwoods Casino is widely reputed to be the largest casino in the Western Hemisphere.

53. Submitted by Dale and Miriam Mast, USSPN State Apostolic Coordinators for Delaware.

54. Submitted by Dale and Miriam Mast, USSPN State Apostolic Coordinators for Delaware.

55. This entire section is quoted from http://www.destatemuseums.org/vc/Dehistory.doc; accessed January 2, 2004.

56. Submitted by Chuck D. Pierce.

57. This entire section is quoted from "Washington DC District History," *SHG Resources,* http://www.shgresources.com/dc/history/; accessed February 17, 2005.

58. Submitted by Ken Malone, USSPN State Apostolic Coordinator for Florida.

59. This section was adapted from an article by Peter O. Muller and D.S. Winsboro, "Florida," *World Book Encyclopedia,* Vol. 7F (Chicago, IL: World Book, Inc., 2004), also includes information from M.C. Bob Leonard, "Florida of the Indians"; http://www.bob-leonard-florida.com/floridanabob/floridians.htm; accessed September 29, 2023.

60. The preceding information about Georgia was submitted by Jacquie Tyre, USSPN State Apostolic Coordinator for Georgia.

61. The following section is quoted from *The Columbia Electronic Encyclopedia,* 6th ed.; http://www.infoplease.com/ce6/us/A0858375.html; accessed October 2, 2023.

62. Submitted by David Bennett, USSPN State Apostolic Coordinator for Hawaii.

63 The following section is quoted from The Columbia Electronic Encyclopedia, 6th ed.; http://www.infoplease.com/ce6/us/A0858564.html; accessed October 2, 2023.

64 Submitted by Stan Kelly, USSPN State Apostolic Coordinator for Idaho.

65 The following section is quoted from *The Columbia Electronic Encyclopedia,* 6th ed.; http://www.infoplease.com/ce6/us/A0858740.html; accessed October 2, 2023.

66 The following section is quoted from The Columbia Electronic Encyclopedia, 6th ed. http://www.infoplease.com/ce6/us/A0858749.html; accessed October 2, 2023.

67 The following section includes portions of the transcript from the Indiana 50-State Tour meeting.

68 The following section is quoted from *The Columbia Electronic Encyclopedia,* 6th ed.; http://www.infoplease.com/ce6/us/A0858787.html; accessed October 2, 2023.

69 The following two sections are from the transcript of a Iowa 50-State Tour meeting where Chuck D. Pierce and Dutch Sheets ministered.

70 Quoted from "Iowa." Last modified: October 9, 2004; http://www.xs64.com/wikixs/ index.php/Iowa#History; accessed February 15, 2005.

71 Ibid.

72 Ibid.

73 Quoted from *The Columbia Electronic Encyclopedia,* 6th ed.; http://www.infoplease.com/ce6/us/A0858887.html; accessed October 2, 2023.

74 Quoted from "Iowa"; http://www.xs64.com/wikixs/ index.php/Iowa#History; accessed February 15, 2005.

ENDNOTES

75 Submitted by Earl Pickard, USSPN State Apostolic Coordinator for Kansas.

76 Submitted by Earl Pickard, USSPN State Apostolic Coordinator for Kansas. Researched and compiled by Alan Vanderkolk. Sources include:

Robert Smith Bader, *Hayseeds, Moralizers & Methodist* (Lawrence, KS: University Press of Kansas, 1988).

David Dary, *Cowboy Culture* (New York: Alfred A. Krnopf, 1981).

J.R. Hollingsworth, *Santa Fe Trail Blazers* (Amarillo, TX: Baxter Lane Co., 1992).

Kansas State Historical Society; www.kshs.org.

Craig Miner, *West of Wichita* (Lawrence, KS: University Press of Kansas, 1986).

The Wichita Eagle: www.kansas.com/mld/eagle.

77 Submitted by Linda Whitaker, USSPN State Apostolic Coordinator for Kentucky. Sources include:

"Asbury Revival 1970," *Lexington Herald Leader* (Lexington, KY); http://www.forerunner.com/forerunner/X0585_Asbury_Revival_1970.html; accessed October 2, 2023.John B. Boles, *Religion in Antebellum Kentucky* (Lexington, KY: The University Press of Kentucky, 1976).

John E. Kleber, Ed., *The Kentucky Encyclopedia* (Lexington, KY: The University Press of Kentucky, 1992).

Carole Marsh, *My First Pocket Guide—Kentucky* (Peach Tree, GA: Gallopade International, 2000).

Linda Sheldon Marshall, "A Historical Presentation for a Council of War in Louisville," A Spiritual Mapping presentation given at Eagles Nest International in Louisville, Kentucky, August 30, 1992.

Mark T. Matson, *Color Atlas of the States—The Family Reference to the USA* (New York: Simon Schuster Macmillan, 1996).

Richard Ulack, Ed., *Atlas of Kentucky* (Lexington, KY: The University Press of Kentucky, 1998).

78 Submitted by Roger and Charlotte Merschbrock, USSPN State Apostolic Coordinators for Louisiana.

79 This section quoted from Columbia Electronic Encyclopedia, 6th ed.; http://www.infoplease.com/ce6/us/A0859363.html; accessed October 2, 2023.

80 Submitted by Richard Brink, USSPN State Apostolic Coordinator for Maine. Sources include:

Dean Bennett, *Maine Dirigo "I Lead"* (Camden, ME: Downeast Books, 1980).

Mary Calvert, *Dawn over the Kennebec* (Lewiston, ME: Twin City Printery, 1983).

Richard Judd, *Maine* (Orono, ME: University of Maine Press, 1995).

Neil Rolde, *An Illustrated History of Maine* (Augusta, ME: State Maine Museum, 1995).

Thomaston Historical Society Plaque on location.

81 Submitted by Chuck D. Pierce.

82 The following section quoted from *The Columbia Electronic Encyclopedia,* 6th ed. Accessed at http://www.infoplease.com/ce6/us/A0859518.html; accessed October 2, 2023.

83 Submitted by Linda Clark, USSPN State Apostolic Coordinator for Massachusetts.

84 The following section is quoted entirely from "Massachusetts State History"; http://www.thingstodo.com/states/MA/history.htm; accessed February 16, 2005.

85 Submitted by Barbara Yoder, USSPN State Apostolic Coordinator for Michigan.

86 The following section is quoted entirely from Global Harvest Ministries. Other sources include:

"America Responds—The Home Front: Muslims in America Part One: Profiling the Proud Americans of 'Little Mecca,'" *NPR;* http://www.npr.org/news/specials/re sponse/home_front/features/2001/oct/muslim/011022.muslim.html; accessed February 25, 2005. George Arney, Programmes, Crossing Continents, The Arab-American community, "The Arab-American Community," *BBC News,* November 1, 2001; http://news. bbc.co.uk/1/hi/programmes/crossing_continents/1630181.stm; accessed February 24, 2005.F. Clever Bald, *Michigan in Four Centuries* (New York: Harper, 1954).

Robin Buckson, "Death Stalks Detroit Children," *The Detroit News* (April 8, 2004); http://www.detnews.com/2004/metro/0404/08/a01-11 6835.htm.

George B. Catlin, *The Story of Detroit* (Detroit, MI: Detroit News, 1923).

James A. Clifton, George L. Cornell, James M. McClurken, *People of the Three Fires: The Ottawa, Potawatomi and Ojibway of Michigan* (Grand Rapids, MI: The Michigan Indian Press, Grand Rapids InterTribal Council, 1986).

Willis F. Dunbar and George S. May, *Michigan: A History of the Wolverine State,* 3rd rev. ed. (Grand Rapids, MI: W.B. Eerdmans Publishing Company, 1995).

Willis F. Dunbar, *Michigan Through the Centuries* (New York: Lewis Historical Publishing Co., 1955).

James E. Fitting, *The Archaeology of Michigan: A Guide to the Prehistory of the Great Lakes Region,* 2nd rev. ed. (Bloomfield Hills, MI: Cranbrook Institute of Science, 1975).

W. Vernon Kinietz, *The Indians of the Western Great Lakes, 1615-1760* (Ann Arbor, MI: The University of Michigan Press, 1991).

Edwin G. Pipp, *The Real Henry Ford;* pamphlet circa 1922.

Betty Sodders, *Michigan Prehistory Mysteries* (Au Train, MI; Avery Color Studios, 1990).

87   Jenny Nolan, "Willow Run and the Arsenal of Democracy" *The Detroit News: Rearview Mirror;* updated December 19, 2002.

88   Lee Iacocca, "Henry Ford: He Produced an Affordable Car, Paid High Wages and Helped Create a Middle Class. Not Bad for an Autocrat," *TIME Magazine,* December 8, 1998.

89   "Famous Masons in History," *Sequin Lodge Newington*; http://www.sequinlevel140.org/famous.htm; accessed February 24, 2005.

90   Gordon Trowbridge, "Racial Divide Widest in U.S.—Fewer Metro Detroit Neighborhoods Are Integrated Than 20 Years Ago," *The Detroit News,* January 14, 2002; https://www.detroitnews.com/story/news/special-reports/2020/04/15/segregation-policies-create-boundaries-between-white-black-suburbs/5142654002/; accessed October 2, 2023.

91   Habeeb Salloum, "Detroit—Arab Capital of North America," *Al Jadid,* Vol. 4, no. 25 (Fall 1998).

92   Brad Heath and Darci McConnell, "Detroit Shrinks to 925,000 Population Loss Since 2000 Is Sharpest of Big U.S. Cities, Erodes State's Clout," *The Detroit News,* July 10, 2003; last accessed February 25, 2005.

93   Louis Aguilar, "Michigan Loses Jobs; Rate Worst in Nation—Analysts Say the State Is Losing Ground as Another 15,000 Positions Are Cut," The Detroit News; http://www.detnews.com/ 2005/business/0501/20/A01-65300.htm; accessed January 20, 2005.

94   Robin Buckson, The Detroit News, April 8, 2004.

95   Brad Heath, "Detroit Is Most Violent Big City: Crime Rate Falls, But Other Cities' Rate Drops Faster," *The Detroit News,* May 25, 2004;

ENDNOTES

http://www.detnews.com/2004/metro/0405/25/d01-162833.htm; accessed December 27, 2004.

96 Submitted by Chuck D. Pierce.

97 The following section is quoted from "Minnesota State History"; http://www.theus50.com/ minnesota/history.shtml; accessed June 9, 2002.

98 This first section was submitted by Chuck D. Pierce.

99 "Mississippi State History"; http://www.segenealogy.com/mississippi/ms_state/history.htm; accessed May 23, 2004.

100 "Testimony of Chief Phillip Martin, Chief of the Mississippi Band of Choctaw Indians Before the Committee on Indian Affairs, United States Senate," March 29, 2000; http://indian.senate.gov/2000hrgs/choctaw_0329/ martin.pdf; accessed March 7, 2005.

101 "Mississippi State History," http://www.segenealogy.com/mississippi/ms_state/history.htm; accessed May 23, 2004.

102 Submitted by Billy Joe Young, USSPN State Apostolic Coordinator for Mississippi.

103 Submitted by Regina Shank, USSPN State Apostolic Coordinator for Missouri. Sources include:

"Bleeding Kansas." *PBS:* Africans in America: Judgment Day, Part 4; http://www.pbs.org/wgbh/aia/part4/4p2952.html; accessed November 12, 2004.

Joni K. Buchner and Cole Younger; http://uproar.fortunecity.com/uproar/231/coleyounger.html; accessed November 15, 2004.

"Civil War in Missouri," *TheTeachersGuide.com;* http://www.theteachersguide.com/Civilwarmo.html; accessed November 9, 2004.

"Civil War in Missouri Facts," *Missouri Commandery of Mollus;* http://home.usmo.com/~momollus/mofacts.htm; accessed November 11, 2004.

R.L. Curry, "State Battles," *Civil War in Miniature,* Chapter 34; http://civilwarmini.com/chapss.htm; accessed November 12, 2004.

Joanne Chiles Eakin, *Tears and Turmoil: Order #11 in Missouri* (Shawnee Mission, KS: Two Trails Publishing, 1996).

William E. Foley, *The Genesis of Missouri: From Wilderness Outpost to Statehood* (Columbia, MO: University of Missouri Press, 1989).

Louis Houck, *A History of Missouri: From the Earliest Explorations and Settlements Until the Admission of the State into the Union* (Chicago, IL: R.R. Donnelley & Sons Company, 1908).

"Kansas-Nebraska Act," *U-S-History.com;* http://www.u-s-history.com/pages/h83.html; accessed November 11, 2004.

Jeff Lindsay, "What was the 1838 Mormon War?" *JeffLindsay.com;* http://www.jefflindsay.com/LDSFAQ/FQ_Missouri.shtml#exterminator; accessed November 14, 2004.

Duane Meyer, *The Heritage of Missouri—A History* (St. Louis, MO: State Publishing Company, Inc., 1963).

"Missouri," *Netstate,* http://www.netstate.com/states/intro/mo_intro.htm; accessed November 12, 2004.

"Missouri State History," *FactMonster.com;* http://www.factmonster.com/ce6/us/A0859686.htm; accessed November 13, 2004.

"Research Collections of the American West: Papers of the St. Louis Fur Trade," *LexisNexis;* http://www.lexisnexis.com/academic/2upa/Awush/StLouisFur.asp; accessed November 13, 2004.

"Saint Charles, Missouri's First Capital," *Saint Louis Front Page;* http://www.slfp.com/SLFP-StCharles.htm; accessed November 12, 2004.

"Slavery Is Founded on the Selfishness of Man's Nature," *EssayCity.com;* http://www.essaycity.com/free_term_papers_and_essays/North_American_History/164.html; accessed November 8, 2004.

ENDNOTES

Kristen Stephensen, "Guerilla Warfare in the Ozarks" Ozarks History Course Syllabus; http://www.republic.k12. mo.us/highschool/teachers/kstephen/oz4d.htm; accessed November 12, 2004.

Donna Theobald, "Haun's Mill Massacre," *PageWise.com;* http://ctct.essortment.com/haunsmillmass_rysw.htm; accessed November 14, 2004.

104 This first section is from the transcript of the Missouri 50-State Tour meeting.

105 Lisa Cozzens, "Impact of Dred Scott," *Welcome to African American History*; http://www.watson.org/~lisa/blackhistory/scott/impact.html; accessed November 12, 2004.

106 "The Fourth Generation," *A Piece of the Family Quilt: The Hall Family;* http://freepages.genealogy.rootsweb.com/~gmfrontporch/hall/d4.htm; accessed November 15, 2004.

107 TheTeachersGuide.com; http://www.theteachersguide.com/civilwarmo.html; accessed November 9, 2004.

108 Submitted by Penny Barney, USSPN State Apostolic Coordinator for Montana.

109 "Ancient Peoples/First Peoples"; http://www.opi.state.mt.us/TeachMTHistory/Firstppls.html; accessed March 7, 2005.

110 "The Fur Traders"; http://www.opi.state.mt.us/TeachMTHistory/furtraders.html; accessed March 7, 2005.

111 "The Gold Seekers"; http://www.opi.state.mt.us/TeachMTHistory/; accessed March 7, 2005.

112 "The Stockgrowers"; http://www.opi.state.mt.us/TeachMTHistory/; accessed March 7, 2005.

113 "The Industrial Miners"; http://www.opi.state.mt.us/TeachMTHistory/; accessed March 7, 2005.

114 "The Homesteaders"; http://www.opi.state.mt.us/TeachMTHistory/homestead.html; accessed March 7, 2005.

115 "World War II and the Cold War"; http://www.opi.state.mt.us/TeachMTHis tory/war.html; accessed March 7, 2005.

116 Submitted by Linelle Kelley, USSPN State Apostolic Coordinator for Nebraska.

117 The following section quoted from *The Columbia Electronic Encyclopedia,* 6th ed.; http://www.infoplease.com/ce6/us/A0859914.html; accessed October 2, 2023.

118 This first section is from the transcript of the Nevada 50-State Tour Meeting.

119 Submitted by Lynnie Walker, USSPN State Apostolic Coordinator for Nevada and Bea Johnson (Santa Fe, NM).

120 "Nevada," *Online Encyclopedia;* http://encarta.msn.com/encyclopedia_761551699_5/Nevada.html#p129; accessed December 28, 2004.

121 *Columbia Electronic Encyclopedia;* http://www.infoplease.com/ce6/us/A0859938.html; accessed December 27, 2004.

122 "Nevada," *Online Encyclopedia;* http://encarta.msn.com/encyclopedia_761551699_5/Nevada.html#p129; accessed December 28, 2004.

123 Submitted by Allen Cook, USSPN State Apostolic Coordinator for New Hampshire.

124 The following sections were submitted by Bea Johnson of Santa Fe, New Mexico. Sources include:

Robert L.A. Adams and Charles E. Clark, "New Hampshire," *World Book Encyclopedia, Vol. 14, N-O* (Chicago, IL: World Book, Inc., 2002).

Grace Jager and Ronald Jager, *The Granite State New Hampshire* (Sun Valley, CA: American Historical Press, 2000).

125 Submitted by John and Sheryl Price, USSPN State Apostolic Coordinators for New Jersey.

126 The following section is quoted from "New Jersey State History"; http://www.theus50.com/newjersey/history.shtml; accessed July 28, 2002.

127 Submitted by Chuck D. Pierce.

128 The information in the following section can be found in "New Mexico," *World Book Encyclopedia,* Vol. 14, N-O (Chicago, IL: World Book, Inc., 2004).

129 Submitted by Joseph Askins, USSPN State Apostolic Co-coordinator for New York.

130 Submitted by Joseph and Vonnie Askins, USSPN State Apostolic Coordinators for New York, and Susan Stanfield, USSPN Communications Assistant.

131 Don Healy, "The Iroquois Confederacy"; http://users.aol.com/donh523/navapage/iroquois.htm; accessed July 11, 2002.

132 "New York City Breaks"; http://www.citybreaksguide.com/New_York_City_Breaks.asp; accessed July 11, 2002.

133 "History of New York State"; http://www.iloveny.com/info_center/state_facts_history_post_ 1900.asp; accessed July 11, 2002.

134 Ibid.

135 Submitted by Otis Lockett Sr., USSPN State Apostolic Coordinator for North Carolina.

136 Joe A. Mobley, "The Way We Lived in North Carolina"; http://www.waywelivednc.com/1820-1870/default.htm; accessed March 8, 2005.

137 Joe A. Mobley, "The Way We Lived in North Carolina"; http://www.waywelivednc.com/1870-1920/overview.htm; accessed March 8, 2005.

138 Joe A. Mobley, "The Way We Lived in North Carolina"; http://www.waywelivednc.com/1820-1870/overview.htm; accessed March 8, 2005.

139 Joe A. Mobley, "The Way We Lived in North Carolina"; http://www.waywelivednc.com/1870-1920/overview.htm; accessed March 8, 2005.

140 Joe A. Mobley, "The Way We Lived in North Carolina"; http://www.waywelivednc.com/1870-1920/default.htm; accessed March 8, 2005.

141 Submitted by James Hessler, USSPN State Apostolic Coordinator for North Dakota.

142 Submitted by Bea Johnson of Santa Fe, New Mexico. Sources include:

"North Dakota," *World Book Encyclopedia,* Vol. 14, N-O (Chicago, IL: World Book, Inc., 2004).

"Summary of North Dakota History," *North Dakota Centennial Blue Book 1889-1989;* http://www.minot.k12.nd.us/mps/cc/ndhistory.html; accessed December 22, 2004.

143 Douglas C. Munski and Jerome D. Tweton, "North Dakota." *World Book Encyclopedia,* Vol. 14, N-O (Chicago, IL: World Book, Inc., 2004).

144 Submitted by John Watson, USSPN State Apostolic Coordinator for Ohio.

145 The following section is quoted from "Ohio History," *The Columbia Electronic Encyclopedia,* 6th ed.; http://www.infoplease.com/ce6/us/A0860112.html; accessed December 29, 2004.

146 Submitted by Chuck D. Pierce.

147 Sources for this section include:

"Oklahoma History"; http://www.state.ok.us/osfdocs/history.html; accessed November 18, 2004.

John Sipes, "The Lodge Pole Massacre Site (Washita, 1868): A Cheyenne Enigma," *Watonga Republican* Newspaper (Watonga, OK: January 15, 1997).

"Welcome to These United States—Oklahoma"; http://www.theseunitedstates.com/oklahoma.html; accessed November 18, 2004.

148 John Sipes, "The Lodge Pole Massacre Site (Washita, 1868): A Cheyenne Enigma," *Watonga Republican* Newspaper (Watonga, OK: January 15, 1997).

149 Submitted by Steve Shultz, USSPN State Apostolic Coordinator for Oregon.

150 The following section is quoted from "Oregon History," *The Columbia Electronic Encyclopedia,* 6th ed.; http://www.infoplease.com/ce6/us/A0860159.html; accessed February 21, 2005.

151 Submitted by John Shuey, USSPN State Apostolic Co-coordinator for Pennsylvania.

152 Submitted by John Shuey, USSPN State Apostolic Co-coordinator for Pennsylvania. Sources include:

Edwin B. Bronner, *William Penn's Holy Experiment: The Founding of Pennsylvania 1681-1701* (Westport: Greenwood Press, 1978).

Darrell Fields, *The Seed of a Nation* (Mechanicsburg, PA: Covenant Press, 2000).

Francis Jennings, *Empire of Fortune: Crowns, Colonies, and Tribes in the Seven Years War in America* (New York: William H. Norton & Co, 1988).

Jean R. Soderlund, *William Penn and the Founding of Pennsylvania* (Philadelphia: University of Pennsylvania Press, 1983).

William Penn Tercentenary Committee, Remember William Penn 1644-1944 (Harrisburg, PA, 1944).

http://www.2be1ask1.com/linklib/us/pennsylvania.html; accessed October 1, 2023. https://americancivilwar.com/getty.html; accessed October 2, 2023.

153 Jean R. Soderlund, *William Penn and the Founding of Pennsylvania* (Philadelphia: University of Pennsylvania Press, 1983), 55.

154 Edwin B. Bronner, *William Penn's Holy Experiment, The Founding of Pennsylvania* (Westport: Greenwood Press, 1978), 6.

155 Darrell Fields, *The Seed of a Nation* (Mechanicsburg, PA: Covenant Press, 2000), 205.

156 Submitted by Chuck D. Pierce.

157 Submitted by Nancy Boyce, USSPN State Apostolic Coordinator for Rhode Island.

158 The following section is quoted from "Rhode Island History," *The Columbia Electronic Encyclopedia,* 6th ed.; http://www.infoplease.com/ce6/us/A0860724.html; accessed February 20, 2005.

159 This section is taken from portions of the transcript of the South Carolina 50-State-Tour meeting.

160 The following two sections were submitted by Frank Seignious, USSPN State Apostolic Coordinator for South Carolina. Sources include:

Walter B. Edgar, *South Carolina a History* (Columbia, SC: University of South Carolina Press, 1998).

Walter B. Edgar, *Partisans and Redcoats: The Southern Conflict That Turned the Tide of the American Revolution* (New York: Harper Collins, 2001).

Walter B. Edgar, from in a lecture March 18, 2003.

Robert J. Winters, *Reviving the Holy City* (Columbus, GA: Brentwood Christian Press, 1995).

161 Erwin Holt, "USSPN Weekly State Prayer Focus for South Carolina," February 22, 2004; http://www.globalharvest.org/index.asp?action=sc; accessed January 18, 2005.

162 Submitted by JoAnn Parrott, USSPN State Mobilizing Coordinator for South Carolina.

163 Submitted by Steve Hickey, USSPN State Apostolic Coordinator for South Dakota.

164 The following section is quoted from "South Dakota History," *The Columbia Electronic Encyclopedia,* 6th ed., http://www.infoplease.com/ce6/us/A0861208.html; accessed February 20, 2005.

165 Submitted by Tammy Alsup, USSPN State Apostolic Coordinator for Tennessee.

166 The following section is quoted from "Tennessee History," *The Columbia Electronic Encyclopedia,* 6th ed.; http://www.infoplease.com/ce6/us/A0861484.html; accessed December 29, 2004.

167 The following section is quoted from The Columbia Electronic Encyclopedia, 6th ed.; http://www.infoplease.com/ce6/us/A0861505.html; accessed March 9, 2005.

168 Submitted by Corky and Sharon Seevinck, USSPN State Apostolic Coordinators for Utah.

169 "Unhappy in Utah," *CBSNEWS.com,* June 3, 2003.

170 Sources for the following section include: Ron Rood and Linda Thatcher, "Brief History of Utah"; http://historytogo.utah.gov/brhistory.html; accessed March 9, 2005; and Vincent Wilson Jr.'s *The Book of the States* (American History Research Associates, 1998).

171 Ron Rood and Linda Thatcher, "Brief History of Utah"; http://historytogo.utah.gov/brhistory.html; accessed March 9, 2005.

172 Submitted by Christie and Katherine Leary, USSPN State Apostolic Coordinators for Vermont.

173 The following section is quoted from "History of Vermont," *The Columbia Electronic Encyclopedia,* 6th ed.; http://www.infoplease.com/ce6/us/A0861780.html; accessed February 20, 2005.

174 Submitted by Chuck D. Pierce.

175 Submitted by Travis Thigpen, USSPN State Apostolic Coordinator for Virginia.

176 The following section is quoted from "Guide to Virginia History," *SHG Resources;* Copyright 2003; http://www.shgresources.com/va/history/; accessed February 20, 2005.

177 Submitted by Burdell Austin, USSPN State Mobilizing Coordinator for Washington. Taken from portions of the transcript from the Washington 50-State Tour meeting.

178 The following section is quoted from "Washington History," The Columbia Electronic Encyclopedia, 6th ed.; http://www.theus50.com/washington/history.shtml#general; accessed October 23, 2004.

179 Submitted by Ron and Nancy Thaxton, USSPN State Apostolic Coordinators for West Virginia.

180 The following section is quoted from "West Virginia History," The Columbia Electronic Encyclopedia, 6th ed.; http://www.infoplease.com/ce6/us/A0861927.html; accessed February 17, 2005.

181 Submitted by Venner Alston, USSPN State Apostolic Co-coordinator for Wisconsin.

ENDNOTES

182 The following section is quoted from "Wisconsin History," *The Columbia Electronic Encyclopedia,* 6th ed.; http://www.infoplease.com/ce6/us/A0861981.html; accessed February 17, 2005.

183 Submitted by Don Hinton, USSPN State Apostolic Coordinator for Wyoming.

184 The following section is quoted from "Wyoming History," *The Columbia Electronic Encyclopedia,* 6th ed.; http://www.infoplease.com/ce6/us/A0862023.html; accessed February 17, 2005.

ABOUT THE AUTHORS

CHUCK D. PIERCE

CHARLES D. "CHUCK" PIERCE leads an apostolic and prophetic ministry in Corinth, Texas. He is President of Glory of Zion International, Kingdom Harvest Alliance, and Global Spheres Inc. These three ministries are housed at Global Spheres Center, which also includes Beulah Acres and the Israel Prayer Garden. He continues to gather and mobilize the worshipping Triumphant Reserve throughout the world. The ministries located at Global Spheres Center participate in regional and national gatherings to develop new Kingdom paradigms. Dr. Pierce also serves as a key bridge between Jew and Gentile as the Lord raises up One New Man. He is known for his accurate prophetic gifting which helps direct nations, cities, churches, and individuals in understanding the times and seasons in which we live. He has written numerous best-selling books and has a degree in Business from Texas A&M, Master's work in Cognitive Systems from the University of North Texas, and a D.Min. from the Wagner Leadership Institute.

DUTCH SHEETS

DUTCH SHEETS is an internationally recognized author and founder of Dutch Sheets Ministries and Give Him 15®. Having been in ministry for over 45 years, Dutch has pastored, taught in Bible colleges, and preached in many nations. He has written 24 books, some of which have been translated into over 30 languages. His international bestseller, *Intercessory Prayer*, has sold over 1 million copies worldwide.

Dutch is a messenger of hope for America, boldly proclaiming that she will experience a Third Great Awakening and turn back to her God-given destiny. He labors to equip the church in governmental intercession, challenging believers to passionate prayer for worldwide revival.

Since expanding the platform in 2020, the GH15 daily prayer YouTube videos, the mobile APP, podcasts, and blog have had over 59 million engagements across multiple media outlets where Dutch has led prayer for the nation. In November 2022, Dutch released a GH15 Devotional Book that is the first in a series. Each 30-day volume contains biblical teachings and insights for daily life, as well as prayers and decrees for our nation.

Dutch treasures time spent with his family and grandchildren. He and Ceci, his wife of 40-plus years, enjoy quiet walks in the woods, reading, fishing, and an occasional walk on the beach. They make their home in beautiful South Carolina.

TIM SHEETS

DR. TIM SHEETS is an apostle, pastor, and author based in southwestern Ohio. He ministers nationally and internationally at conferences, churches, seminars, and Bible schools. He is a graduate of Christ for the Nations Institute and has a Doctorate of Divinity from Christian Life School of Theology.

He is the author of: *Angel Armies; Angel Armies on Assignment; Planting the Heavens; Heaven Made Real; The New Era of Glory; Ninjas with Feathers; Prayers and Decrees That Activate Angel Armies;* as well as *Come Home* and *God's Got This,* both coauthored with his daughter, Rachel Shafer.

Dr. Sheets is the founder of AwakeningNow Prayer Network and the pastor of Oasis Church in Middletown, Ohio.

Dr. Sheets resides with his wife, Carol, in Lebanon, Ohio. They have two children, Rachel (Mark) Shafer, and Joshua (Jessica) Sheets, and 7 grandchildren (Madeline, Lily, Jude, Jaidin, Joelle, Sam, and Grace).

TIM SHEETS MINISTRIES

6927 Lefferson Road

Middletown, OH 45044

TimSheets.org

Phone: 513-424-7150

YOUR Prophetic COMMUNITY

Sign up for a **FREE** subscription to the Destiny Image digital magazine and get awesome content delivered directly to your inbox!

destinyimage.com/signup

Sign up for Cutting-Edge Messages that Supernaturally Empower You

- Gain valuable insights and guidance based on biblical principles
- Deepen your faith and understanding of God's plan for your life
- Receive regular updates and prophetic messages
- Connect with a community of believers who share your values and beliefs

Experience Fresh Video Content that Reveals Your Prophetic Inheritance

- Receive prophetic messages and insights
- Connect with a powerful tool for spiritual growth and development
- Stay connected and inspired on your faith journey

Listen to Powerful Podcasts that Propel You into God's Presence Every Day

- Deepen your understanding of God's prophetic assignment
- Experience God's revival power throughout your day
- Learn how to grow spiritually in your walk with God

Check out
our **Destiny Image**
bestsellers page at
destinyimage.com/bestsellers

for cutting-edge,
prophetic messages
that will supernaturally
empower you and the
body of Christ.

In the Right Hands, This Book Will Change Lives!

Most of the people who need this message will not be looking for this book. To change their lives, you need to **put a copy of this book in their hands.**

Our ministry is constantly seeking methods to find the people who need this anointed message to change their lives. **Will you help us reach these people?**

Extend this ministry by sowing three, five, ten, or *even more* books today and change people's lives for the better! Your generosity will be part of catalyzing the Great Awakening that many have been prophesying and praying for.